Story & Art by
Taeko Watanabe

Contents

Story Thus Far

I t is the end of the Bakufu era, the third year of Bunkyu (1863) in Kyoto. The Shinsengumi is a band of warriors formed to protect the shogun.

Tominaga Sei, the daughter of a former Bakufu *bushi*, joined the Shinsengumi disguised as a boy by the name of Kamiya Seizaburo to avenge her father and brother. She has continued her training under the only person in the Shinsengumi who knows her true identity, Okita Soji, and she aspires to become a true *bushi*.

Sei feels trapped between her female self and *bushi* self ever since she played the role of a woman in the Terayada Inn infiltration mission. Okita has also begun to look upon Sei as a woman, but, despite his growing feelings for her, he heartlessly brushes off her affection.

Sei makes up her mind to travel to Senjuan to become a nun. While there, she is advised by the nun Suigetsu that love isn't all about one-sided yearning. Sei decides to return to the Shinsengumi and falls asleep at the dojo. After a frantic search, Okita weeps tears of love upon discovering that she has returned…

Characters

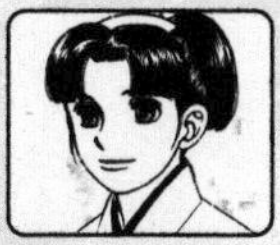

Tominaga Sei
She disguises herself as a boy to enter the Mibu-Roshi. She trains under Soji, aspiring to become a true *bushi*. But secretly, she is in love with Soji.

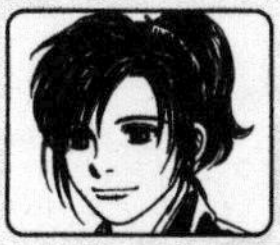

Okita Soji
Assistant vice captain of the Shinsengumi and licensed master of the Ten'nen Rishin-ryu. He supports the troop alongside Kondo and Hijikata and guides Seizaburo with a kind yet firm hand.

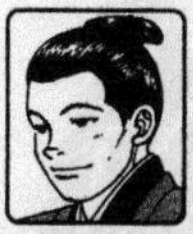

Kondo Isami
Captain of the Shinsengumi and fourth grandmaster of the Ten'nen Rishin-ryu. A passionate, warm and well-respected leader.

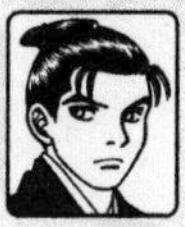

Hijikata Toshizo
Vice captain of the Shinsengumi. He commands both the group and himself with a rigid strictness. He is also known as the "Oni vice captain."

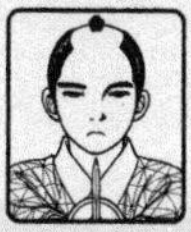

Saito Hajime
Assistant Vice Captain. He was a friend of Sei's older brother. Sei is attached to him in place of her lost brother.

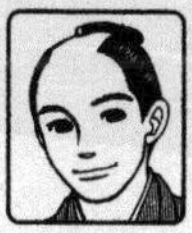

Tominaga Yuma
Sei's older brother and Saito's friend at the same dojo. He was killed with his father by thugs who want to overthrow the Bakufu.

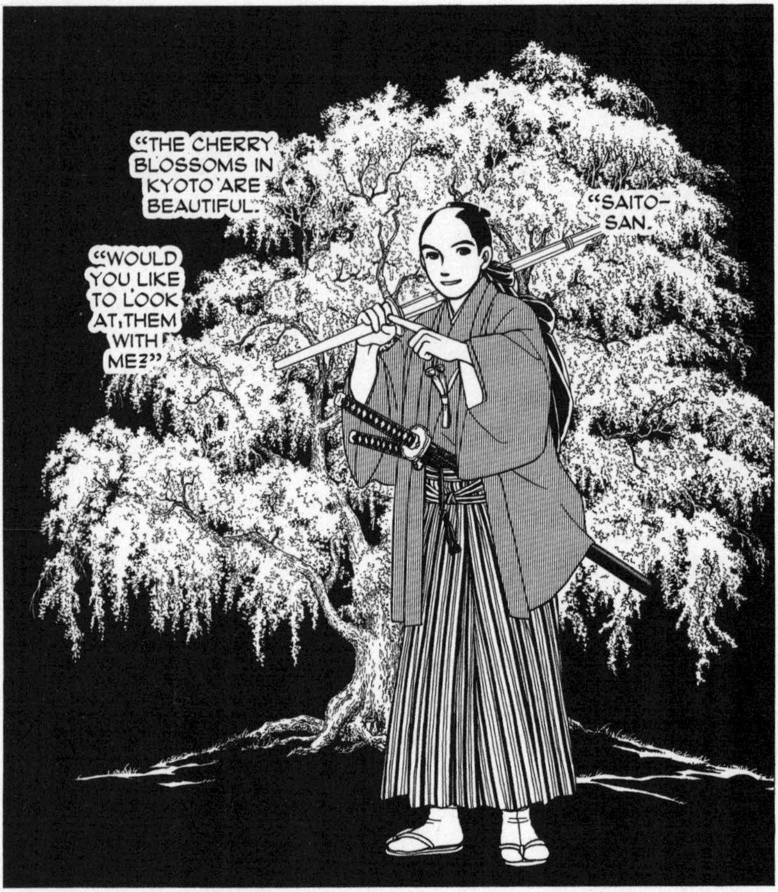
"SAITO-SAN.
"THE CHERRY BLOSSOMS IN KYOTO ARE BEAUTIFUL.
"WOULD YOU LIKE TO LOOK AT THEM WITH ME?"

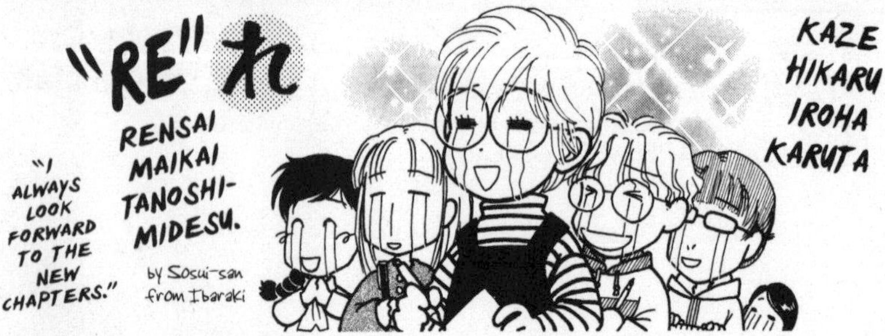
KAZE HIKARU IROHA KARUTA
"RE" れ
RENSAI MAIKAI TANOSHI-MIDESU.
"I ALWAYS LOOK FORWARD TO THE NEW CHAPTERS."
by Sosui-san from Ibaraki

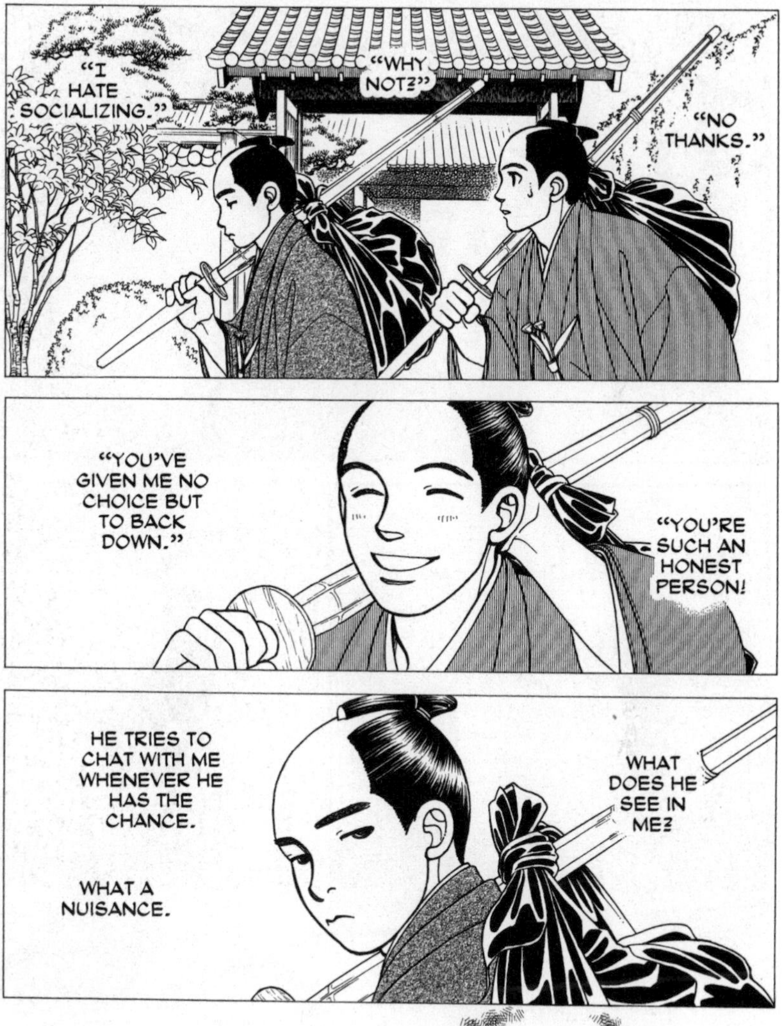
"NO THANKS."
"WHY NOT?"
"I HATE SOCIALIZING."
"YOU'RE SUCH AN HONEST PERSON!
"YOU'VE GIVEN ME NO CHOICE BUT TO BACK DOWN."
WHAT DOES HE SEE IN ME?
HE TRIES TO CHAT WITH ME WHENEVER HE HAS THE CHANCE.
WHAT A NUISANCE.
TOMINAGA YUMA...

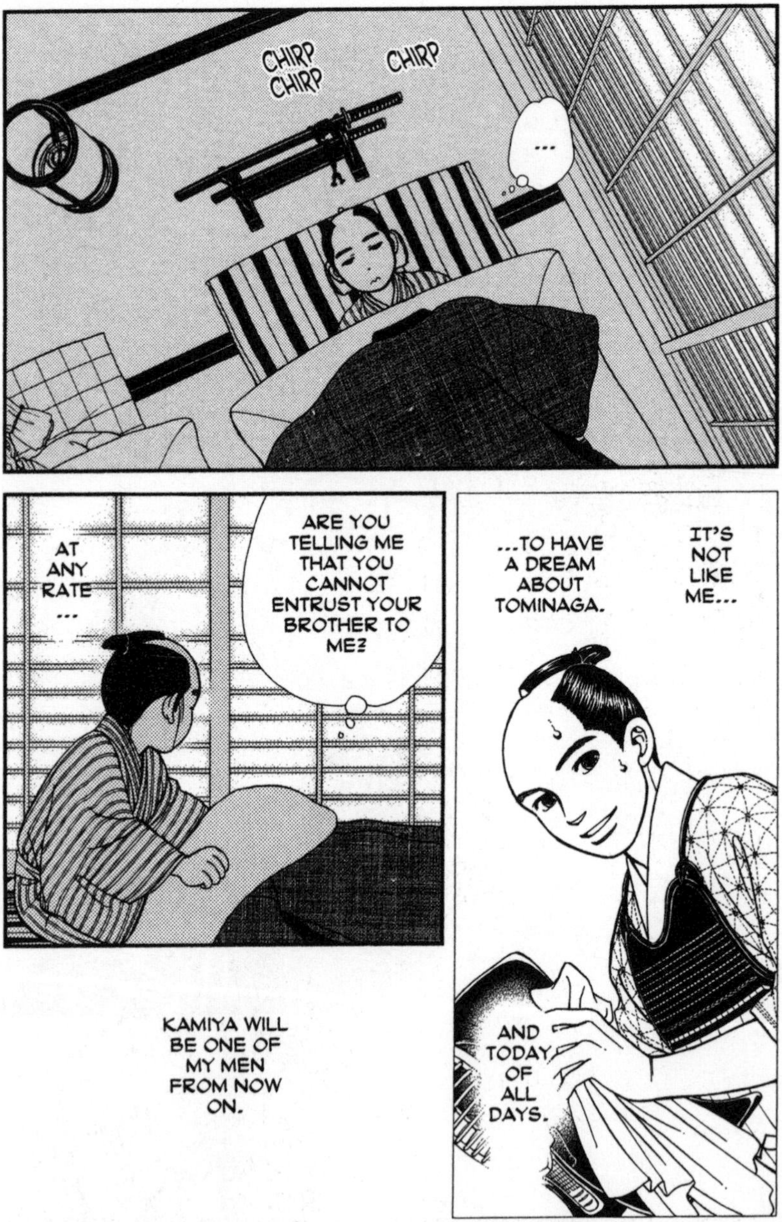
CHIRP
CHIRP CHIRP
...
IT'S NOT LIKE ME...
...TO HAVE A DREAM ABOUT TOMINAGA.
AND TODAY OF ALL DAYS.
ARE YOU TELLING ME THAT YOU CANNOT ENTRUST YOUR BROTHER TO ME?
AT ANY RATE...
KAMIYA WILL BE ONE OF MY MEN FROM NOW ON.

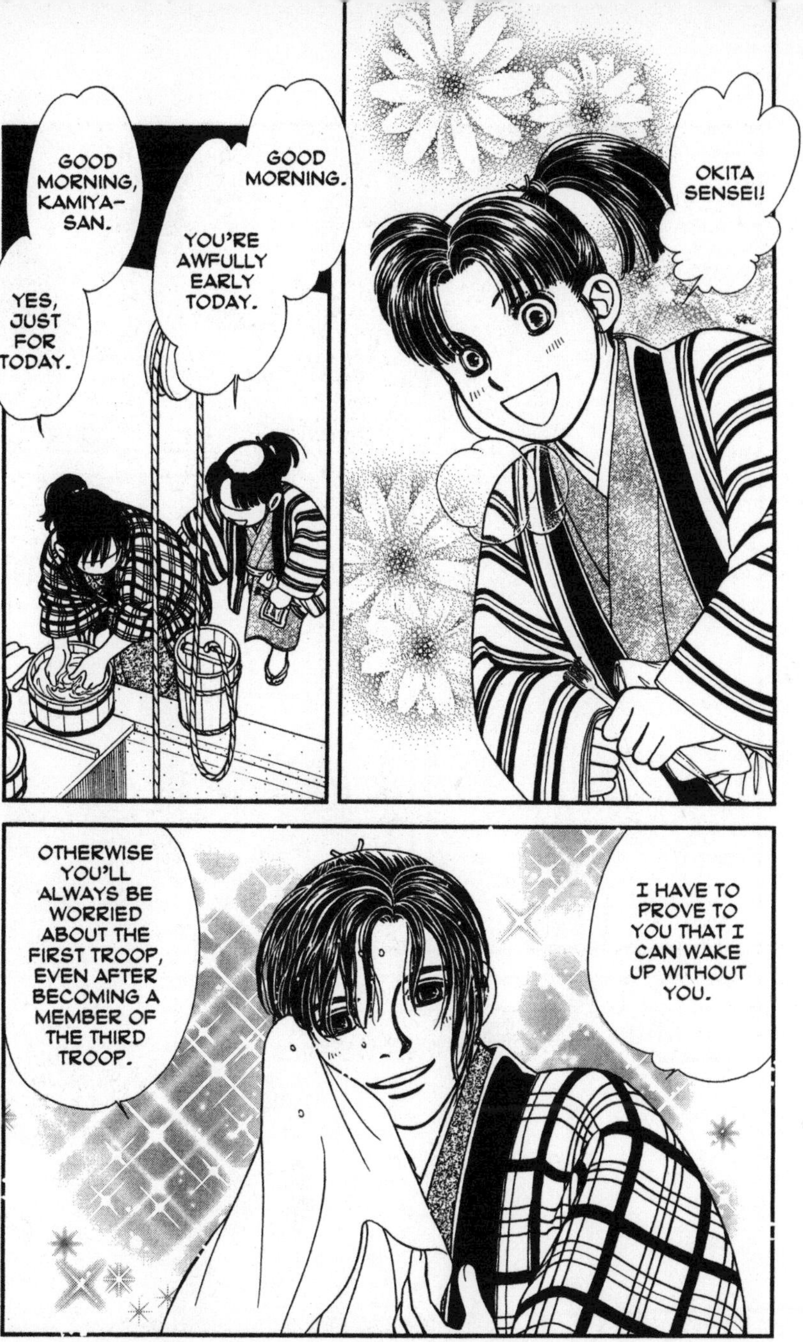
OKITA SENSEI!
GOOD MORNING.
GOOD MORNING, KAMIYA-SAN.
YOU'RE AWFULLY EARLY TODAY.
YES, JUST FOR TODAY.
I HAVE TO PROVE TO YOU THAT I CAN WAKE UP WITHOUT YOU.
OTHERWISE YOU'LL ALWAYS BE WORRIED ABOUT THE FIRST TROOP, EVEN AFTER BECOMING A MEMBER OF THE THIRD TROOP.

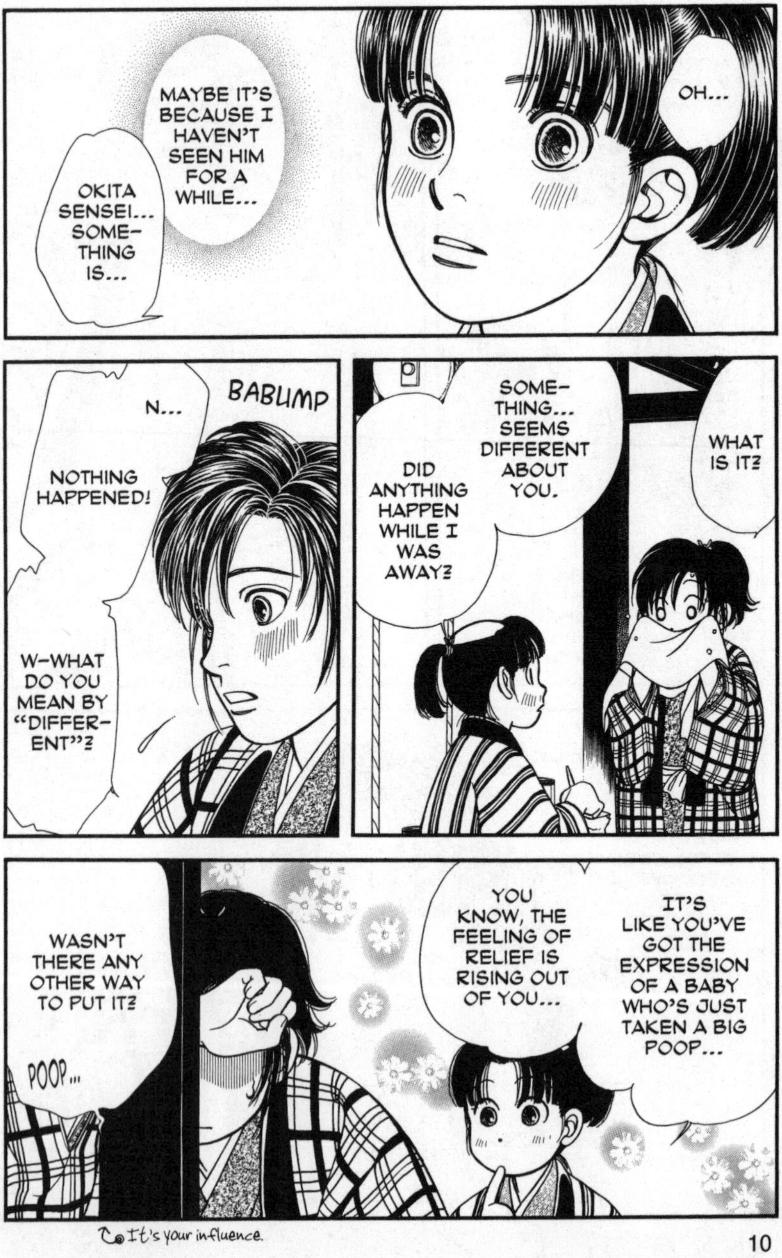
OH...
MAYBE IT'S BECAUSE I HAVEN'T SEEN HIM FOR A WHILE...
OKITA SENSEI... SOME-THING IS...
WHAT IS IT?
SOME-THING... SEEMS DIFFERENT ABOUT YOU.
DID ANYTHING HAPPEN WHILE I WAS AWAY?
BABUMP
N...
NOTHING HAPPENED!
W-WHAT DO YOU MEAN BY "DIFFER-ENT"?
IT'S LIKE YOU'VE GOT THE EXPRESSION OF A BABY WHO'S JUST TAKEN A BIG POOP...
YOU KNOW, THE FEELING OF RELIEF IS RISING OUT OF YOU...
WASN'T THERE ANY OTHER WAY TO PUT IT?
POOP...

It's your influence.

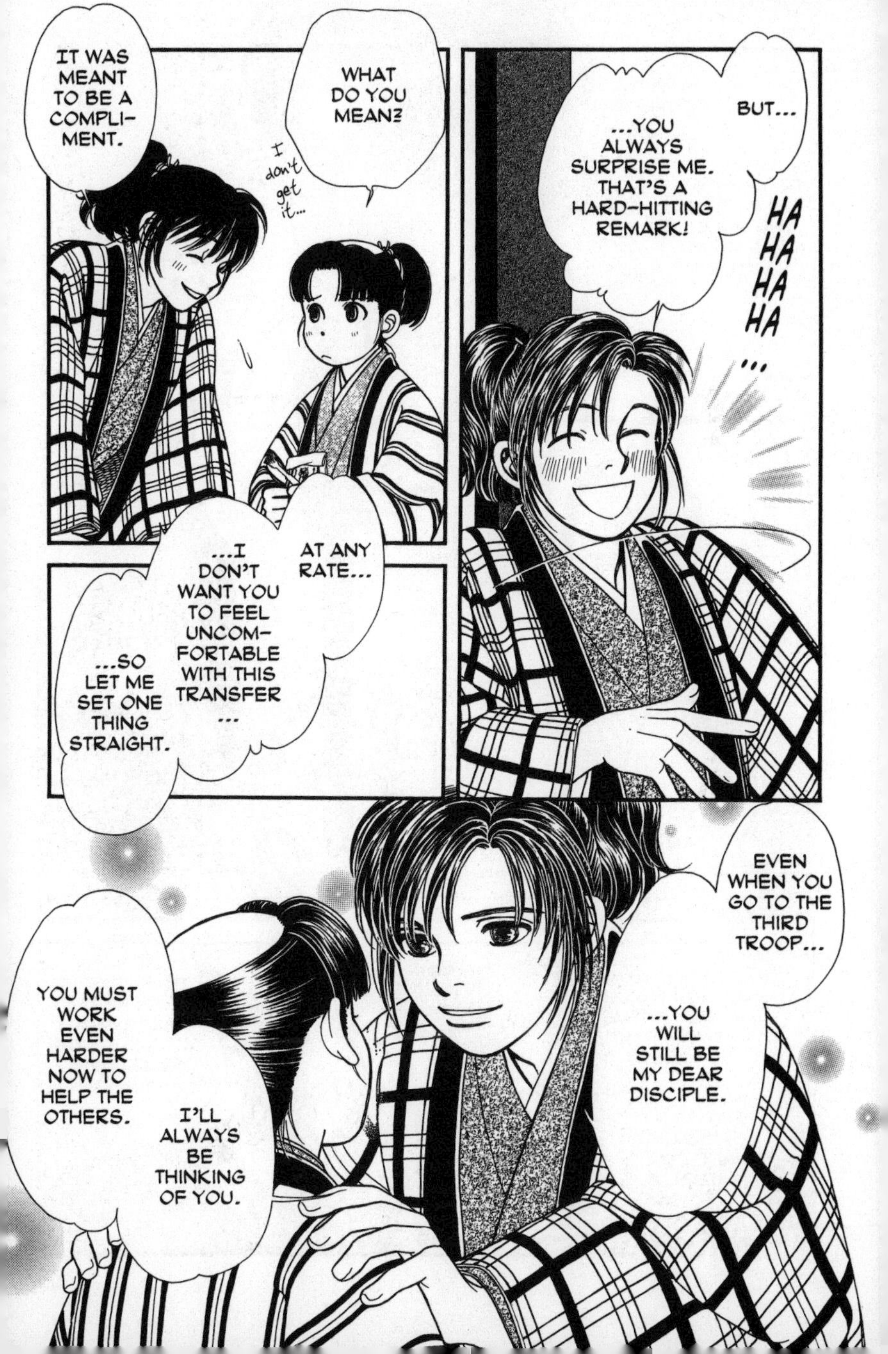
BUT...
...YOU ALWAYS SURPRISE ME. THAT'S A HARD-HITTING REMARK!
HA HA HA HA...
WHAT DO YOU MEAN?
I don't get it...
IT WAS MEANT TO BE A COMPLIMENT.
AT ANY RATE...
...I DON'T WANT YOU TO FEEL UNCOMFORTABLE WITH THIS TRANSFER...
...SO LET ME SET ONE THING STRAIGHT.
EVEN WHEN YOU GO TO THE THIRD TROOP...
...YOU WILL STILL BE MY DEAR DISCIPLE.
YOU MUST WORK EVEN HARDER NOW TO HELP THE OTHERS.
I'LL ALWAYS BE THINKING OF YOU.

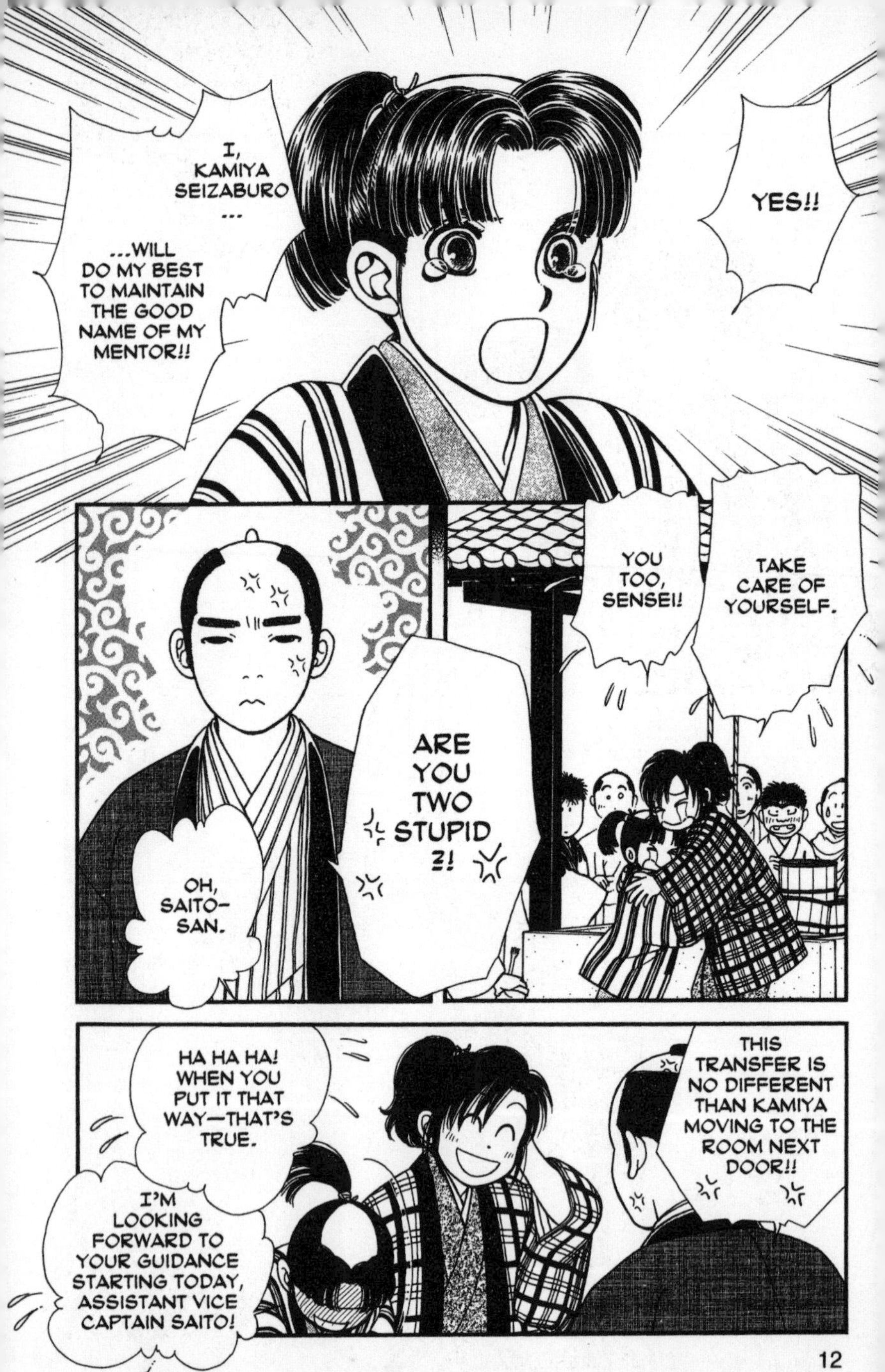
YES!!
I, KAMIYA SEIZABURO...
...WILL DO MY BEST TO MAINTAIN THE GOOD NAME OF MY MENTOR!!
TAKE CARE OF YOURSELF.
YOU TOO, SENSEI!
ARE YOU TWO STUPID?!
OH, SAITO-SAN.
THIS TRANSFER IS NO DIFFERENT THAN KAMIYA MOVING TO THE ROOM NEXT DOOR!!
HA HA HA! WHEN YOU PUT IT THAT WAY—THAT'S TRUE.
I'M LOOKING FORWARD TO YOUR GUIDANCE STARTING TODAY, ASSISTANT VICE CAPTAIN SAITO!

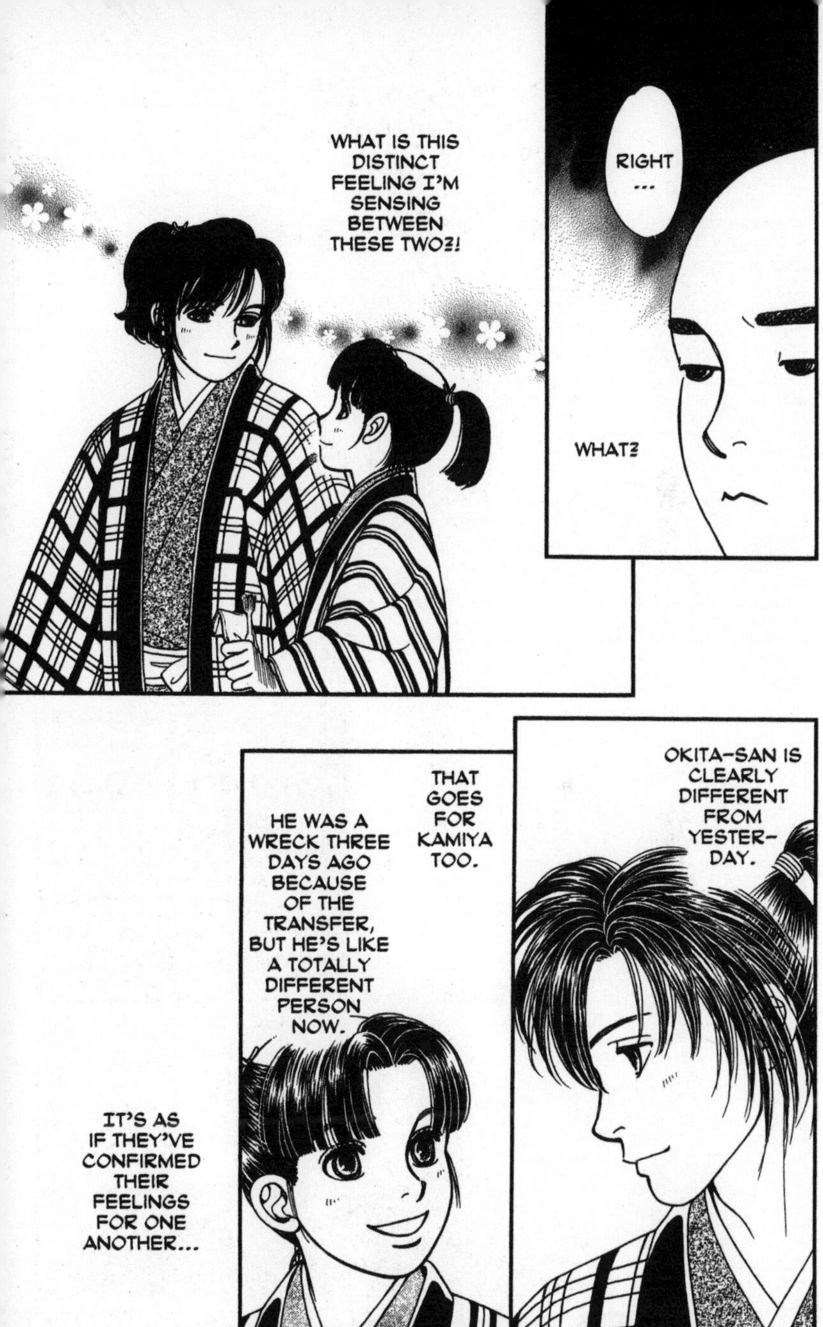
RIGHT ...
WHAT?
WHAT IS THIS DISTINCT FEELING I'M SENSING BETWEEN THESE TWO?!
OKITA-SAN IS CLEARLY DIFFERENT FROM YESTER-DAY.
THAT GOES FOR KAMIYA TOO.
HE WAS A WRECK THREE DAYS AGO BECAUSE OF THE TRANSFER, BUT HE'S LIKE A TOTALLY DIFFERENT PERSON NOW.
IT'S AS IF THEY'VE CONFIRMED THEIR FEELINGS FOR ONE ANOTHER...

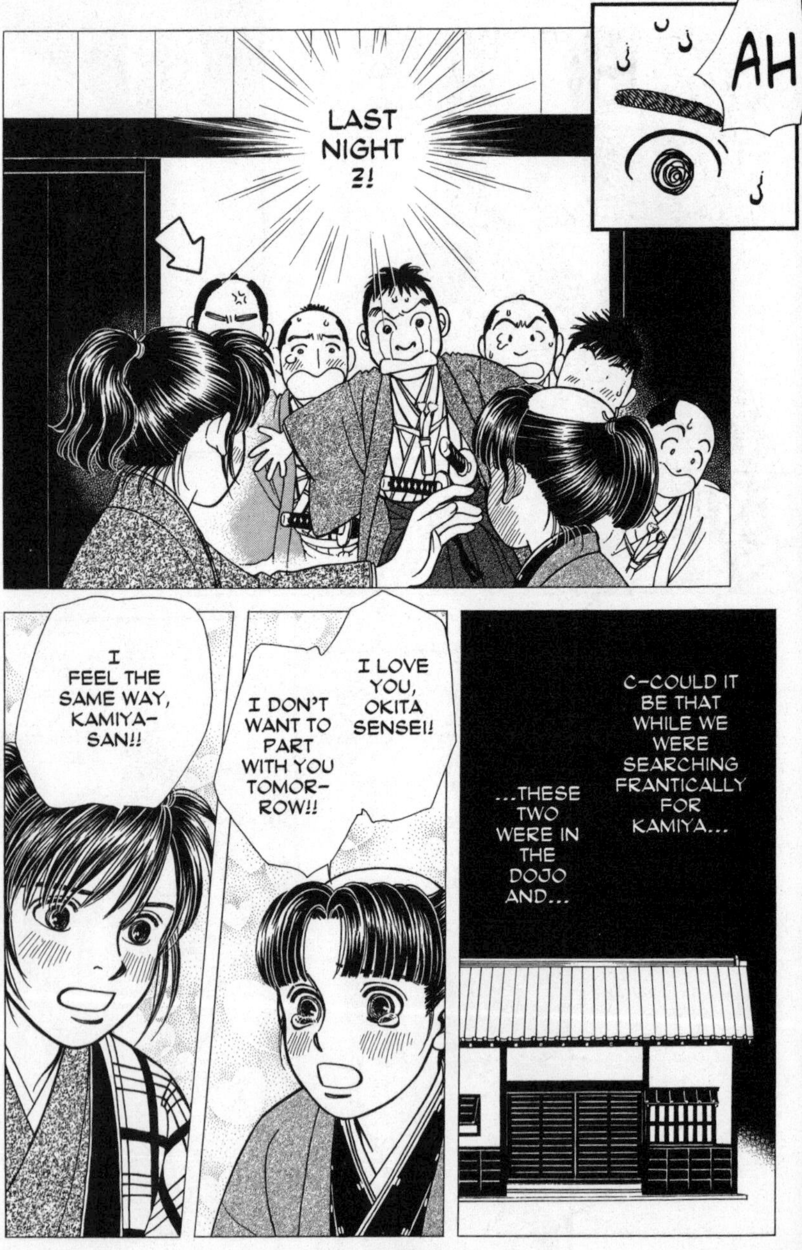
AH
LAST NIGHT?!
C-COULD IT BE THAT WHILE WE WERE SEARCHING FRANTICALLY FOR KAMIYA...
...THESE TWO WERE IN THE DOJO AND...
I LOVE YOU, OKITA SENSEI!!
I DON'T WANT TO PART WITH YOU TOMORROW!!
I FEEL THE SAME WAY, KAMIYA-SAN!!

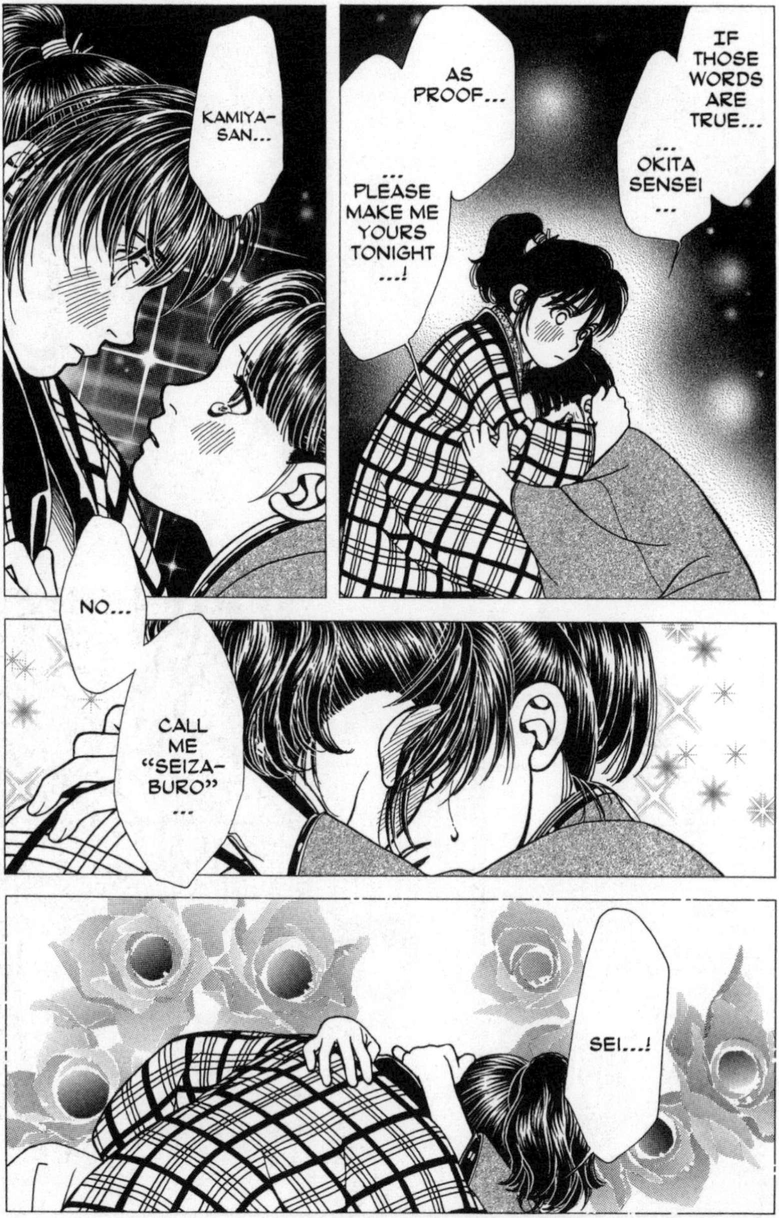
IF THOSE WORDS ARE TRUE...
... OKITA SENSEI ...
AS PROOF...
... PLEASE MAKE ME YOURS TONIGHT ...!
KAMIYA-SAN...
NO...
CALL ME "SEIZA-BURO" ...
SEI...!

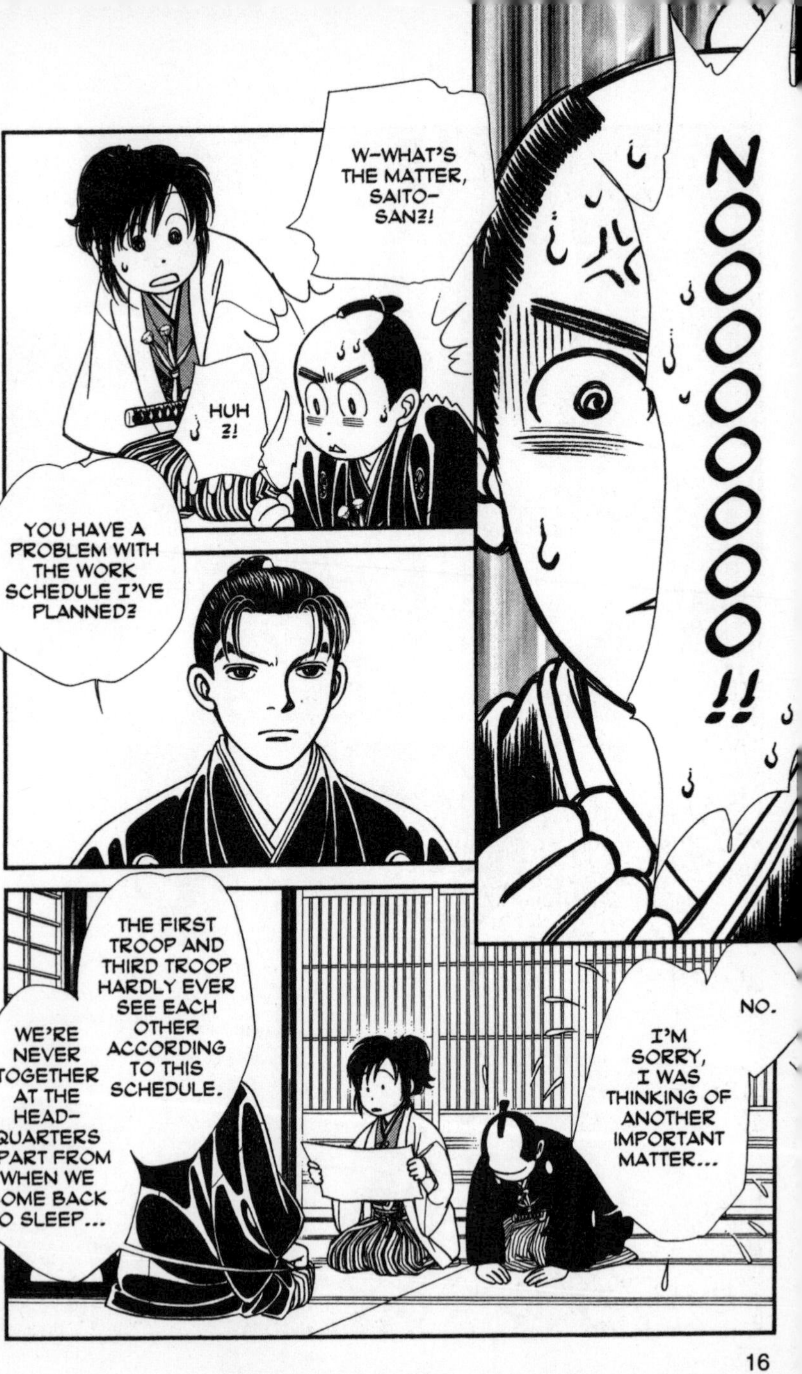

NOOOOOOOOO!!
W-WHAT'S THE MATTER, SAITO-SAN?!
HUH ?!
YOU HAVE A PROBLEM WITH THE WORK SCHEDULE I'VE PLANNED?
NO.
I'M SORRY, I WAS THINKING OF ANOTHER IMPORTANT MATTER...
THE FIRST TROOP AND THIRD TROOP HARDLY EVER SEE EACH OTHER ACCORDING TO THIS SCHEDULE.
WE'RE NEVER TOGETHER AT THE HEAD-QUARTERS APART FROM WHEN WE COME BACK TO SLEEP...

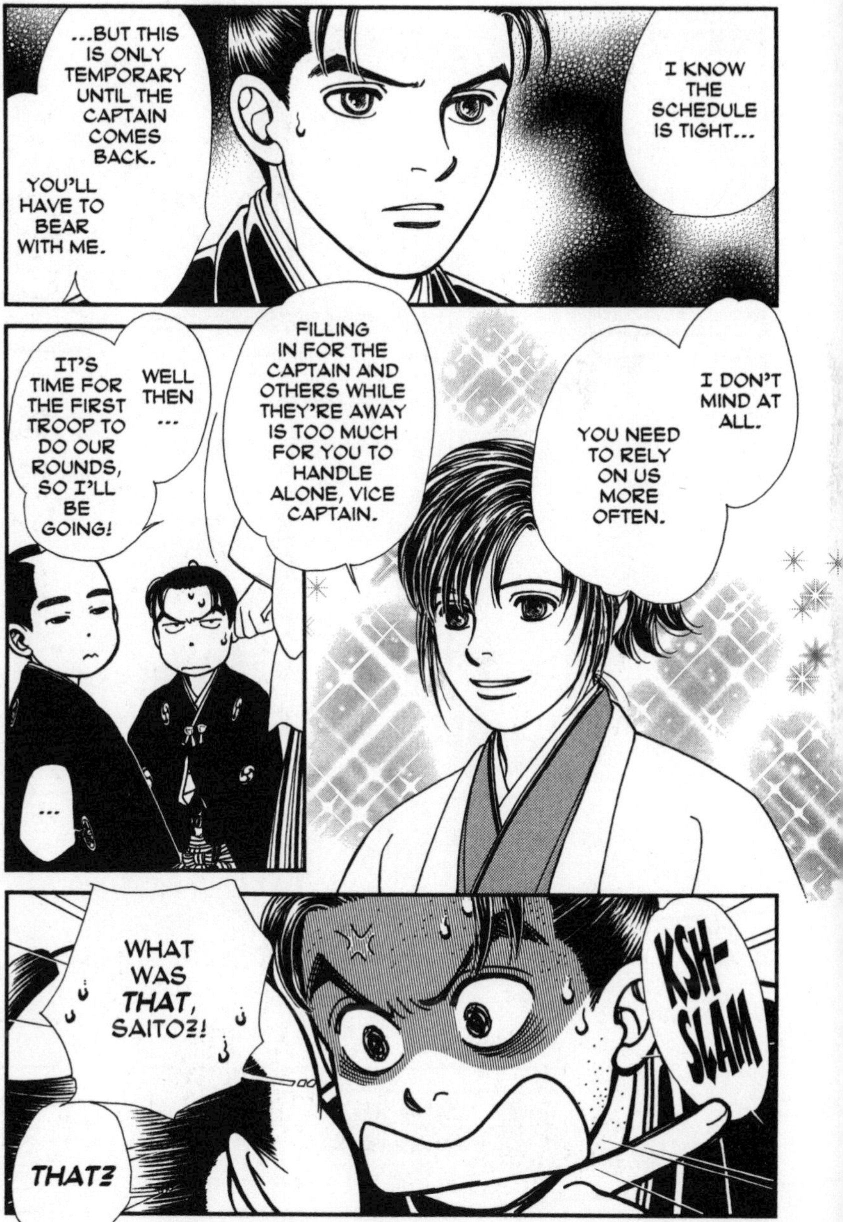
I KNOW THE SCHEDULE IS TIGHT...
...BUT THIS IS ONLY TEMPORARY UNTIL THE CAPTAIN COMES BACK.
YOU'LL HAVE TO BEAR WITH ME.
I DON'T MIND AT ALL.
YOU NEED TO RELY ON US MORE OFTEN.
FILLING IN FOR THE CAPTAIN AND OTHERS WHILE THEY'RE AWAY IS TOO MUCH FOR YOU TO HANDLE ALONE, VICE CAPTAIN.
WELL THEN...
IT'S TIME FOR THE FIRST TROOP TO DO OUR ROUNDS, SO I'LL BE GOING!
...
KSH-SLAM
WHAT WAS *THAT*, SAITO?!
THAT?

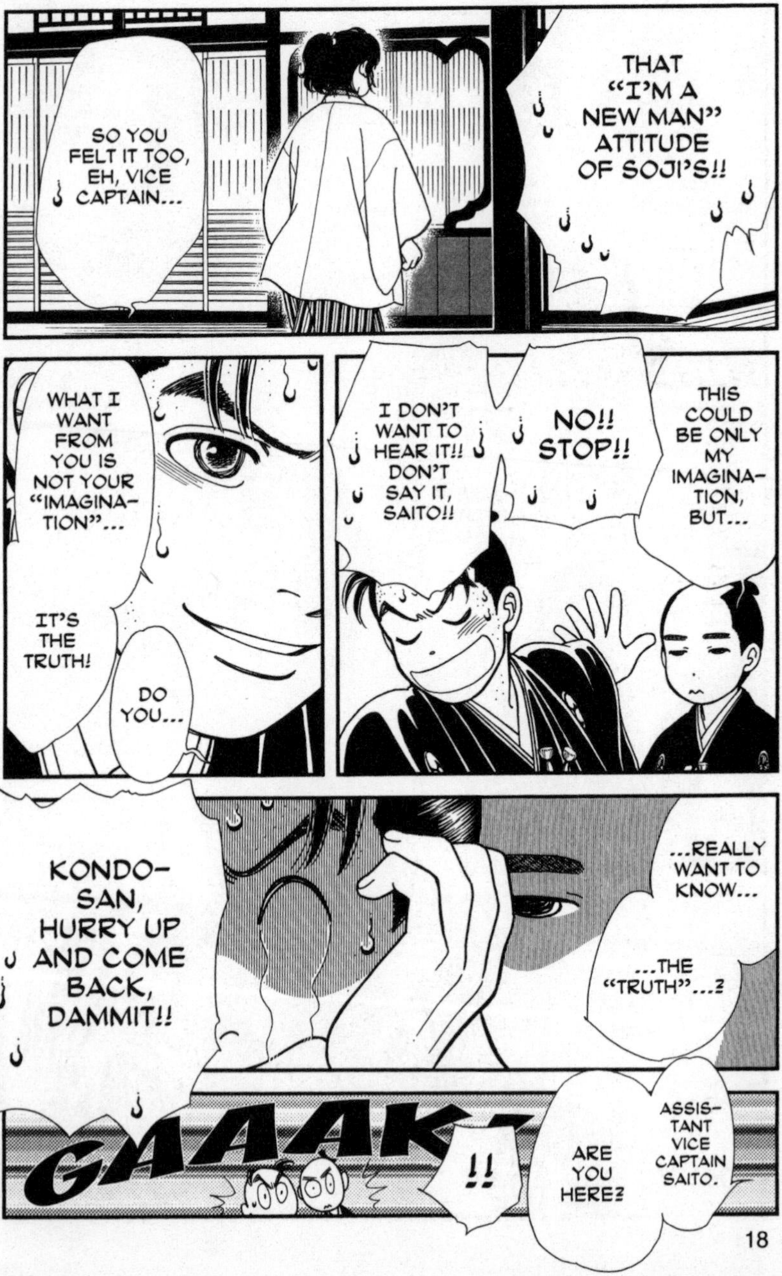
THAT "I'M A NEW MAN" ATTITUDE OF SOJI'S!!
SO YOU FELT IT TOO, EH, VICE CAPTAIN...
THIS COULD BE ONLY MY IMAGINATION, BUT...
NO!! STOP!!
I DON'T WANT TO HEAR IT!! DON'T SAY IT, SAITO!!
WHAT I WANT FROM YOU IS NOT YOUR "IMAGINATION"...
IT'S THE TRUTH!
DO YOU...
...REALLY WANT TO KNOW...
...THE "TRUTH"...?
KONDO-SAN, HURRY UP AND COME BACK, DAMMIT!!
ASSISTANT VICE CAPTAIN SAITO.
ARE YOU HERE?
!!
GAAAK!

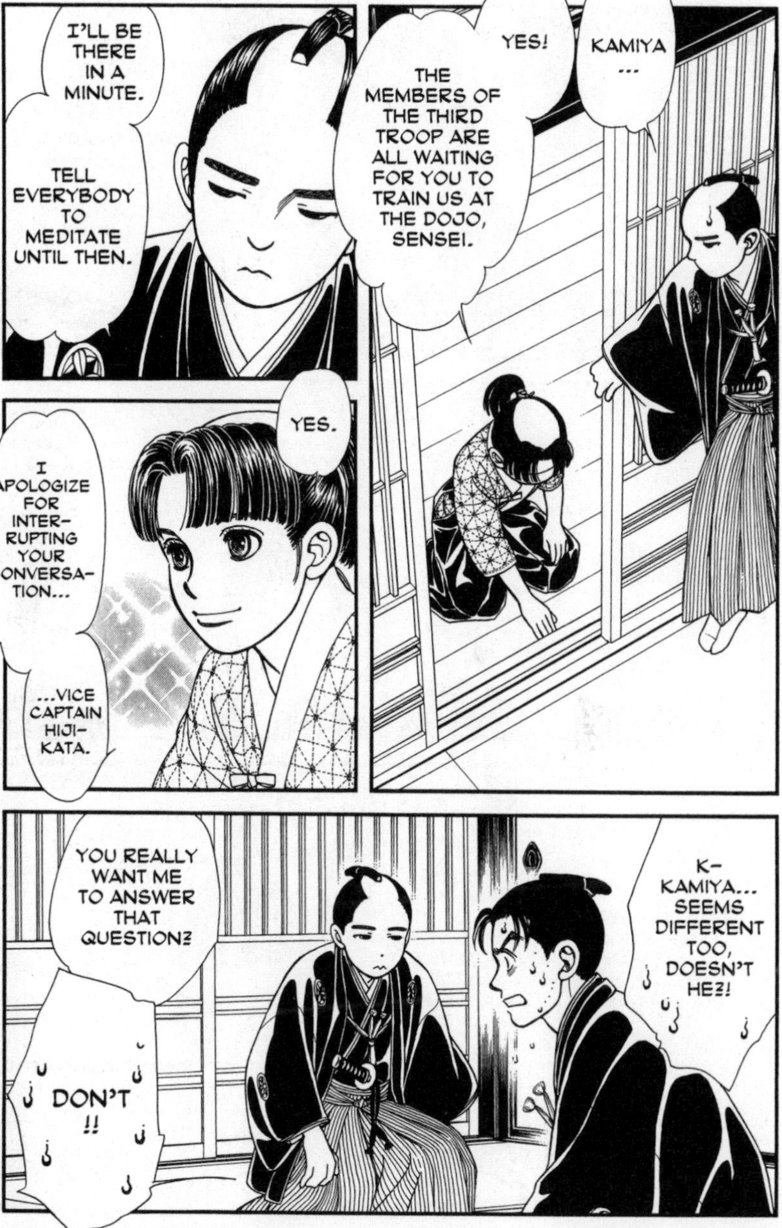
KAMIYA ...
YES!
THE MEMBERS OF THE THIRD TROOP ARE ALL WAITING FOR YOU TO TRAIN US AT THE DOJO, SENSEI.
I'LL BE THERE IN A MINUTE.
TELL EVERYBODY TO MEDITATE UNTIL THEN.
YES.
I APOLOGIZE FOR INTER-RUPTING YOUR CONVERSA-TION...
...VICE CAPTAIN HIJI-KATA.
K-KAMIYA... SEEMS DIFFERENT TOO, DOESN'T HE?!
YOU REALLY WANT ME TO ANSWER THAT QUESTION?
DON'T!!

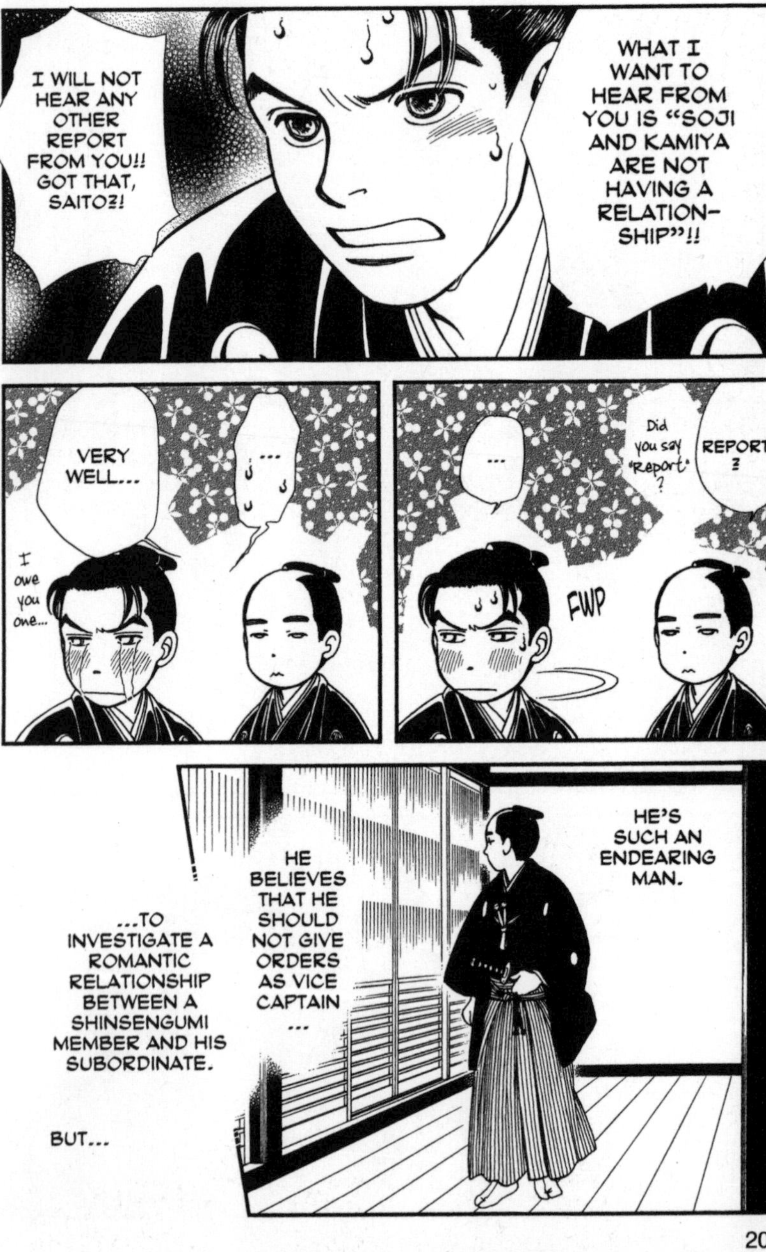
WHAT I WANT TO HEAR FROM YOU IS "SOJI AND KAMIYA ARE NOT HAVING A RELATIONSHIP"!!
I WILL NOT HEAR ANY OTHER REPORT FROM YOU!! GOT THAT, SAITO?!
REPORT?
Did you say "Report"?
...
FWP
...
VERY WELL...
I owe you one...
HE'S SUCH AN ENDEARING MAN.
HE BELIEVES THAT HE SHOULD NOT GIVE ORDERS AS VICE CAPTAIN ...
...TO INVESTIGATE A ROMANTIC RELATIONSHIP BETWEEN A SHINSENGUMI MEMBER AND HIS SUBORDINATE.
BUT...

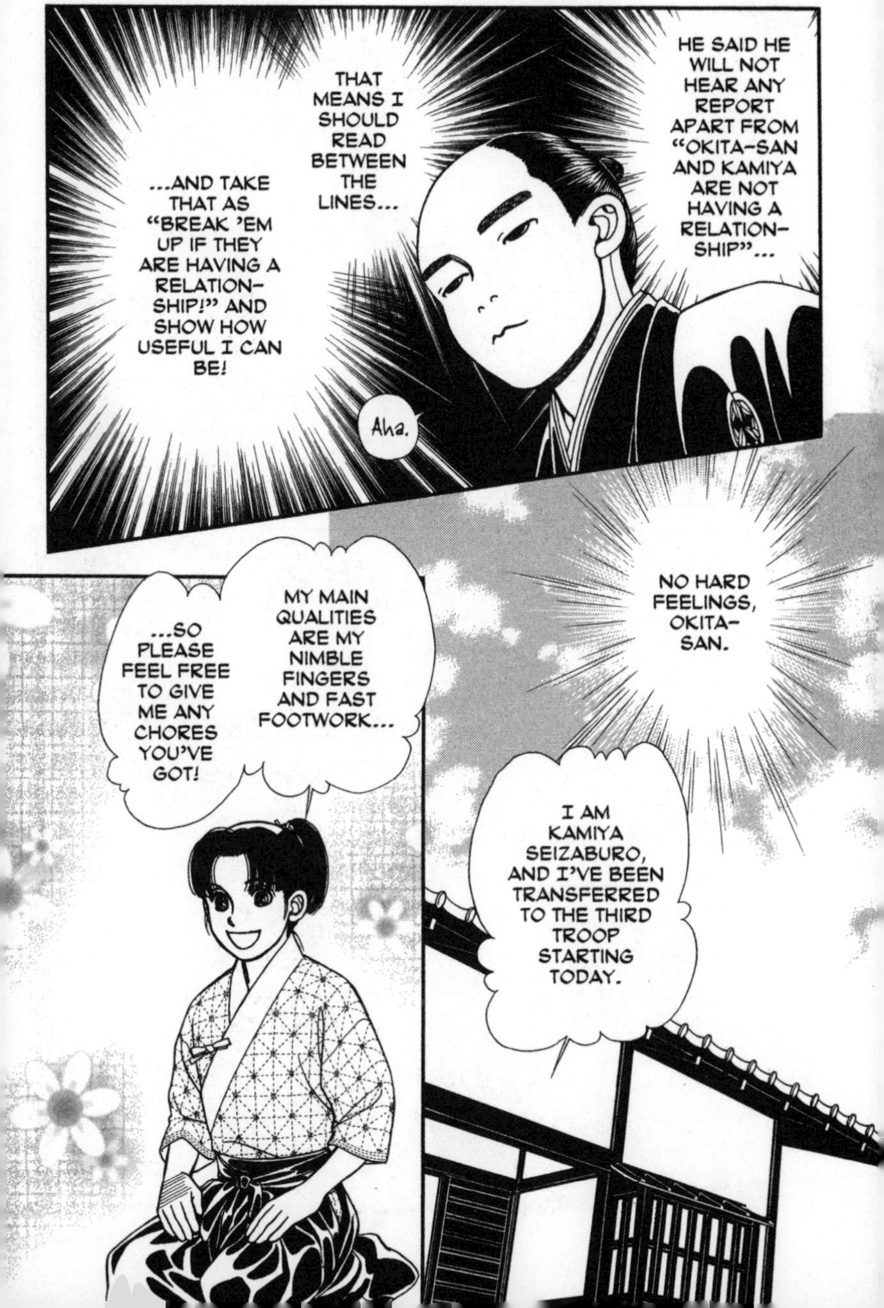
HE SAID HE WILL NOT HEAR ANY REPORT APART FROM "OKITA-SAN AND KAMIYA ARE NOT HAVING A RELATION-SHIP"...
THAT MEANS I SHOULD READ BETWEEN THE LINES...
...AND TAKE THAT AS "BREAK 'EM UP IF THEY ARE HAVING A RELATION-SHIP!" AND SHOW HOW USEFUL I CAN BE!
Aha.
NO HARD FEELINGS, OKITA-SAN.
I AM KAMIYA SEIZABURO, AND I'VE BEEN TRANSFERRED TO THE THIRD TROOP STARTING TODAY.
MY MAIN QUALITIES ARE MY NIMBLE FINGERS AND FAST FOOTWORK...
...SO PLEASE FEEL FREE TO GIVE ME ANY CHORES YOU'VE GOT!

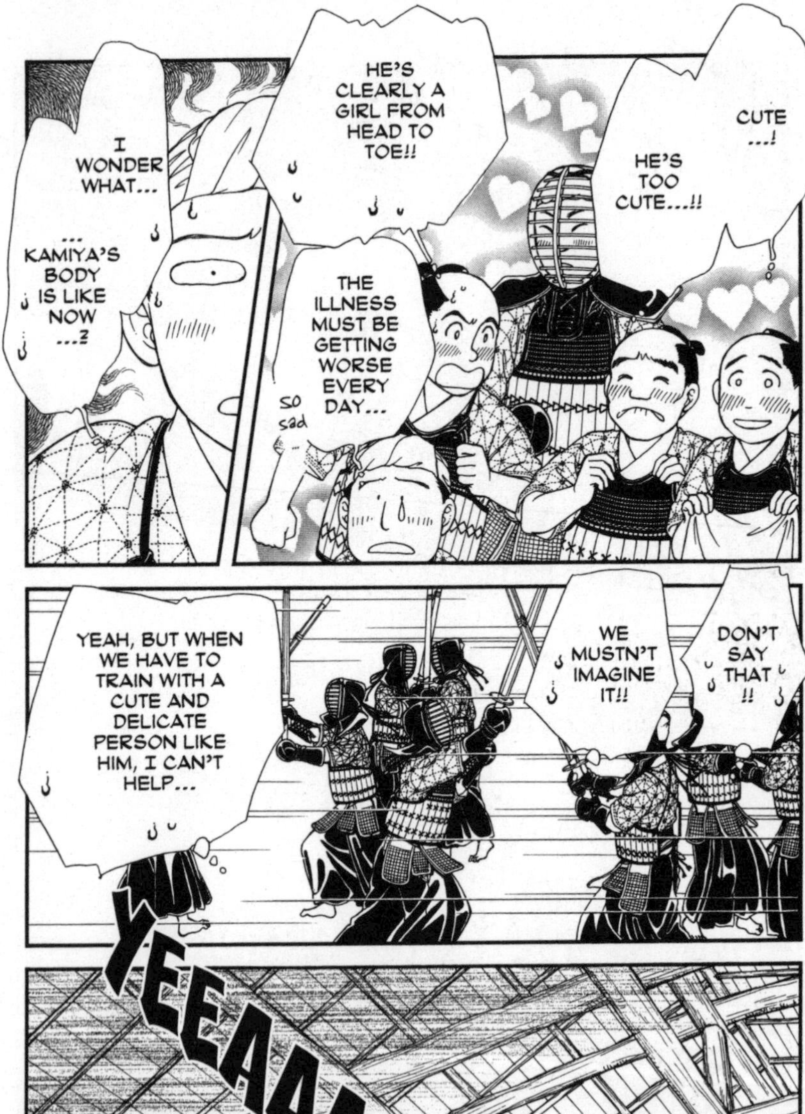
CUTE ...!
HE'S TOO CUTE...!!
HE'S CLEARLY A GIRL FROM HEAD TO TOE!!
THE ILLNESS MUST BE GETTING WORSE EVERY DAY...
SO sad
I WONDER WHAT...
...KAMIYA'S BODY IS LIKE NOW ...?
DON'T SAY THAT !!
WE MUSTN'T IMAGINE IT!!
YEAH, BUT WHEN WE HAVE TO TRAIN WITH A CUTE AND DELICATE PERSON LIKE HIM, I CAN'T HELP...
YEEAAAAAH!

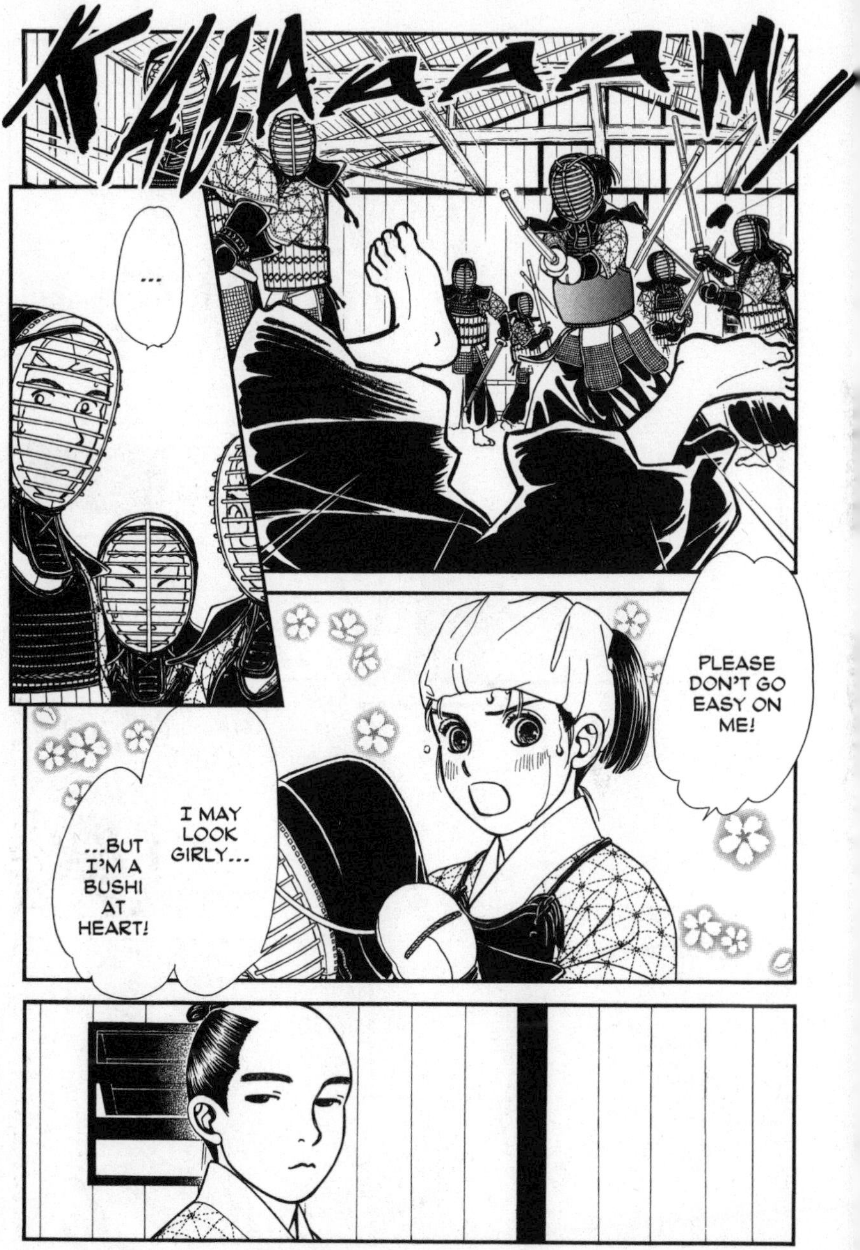
KABAAAAM!!
...
PLEASE DON'T GO EASY ON ME!
I MAY LOOK GIRLY...
...BUT I'M A BUSHI AT HEART!

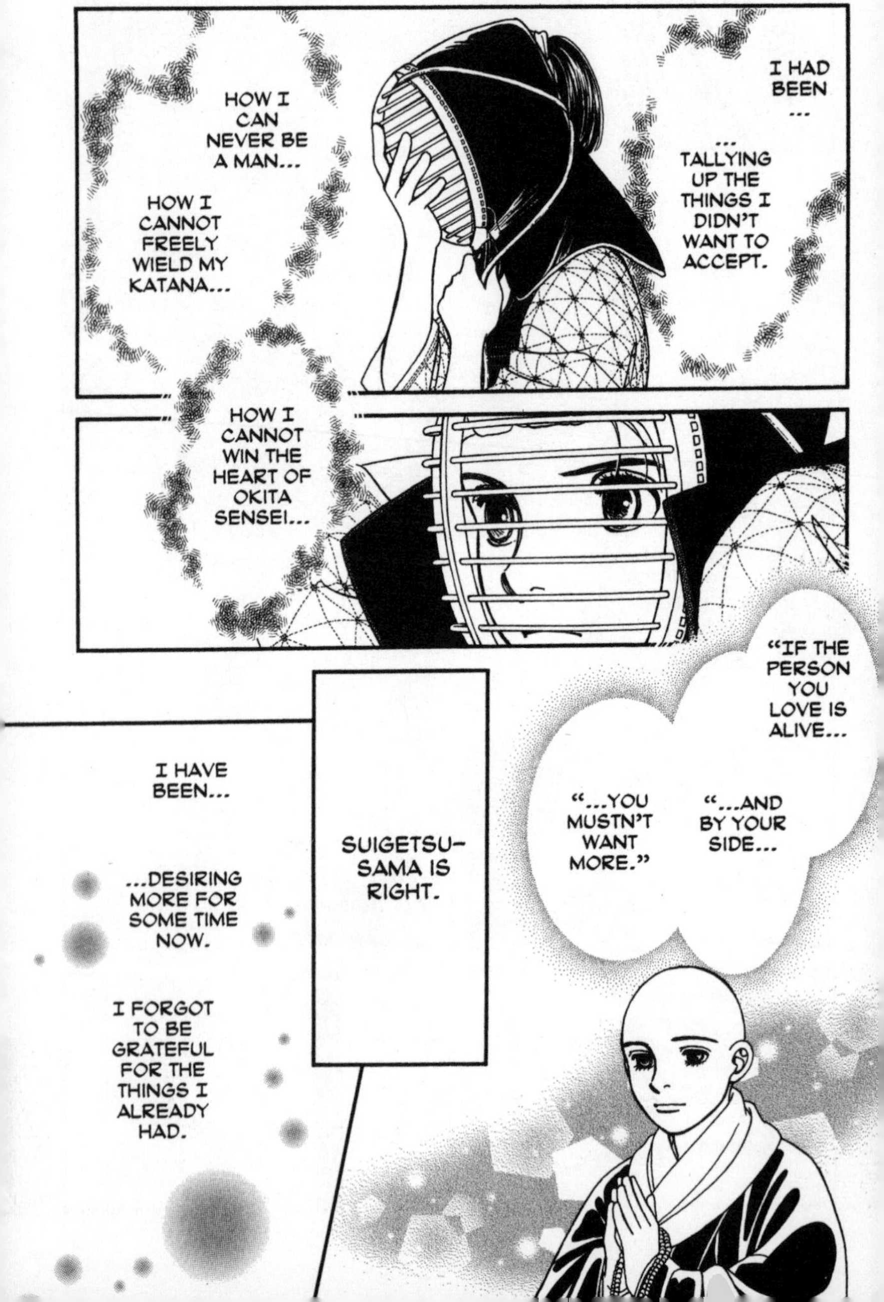
I HAD BEEN ...
... TALLYING UP THE THINGS I DIDN'T WANT TO ACCEPT.
HOW I CAN NEVER BE A MAN...
HOW I CANNOT FREELY WIELD MY KATANA...
HOW I CANNOT WIN THE HEART OF OKITA SENSEI...
“IF THE PERSON YOU LOVE IS ALIVE...
“...AND BY YOUR SIDE...
“...YOU MUSTN'T WANT MORE.”
SUIGETSU-SAMA IS RIGHT.
I HAVE BEEN...
...DESIRING MORE FOR SOME TIME NOW.
I FORGOT TO BE GRATEFUL FOR THE THINGS I ALREADY HAD.

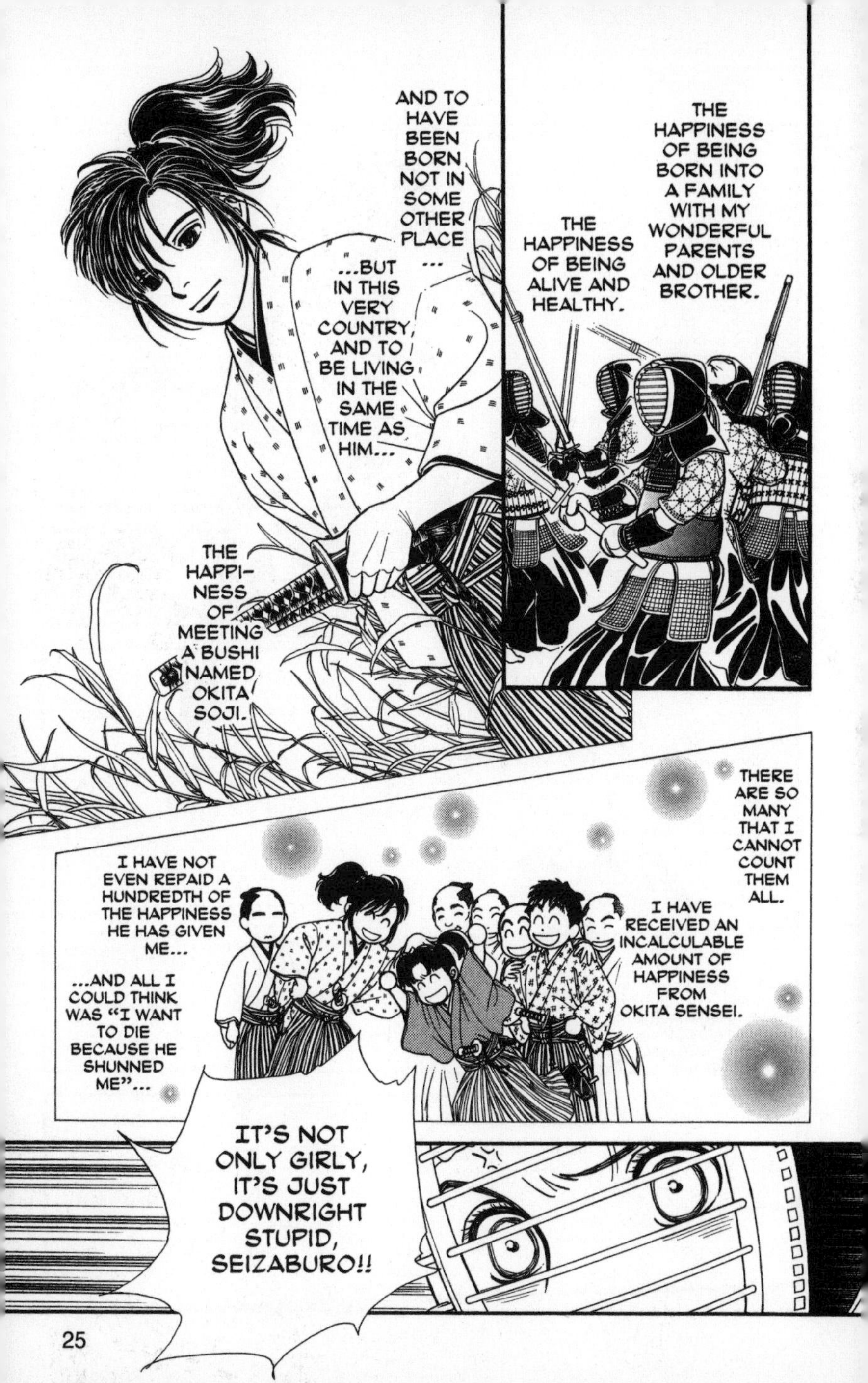
THE HAPPINESS OF BEING BORN INTO A FAMILY WITH MY WONDERFUL PARENTS AND OLDER BROTHER.
THE HAPPINESS OF BEING ALIVE AND HEALTHY.
AND TO HAVE BEEN BORN NOT IN SOME OTHER PLACE...
...BUT IN THIS VERY COUNTRY, AND TO BE LIVING IN THE SAME TIME AS HIM...
THE HAPPI-NESS OF MEETING A BUSHI NAMED OKITA SOJI.
THERE ARE SO MANY THAT I CANNOT COUNT THEM ALL.
I HAVE RECEIVED AN INCALCULABLE AMOUNT OF HAPPINESS FROM OKITA SENSEI.
I HAVE NOT EVEN REPAID A HUNDREDTH OF THE HAPPINESS HE HAS GIVEN ME...
...AND ALL I COULD THINK WAS "I WANT TO DIE BECAUSE HE SHUNNED ME"...
IT'S NOT ONLY GIRLY, IT'S JUST DOWNRIGHT STUPID, SEIZABURO!!

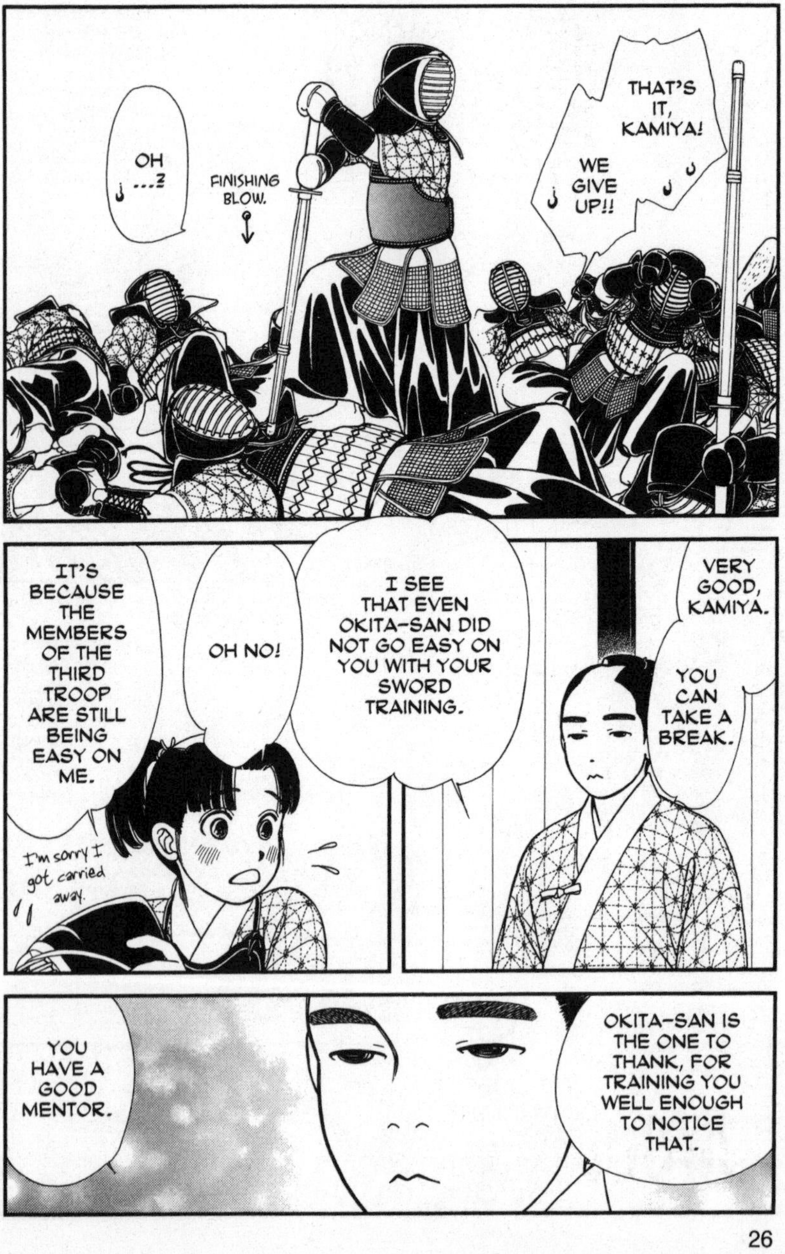
THAT'S IT, KAMIYA! WE GIVE UP!!
FINISHING BLOW.
OH ...
VERY GOOD, KAMIYA.
YOU CAN TAKE A BREAK.
I SEE THAT EVEN OKITA-SAN DID NOT GO EASY ON YOU WITH YOUR SWORD TRAINING.
OH NO!
IT'S BECAUSE THE MEMBERS OF THE THIRD TROOP ARE STILL BEING EASY ON ME.
I'm sorry I got carried away.
OKITA-SAN IS THE ONE TO THANK, FOR TRAINING YOU WELL ENOUGH TO NOTICE THAT.
YOU HAVE A GOOD MENTOR.

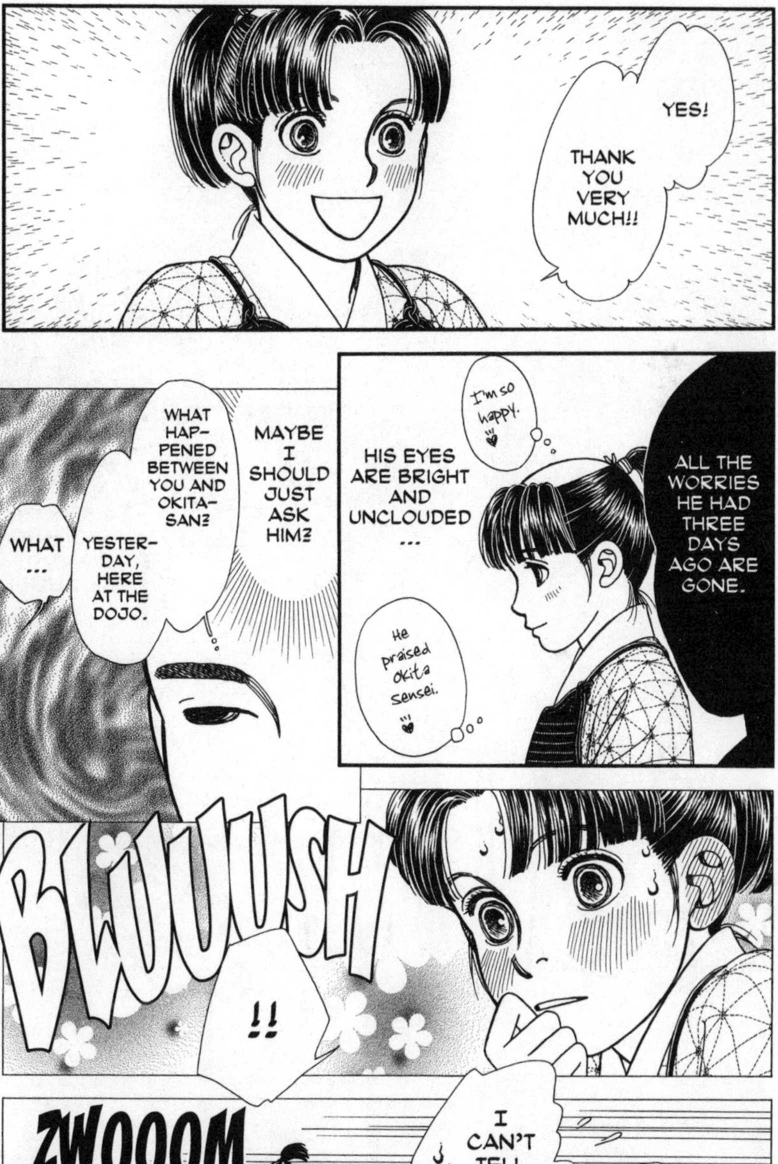
YES!
THANK YOU VERY MUCH!!
ALL THE WORRIES HE HAD THREE DAYS AGO ARE GONE.
I'm so happy.
HIS EYES ARE BRIGHT AND UNCLOUDED...
He praised Okita sensei.
MAYBE I SHOULD JUST ASK HIM?
WHAT HAP-PENED BETWEEN YOU AND OKITA-SAN?
YESTER-DAY, HERE AT THE DOJO.
WHAT...
BLUUUSH
!!
I CAN'T TELL YOU!
ZWOOOM

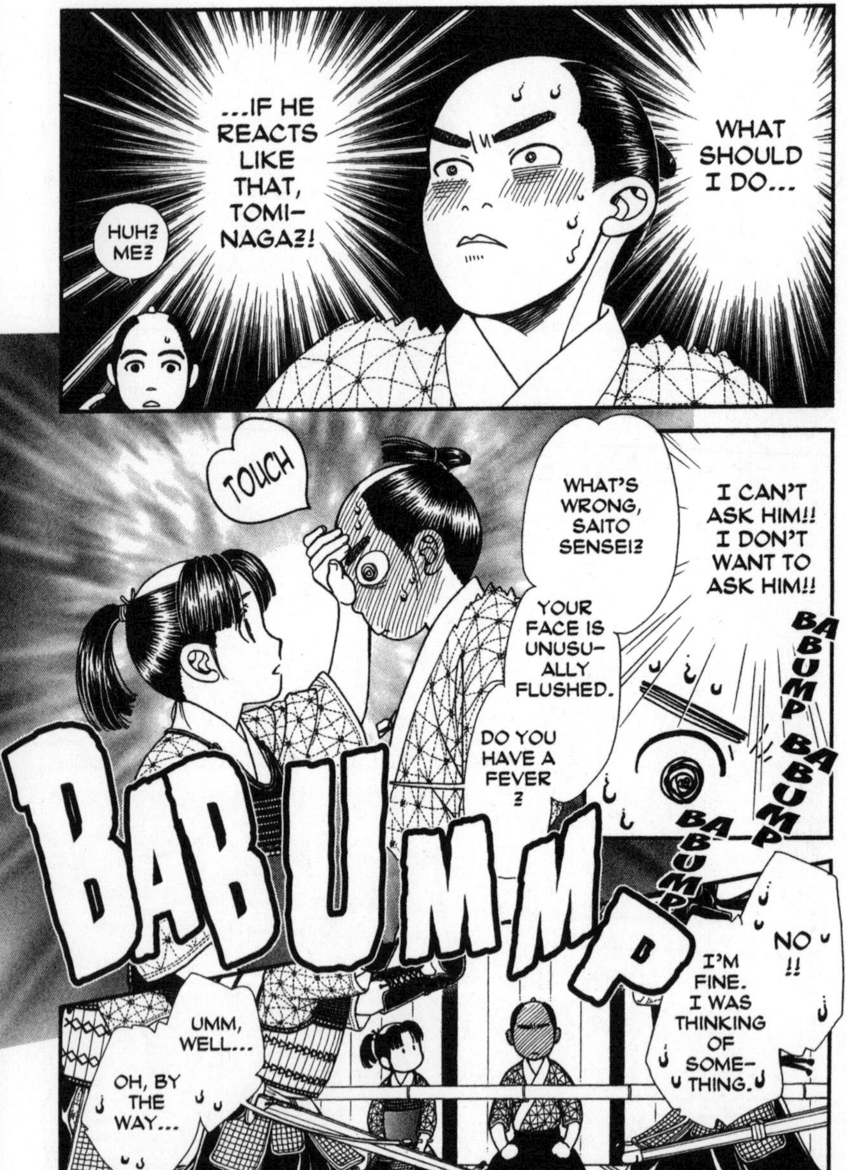
WHAT SHOULD I DO...
...IF HE REACTS LIKE THAT, TOMI-NAGA?!
HUH? ME?
I CAN'T ASK HIM!! I DON'T WANT TO ASK HIM!!
BABUMP BABUMP
BABUMP
WHAT'S WRONG, SAITO SENSEI?
YOUR FACE IS UNUSU-ALLY FLUSHED.
DO YOU HAVE A FEVER?
TOUCH
BABUMP
NO!!
I'M FINE. I WAS THINKING OF SOME-THING.
UMM, WELL...
OH, BY THE WAY...

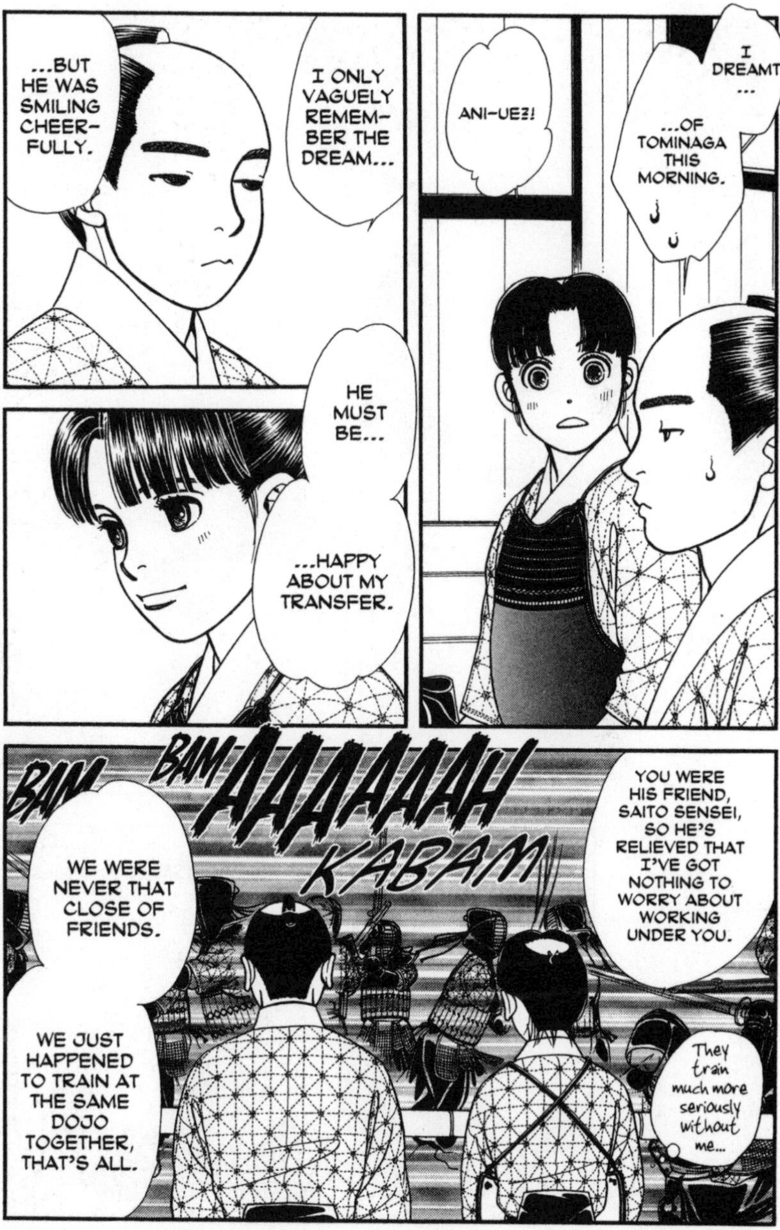
I DREAMT...
...OF TOMINAGA THIS MORNING.
ANI-UE?!
I ONLY VAGUELY REMEMBER THE DREAM...
...BUT HE WAS SMILING CHEERFULLY.
HE MUST BE...
...HAPPY ABOUT MY TRANSFER.
YOU WERE HIS FRIEND, SAITO SENSEI, SO HE'S RELIEVED THAT I'VE GOT NOTHING TO WORRY ABOUT WORKING UNDER YOU.
AAAAAAH
BAM
BAM
KABAM
WE WERE NEVER THAT CLOSE OF FRIENDS.
They train much more seriously without me...
WE JUST HAPPENED TO TRAIN AT THE SAME DOJO TOGETHER, THAT'S ALL.

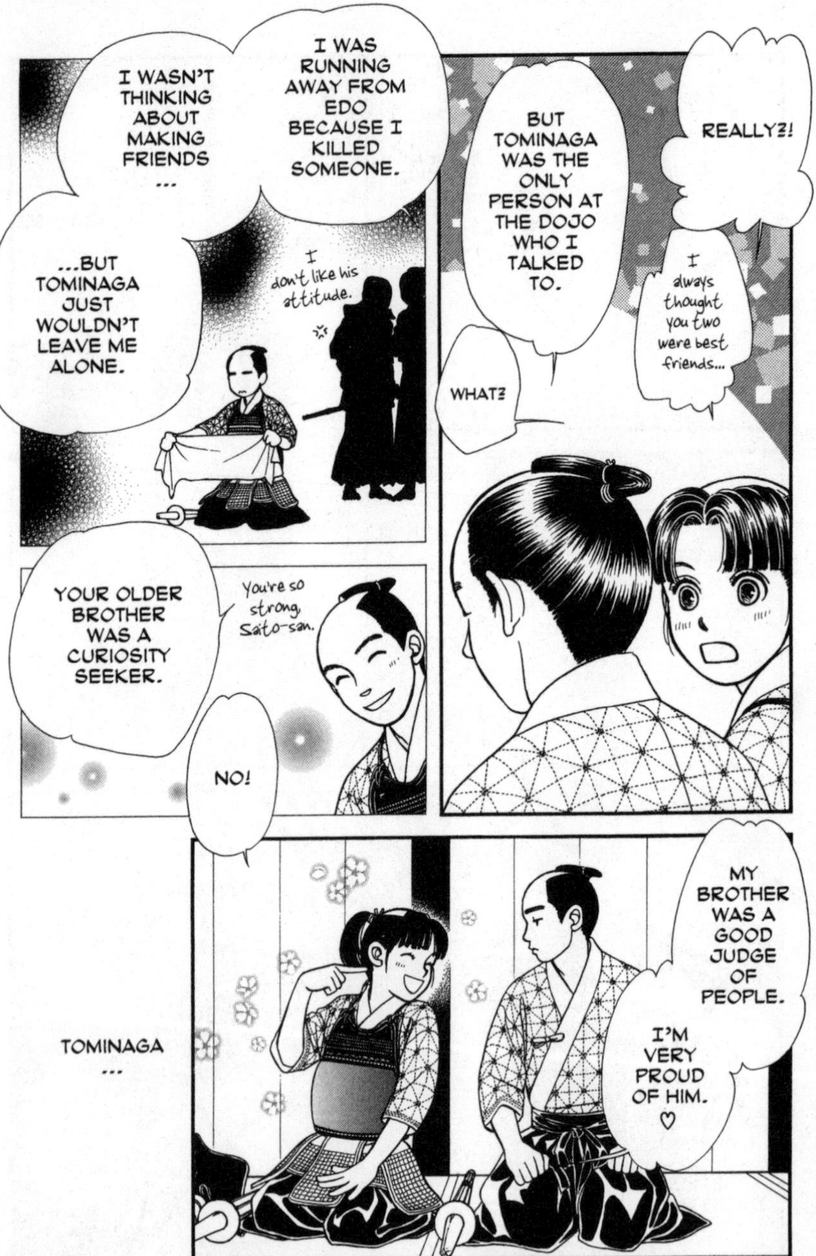
BUT TOMINAGA WAS THE ONLY PERSON AT THE DOJO WHO I TALKED TO.
REALLY?!
I always thought you two were best friends...
WHAT?
I WASN'T THINKING ABOUT MAKING FRIENDS ...
I WAS RUNNING AWAY FROM EDO BECAUSE I KILLED SOMEONE.
...BUT TOMINAGA JUST WOULDN'T LEAVE ME ALONE.
I don't like his attitude.
You're so strong, Saito-san.
YOUR OLDER BROTHER WAS A CURIOSITY SEEKER.
NO!
MY BROTHER WAS A GOOD JUDGE OF PEOPLE.
I'M VERY PROUD OF HIM. ♡
TOMINAGA ...

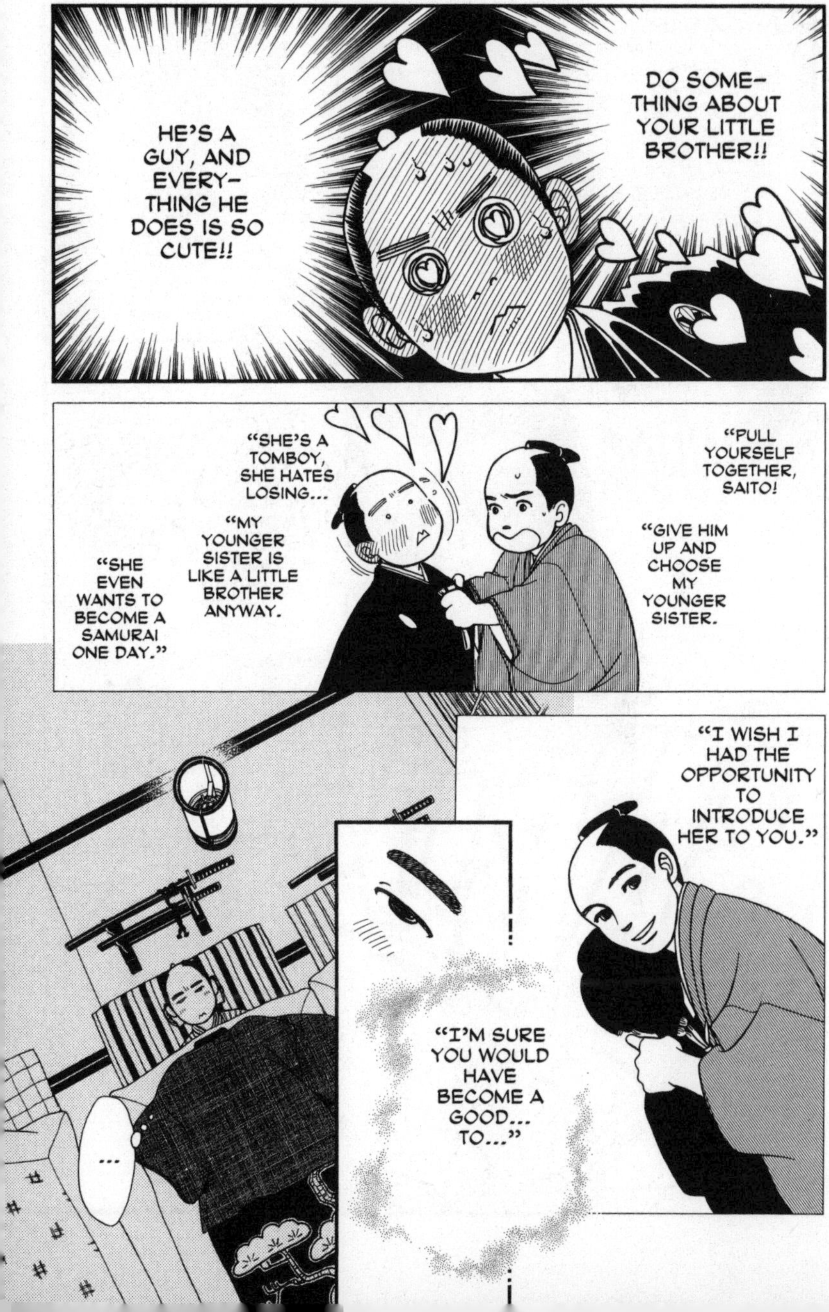
DO SOME-THING ABOUT YOUR LITTLE BROTHER!!
HE'S A GUY, AND EVERY-THING HE DOES IS SO CUTE!!
"PULL YOURSELF TOGETHER, SAITO!
"GIVE HIM UP AND CHOOSE MY YOUNGER SISTER.
"SHE'S A TOMBOY, SHE HATES LOSING...
"MY YOUNGER SISTER IS LIKE A LITTLE BROTHER ANYWAY.
"SHE EVEN WANTS TO BECOME A SAMURAI ONE DAY."
"I WISH I HAD THE OPPORTUNITY TO INTRODUCE HER TO YOU."
"I'M SURE YOU WOULD HAVE BECOME A GOOD... TO..."
...

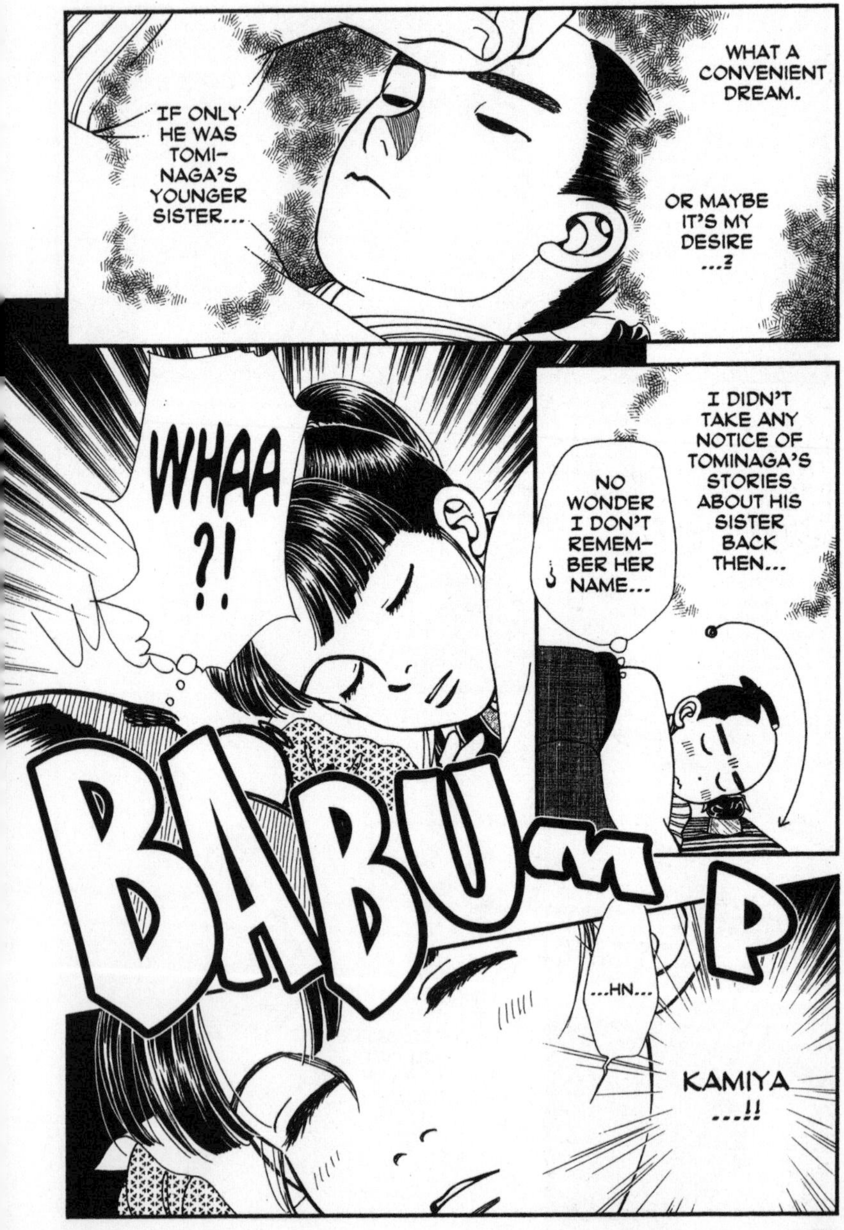
WHAT A CONVENIENT DREAM.
IF ONLY HE WAS TOMI-NAGA'S YOUNGER SISTER...
OR MAYBE IT'S MY DESIRE ...?
I DIDN'T TAKE ANY NOTICE OF TOMINAGA'S STORIES ABOUT HIS SISTER BACK THEN...
NO WONDER I DON'T REMEM-BER HER NAME...
WHAA ?!
BABUmP
...HN...
KAMIYA ...!!

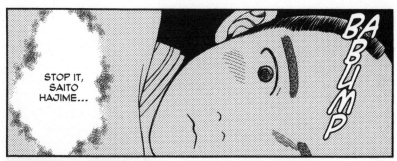

BA BUMP
STOP IT, SAITO HAJIME...
NO MATTER HOW CUTE HE MAY BE, HE'S A MAN.
BA BUMP
SHUDO LOVE IS ONLY TRUE WHEN YOU KEEP IT HIDDEN INSIDE YOU.
BA BUMP
TOUCH HIM AND IT'LL ONLY BE A SELFISH DESIRE FOR LUST...
BA BUMP
I DON'T CARE!!

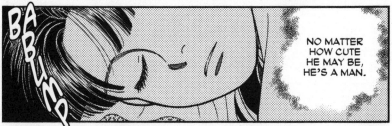

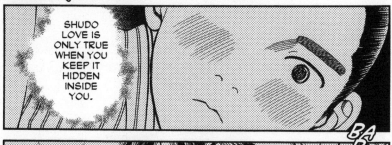

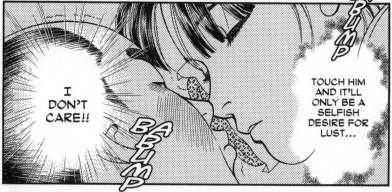

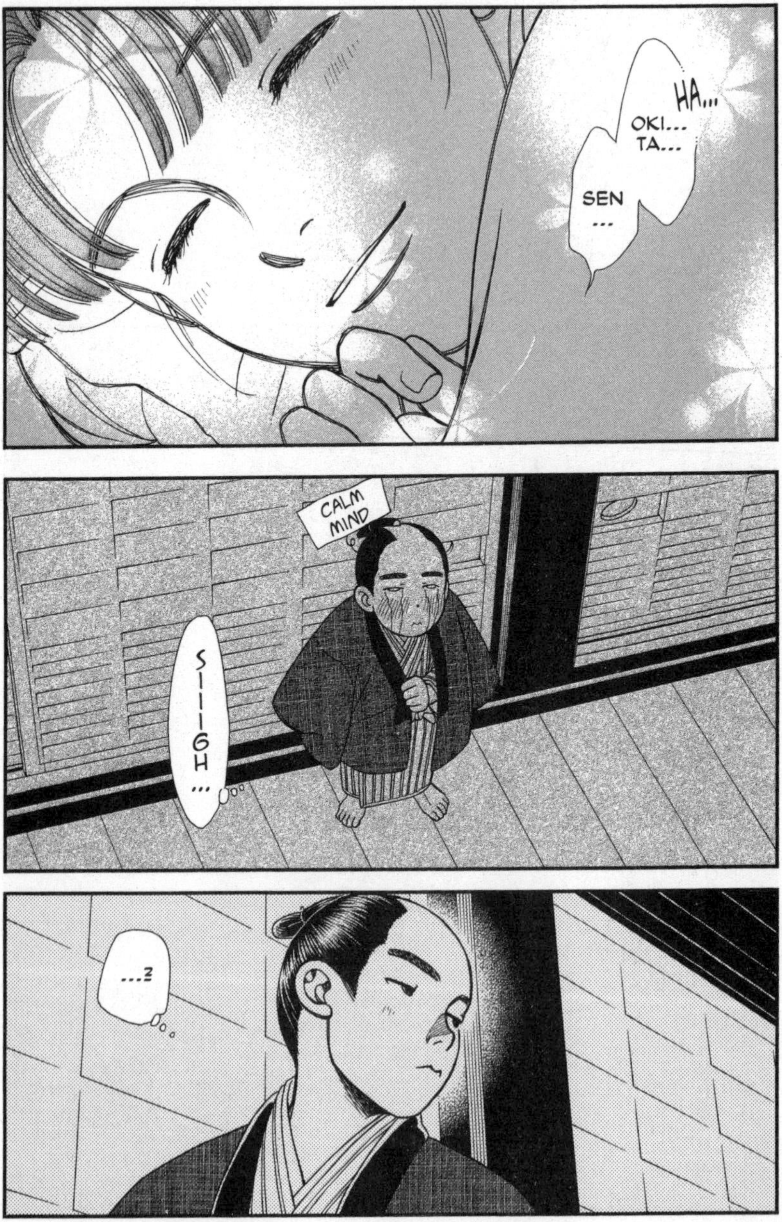
HA...
OKI... TA...
SEN ...
CALM MIND
SIIIGH ...
...Z

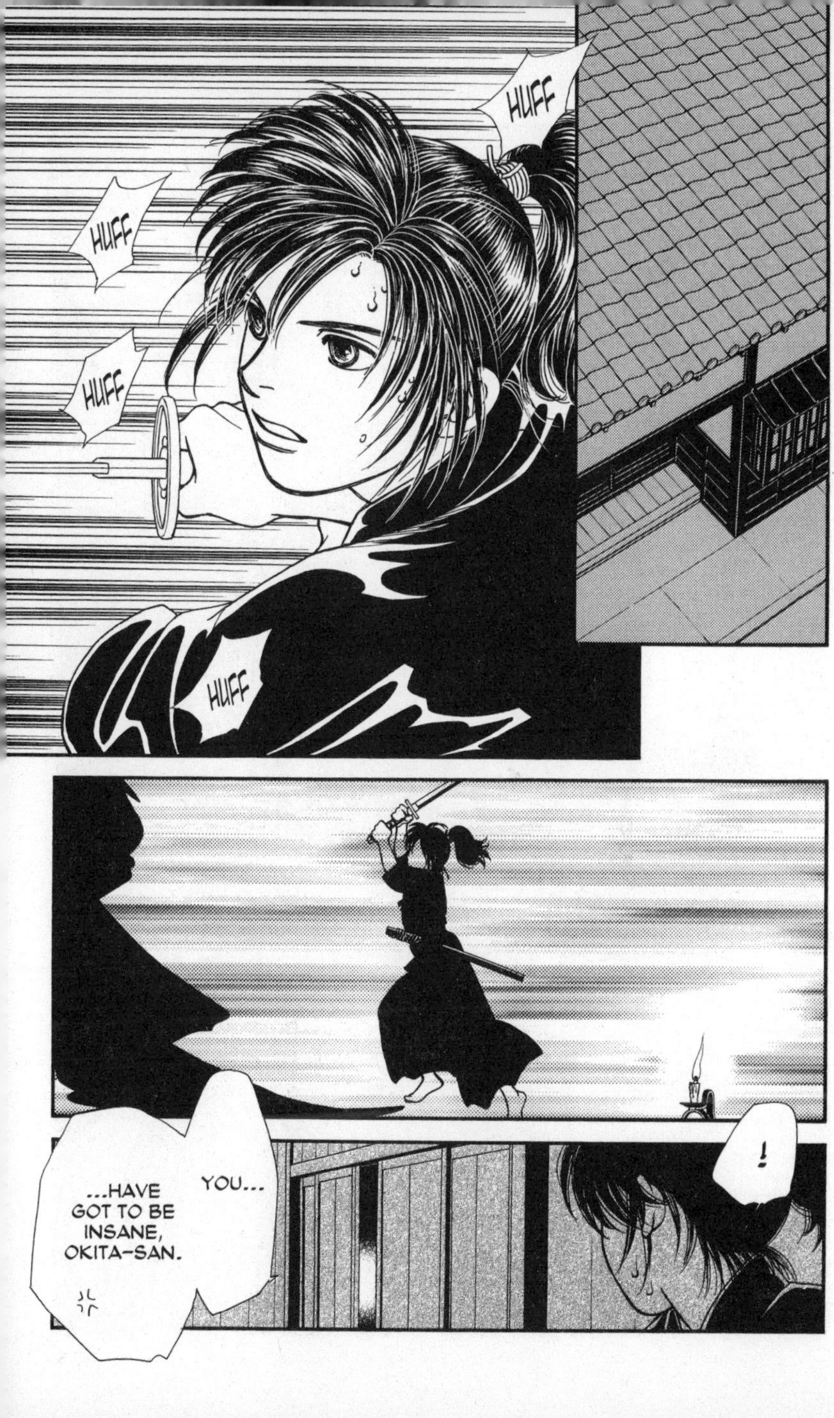
HUFF
HUFF
HUFF
HUFF
!
YOU...
...HAVE GOT TO BE INSANE, OKITA-SAN.

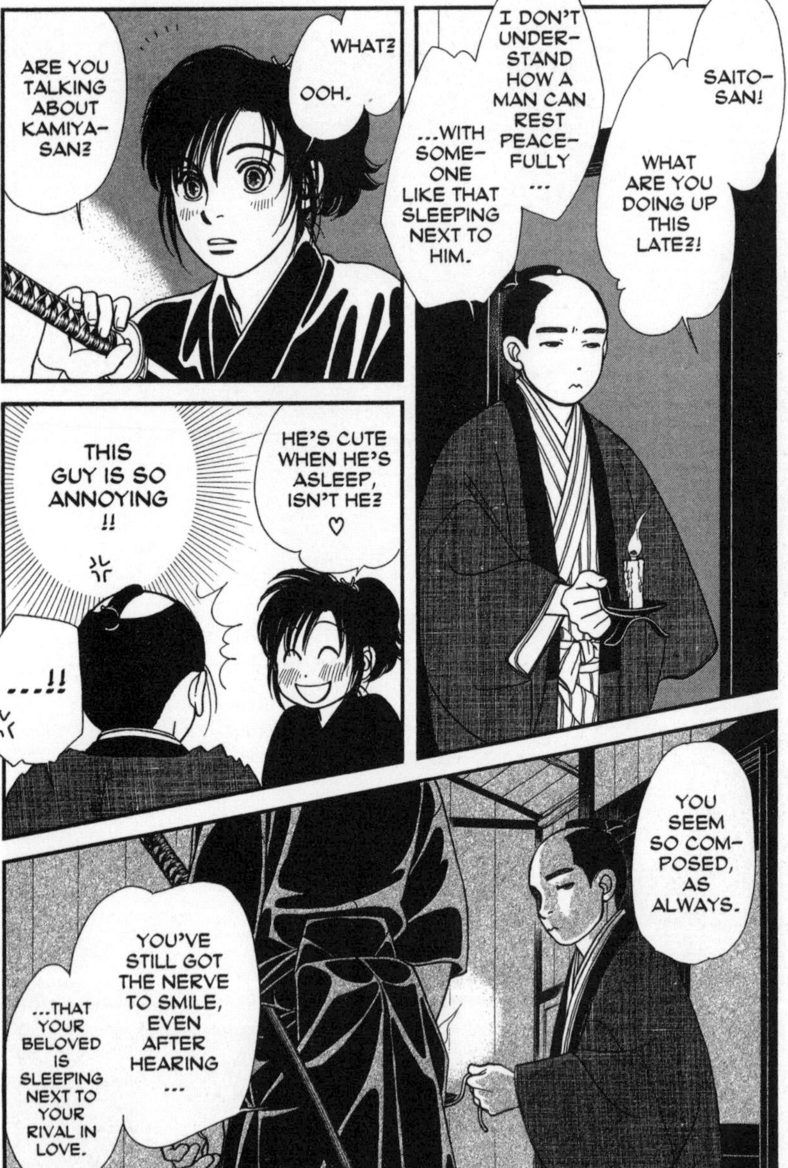
SAITO-SAN!
WHAT ARE YOU DOING UP THIS LATE?!
I DON'T UNDERSTAND HOW A MAN CAN REST PEACEFULLY...
...WITH SOMEONE LIKE THAT SLEEPING NEXT TO HIM.
WHAT?
OOH.
ARE YOU TALKING ABOUT KAMIYA-SAN?
HE'S CUTE WHEN HE'S ASLEEP, ISN'T HE? ♡
THIS GUY IS SO ANNOYING!!
...!!
YOU SEEM SO COMPOSED, AS ALWAYS.
YOU'VE STILL GOT THE NERVE TO SMILE, EVEN AFTER HEARING...
...THAT YOUR BELOVED IS SLEEPING NEXT TO YOUR RIVAL IN LOVE.

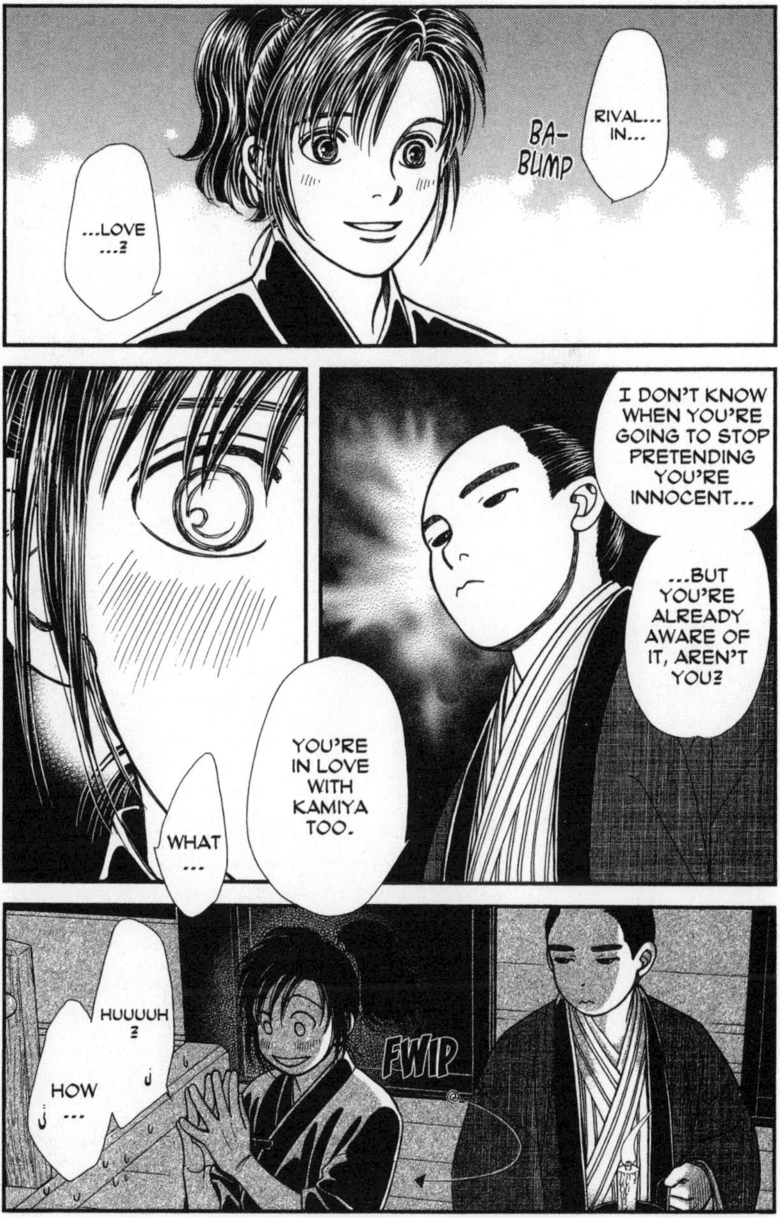
RIVAL... IN...
BA-BUMP
...LOVE ...?
I DON'T KNOW WHEN YOU'RE GOING TO STOP PRETENDING YOU'RE INNOCENT...
...BUT YOU'RE ALREADY AWARE OF IT, AREN'T YOU?
YOU'RE IN LOVE WITH KAMIYA TOO.
WHAT ...
FWIP
HUUUUH?
HOW ...

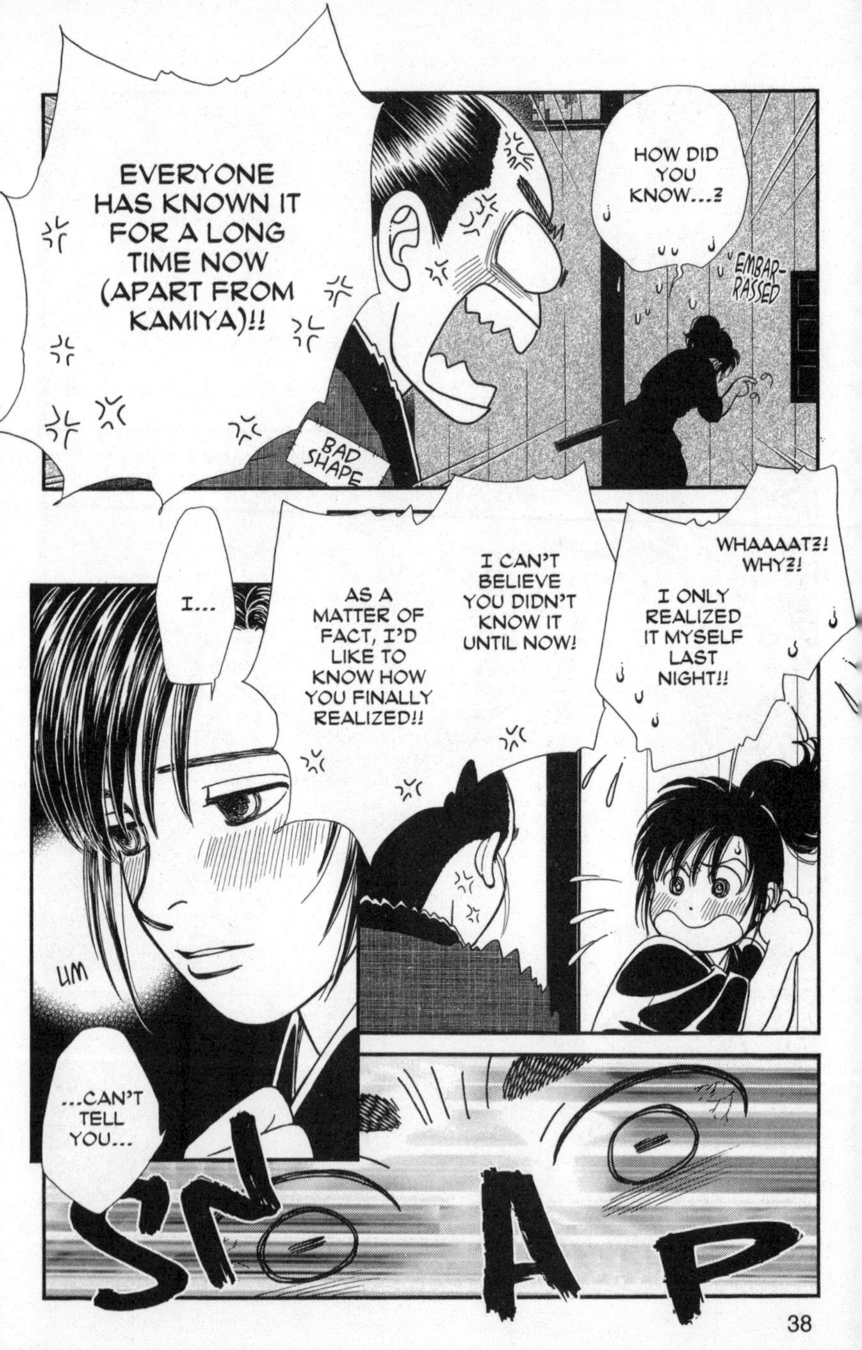
HOW DID YOU KNOW...?
EMBARRASSED
EVERYONE HAS KNOWN IT FOR A LONG TIME NOW (APART FROM KAMIYA)!!
BAD SHAPE
WHAAAAT?! WHY?!
I ONLY REALIZED IT MYSELF LAST NIGHT!!
I CAN'T BELIEVE YOU DIDN'T KNOW IT UNTIL NOW!
AS A MATTER OF FACT, I'D LIKE TO KNOW HOW YOU FINALLY REALIZED!!
I...
UM
...CAN'T TELL YOU...
SNAP

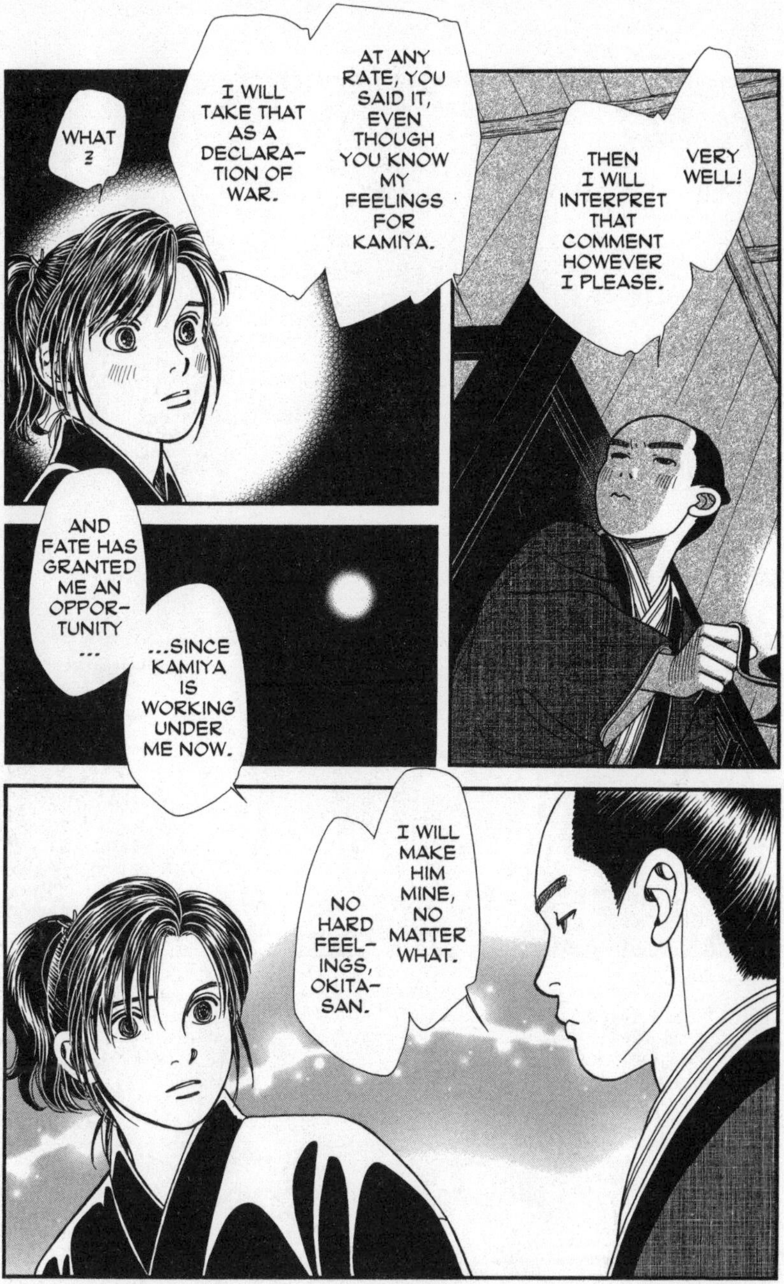
VERY WELL!
THEN I WILL INTERPRET THAT COMMENT HOWEVER I PLEASE.
AT ANY RATE, YOU SAID IT, EVEN THOUGH YOU KNOW MY FEELINGS FOR KAMIYA.
I WILL TAKE THAT AS A DECLARATION OF WAR.
WHAT?
AND FATE HAS GRANTED ME AN OPPORTUNITY...
...SINCE KAMIYA IS WORKING UNDER ME NOW.
I WILL MAKE HIM MINE, NO MATTER WHAT.
NO HARD FEELINGS, OKITA-SAN.

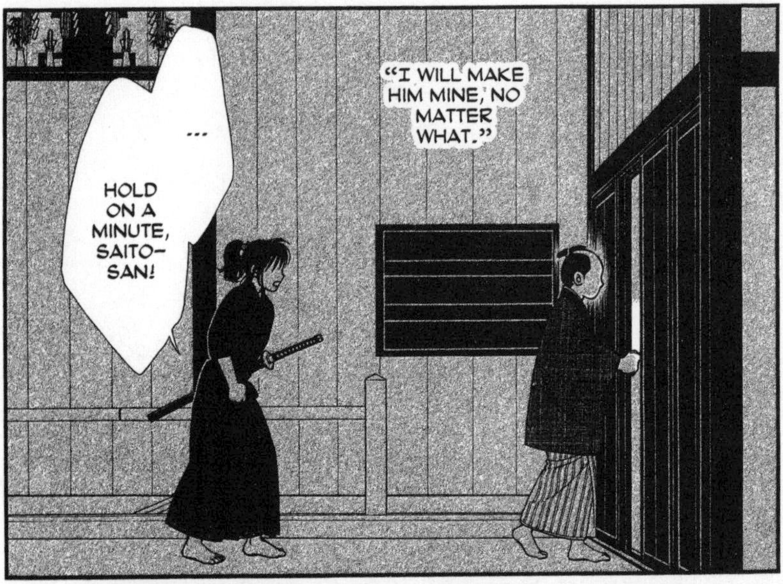
"I WILL MAKE HIM MINE, NO MATTER WHAT."
...
HOLD ON A MINUTE, SAITO-SAN!

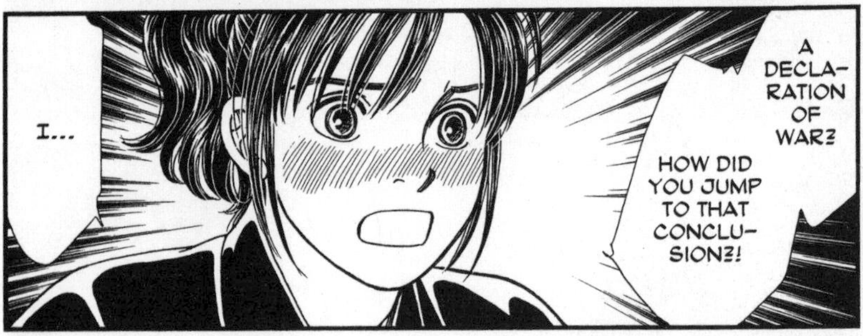
A DECLARATION OF WAR?
HOW DID YOU JUMP TO THAT CONCLUSION?!
I...

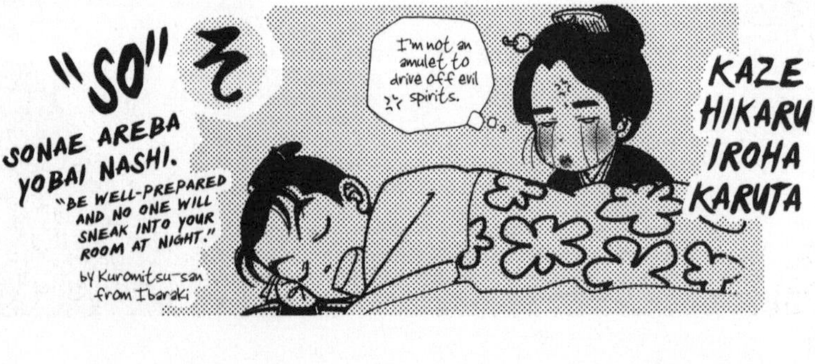
KAZE HIKARU IROHA KARUTA
I'm not an amulet to drive off evil spirits.
"SO" そ
SONAE AREBA YOBAI NASHI.
"BE WELL-PREPARED AND NO ONE WILL SNEAK INTO YOUR ROOM AT NIGHT."
by Kuromitsu-san from Ibaraki

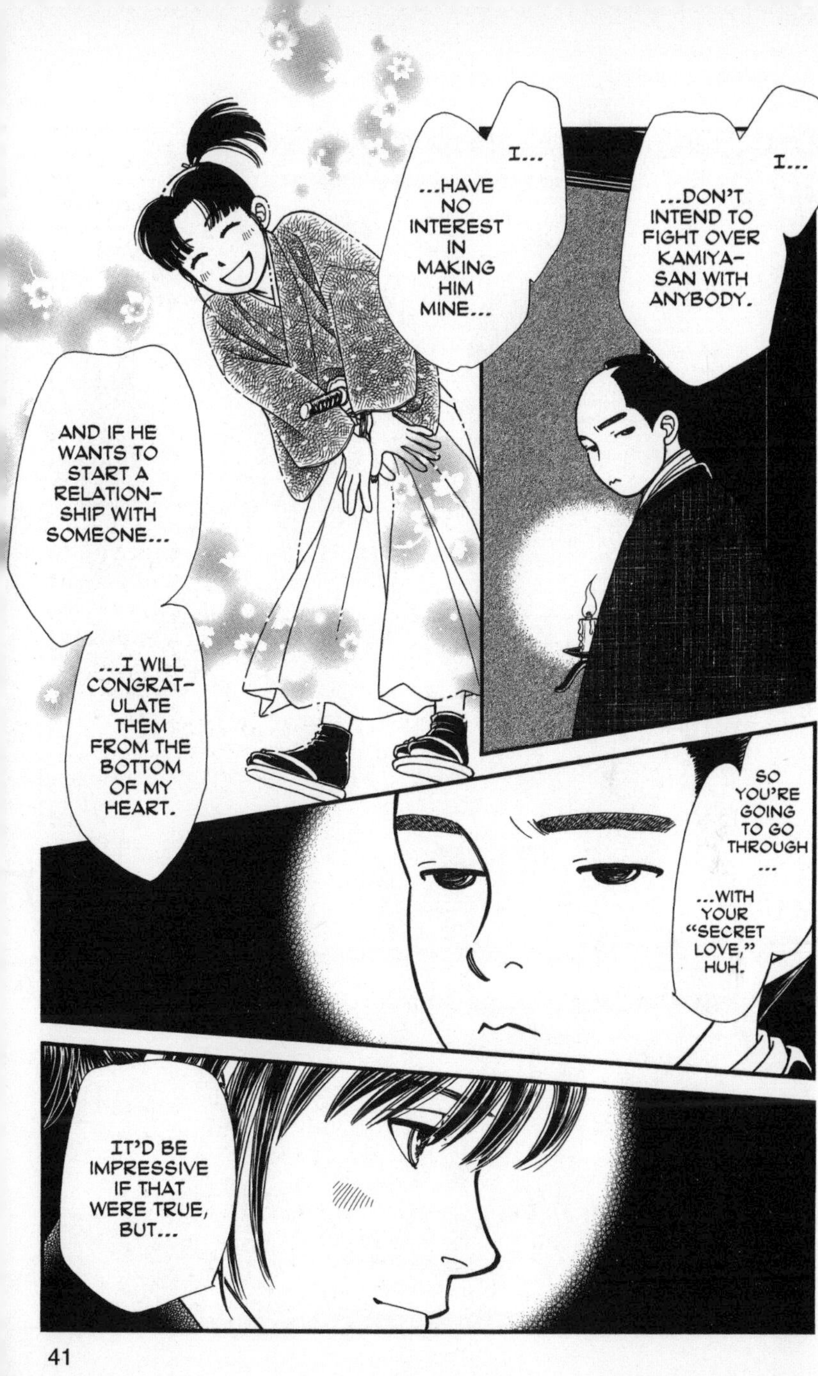
I...
...DON'T INTEND TO FIGHT OVER KAMIYA-SAN WITH ANYBODY.
I...
...HAVE NO INTEREST IN MAKING HIM MINE...
AND IF HE WANTS TO START A RELATION-SHIP WITH SOMEONE...
...I WILL CONGRAT-ULATE THEM FROM THE BOTTOM OF MY HEART.
SO YOU'RE GOING TO GO THROUGH...
...WITH YOUR "SECRET LOVE," HUH.
IT'D BE IMPRESSIVE IF THAT WERE TRUE, BUT...

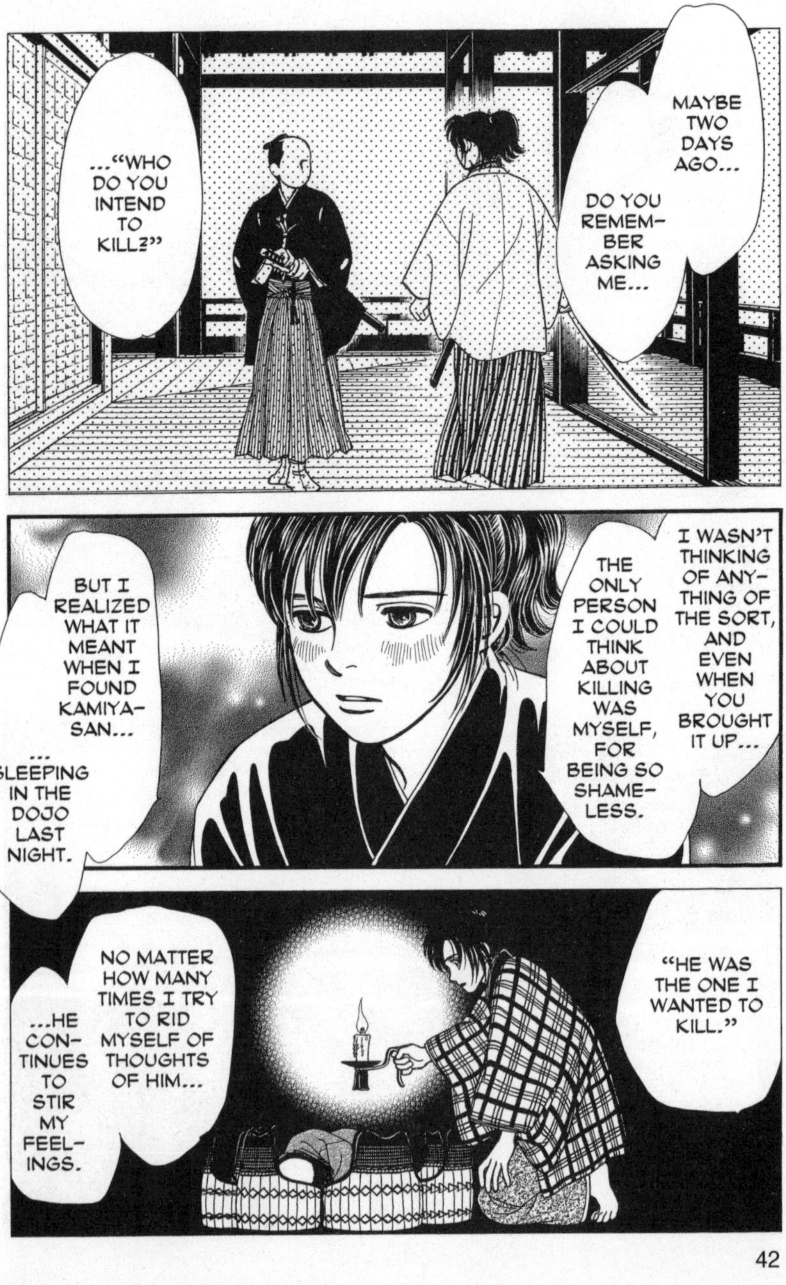
MAYBE TWO DAYS AGO...
DO YOU REMEMBER ASKING ME...
...“WHO DO YOU INTEND TO KILL?”
I WASN’T THINKING OF ANYTHING OF THE SORT, AND EVEN WHEN YOU BROUGHT IT UP...
THE ONLY PERSON I COULD THINK ABOUT KILLING WAS MYSELF, FOR BEING SO SHAMELESS.
BUT I REALIZED WHAT IT MEANT WHEN I FOUND KAMIYA-SAN...
...SLEEPING IN THE DOJO LAST NIGHT.
“HE WAS THE ONE I WANTED TO KILL.”
NO MATTER HOW MANY TIMES I TRY TO RID MYSELF OF THOUGHTS OF HIM...
...HE CONTINUES TO STIR MY FEELINGS.

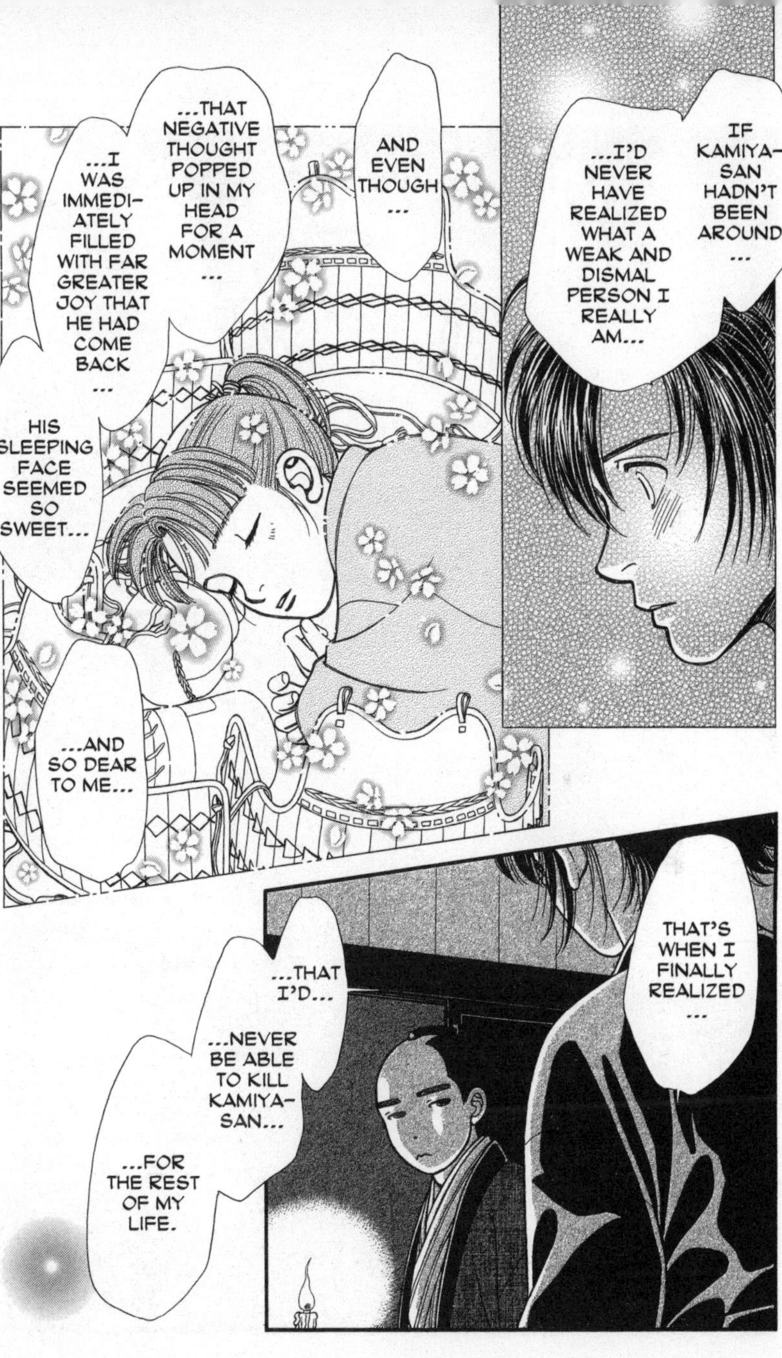
IF KAMIYA-SAN HADN'T BEEN AROUND...
...I'D NEVER HAVE REALIZED WHAT A WEAK AND DISMAL PERSON I REALLY AM...
AND EVEN THOUGH...
...THAT NEGATIVE THOUGHT POPPED UP IN MY HEAD FOR A MOMENT...
...I WAS IMMEDIATELY FILLED WITH FAR GREATER JOY THAT HE HAD COME BACK...
HIS SLEEPING FACE SEEMED SO SWEET...
...AND SO DEAR TO ME...
THAT'S WHEN I FINALLY REALIZED...
...THAT I'D...
...NEVER BE ABLE TO KILL KAMIYA-SAN...
...FOR THE REST OF MY LIFE.

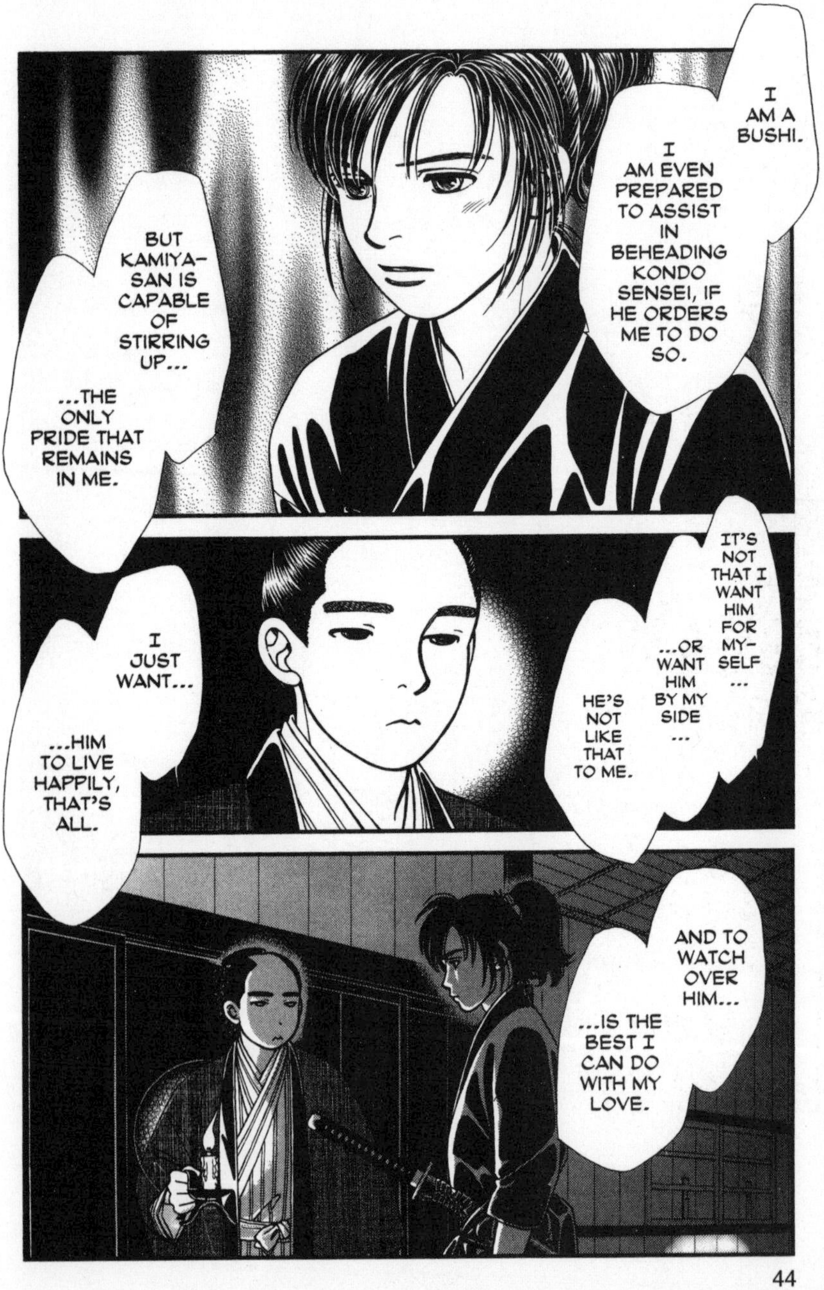
I AM A BUSHI.
I AM EVEN PREPARED TO ASSIST IN BEHEADING KONDO SENSEI, IF HE ORDERS ME TO DO SO.
BUT KAMIYA-SAN IS CAPABLE OF STIRRING UP...
...THE ONLY PRIDE THAT REMAINS IN ME.
IT'S NOT THAT I WANT HIM FOR MYSELF...
...OR WANT HIM BY MY SIDE...
HE'S NOT LIKE THAT TO ME.
I JUST WANT...
...HIM TO LIVE HAPPILY, THAT'S ALL.
AND TO WATCH OVER HIM...
...IS THE BEST I CAN DO WITH MY LOVE.

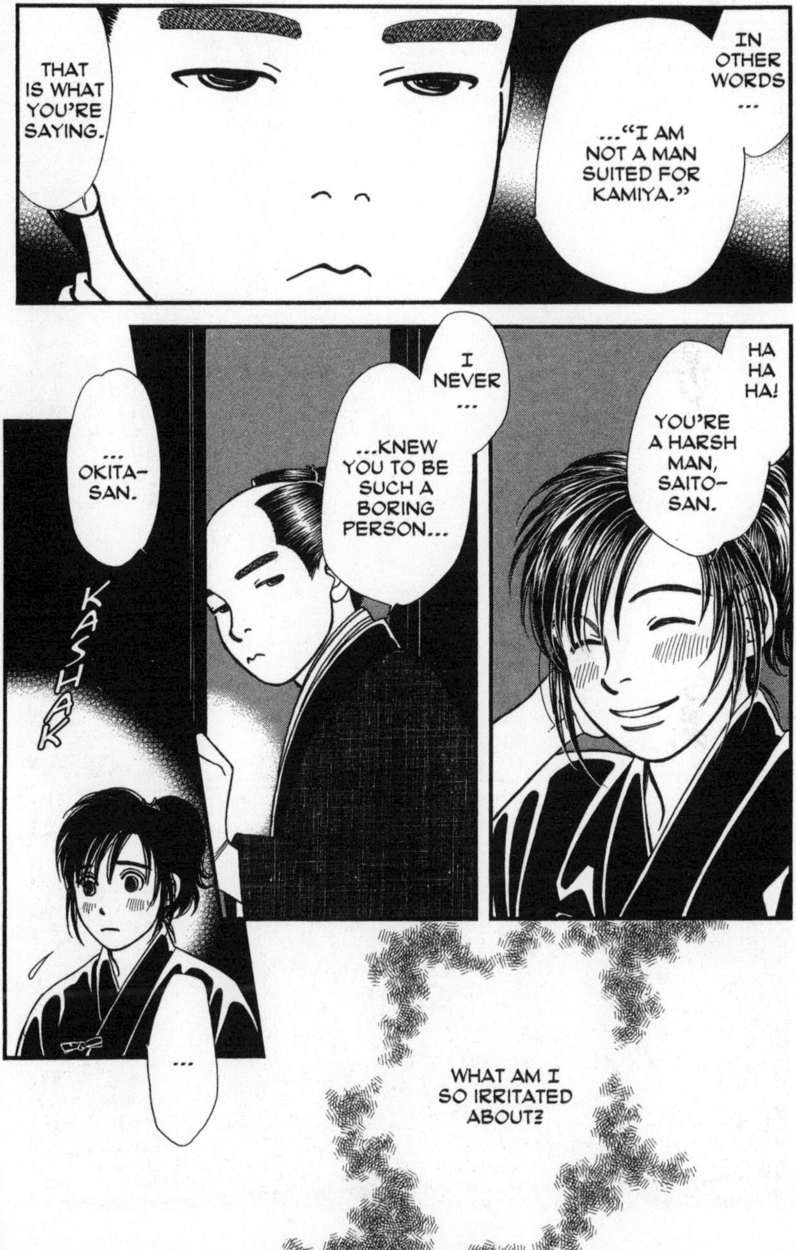
IN OTHER WORDS ...
...“I AM NOT A MAN SUITED FOR KAMIYA.”
THAT IS WHAT YOU’RE SAYING.
HA HA HA!
YOU’RE A HARSH MAN, SAITO-SAN.
I NEVER ...
...KNEW YOU TO BE SUCH A BORING PERSON...
... OKITA-SAN.
KASHAK
...
WHAT AM I SO IRRITATED ABOUT?

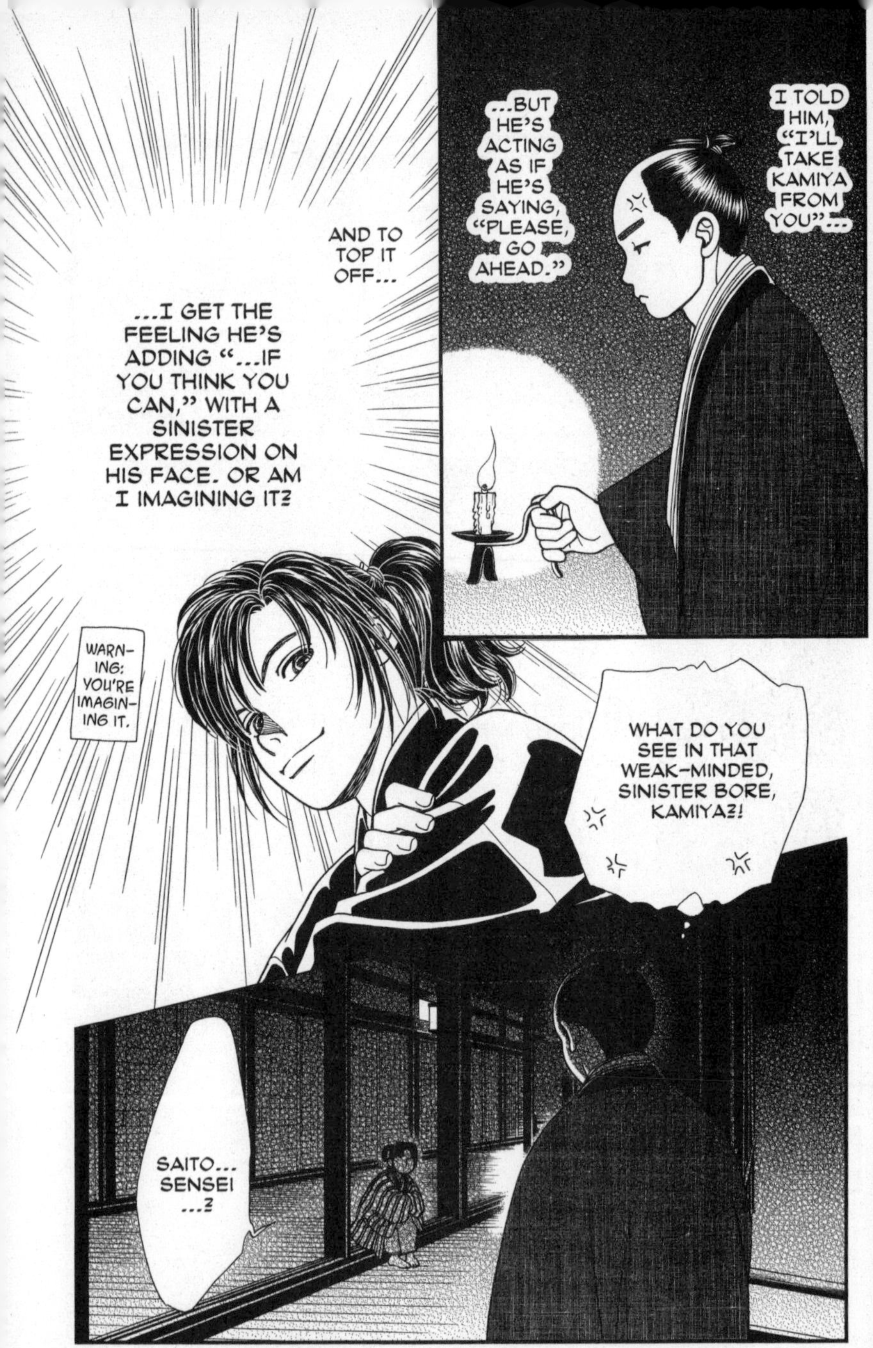
I TOLD HIM, "I'LL TAKE KAMIYA FROM YOU"...
...BUT HE'S ACTING AS IF HE'S SAYING, "PLEASE, GO AHEAD."
AND TO TOP IT OFF...
...I GET THE FEELING HE'S ADDING "...IF YOU THINK YOU CAN," WITH A SINISTER EXPRESSION ON HIS FACE. OR AM I IMAGINING IT?
WARNING: YOU'RE IMAGINING IT.
WHAT DO YOU SEE IN THAT WEAK-MINDED, SINISTER BORE, KAMIYA?!
SAITO... SENSEI...?

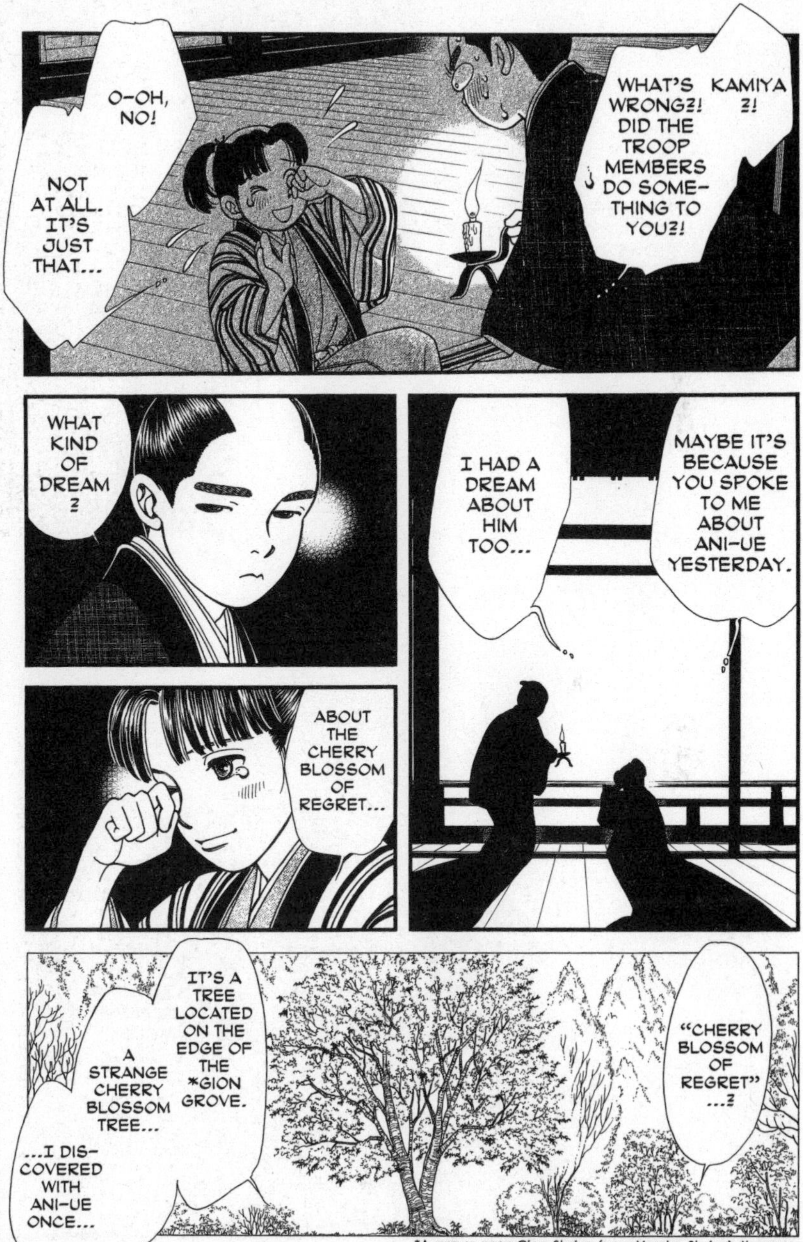
KAMIYA ?!
WHAT'S WRONG?! DID THE TROOP MEMBERS DO SOME-THING TO YOU?!
O-OH, NO!
NOT AT ALL. IT'S JUST THAT...
MAYBE IT'S BECAUSE YOU SPOKE TO ME ABOUT ANI-UE YESTERDAY.
I HAD A DREAM ABOUT HIM TOO...
WHAT KIND OF DREAM ?
ABOUT THE CHERRY BLOSSOM OF REGRET...
"CHERRY BLOSSOM OF REGRET" ...?
IT'S A TREE LOCATED ON THE EDGE OF THE *GION GROVE.
A STRANGE CHERRY BLOSSOM TREE...
...I DIS-COVERED WITH ANI-UE ONCE...

*A grove near Gion Shrine (now Yasaka Shrine). It was a place famous for nighttime cherry blossom viewing.

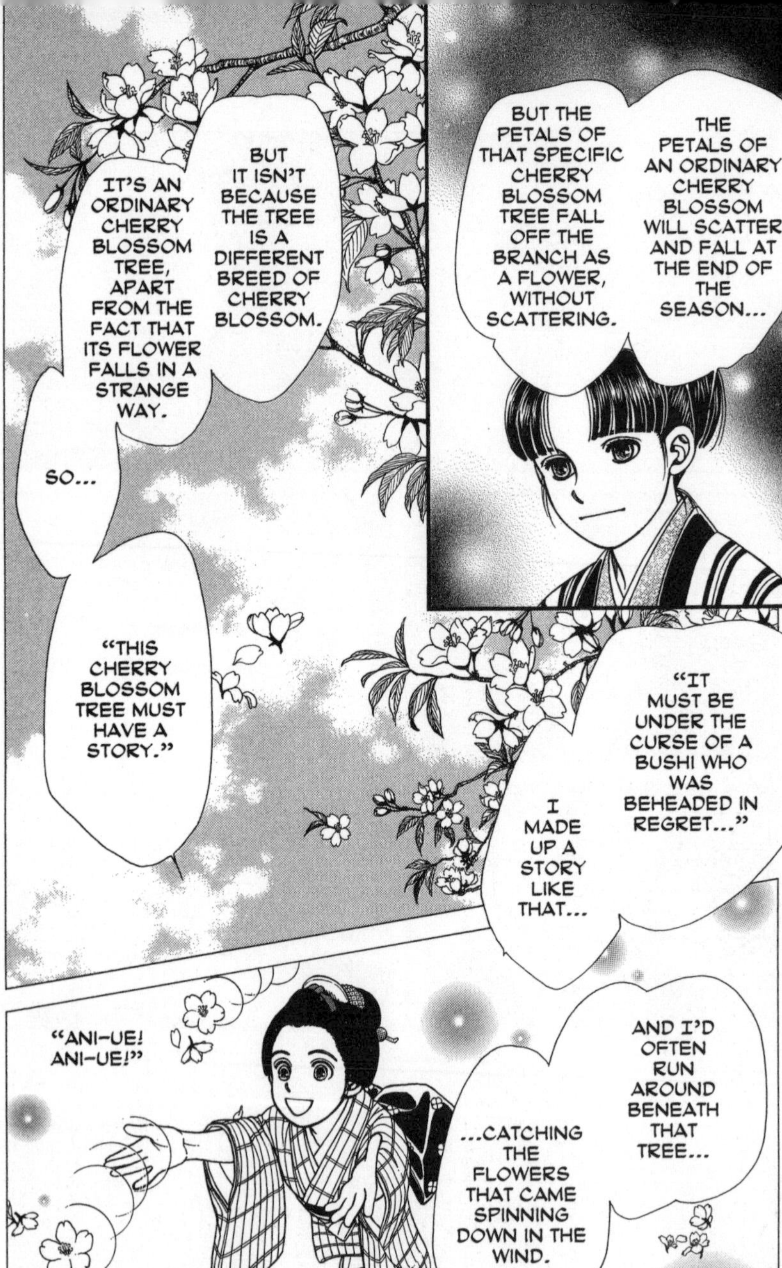
THE PETALS OF AN ORDINARY CHERRY BLOSSOM WILL SCATTER AND FALL AT THE END OF THE SEASON...
BUT THE PETALS OF THAT SPECIFIC CHERRY BLOSSOM TREE FALL OFF THE BRANCH AS A FLOWER, WITHOUT SCATTERING.
BUT IT ISN'T BECAUSE THE TREE IS A DIFFERENT BREED OF CHERRY BLOSSOM.
IT'S AN ORDINARY CHERRY BLOSSOM TREE, APART FROM THE FACT THAT ITS FLOWER FALLS IN A STRANGE WAY.
SO...
"THIS CHERRY BLOSSOM TREE MUST HAVE A STORY."
"IT MUST BE UNDER THE CURSE OF A BUSHI WHO WAS BEHEADED IN REGRET..."
I MADE UP A STORY LIKE THAT...
AND I'D OFTEN RUN AROUND BENEATH THAT TREE...
...CATCHING THE FLOWERS THAT CAME SPINNING DOWN IN THE WIND.
"ANI-UE! ANI-UE!"

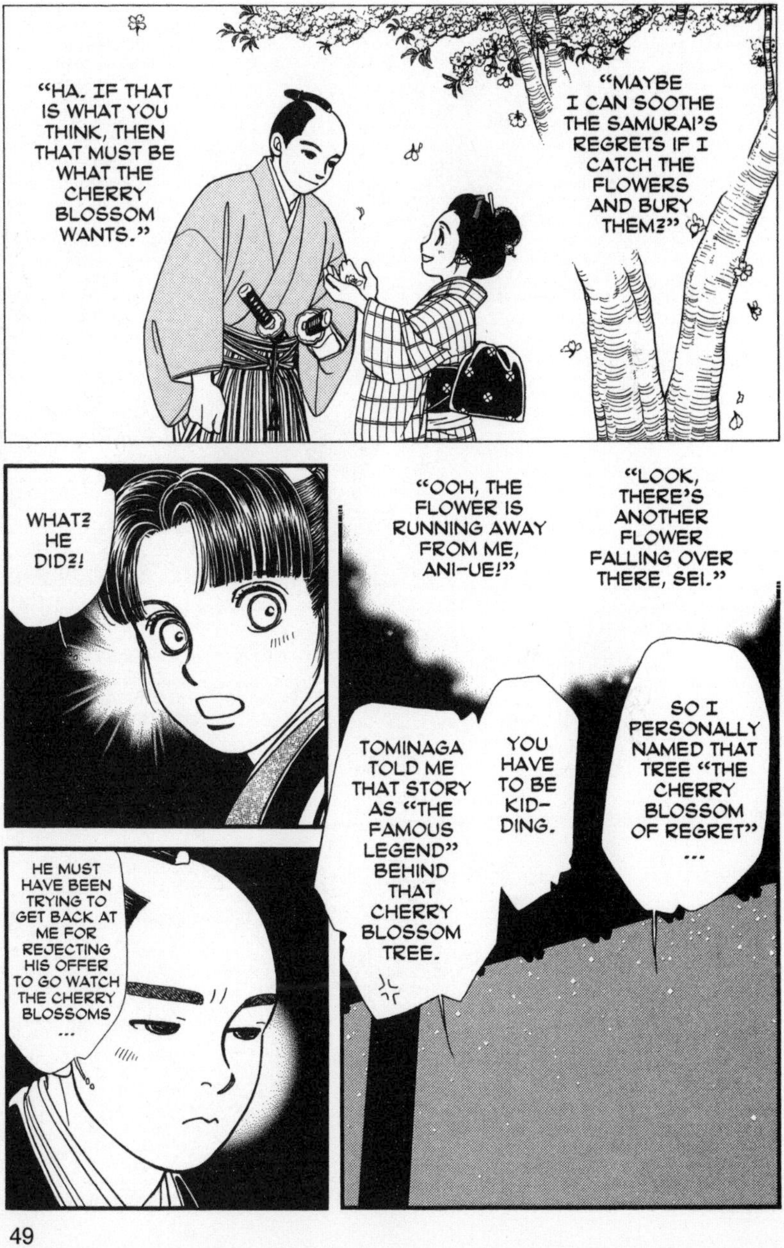
"MAYBE I CAN SOOTHE THE SAMURAI'S REGRETS IF I CATCH THE FLOWERS AND BURY THEM?"
"HA. IF THAT IS WHAT YOU THINK, THEN THAT MUST BE WHAT THE CHERRY BLOSSOM WANTS."
"LOOK, THERE'S ANOTHER FLOWER FALLING OVER THERE, SEI."
"OOH, THE FLOWER IS RUNNING AWAY FROM ME, ANI-UE!"
SO I PERSONALLY NAMED THAT TREE "THE CHERRY BLOSSOM OF REGRET"...
YOU HAVE TO BE KID-DING.
TOMINAGA TOLD ME THAT STORY AS "THE FAMOUS LEGEND" BEHIND THAT CHERRY BLOSSOM TREE.
WHAT? HE DID?!
HE MUST HAVE BEEN TRYING TO GET BACK AT ME FOR REJECTING HIS OFFER TO GO WATCH THE CHERRY BLOSSOMS...

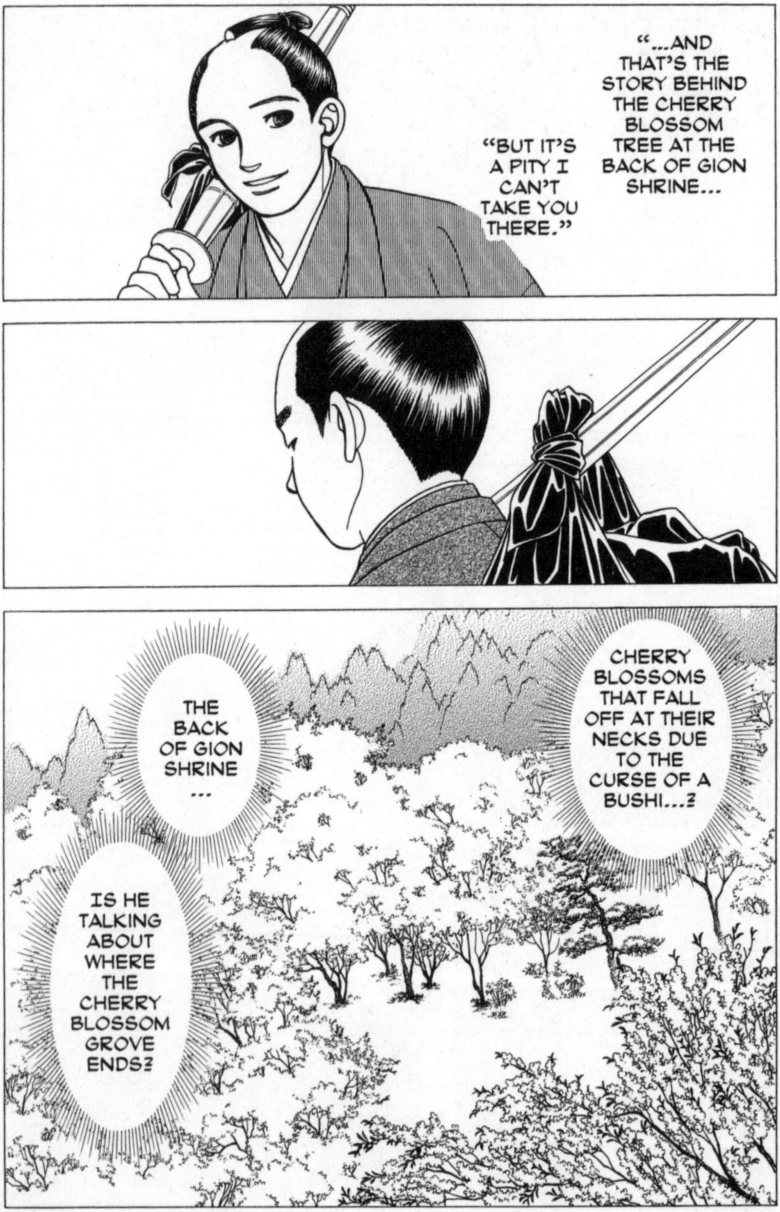
"...AND THAT'S THE STORY BEHIND THE CHERRY BLOSSOM TREE AT THE BACK OF GION SHRINE...
"BUT IT'S A PITY I CAN'T TAKE YOU THERE."
CHERRY BLOSSOMS THAT FALL OFF AT THEIR NECKS DUE TO THE CURSE OF A BUSHI...?
THE BACK OF GION SHRINE...
IS HE TALKING ABOUT WHERE THE CHERRY BLOSSOM GROVE ENDS?

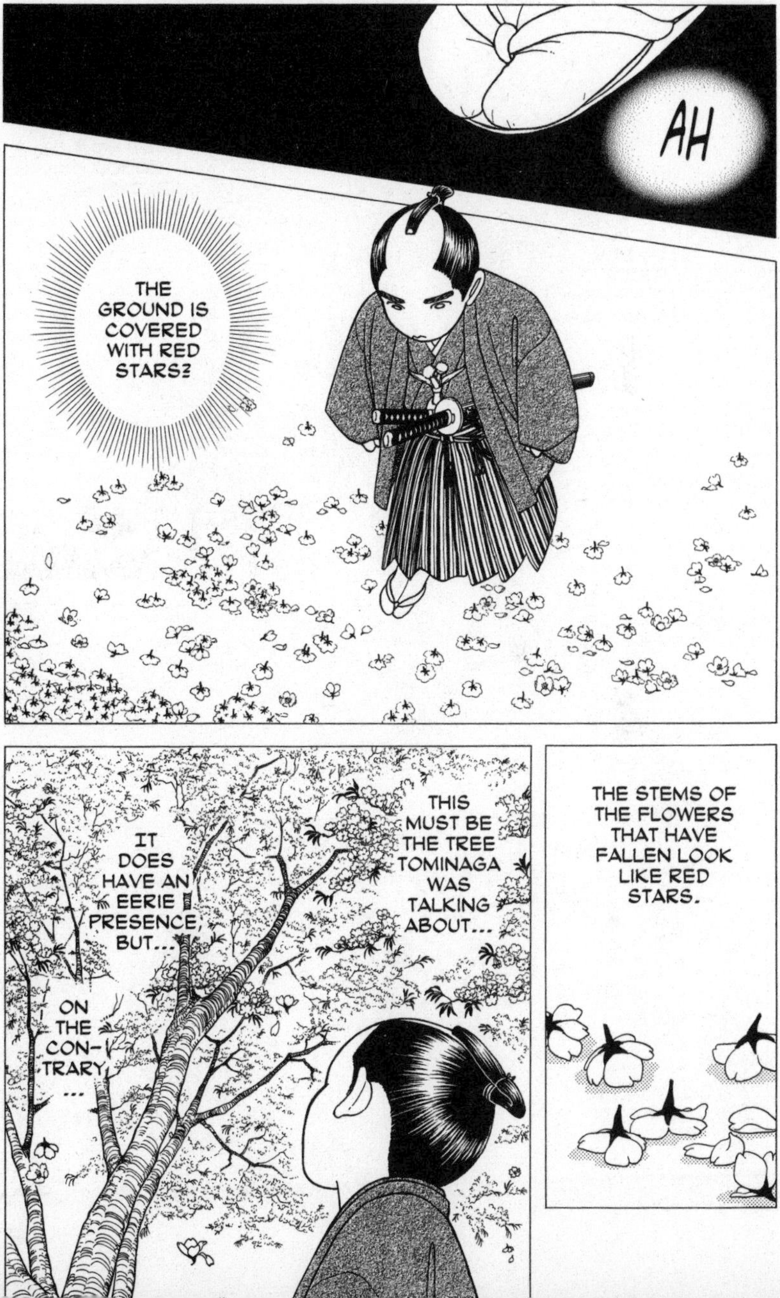
AH
THE GROUND IS COVERED WITH RED STARS?
THE STEMS OF THE FLOWERS THAT HAVE FALLEN LOOK LIKE RED STARS.
THIS MUST BE THE TREE TOMINAGA WAS TALKING ABOUT...
IT DOES HAVE AN EERIE PRESENCE, BUT...
ON THE CON-TRARY ...

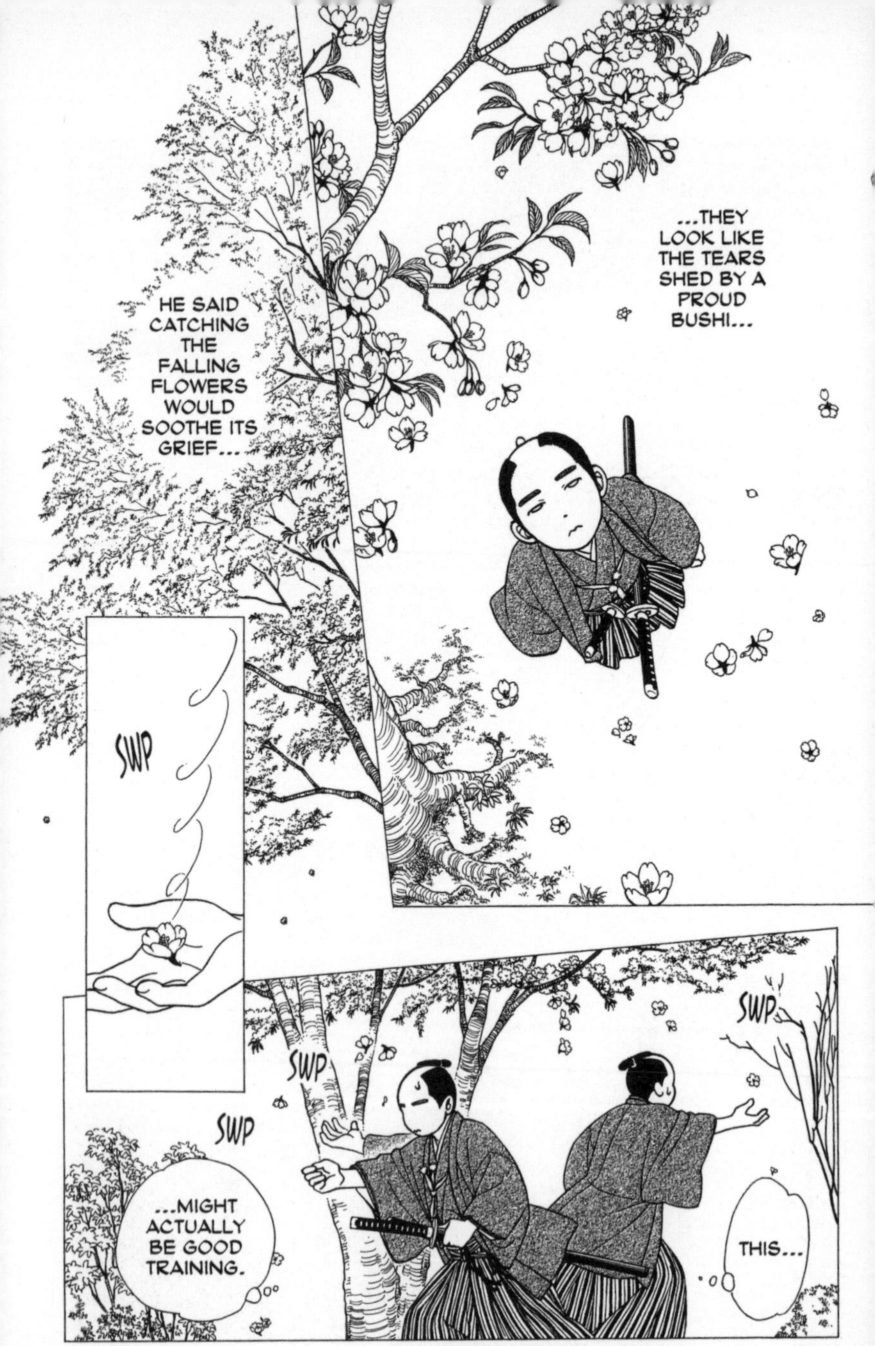
...THEY LOOK LIKE THE TEARS SHED BY A PROUD BUSHI...
HE SAID CATCHING THE FALLING FLOWERS WOULD SOOTHE ITS GRIEF...
SWP
SWP
SWP
SWP
THIS...
...MIGHT ACTUALLY BE GOOD TRAINING.

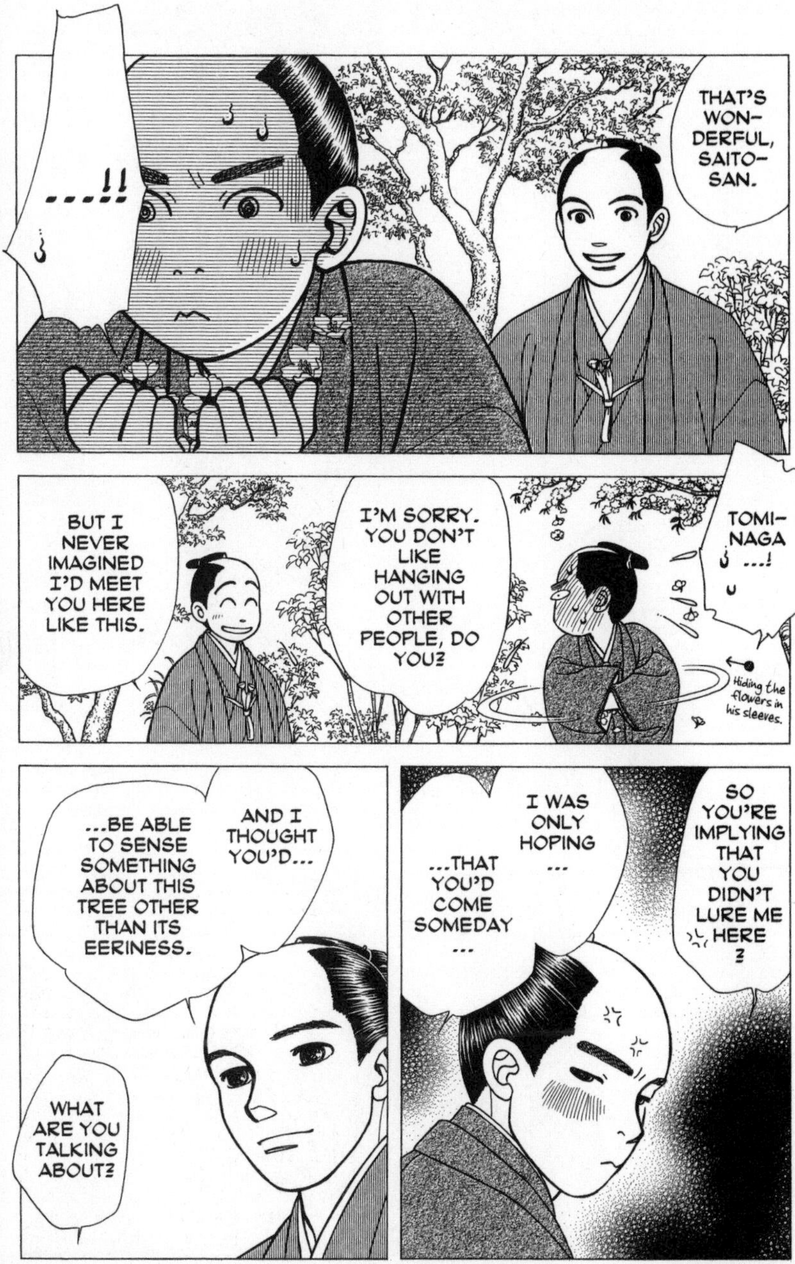
THAT'S WON-DERFUL, SAITO-SAN.
...!!
TOMI-NAGA ...!
Hiding the flowers in his sleeves.
I'M SORRY. YOU DON'T LIKE HANGING OUT WITH OTHER PEOPLE, DO YOU?
BUT I NEVER IMAGINED I'D MEET YOU HERE LIKE THIS.
SO YOU'RE IMPLYING THAT YOU DIDN'T LURE ME HERE?
I WAS ONLY HOPING...
...THAT YOU'D COME SOMEDAY...
AND I THOUGHT YOU'D...
...BE ABLE TO SENSE SOMETHING ABOUT THIS TREE OTHER THAN ITS EERINESS.
WHAT ARE YOU TALKING ABOUT?

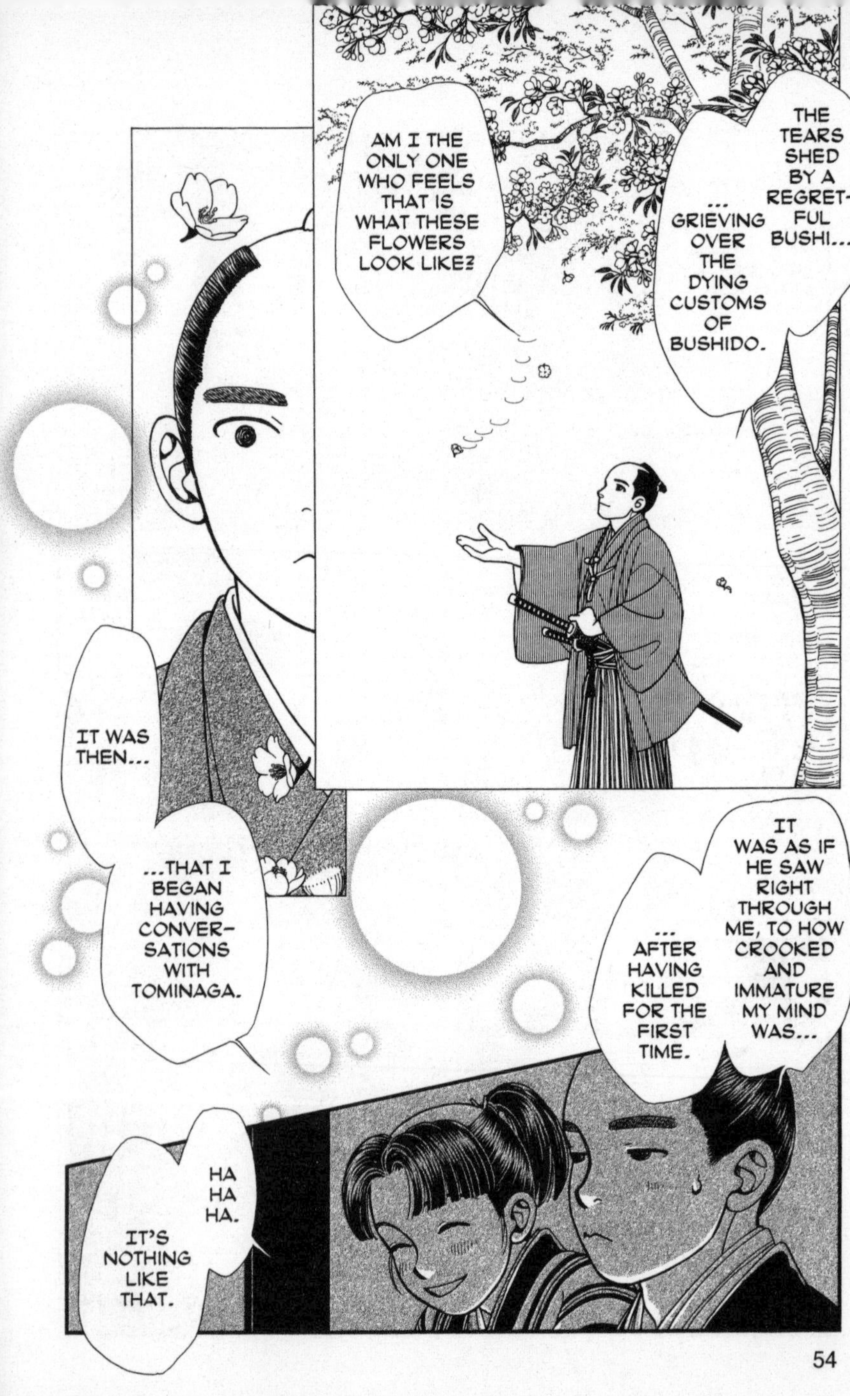

THE TEARS SHED BY A REGRETFUL BUSHI...
...GRIEVING OVER THE DYING CUSTOMS OF BUSHIDO.
AM I THE ONLY ONE WHO FEELS THAT IS WHAT THESE FLOWERS LOOK LIKE?
IT WAS THEN...
...THAT I BEGAN HAVING CONVERSATIONS WITH TOMINAGA.
IT WAS AS IF HE SAW RIGHT THROUGH ME, TO HOW CROOKED AND IMMATURE MY MIND WAS...
...AFTER HAVING KILLED FOR THE FIRST TIME.
HA HA HA. IT'S NOTHING LIKE THAT.

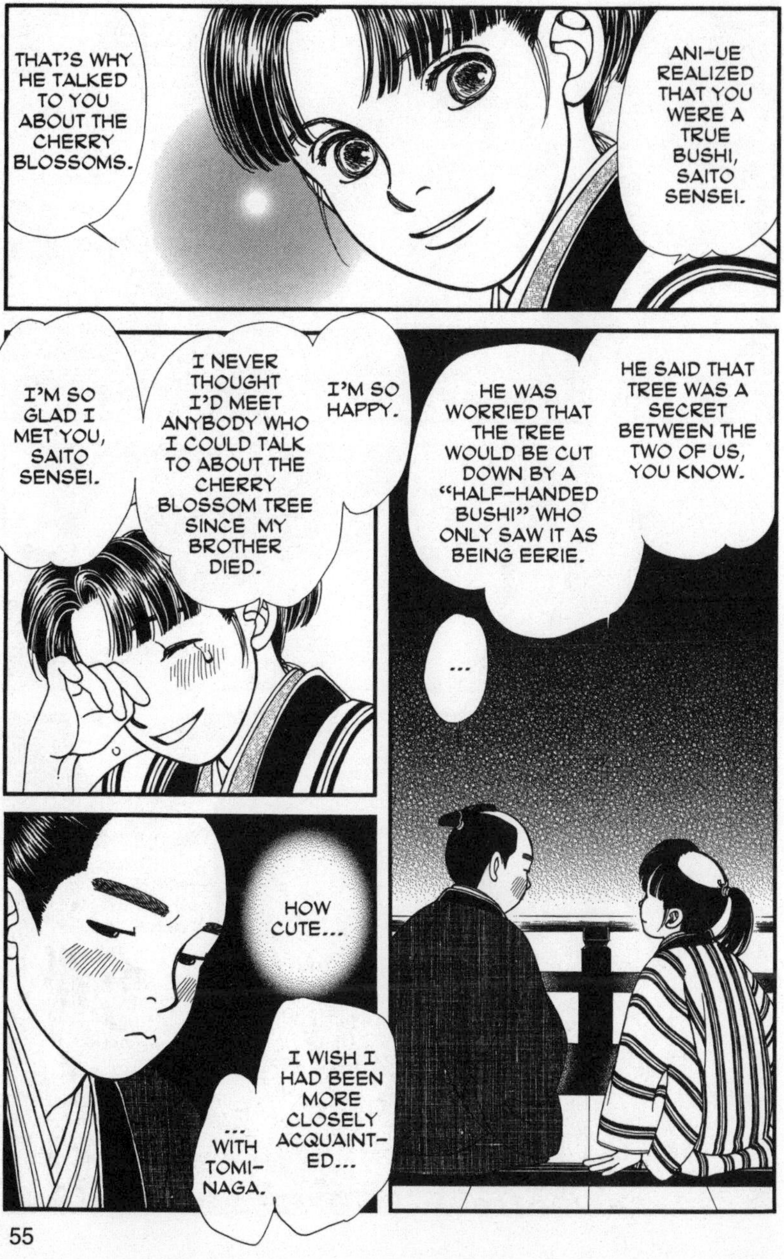
ANI-UE REALIZED THAT YOU WERE A TRUE BUSHI, SAITO SENSEI.
THAT'S WHY HE TALKED TO YOU ABOUT THE CHERRY BLOSSOMS.
HE SAID THAT TREE WAS A SECRET BETWEEN THE TWO OF US, YOU KNOW.
HE WAS WORRIED THAT THE TREE WOULD BE CUT DOWN BY A "HALF-HANDED BUSHI" WHO ONLY SAW IT AS BEING EERIE.
...
I'M SO HAPPY.
I NEVER THOUGHT I'D MEET ANYBODY WHO I COULD TALK TO ABOUT THE CHERRY BLOSSOM TREE SINCE MY BROTHER DIED.
I'M SO GLAD I MET YOU, SAITO SENSEI.
HOW CUTE...
I WISH I HAD BEEN MORE CLOSELY ACQUAINT-ED...
...WITH TOMI-NAGA.

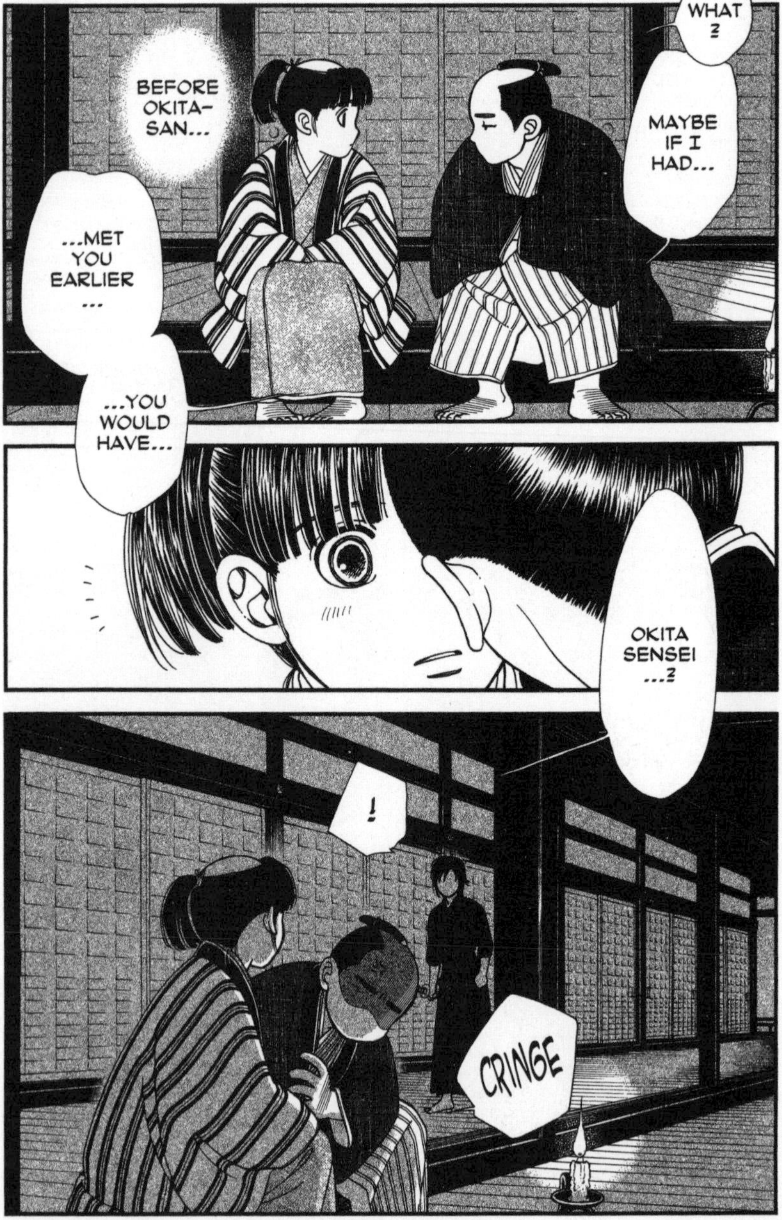
WHAT ?
MAYBE IF I HAD...
BEFORE OKITA-SAN...
...MET YOU EARLIER ...
...YOU WOULD HAVE...
OKITA SENSEI ...?
!
CRINGE

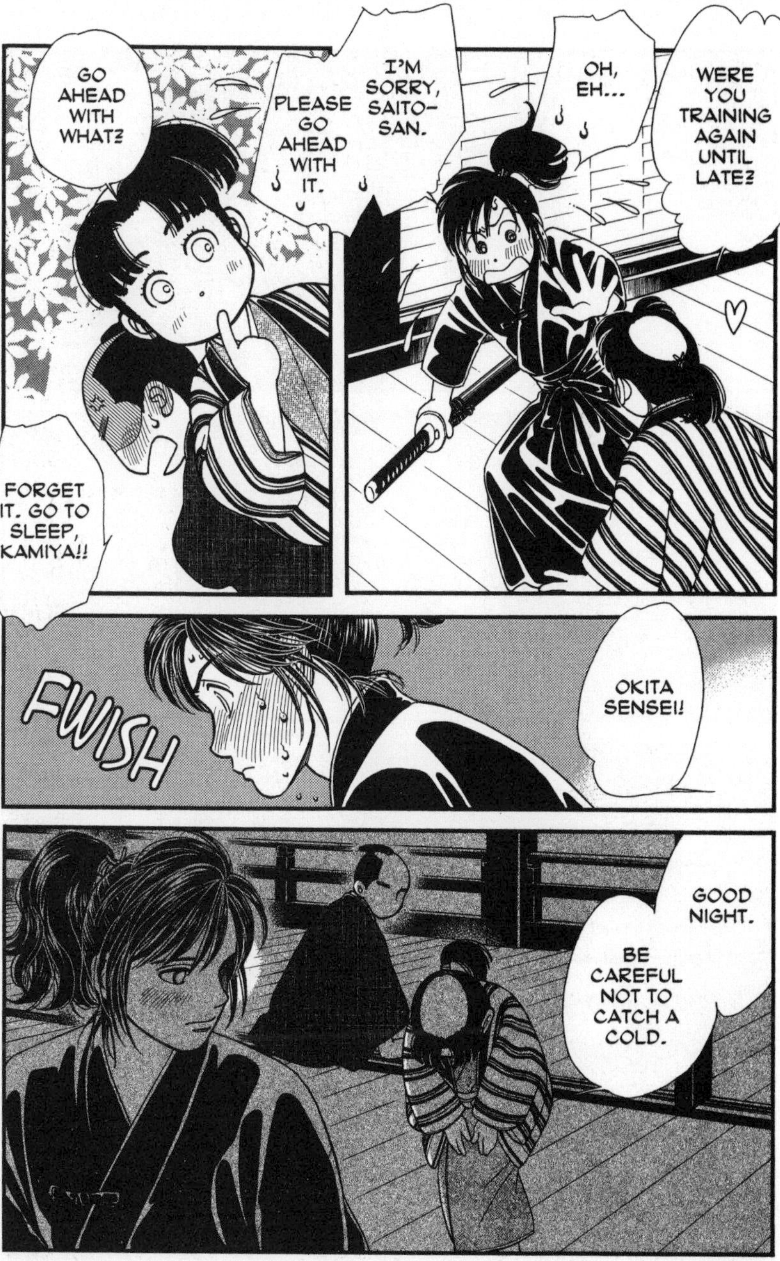
WERE YOU TRAINING AGAIN UNTIL LATE?
OH, EH...
I'M SORRY, SAITO-SAN.
PLEASE GO AHEAD WITH IT.
GO AHEAD WITH WHAT?
FORGET IT. GO TO SLEEP, KAMIYA!!
OKITA SENSEI!
FWISH
GOOD NIGHT.
BE CAREFUL NOT TO CATCH A COLD.

GOOD NIGHT.
YOU TAKE CARE TOO...
...KAMIYA-SAN.
YES!
SHING
HE MUST HAVE DONE IT ON PURPOSE !!
SAITO SENSEI!
I THINK I'M GLAD I WAS TRANSFERRED TO THE THIRD TROOP.
WHY'S THAT?

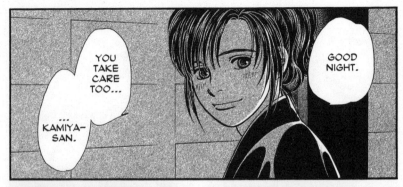

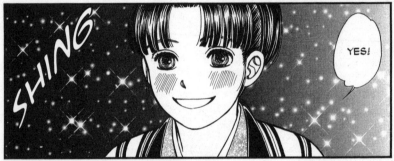

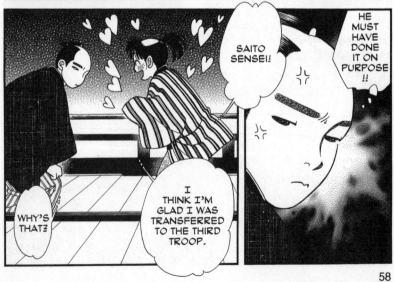

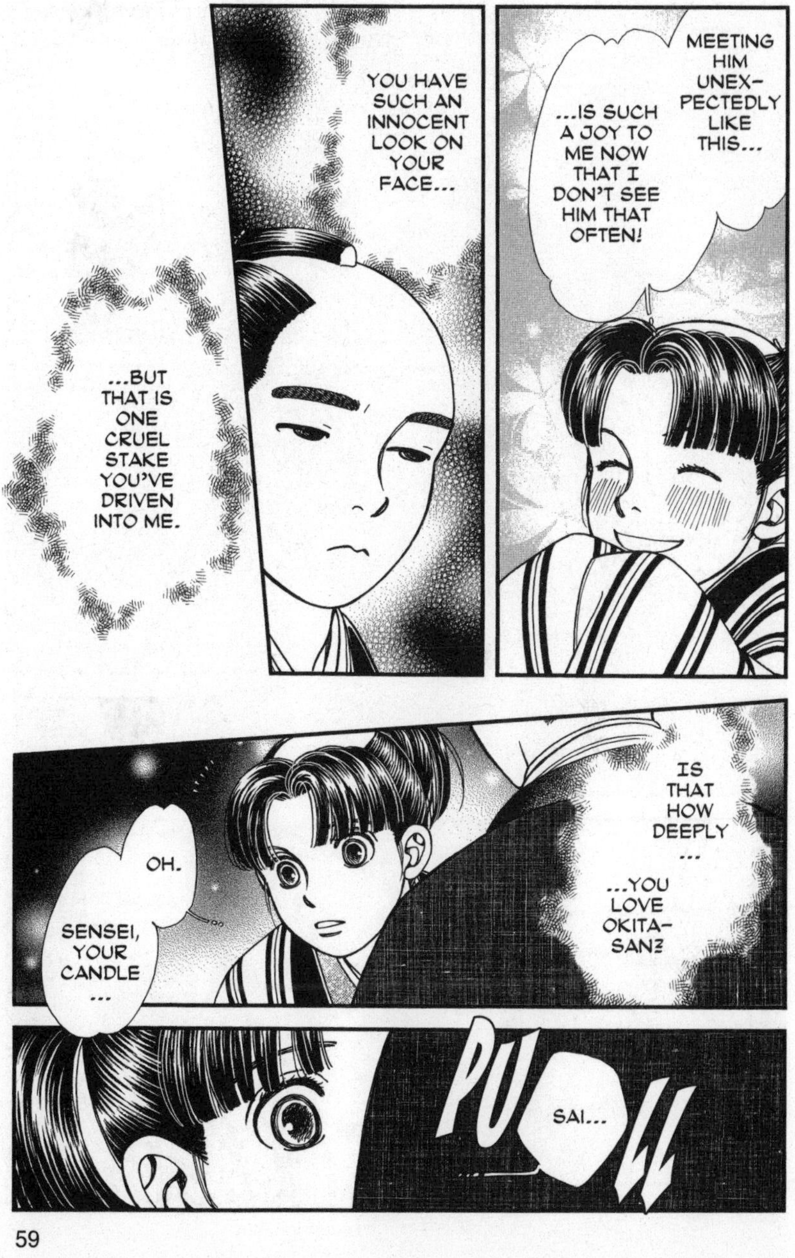
MEETING HIM UNEX-PECTEDLY LIKE THIS...
...IS SUCH A JOY TO ME NOW THAT I DON'T SEE HIM THAT OFTEN!
YOU HAVE SUCH AN INNOCENT LOOK ON YOUR FACE...
...BUT THAT IS ONE CRUEL STAKE YOU'VE DRIVEN INTO ME.
IS THAT HOW DEEPLY...
...YOU LOVE OKITA-SAN?
OH.
SENSEI, YOUR CANDLE...
SAI...

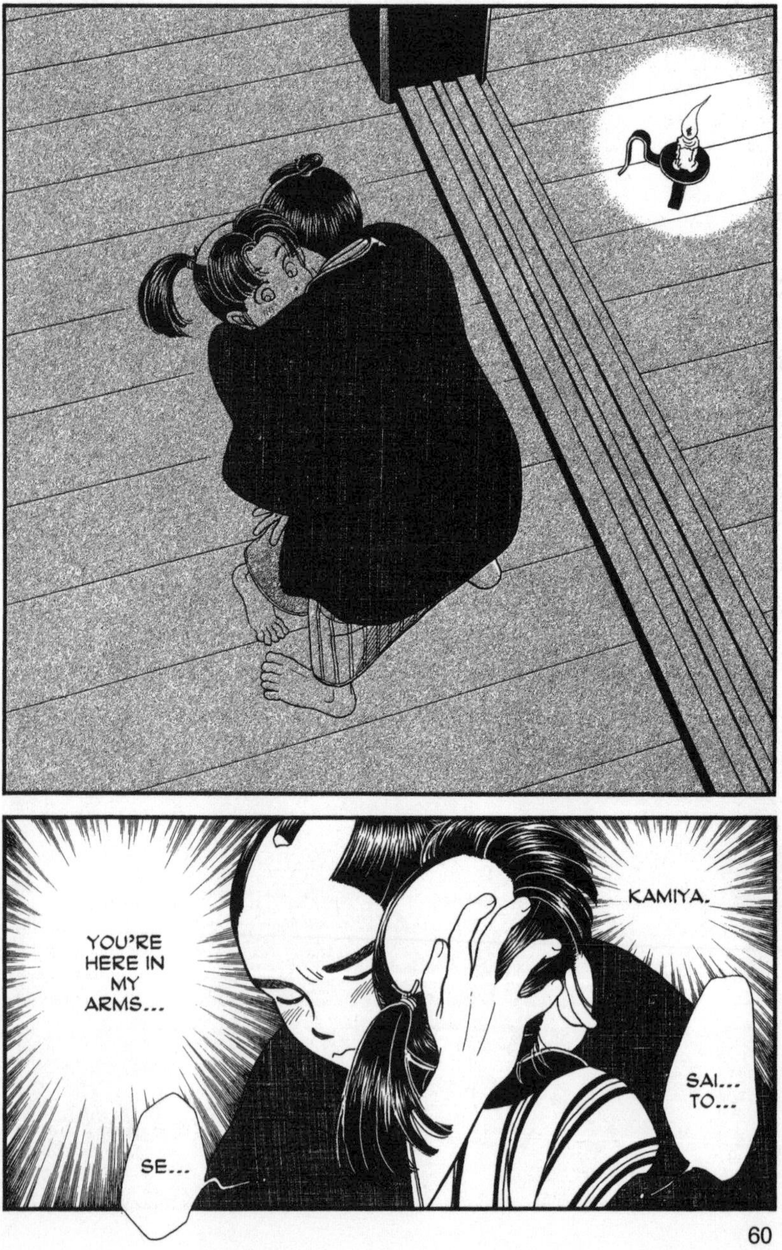
KAMIYA.
SAI... TO...
YOU'RE HERE IN MY ARMS...
SE...

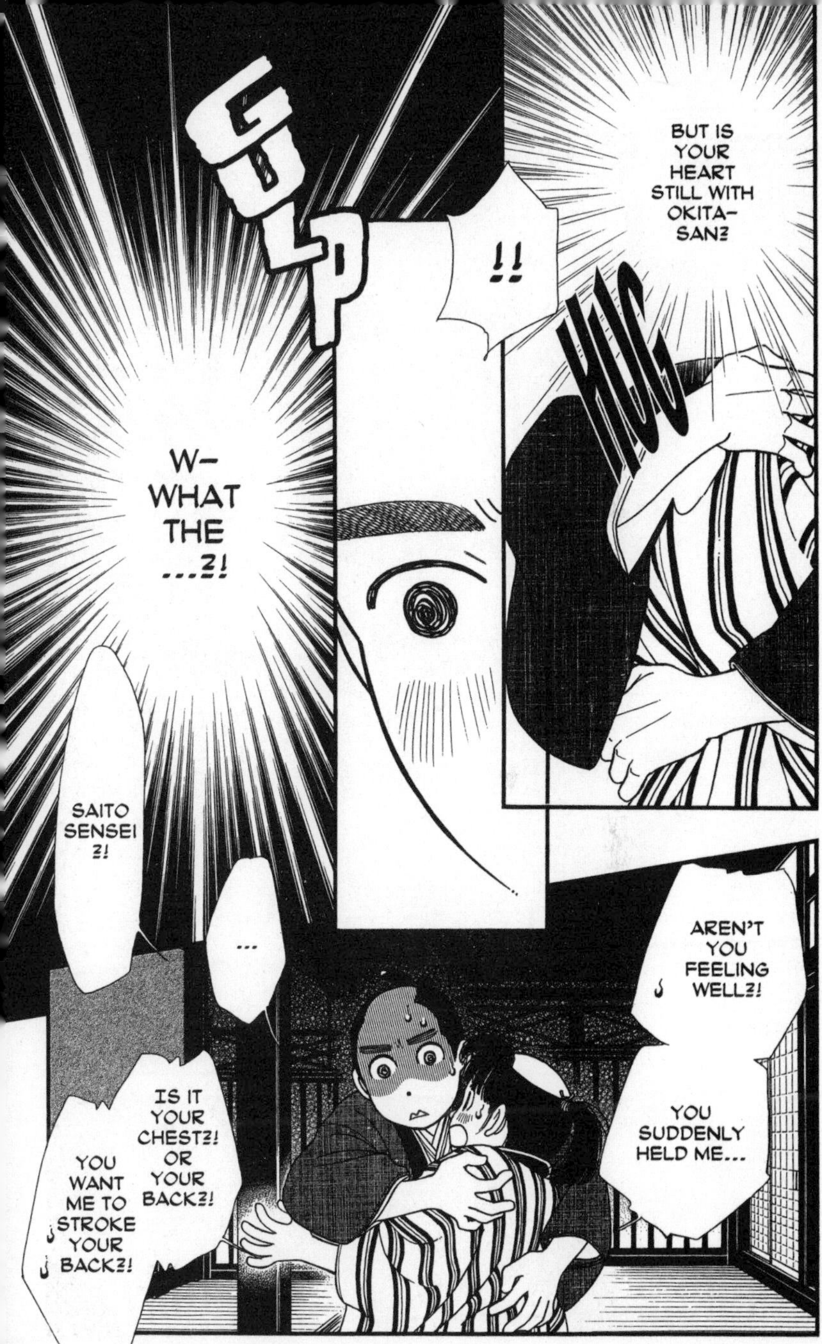
BUT IS YOUR HEART STILL WITH OKITA-SAN?
HUG
!!
GULP
W-WHAT THE ...?!
SAITO SENSEI?!
...
AREN'T YOU FEELING WELL?!
YOU SUDDENLY HELD ME...
IS IT YOUR CHEST?! OR YOUR BACK?!
YOU WANT ME TO STROKE YOUR BACK?!

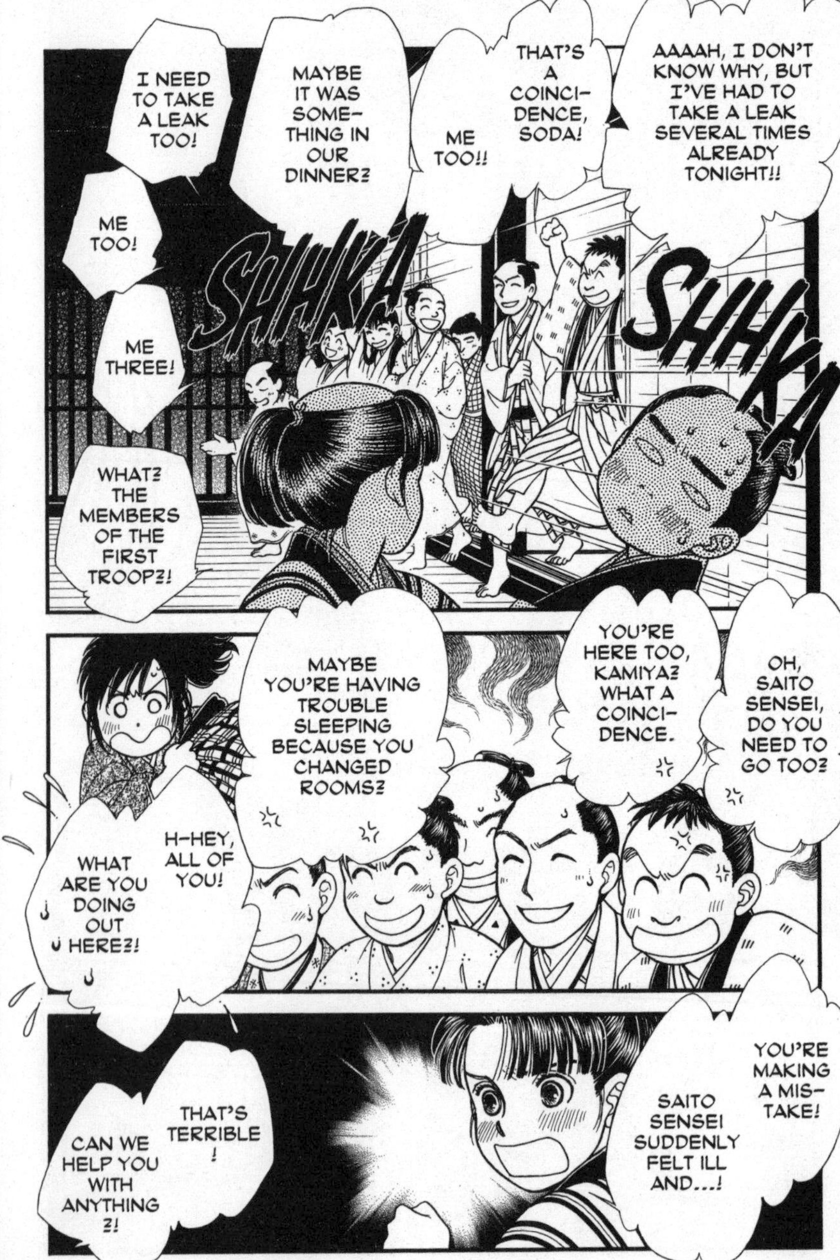
AAAAH, I DON'T KNOW WHY, BUT I'VE HAD TO TAKE A LEAK SEVERAL TIMES ALREADY TONIGHT!!
THAT'S A COINCIDENCE, SODA!
ME TOO!!
MAYBE IT WAS SOMETHING IN OUR DINNER?
I NEED TO TAKE A LEAK TOO!
SHHKA
SHHKA
ME TOO!
ME THREE!
WHAT? THE MEMBERS OF THE FIRST TROOP?!
OH, SAITO SENSEI, DO YOU NEED TO GO TOO?
YOU'RE HERE TOO, KAMIYA? WHAT A COINCIDENCE.
MAYBE YOU'RE HAVING TROUBLE SLEEPING BECAUSE YOU CHANGED ROOMS?
H-HEY, ALL OF YOU!
WHAT ARE YOU DOING OUT HERE?!
YOU'RE MAKING A MISTAKE!
SAITO SENSEI SUDDENLY FELT ILL AND...!
THAT'S TERRIBLE!
CAN WE HELP YOU WITH ANYTHING?!

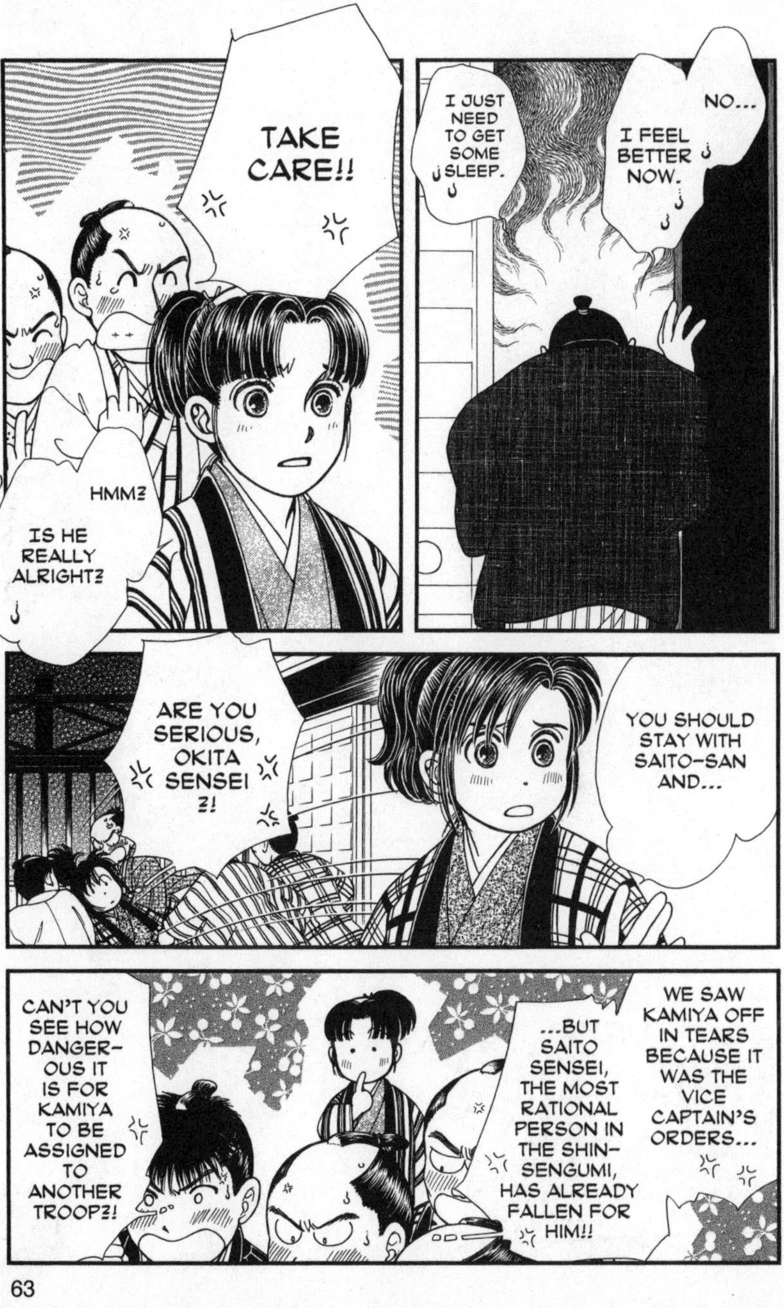
NO... I FEEL BETTER NOW.
I JUST NEED TO GET SOME SLEEP.
TAKE CARE!!
HMM? IS HE REALLY ALRIGHT?
(ha ha)
YOU SHOULD STAY WITH SAITO-SAN AND...
ARE YOU SERIOUS, OKITA SENSEI?!
WE SAW KAMIYA OFF IN TEARS BECAUSE IT WAS THE VICE CAPTAIN'S ORDERS...
...BUT SAITO SENSEI, THE MOST RATIONAL PERSON IN THE SHINSENGUMI, HAS ALREADY FALLEN FOR HIM!!
CAN'T YOU SEE HOW DANGEROUS IT IS FOR KAMIYA TO BE ASSIGNED TO ANOTHER TROOP?!

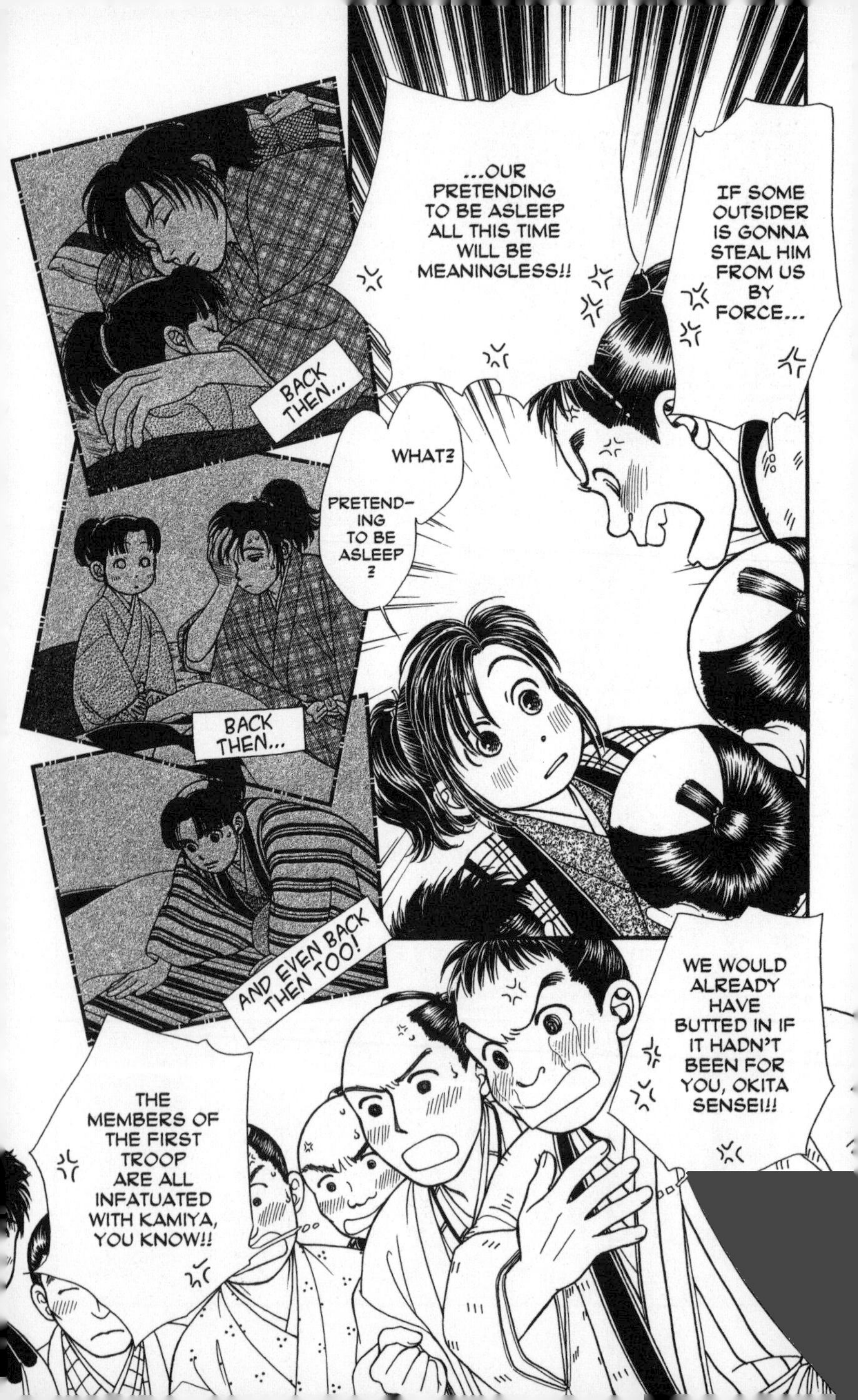
IF SOME OUTSIDER IS GONNA STEAL HIM FROM US BY FORCE...
...OUR PRETENDING TO BE ASLEEP ALL THIS TIME WILL BE MEANINGLESS!!
WHAT?
PRETENDING TO BE ASLEEP?
BACK THEN...
BACK THEN...
AND EVEN BACK THEN TOO!
WE WOULD ALREADY HAVE BUTTED IN IF IT HADN'T BEEN FOR YOU, OKITA SENSEI!!
THE MEMBERS OF THE FIRST TROOP ARE ALL INFATUATED WITH KAMIYA, YOU KNOW!!

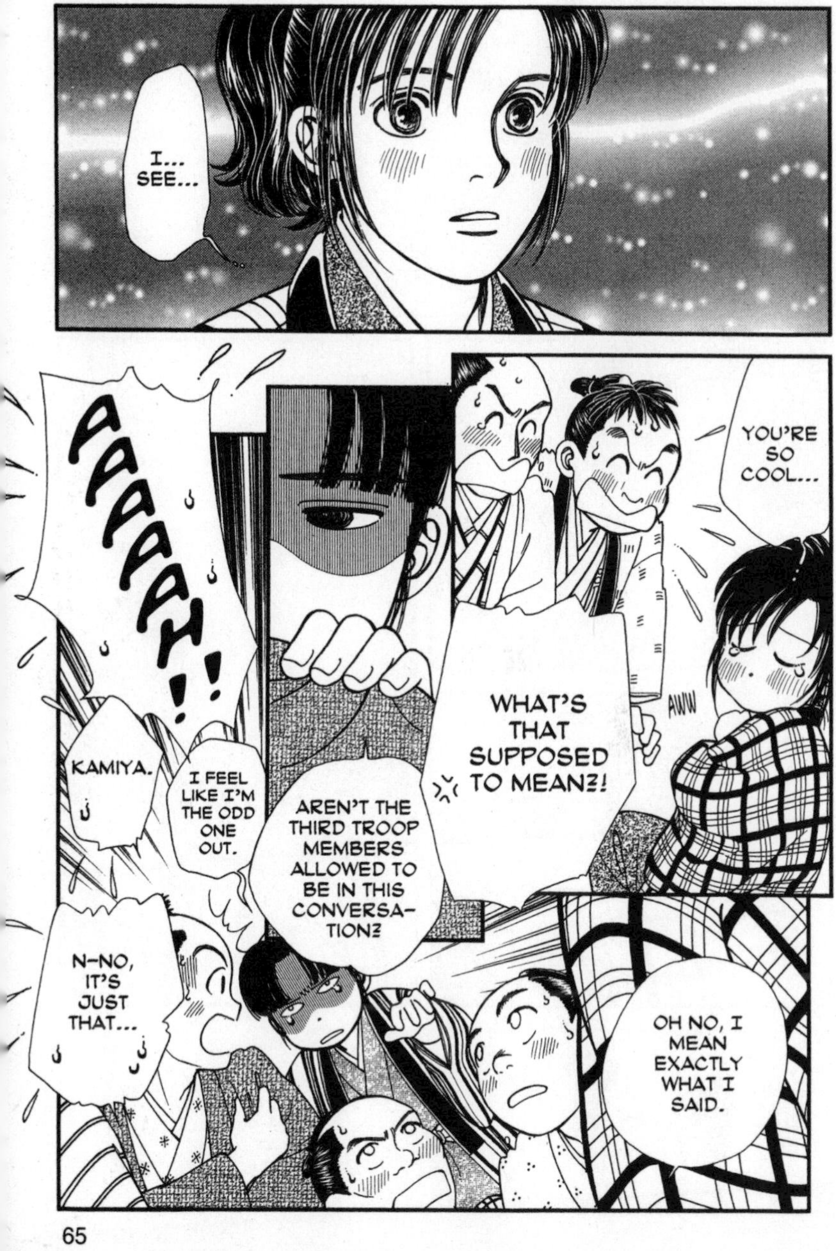
I... SEE...
YOU'RE SO COOL...
AWW
WHAT'S THAT SUPPOSED TO MEAN?!
AAAAAH!!
KAMIYA.
I FEEL LIKE I'M THE ODD ONE OUT.
AREN'T THE THIRD TROOP MEMBERS ALLOWED TO BE IN THIS CONVERSA-TION?
OH NO, I MEAN EXACTLY WHAT I SAID.
N-NO, IT'S JUST THAT...

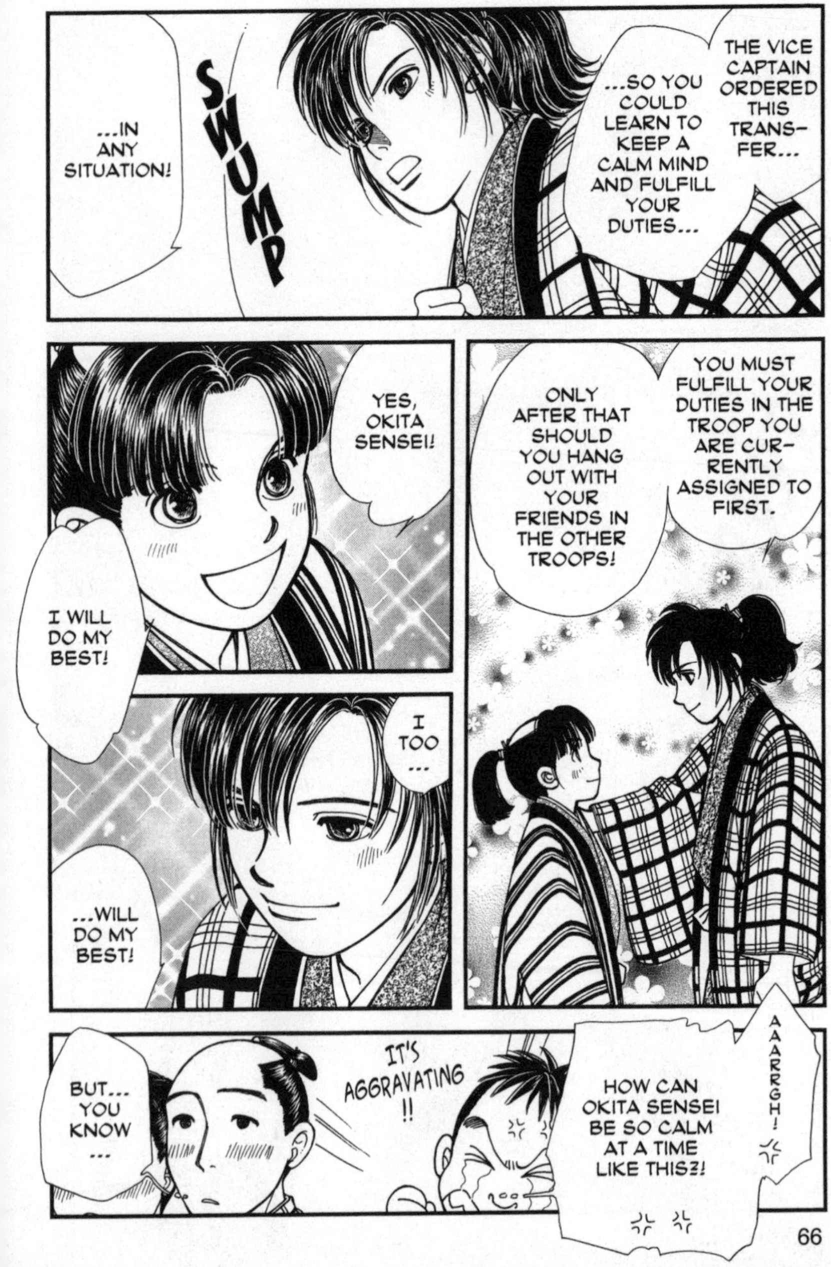
THE VICE CAPTAIN ORDERED THIS TRANSFER...
...SO YOU COULD LEARN TO KEEP A CALM MIND AND FULFILL YOUR DUTIES...
SWUMP
...IN ANY SITUATION!
YOU MUST FULFILL YOUR DUTIES IN THE TROOP YOU ARE CURRENTLY ASSIGNED TO FIRST.
ONLY AFTER THAT SHOULD YOU HANG OUT WITH YOUR FRIENDS IN THE OTHER TROOPS!
YES, OKITA SENSEI!
I WILL DO MY BEST!
I TOO...
...WILL DO MY BEST!
AAARGH!
HOW CAN OKITA SENSEI BE SO CALM AT A TIME LIKE THIS?!
IT'S AGGRAVATING!!
BUT... YOU KNOW...

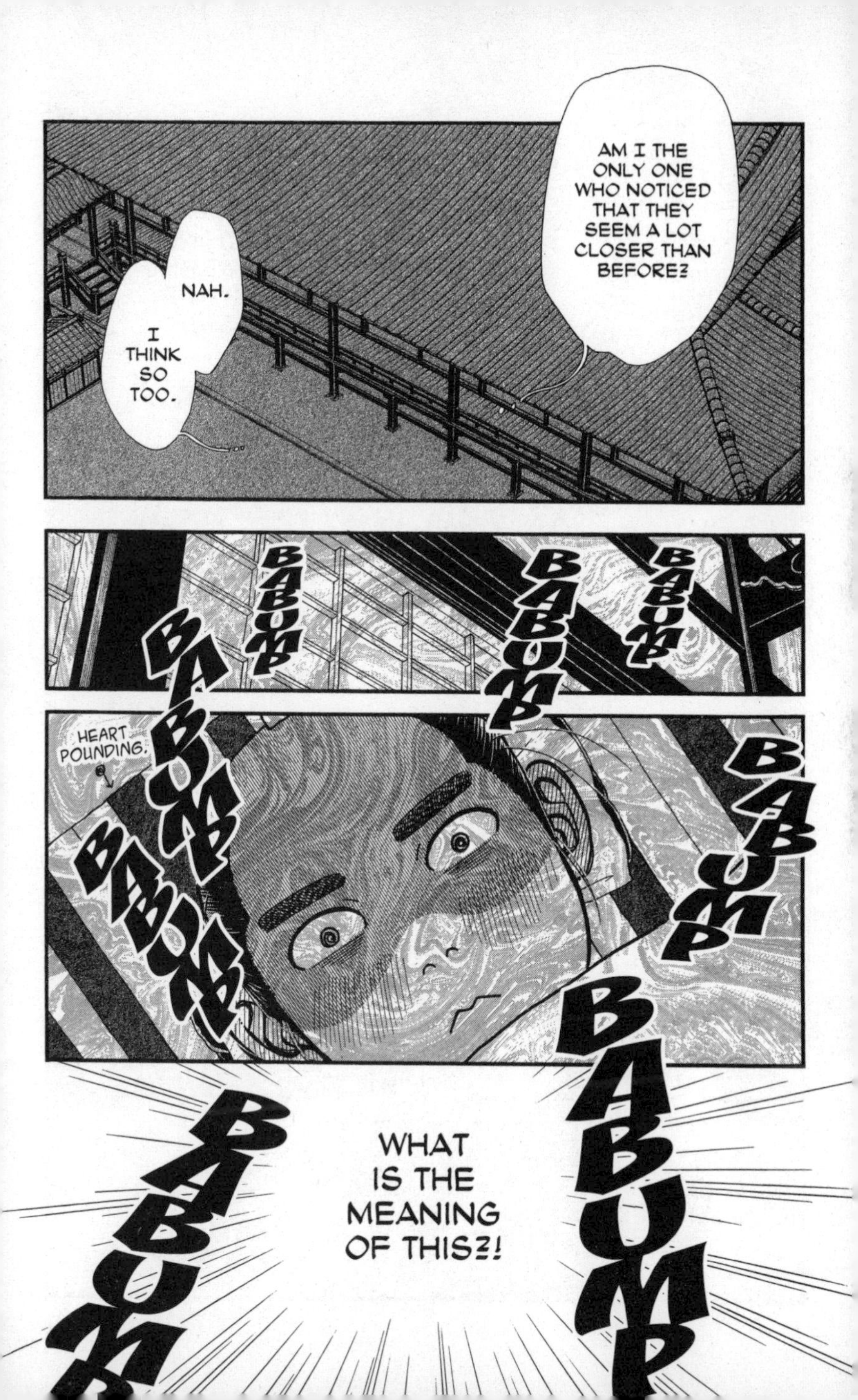
AM I THE ONLY ONE WHO NOTICED THAT THEY SEEM A LOT CLOSER THAN BEFORE?
NAH.
I THINK SO TOO.
BABUMP
BABUMP
BABUMP
BABUMP
BABUMP
HEART POUNDING.
BABUMP
BABUMP
WHAT IS THE MEANING OF THIS?!

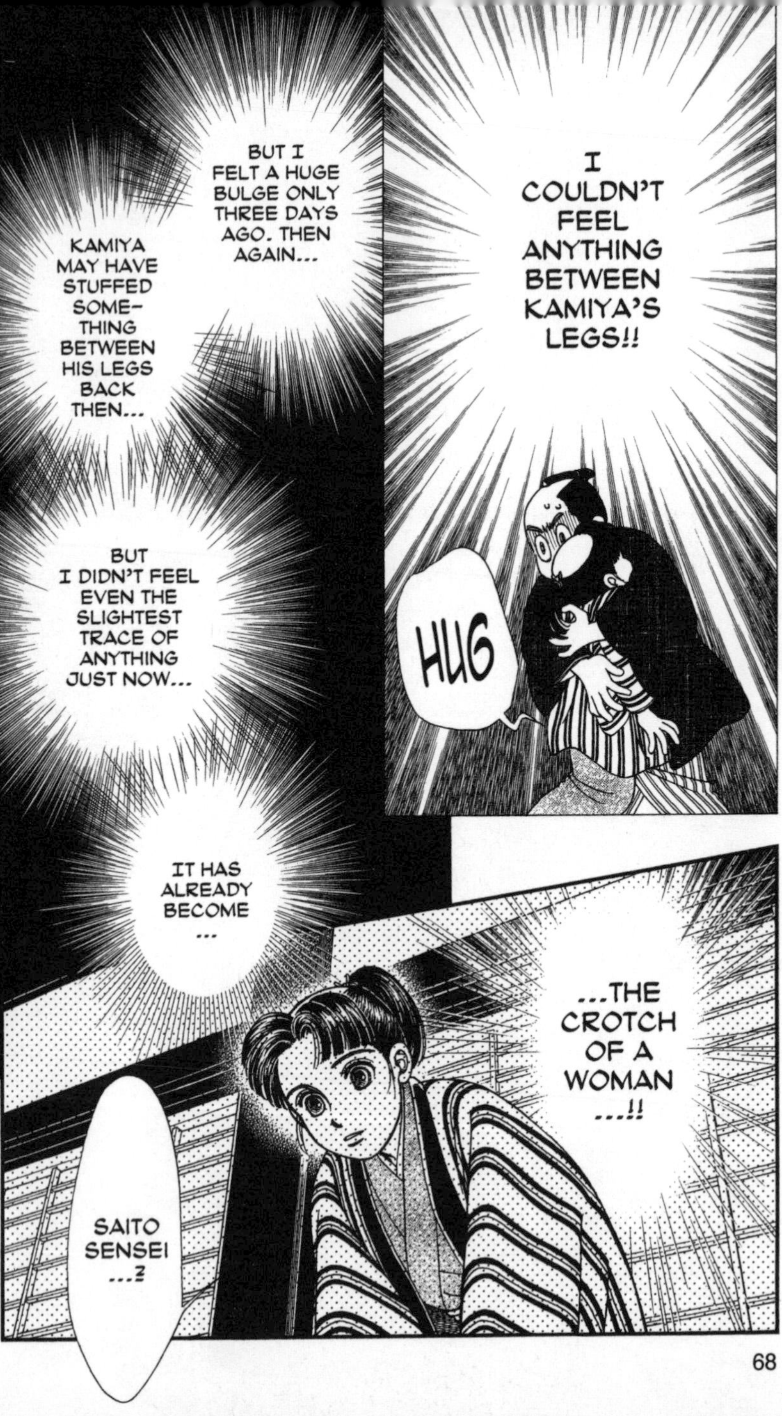
I COULDN'T FEEL ANYTHING BETWEEN KAMIYA'S LEGS!!
HUG
BUT I FELT A HUGE BULGE ONLY THREE DAYS AGO. THEN AGAIN...
KAMIYA MAY HAVE STUFFED SOME-THING BETWEEN HIS LEGS BACK THEN...
BUT I DIDN'T FEEL EVEN THE SLIGHTEST TRACE OF ANYTHING JUST NOW...
IT HAS ALREADY BECOME ...
...THE CROTCH OF A WOMAN ...!!
SAITO SENSEI ...?

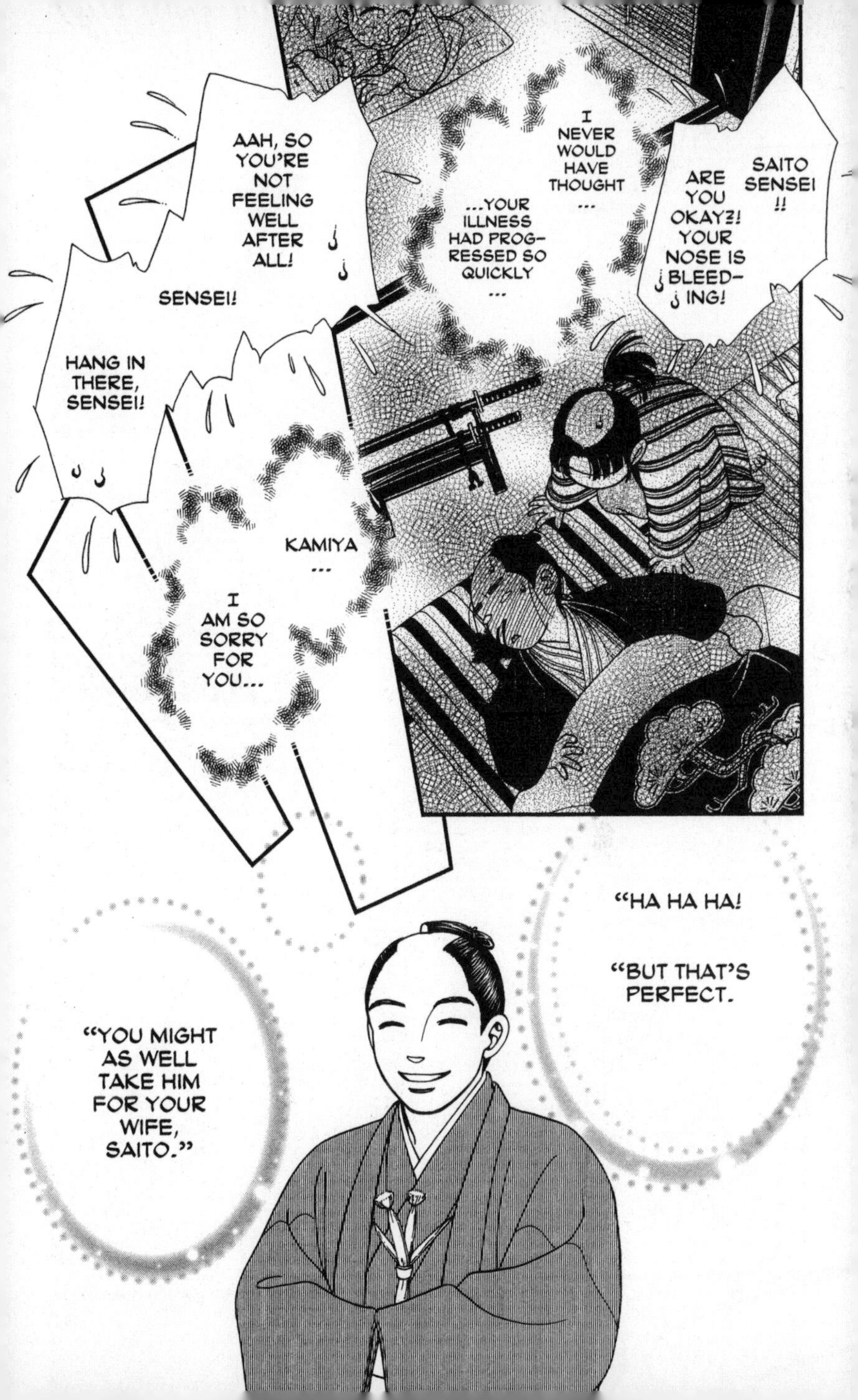
SAITO SENSEI!!
ARE YOU OKAY?! YOUR NOSE IS BLEEDING!
I NEVER WOULD HAVE THOUGHT...
...YOUR ILLNESS HAD PROGRESSED SO QUICKLY...
AAH, SO YOU'RE NOT FEELING WELL AFTER ALL!
SENSEI!
HANG IN THERE, SENSEI!
KAMIYA...
I AM SO SORRY FOR YOU...
"HA HA HA!
"BUT THAT'S PERFECT.
"YOU MIGHT AS WELL TAKE HIM FOR YOUR WIFE, SAITO."

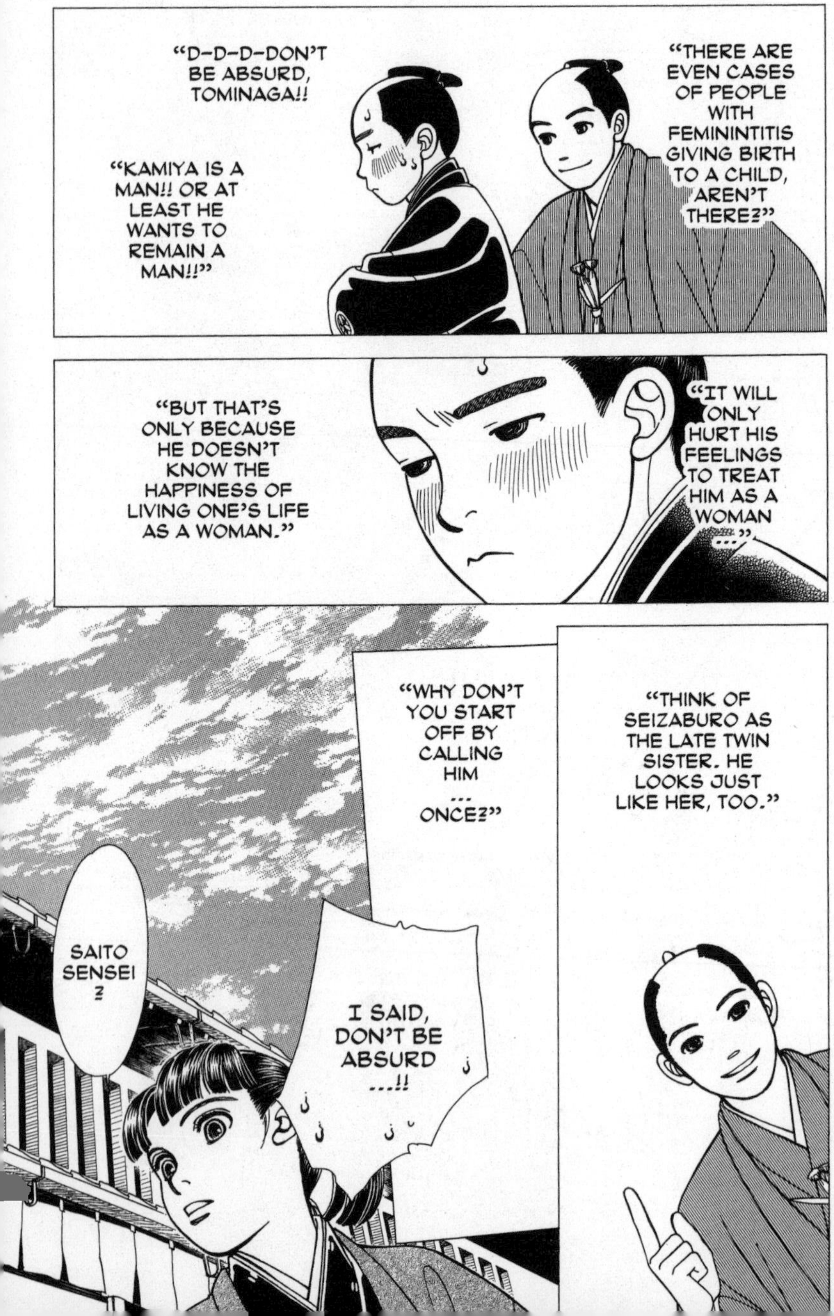
"THERE ARE EVEN CASES OF PEOPLE WITH FEMININTITIS GIVING BIRTH TO A CHILD, AREN'T THERE?"
"D-D-D-DON'T BE ABSURD, TOMINAGA!!
"KAMIYA IS A MAN!! OR AT LEAST HE WANTS TO REMAIN A MAN!!"
"IT WILL ONLY HURT HIS FEELINGS TO TREAT HIM AS A WOMAN ..."
"BUT THAT'S ONLY BECAUSE HE DOESN'T KNOW THE HAPPINESS OF LIVING ONE'S LIFE AS A WOMAN."
"THINK OF SEIZABURO AS THE LATE TWIN SISTER. HE LOOKS JUST LIKE HER, TOO."
"WHY DON'T YOU START OFF BY CALLING HIM ... ONCE?"
I SAID, DON'T BE ABSURD ...!!
SAITO SENSEI?

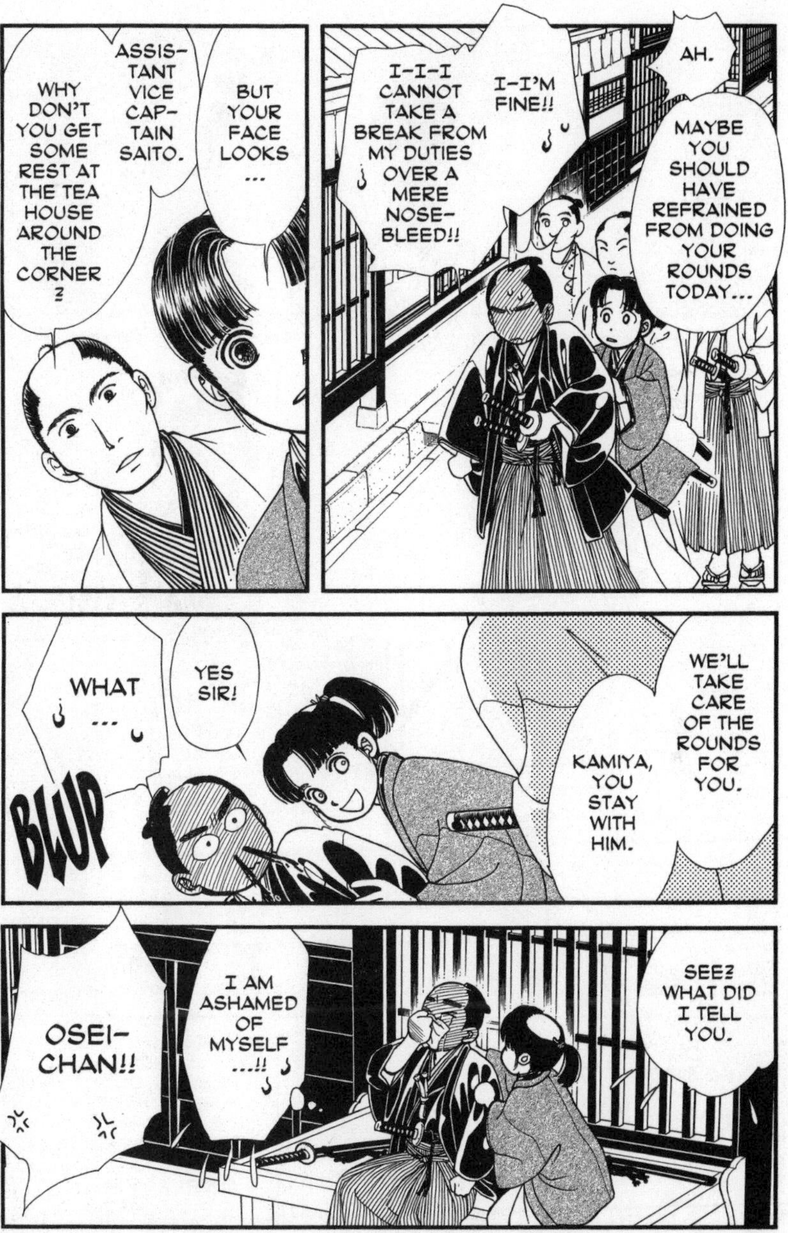
AH.
MAYBE YOU SHOULD HAVE REFRAINED FROM DOING YOUR ROUNDS TODAY...
I-I'M FINE!!
I-I-I CANNOT TAKE A BREAK FROM MY DUTIES OVER A MERE NOSE-BLEED!!
BUT YOUR FACE LOOKS ...
ASSISTANT VICE CAPTAIN SAITO.
WHY DON'T YOU GET SOME REST AT THE TEA HOUSE AROUND THE CORNER?
WE'LL TAKE CARE OF THE ROUNDS FOR YOU.
KAMIYA, YOU STAY WITH HIM.
YES SIR!
WHAT ...
BLUP
SEE? WHAT DID I TELL YOU.
I AM ASHAMED OF MYSELF ...!!
OSEI-CHAN!!

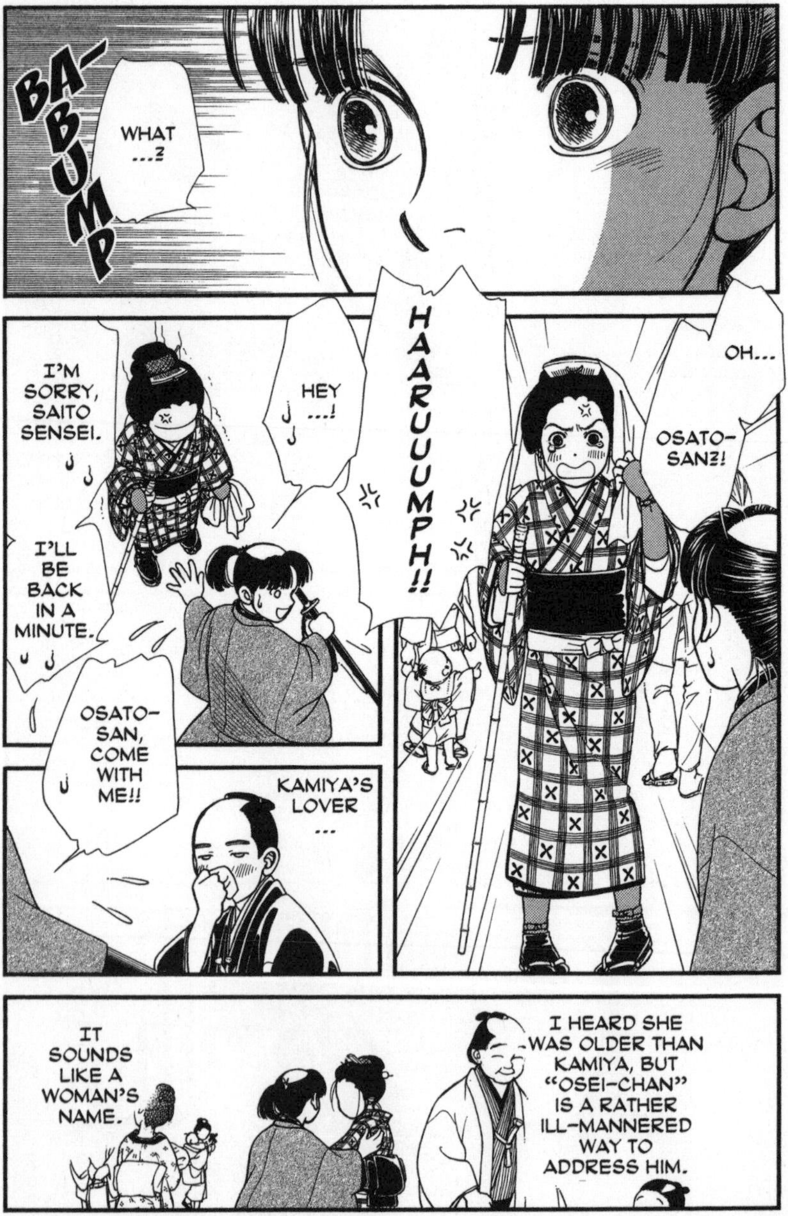
BA-BUMP
WHAT ...?
OH...
OSATO-SAN?!
HAARUUUMPH!!
HEY ...!
I'M SORRY, SAITO SENSEI.
I'LL BE BACK IN A MINUTE.
OSATO-SAN, COME WITH ME!!
KAMIYA'S LOVER ...
I HEARD SHE WAS OLDER THAN KAMIYA, BUT "OSEI-CHAN" IS A RATHER ILL-MANNERED WAY TO ADDRESS HIM.
IT SOUNDS LIKE A WOMAN'S NAME.

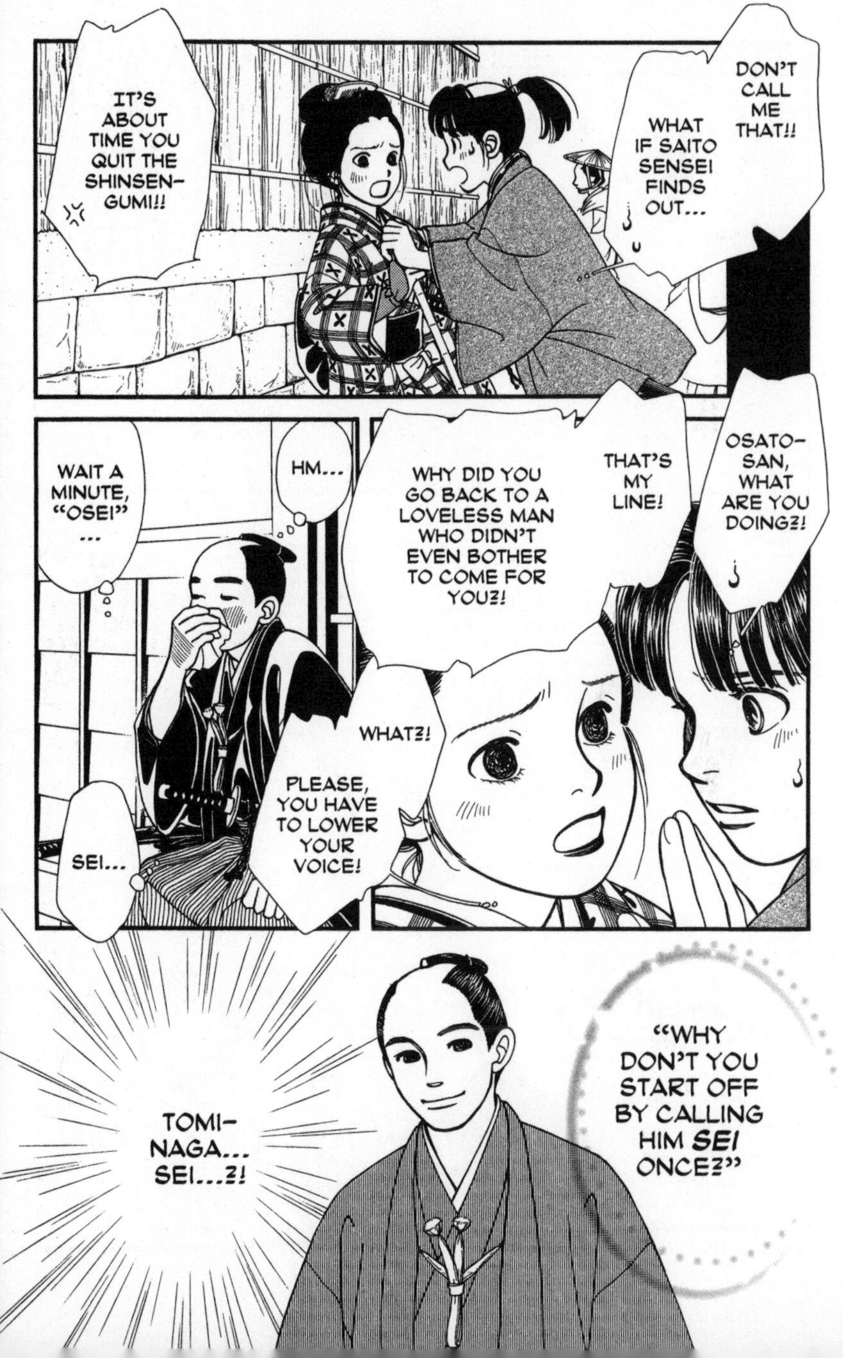
DON'T CALL ME THAT!!
WHAT IF SAITO SENSEI FINDS OUT...
IT'S ABOUT TIME YOU QUIT THE SHINSEN-GUMI!!
OSATO-SAN, WHAT ARE YOU DOING?!
THAT'S MY LINE!
WHY DID YOU GO BACK TO A LOVELESS MAN WHO DIDN'T EVEN BOTHER TO COME FOR YOU?!
WHAT?!
PLEASE, YOU HAVE TO LOWER YOUR VOICE!
HM...
WAIT A MINUTE, "OSEI" ...
SEI...
"WHY DON'T YOU START OFF BY CALLING HIM *SEI* ONCE?"
TOMI-NAGA... SEI...?!

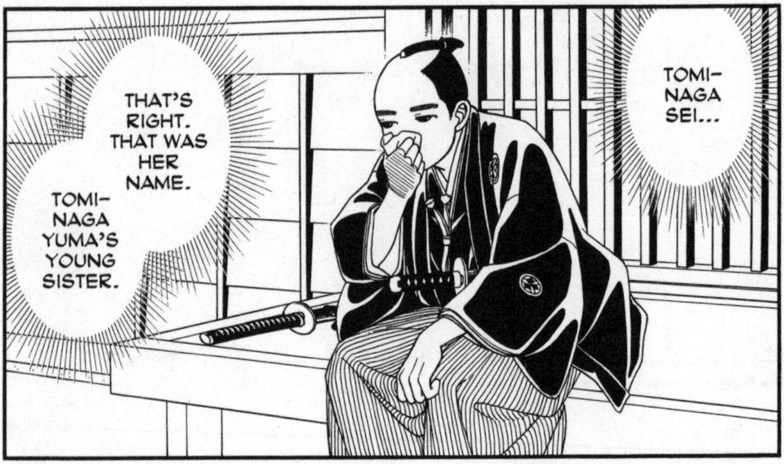
TOMI-NAGA SEI...
THAT'S RIGHT. THAT WAS HER NAME.
TOMI-NAGA YUMA'S YOUNG SISTER.

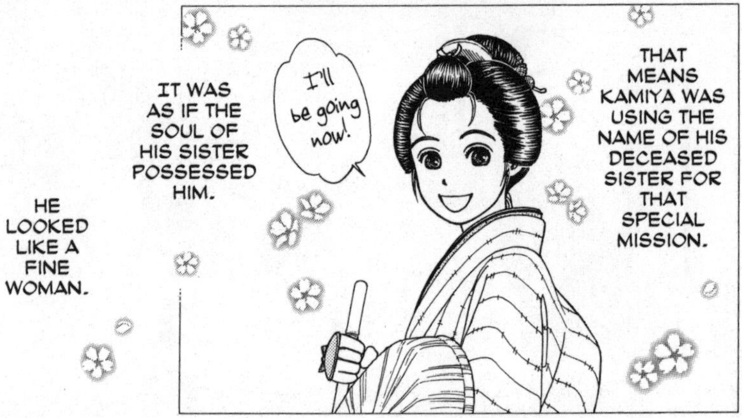
THAT MEANS KAMIYA WAS USING THE NAME OF HIS DECEASED SISTER FOR THAT SPECIAL MISSION.
I'll be going now!
IT WAS AS IF THE SOUL OF HIS SISTER POSSESSED HIM.
HE LOOKED LIKE A FINE WOMAN.

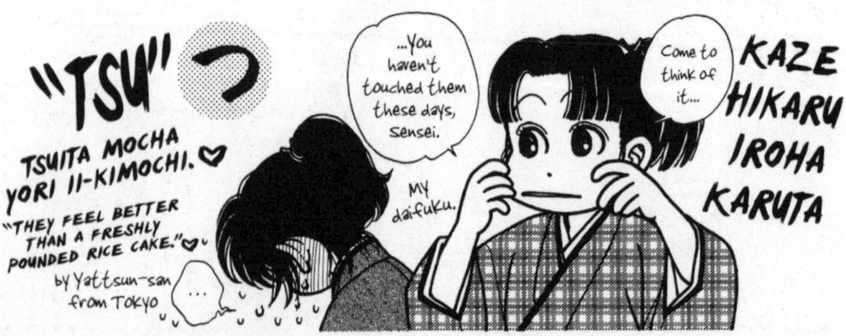
KAZE HIKARU IROHA KARUTA
Come to think of it...
...You haven't touched them these days, Sensei.
My daifuku.
...
"TSU" つ
TSUITA MOCHA YORI II-KIMOCHI.
"THEY FEEL BETTER THAN A FRESHLY POUNDED RICE CAKE."
by Yattsun-san from TOKYO

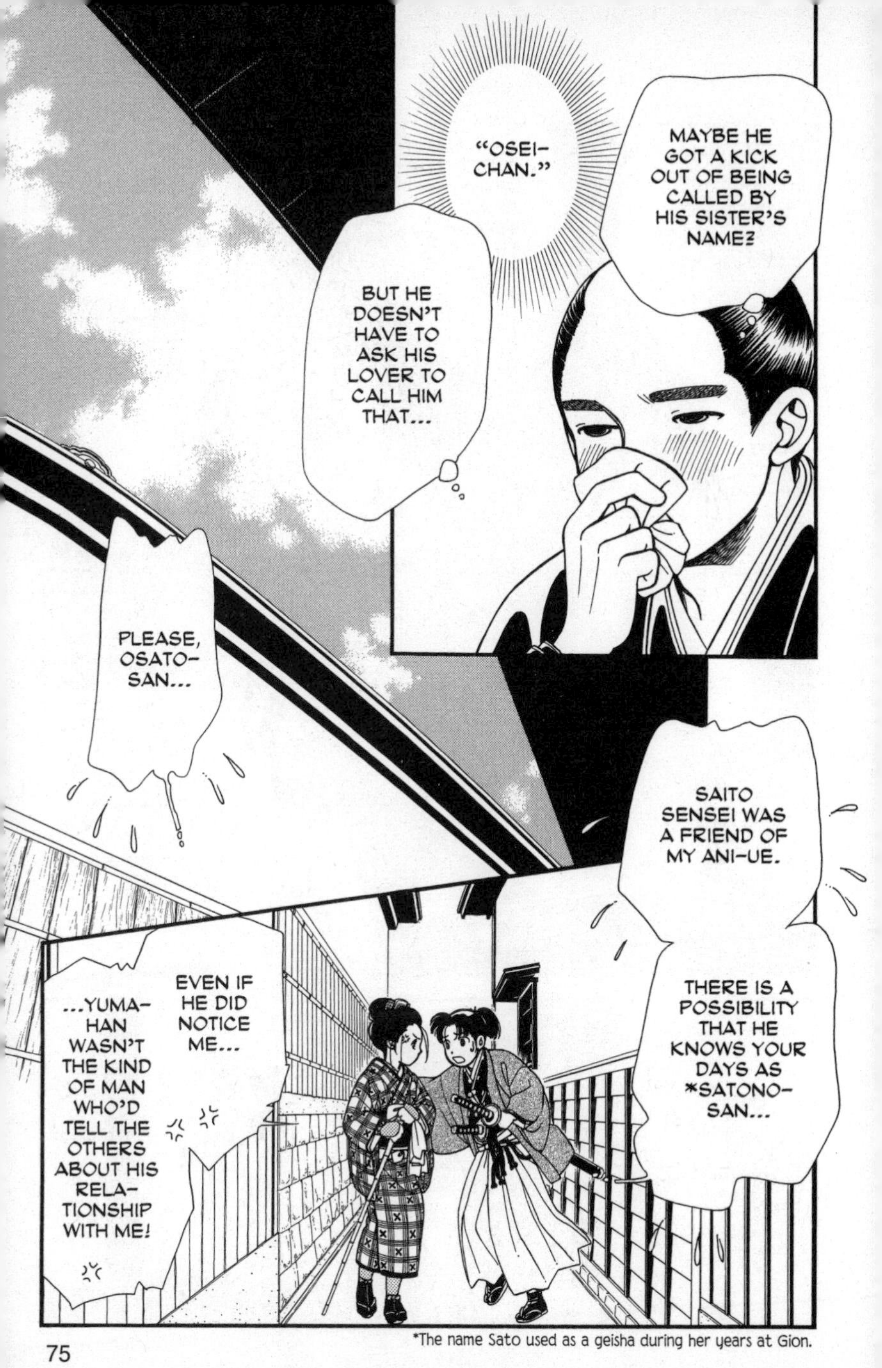

MAYBE HE GOT A KICK OUT OF BEING CALLED BY HIS SISTER'S NAME?
"OSEI-CHAN."
BUT HE DOESN'T HAVE TO ASK HIS LOVER TO CALL HIM THAT...
PLEASE, OSATO-SAN...
SAITO SENSEI WAS A FRIEND OF MY ANI-UE.
THERE IS A POSSIBILITY THAT HE KNOWS YOUR DAYS AS *SATONO-SAN...
EVEN IF HE DID NOTICE ME...
...YUMA-HAN WASN'T THE KIND OF MAN WHO'D TELL THE OTHERS ABOUT HIS RELATIONSHIP WITH ME!

*The name Sato used as a geisha during her years at Gion.

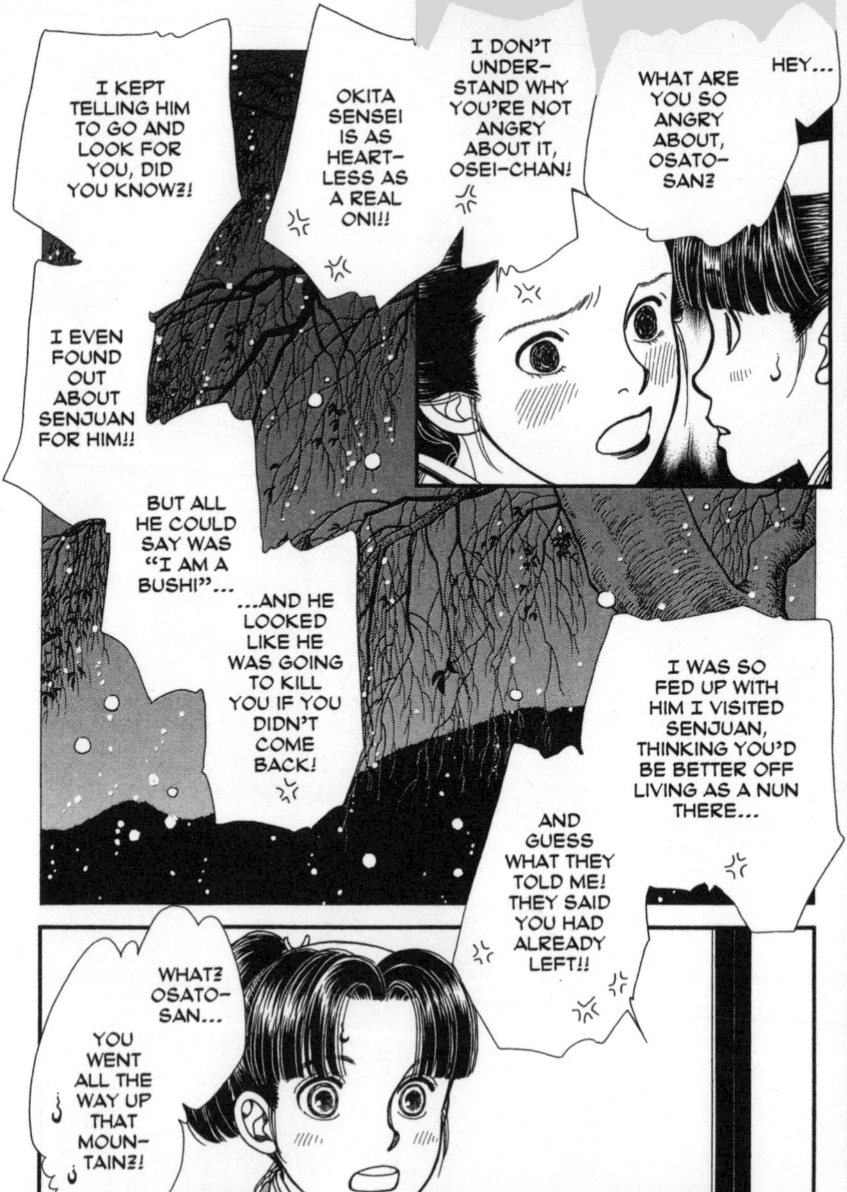
HEY...
WHAT ARE YOU SO ANGRY ABOUT, OSATO-SAN?
I DON'T UNDER-STAND WHY YOU'RE NOT ANGRY ABOUT IT, OSEI-CHAN!
OKITA SENSEI IS AS HEART-LESS AS A REAL ONI!!
I KEPT TELLING HIM TO GO AND LOOK FOR YOU, DID YOU KNOW?!
I EVEN FOUND OUT ABOUT SENJUAN FOR HIM!!
BUT ALL HE COULD SAY WAS "I AM A BUSHI"...
...AND HE LOOKED LIKE HE WAS GOING TO KILL YOU IF YOU DIDN'T COME BACK!
I WAS SO FED UP WITH HIM I VISITED SENJUAN, THINKING YOU'D BE BETTER OFF LIVING AS A NUN THERE...
AND GUESS WHAT THEY TOLD ME! THEY SAID YOU HAD ALREADY LEFT!!
WHAT? OSATO-SAN...
YOU WENT ALL THE WAY UP THAT MOUN-TAIN?!

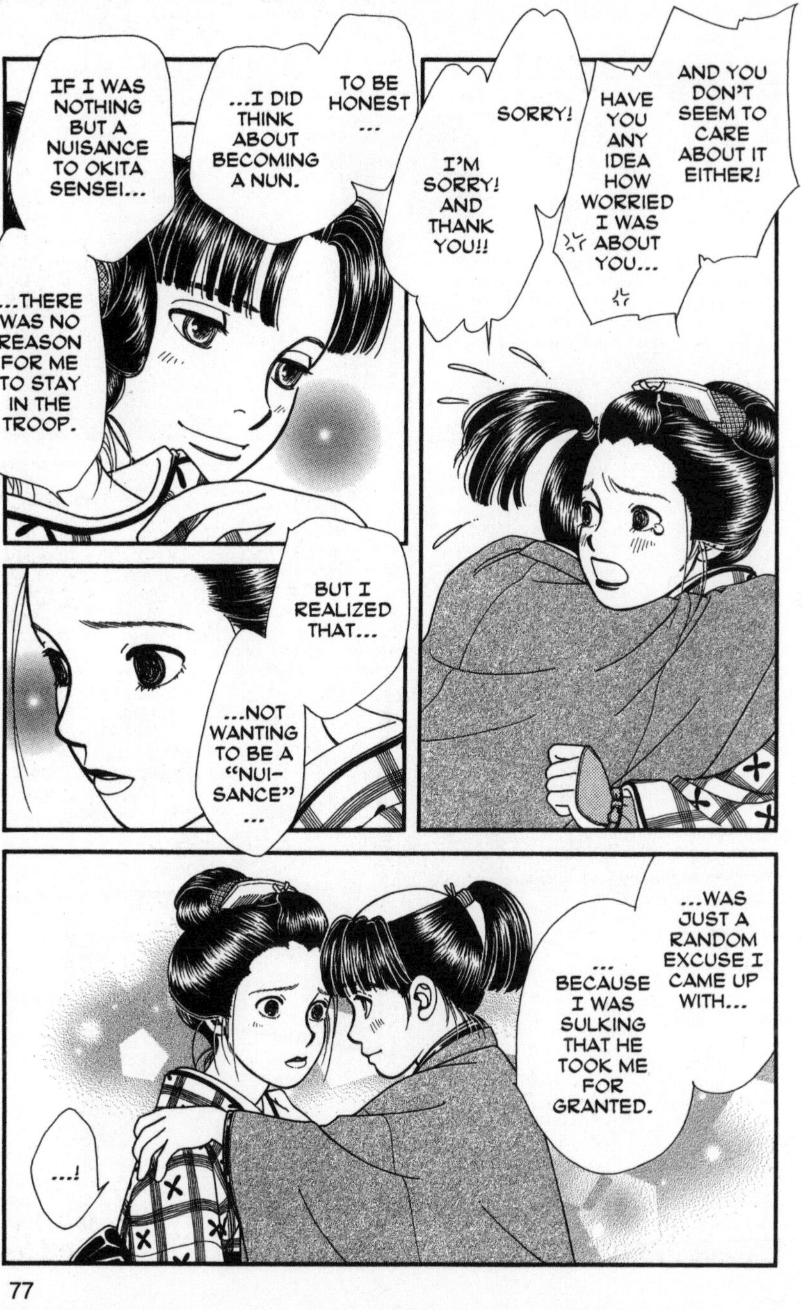
AND YOU DON'T SEEM TO CARE ABOUT IT EITHER!
HAVE YOU ANY IDEA HOW WORRIED I WAS ABOUT YOU...
SORRY!
I'M SORRY! AND THANK YOU!!
TO BE HONEST...
...I DID THINK ABOUT BECOMING A NUN.
IF I WAS NOTHING BUT A NUISANCE TO OKITA SENSEI...
...THERE WAS NO REASON FOR ME TO STAY IN THE TROOP.
BUT I REALIZED THAT...
...NOT WANTING TO BE A "NUI-SANCE"...
...WAS JUST A RANDOM EXCUSE I CAME UP WITH...
...BECAUSE I WAS SULKING THAT HE TOOK ME FOR GRANTED.
...!

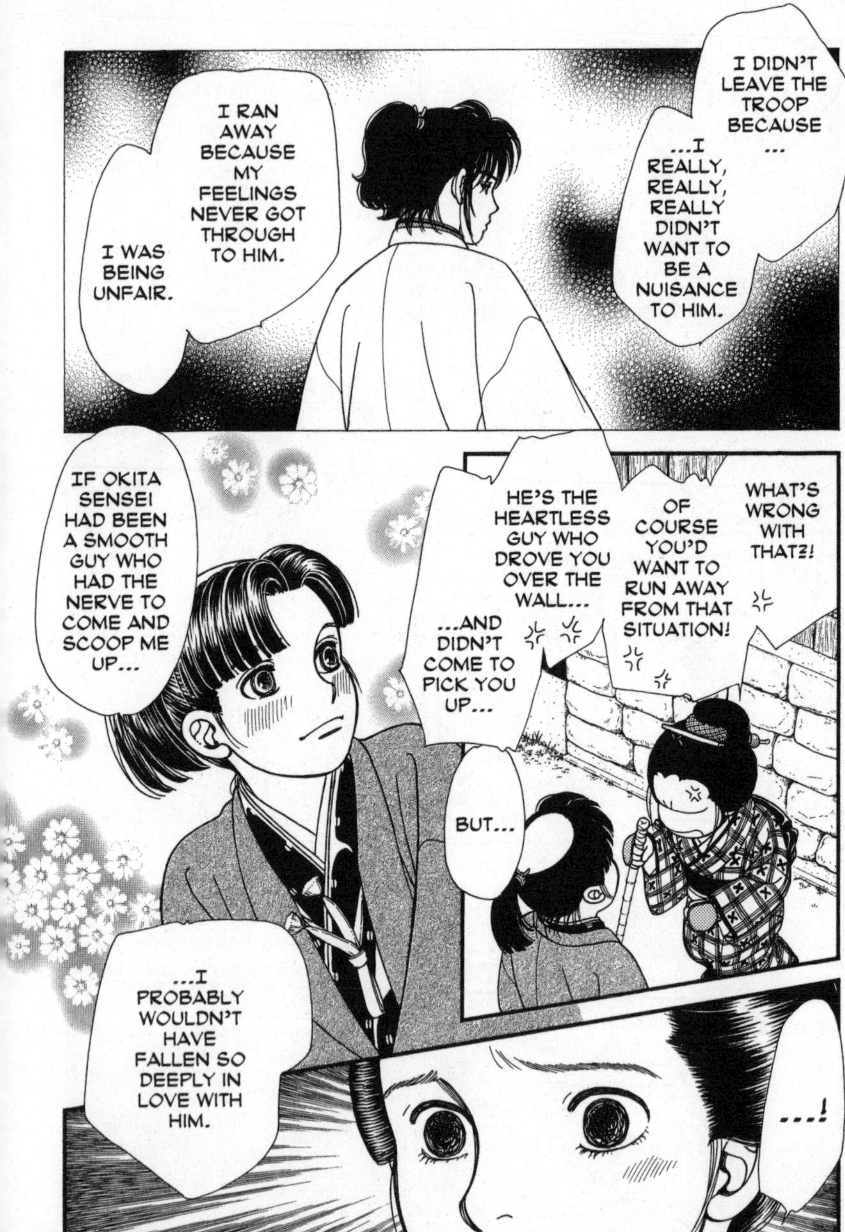
I DIDN'T LEAVE THE TROOP BECAUSE ...
...I REALLY, REALLY, REALLY DIDN'T WANT TO BE A NUISANCE TO HIM.
I RAN AWAY BECAUSE MY FEELINGS NEVER GOT THROUGH TO HIM.
I WAS BEING UNFAIR.
WHAT'S WRONG WITH THAT?!
OF COURSE YOU'D WANT TO RUN AWAY FROM THAT SITUATION!
HE'S THE HEARTLESS GUY WHO DROVE YOU OVER THE WALL...
...AND DIDN'T COME TO PICK YOU UP...
BUT...
IF OKITA SENSEI HAD BEEN A SMOOTH GUY WHO HAD THE NERVE TO COME AND SCOOP ME UP...
...I PROBABLY WOULDN'T HAVE FALLEN SO DEEPLY IN LOVE WITH HIM.
...!

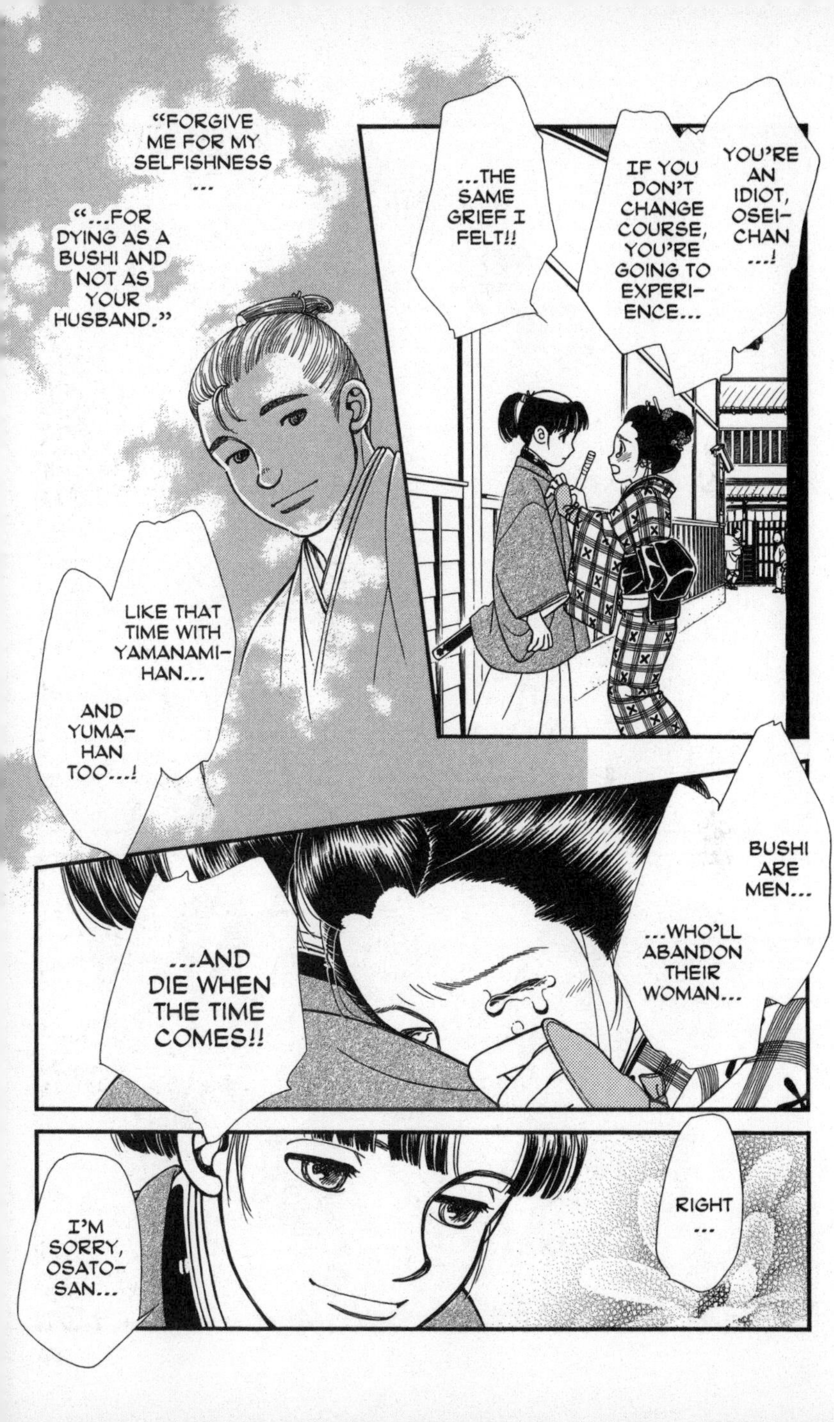
YOU'RE AN IDIOT, OSEI-CHAN...!
IF YOU DON'T CHANGE COURSE, YOU'RE GOING TO EXPERIENCE...
...THE SAME GRIEF I FELT!!
"FORGIVE ME FOR MY SELFISHNESS...
"...FOR DYING AS A BUSHI AND NOT AS YOUR HUSBAND."
LIKE THAT TIME WITH YAMANAMI-HAN...
AND YUMA-HAN TOO...!
BUSHI ARE MEN...
...WHO'LL ABANDON THEIR WOMAN...
...AND DIE WHEN THE TIME COMES!!
RIGHT...
I'M SORRY, OSATO-SAN...

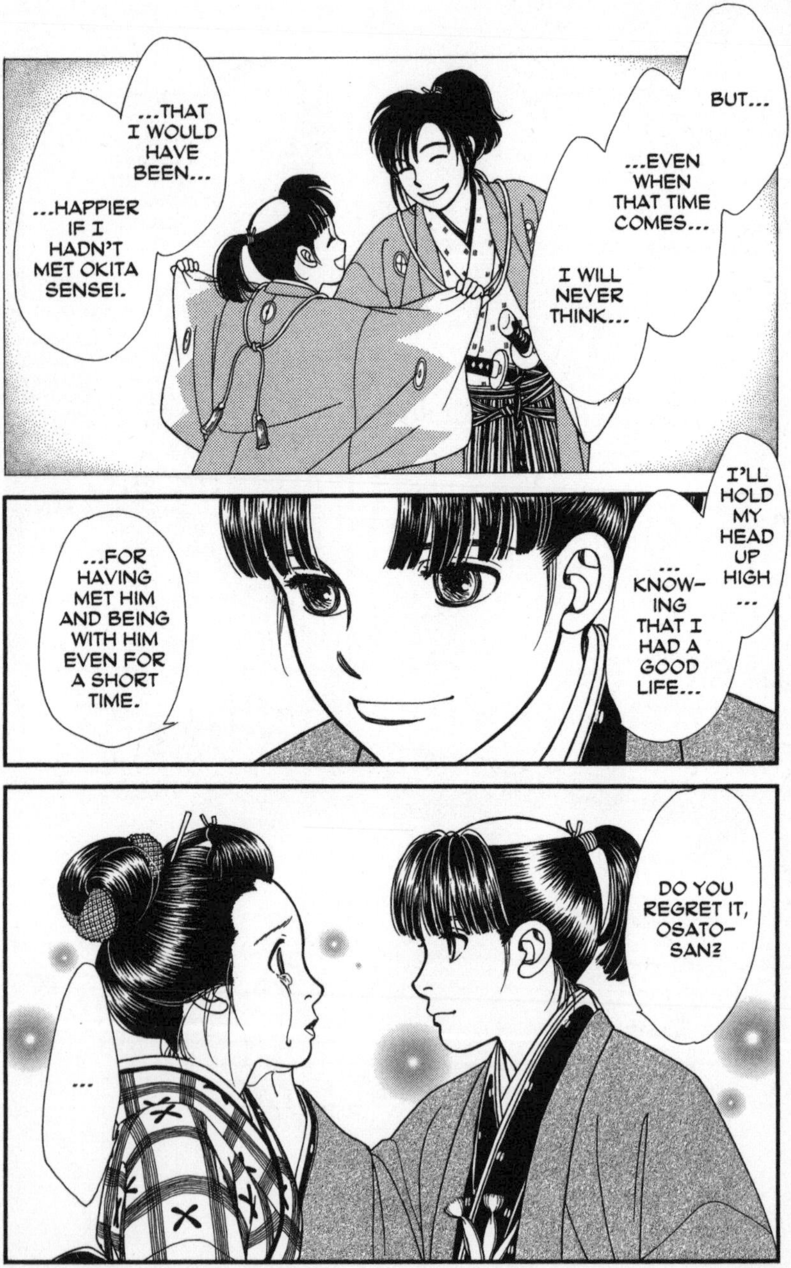
BUT...
...EVEN WHEN THAT TIME COMES...
I WILL NEVER THINK...
...THAT I WOULD HAVE BEEN...
...HAPPIER IF I HADN'T MET OKITA SENSEI.
I'LL HOLD MY HEAD UP HIGH...
...KNOWING THAT I HAD A GOOD LIFE...
...FOR HAVING MET HIM AND BEING WITH HIM EVEN FOR A SHORT TIME.
DO YOU REGRET IT, OSATO-SAN?
...

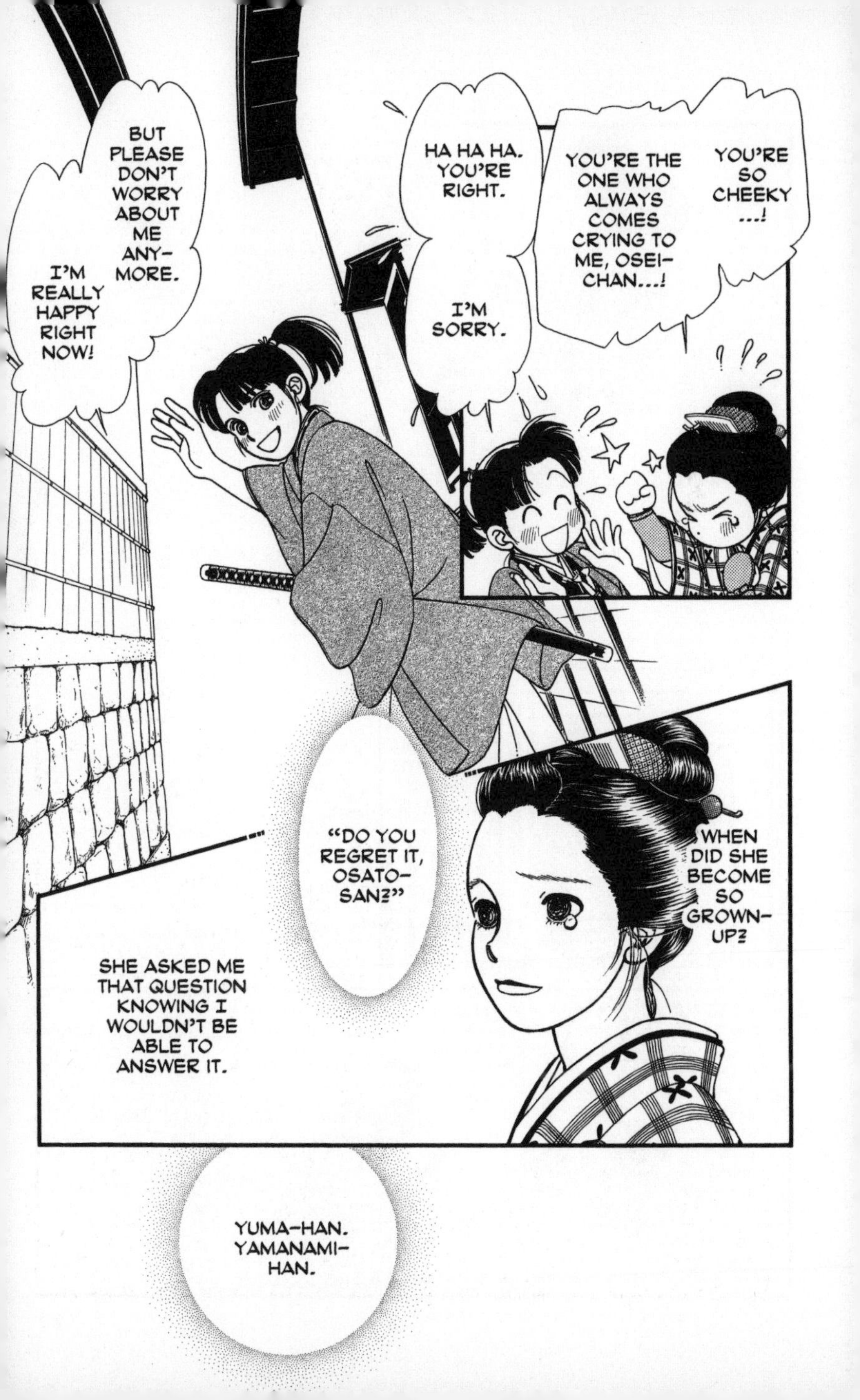
YOU'RE SO CHEEKY ...!
YOU'RE THE ONE WHO ALWAYS COMES CRYING TO ME, OSEI-CHAN...!
HA HA HA. YOU'RE RIGHT.
I'M SORRY.
BUT PLEASE DON'T WORRY ABOUT ME ANYMORE.
I'M REALLY HAPPY RIGHT NOW!
WHEN DID SHE BECOME SO GROWN-UP?
"DO YOU REGRET IT, OSATO-SAN?"
SHE ASKED ME THAT QUESTION KNOWING I WOULDN'T BE ABLE TO ANSWER IT.
YUMA-HAN. YAMANAMI-HAN.

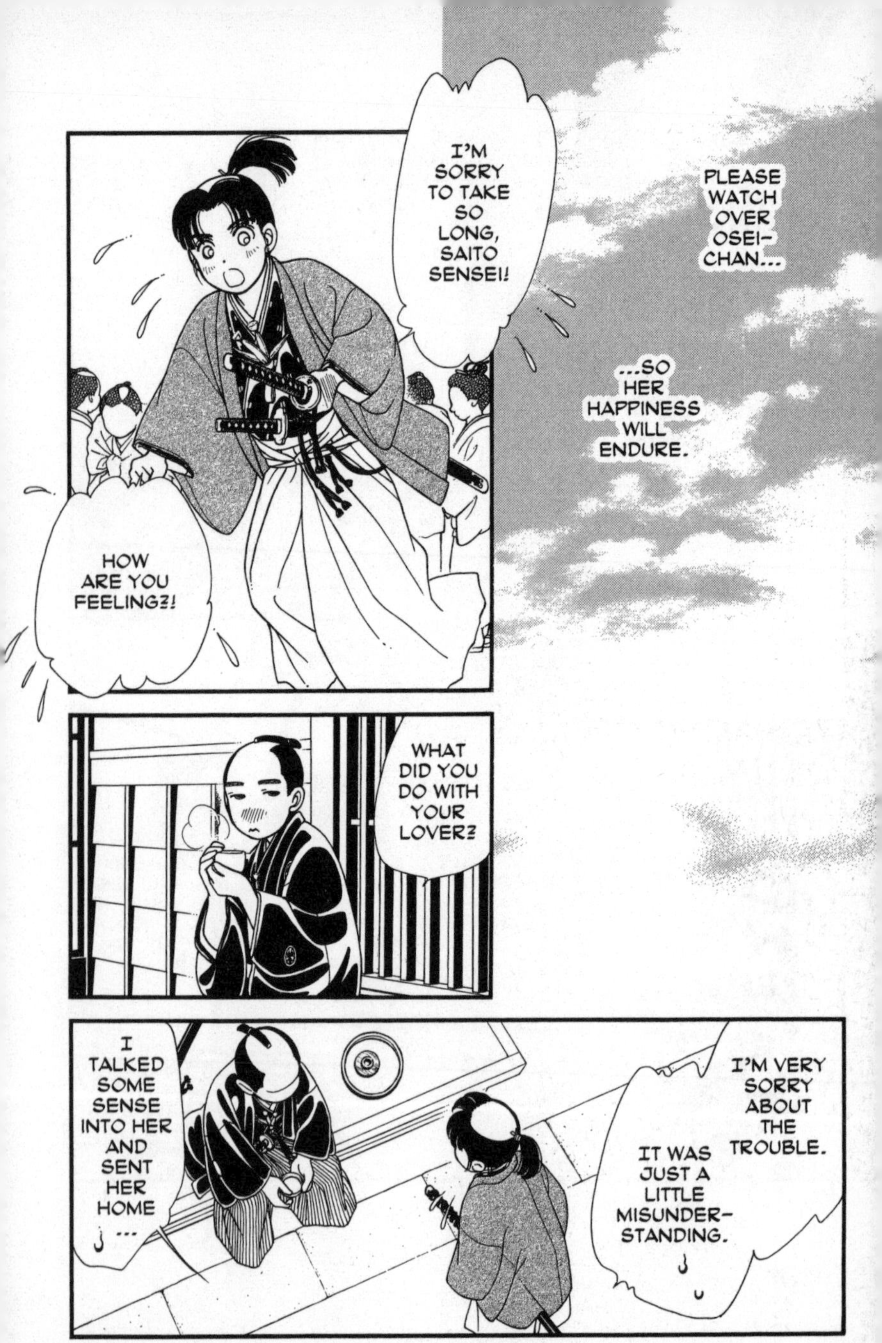
PLEASE WATCH OVER OSEI-CHAN...
...SO HER HAPPINESS WILL ENDURE.
I'M SORRY TO TAKE SO LONG, SAITO SENSEI!
HOW ARE YOU FEELING?!
WHAT DID YOU DO WITH YOUR LOVER?
I'M VERY SORRY ABOUT THE TROUBLE.
IT WAS JUST A LITTLE MISUNDER-STANDING.
I TALKED SOME SENSE INTO HER AND SENT HER HOME...

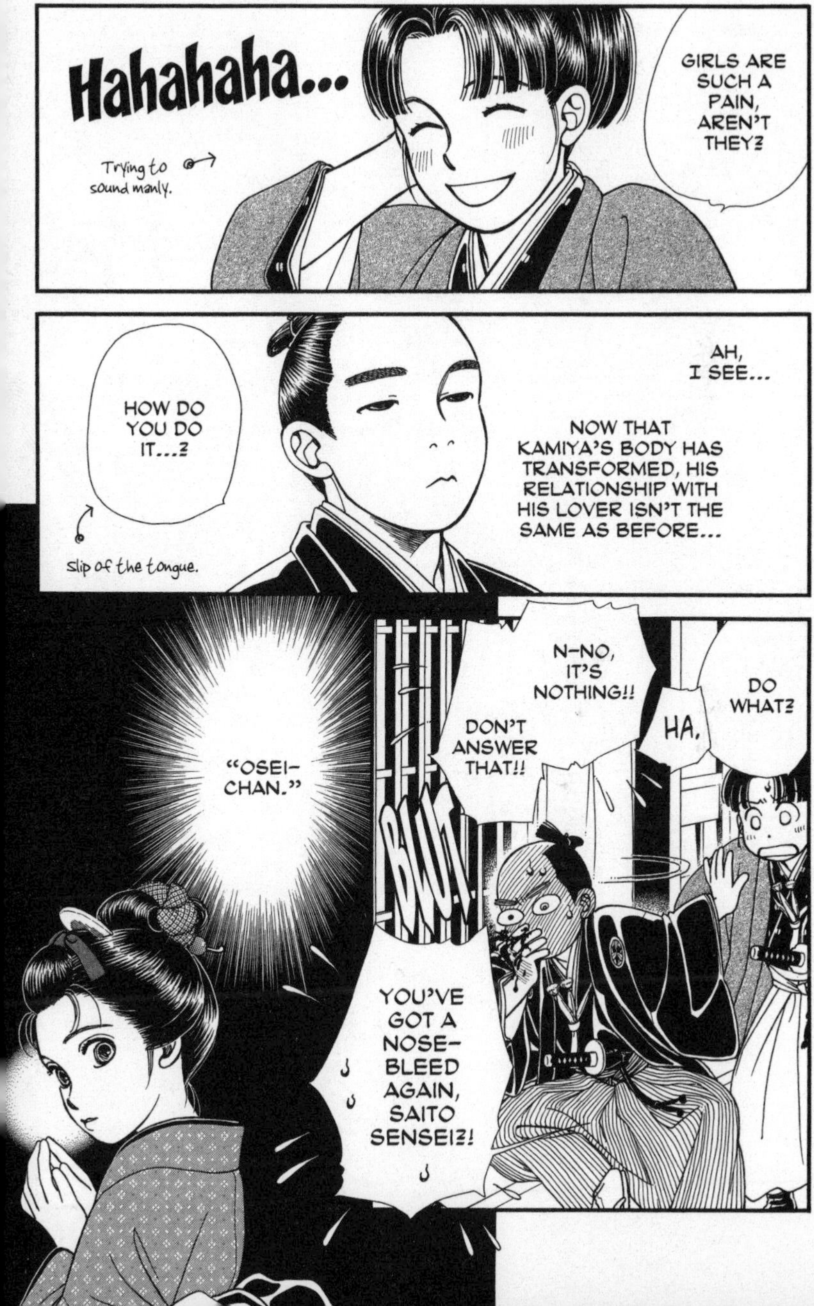
GIRLS ARE SUCH A PAIN, AREN'T THEY?
Hahahaha...
Trying to sound manly.
AH, I SEE...
NOW THAT KAMIYA'S BODY HAS TRANSFORMED, HIS RELATIONSHIP WITH HIS LOVER ISN'T THE SAME AS BEFORE...
HOW DO YOU DO IT...?
slip of the tongue.
DO WHAT?
HA,
N-NO, IT'S NOTHING!!
DON'T ANSWER THAT!!
YOU'VE GOT A NOSE-BLEED AGAIN, SAITO SENSEI!?!
"OSEI-CHAN."

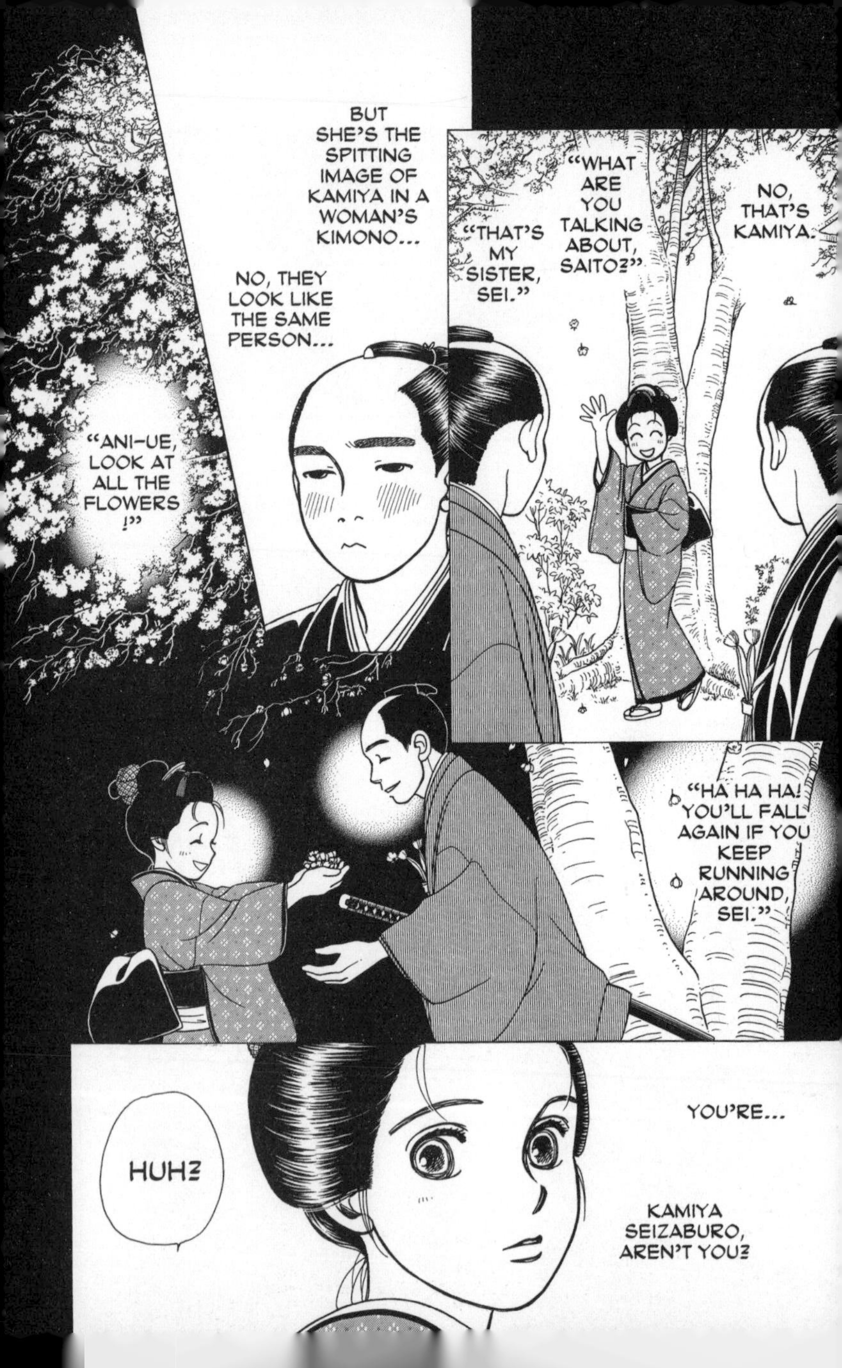
BUT SHE'S THE SPITTING IMAGE OF KAMIYA IN A WOMAN'S KIMONO...
NO, THEY LOOK LIKE THE SAME PERSON...
NO, THAT'S KAMIYA.
"WHAT ARE YOU TALKING ABOUT, SAITO?"
"THAT'S MY SISTER, SEI."
"HA HA HA! YOU'LL FALL AGAIN IF YOU KEEP RUNNING AROUND, SEI."
"ANI-UE, LOOK AT ALL THE FLOWERS!"
YOU'RE...
KAMIYA SEIZABURO, AREN'T YOU?
HUH?

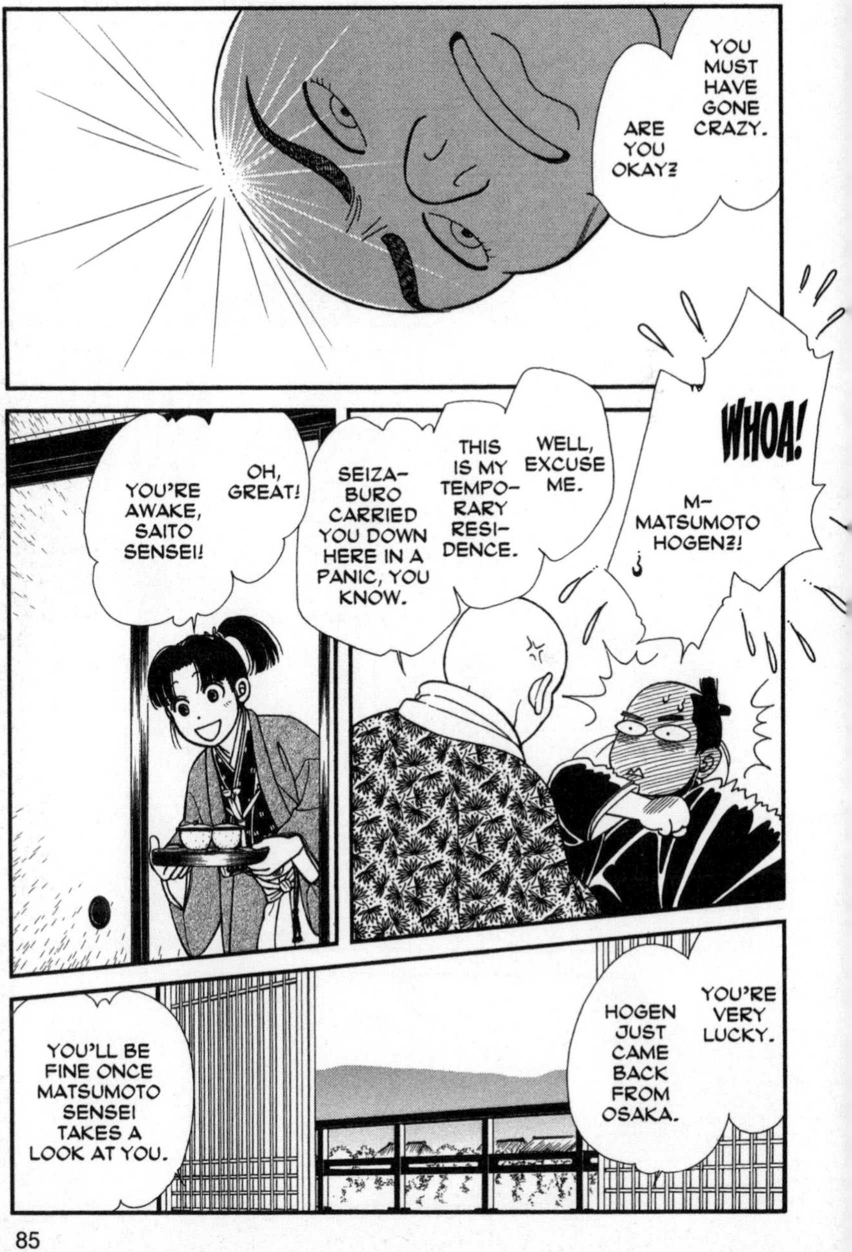
YOU MUST HAVE GONE CRAZY.
ARE YOU OKAY?!
WHOA!
M-MATSUMOTO HOGEN?!
WELL, EXCUSE ME.
THIS IS MY TEMPORARY RESIDENCE.
SEIZABURO CARRIED YOU DOWN HERE IN A PANIC, YOU KNOW.
OH, GREAT!
YOU'RE AWAKE, SAITO SENSEI!
YOU'RE VERY LUCKY.
HOGEN JUST CAME BACK FROM OSAKA.
YOU'LL BE FINE ONCE MATSUMOTO SENSEI TAKES A LOOK AT YOU.

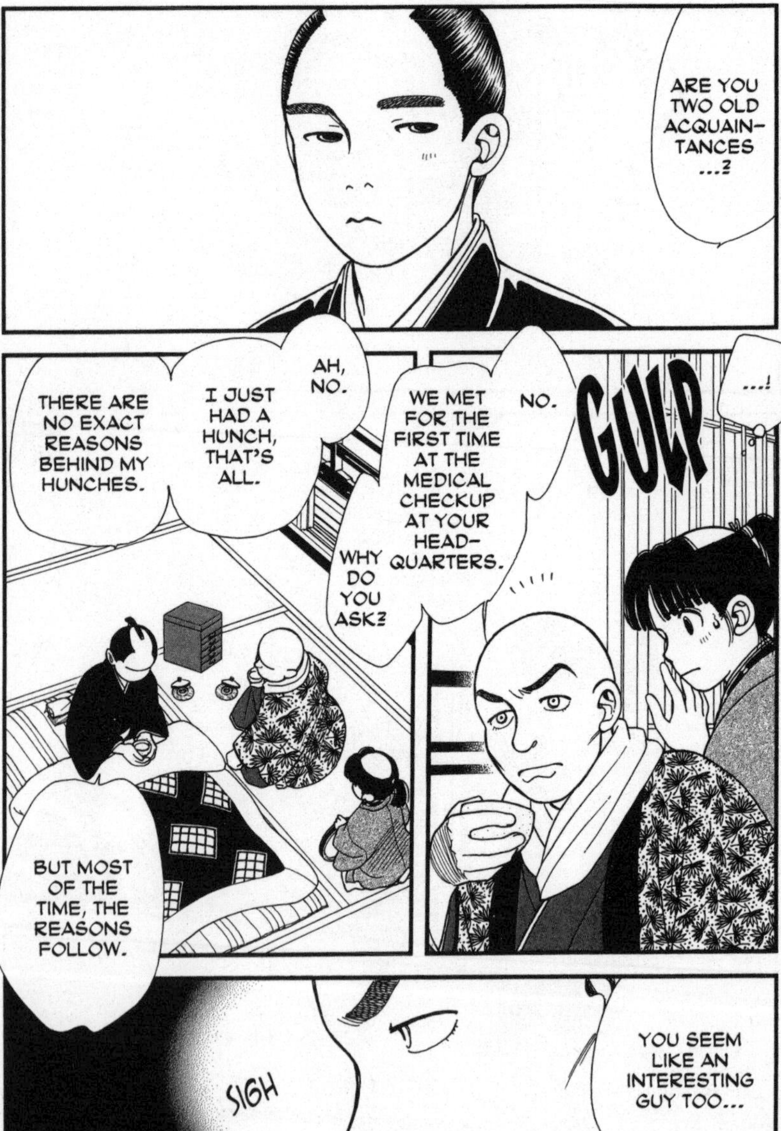

ARE YOU TWO OLD ACQUAINTANCES ...?
...!
GULP
NO.
WE MET FOR THE FIRST TIME AT THE MEDICAL CHECKUP AT YOUR HEADQUARTERS.
WHY DO YOU ASK?
AH, NO.
I JUST HAD A HUNCH, THAT'S ALL.
THERE ARE NO EXACT REASONS BEHIND MY HUNCHES.
BUT MOST OF THE TIME, THE REASONS FOLLOW.
YOU SEEM LIKE AN INTERESTING GUY TOO...
SIGH

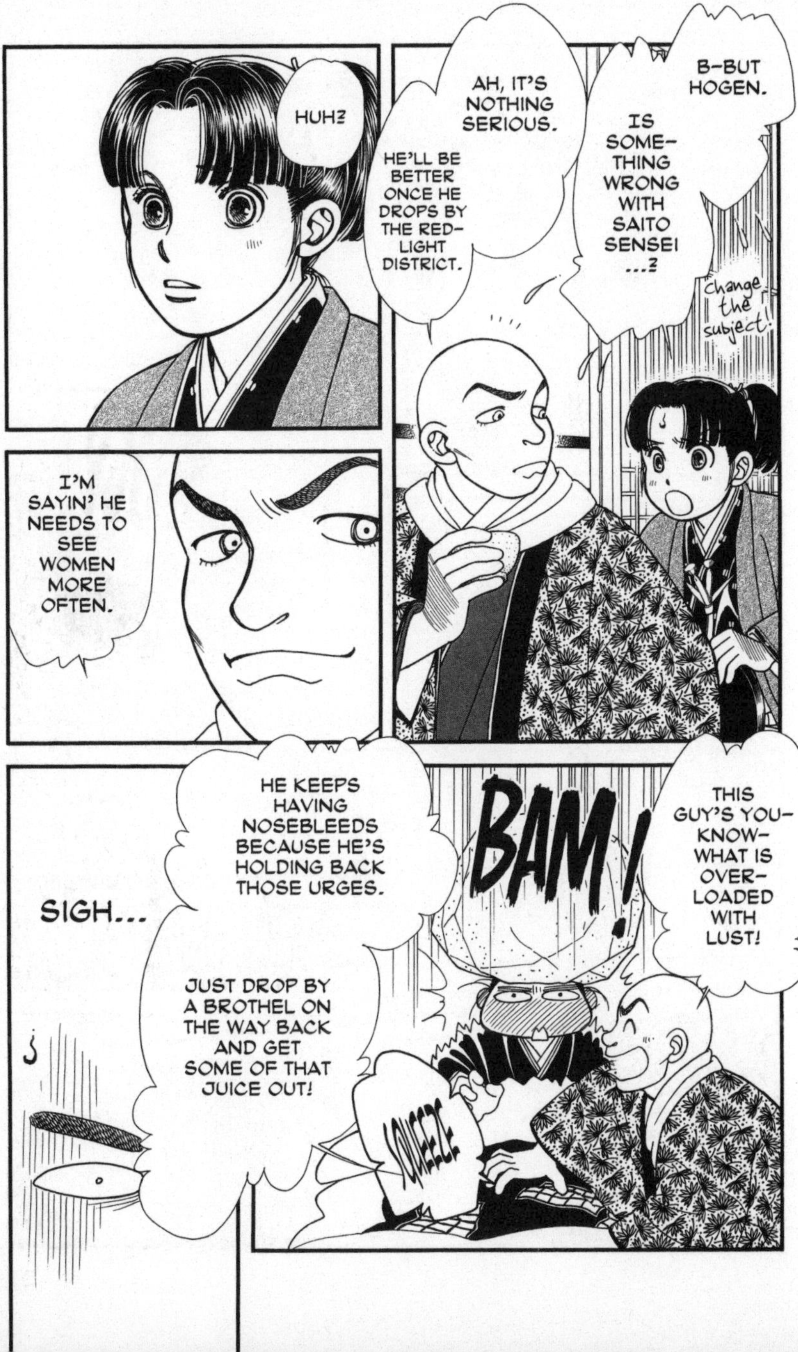
B-BUT HOGEN.
IS SOME-THING WRONG WITH SAITO SENSEI...?
change the subject!
AH, IT'S NOTHING SERIOUS.
HE'LL BE BETTER ONCE HE DROPS BY THE RED-LIGHT DISTRICT.
HUH?
I'M SAYIN' HE NEEDS TO SEE WOMEN MORE OFTEN.
THIS GUY'S YOU-KNOW-WHAT IS OVER-LOADED WITH LUST!
BAM!
HE KEEPS HAVING NOSEBLEEDS BECAUSE HE'S HOLDING BACK THOSE URGES.
JUST DROP BY A BROTHEL ON THE WAY BACK AND GET SOME OF THAT JUICE OUT!
SQUEEZE
SIGH...

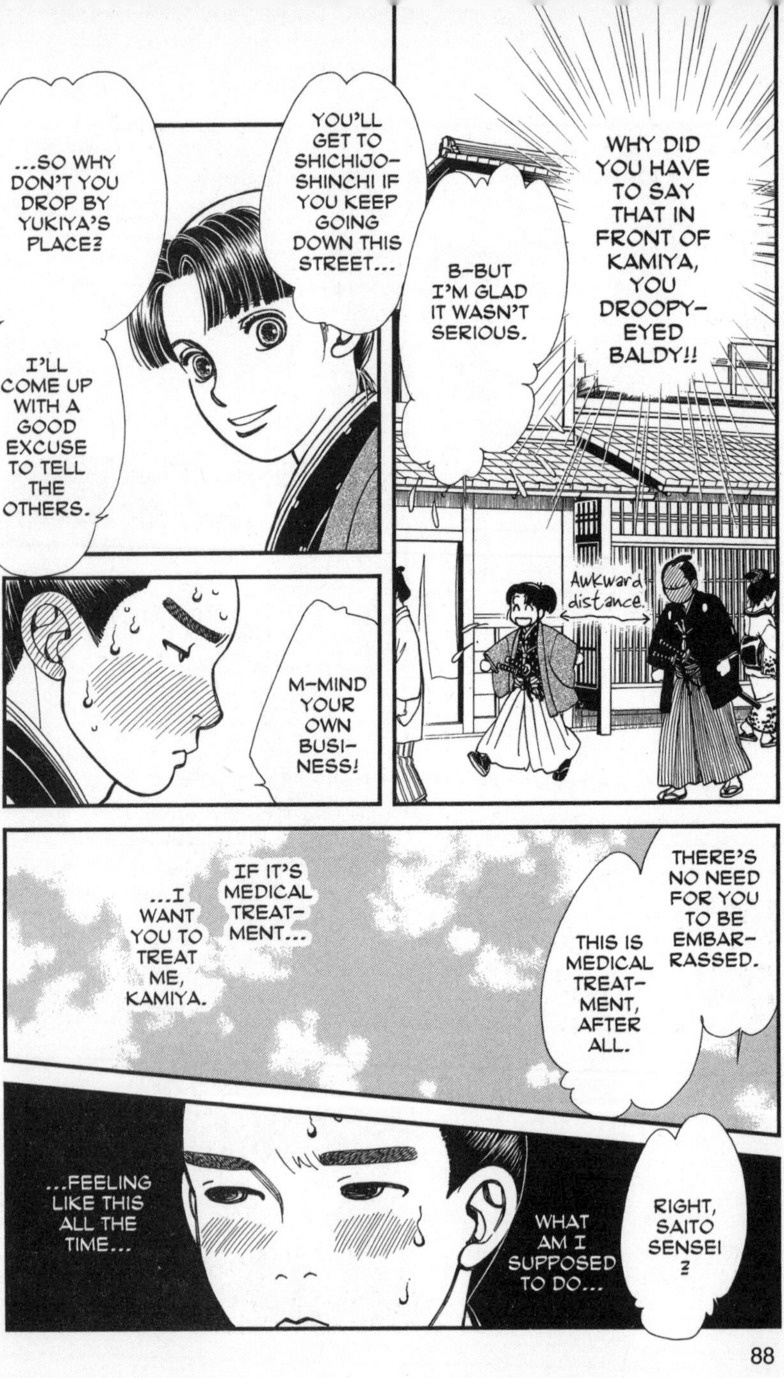
WHY DID YOU HAVE TO SAY THAT IN FRONT OF KAMIYA, YOU DROOPY-EYED BALDY!!
B-BUT I'M GLAD IT WASN'T SERIOUS.
Awkward distance
YOU'LL GET TO SHICHIJO-SHINCHI IF YOU KEEP GOING DOWN THIS STREET...
...SO WHY DON'T YOU DROP BY YUKIYA'S PLACE?
I'LL COME UP WITH A GOOD EXCUSE TO TELL THE OTHERS.
M-MIND YOUR OWN BUSI-NESS!
THERE'S NO NEED FOR YOU TO BE EMBAR-RASSED.
THIS IS MEDICAL TREAT-MENT, AFTER ALL.
IF IT'S MEDICAL TREAT-MENT...
...I WANT YOU TO TREAT ME, KAMIYA.
RIGHT, SAITO SENSEI?
WHAT AM I SUPPOSED TO DO...
...FEELING LIKE THIS ALL THE TIME...

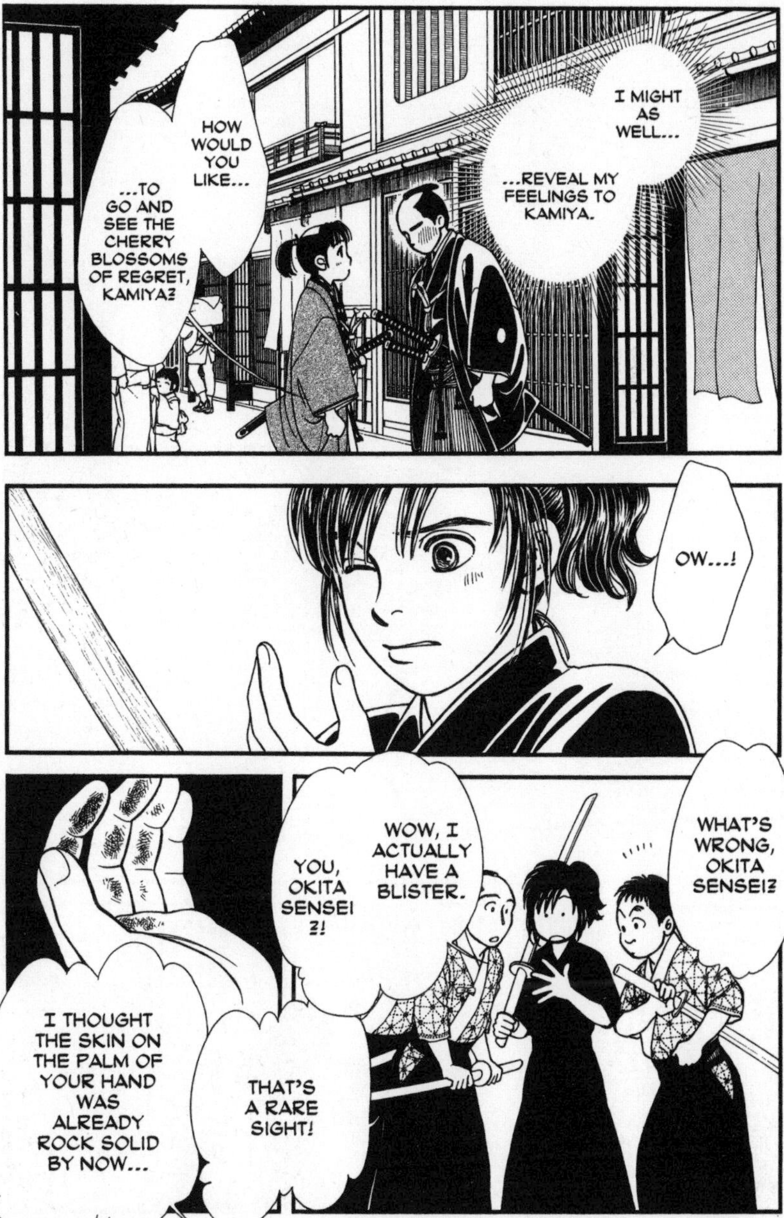
I MIGHT AS WELL...
...REVEAL MY FEELINGS TO KAMIYA.
HOW WOULD YOU LIKE...
...TO GO AND SEE THE CHERRY BLOSSOMS OF REGRET, KAMIYA?
OW...!
WHAT'S WRONG, OKITA SENSEI?
WOW, I ACTUALLY HAVE A BLISTER.
YOU, OKITA SENSEI ?!
THAT'S A RARE SIGHT!
I THOUGHT THE SKIN ON THE PALM OF YOUR HAND WAS ALREADY ROCK SOLID BY NOW...

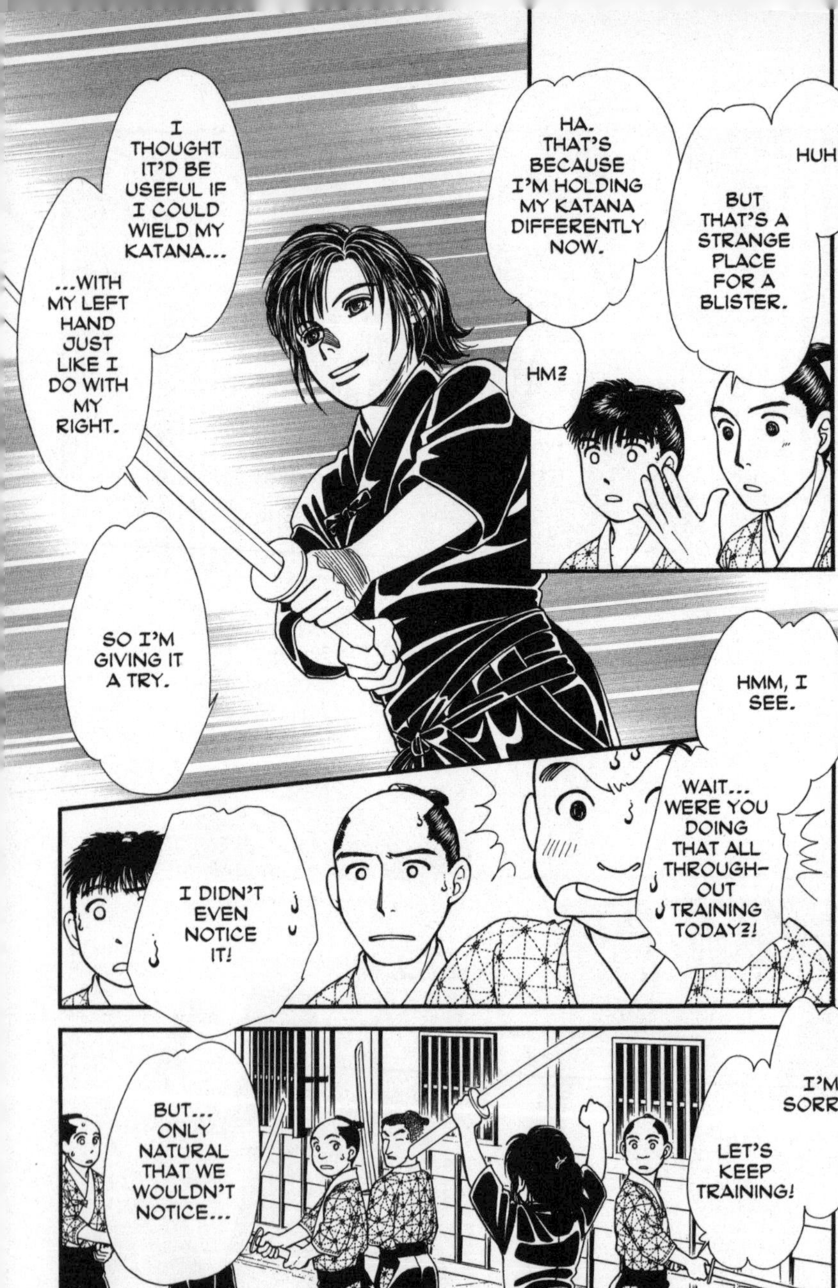
HUH? BUT THAT'S A STRANGE PLACE FOR A BLISTER.
HM?
HA. THAT'S BECAUSE I'M HOLDING MY KATANA DIFFERENTLY NOW.
I THOUGHT IT'D BE USEFUL IF I COULD WIELD MY KATANA...
...WITH MY LEFT HAND JUST LIKE I DO WITH MY RIGHT.
SO I'M GIVING IT A TRY.
HMM, I SEE.
WAIT... WERE YOU DOING THAT ALL THROUGH-OUT TRAINING TODAY?!
I DIDN'T EVEN NOTICE IT!
I'M SORRY.
LET'S KEEP TRAINING!
BUT... ONLY NATURAL THAT WE WOULDN'T NOTICE...

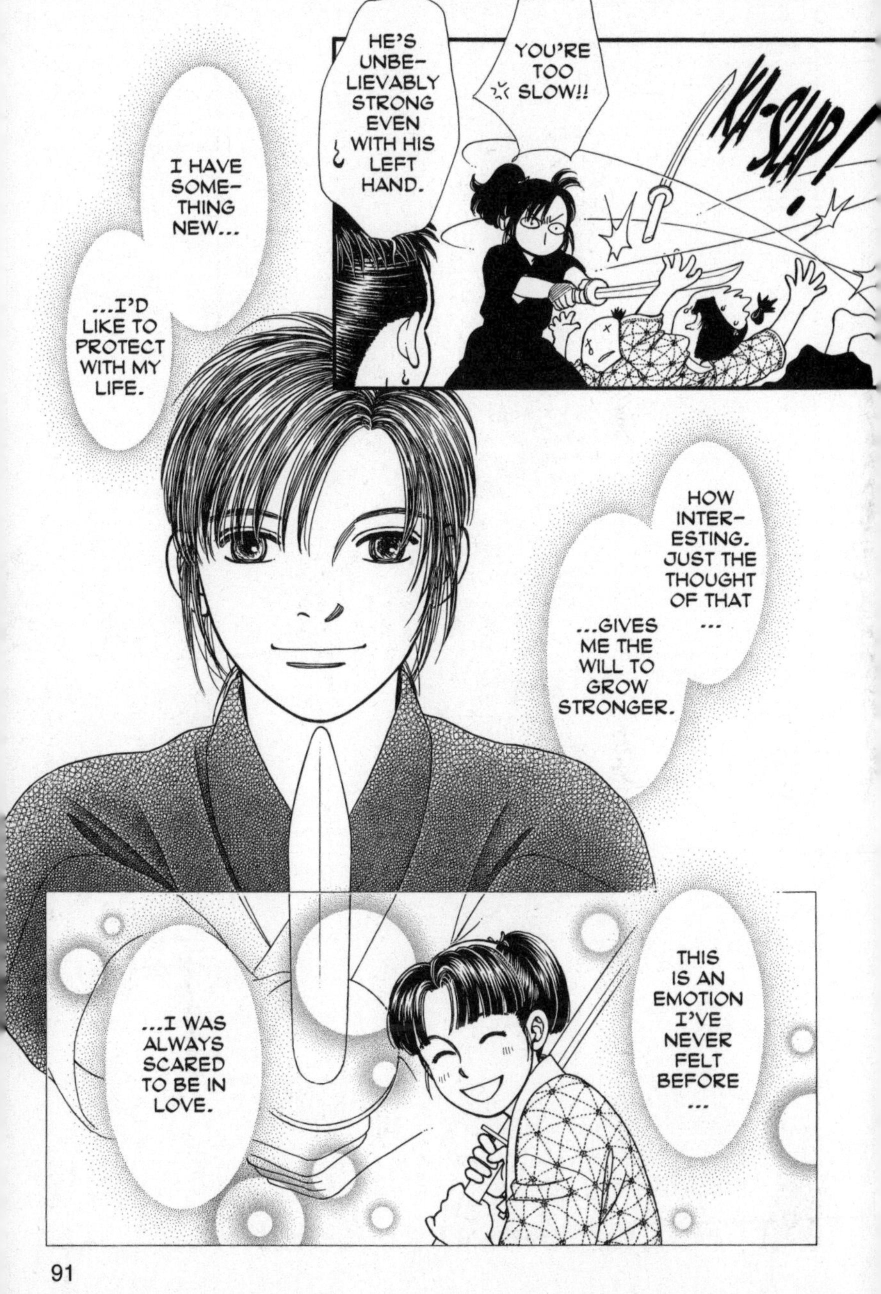
KA-SLAP!
YOU'RE TOO SLOW!!
HE'S UNBE-LIEVABLY STRONG EVEN WITH HIS LEFT HAND.
I HAVE SOME-THING NEW...
...I'D LIKE TO PROTECT WITH MY LIFE.
HOW INTER-ESTING. JUST THE THOUGHT OF THAT ...
...GIVES ME THE WILL TO GROW STRONGER.
THIS IS AN EMOTION I'VE NEVER FELT BEFORE ...
...I WAS ALWAYS SCARED TO BE IN LOVE.

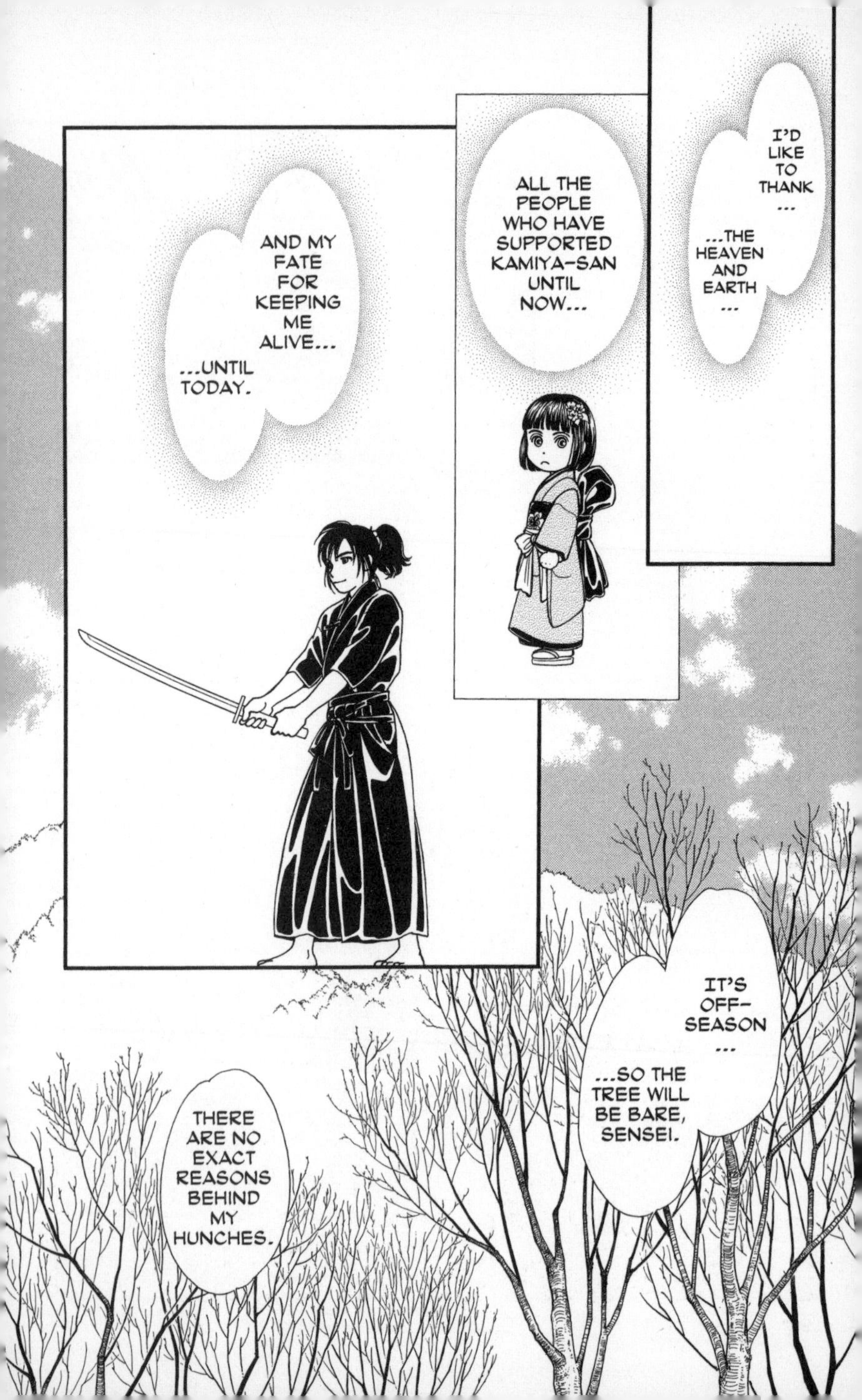
I'D LIKE TO THANK...
...THE HEAVEN AND EARTH...
ALL THE PEOPLE WHO HAVE SUPPORTED KAMIYA-SAN UNTIL NOW...
AND MY FATE FOR KEEPING ME ALIVE...
...UNTIL TODAY.
IT'S OFF-SEASON...
...SO THE TREE WILL BE BARE, SENSEI.
THERE ARE NO EXACT REASONS BEHIND MY HUNCHES.

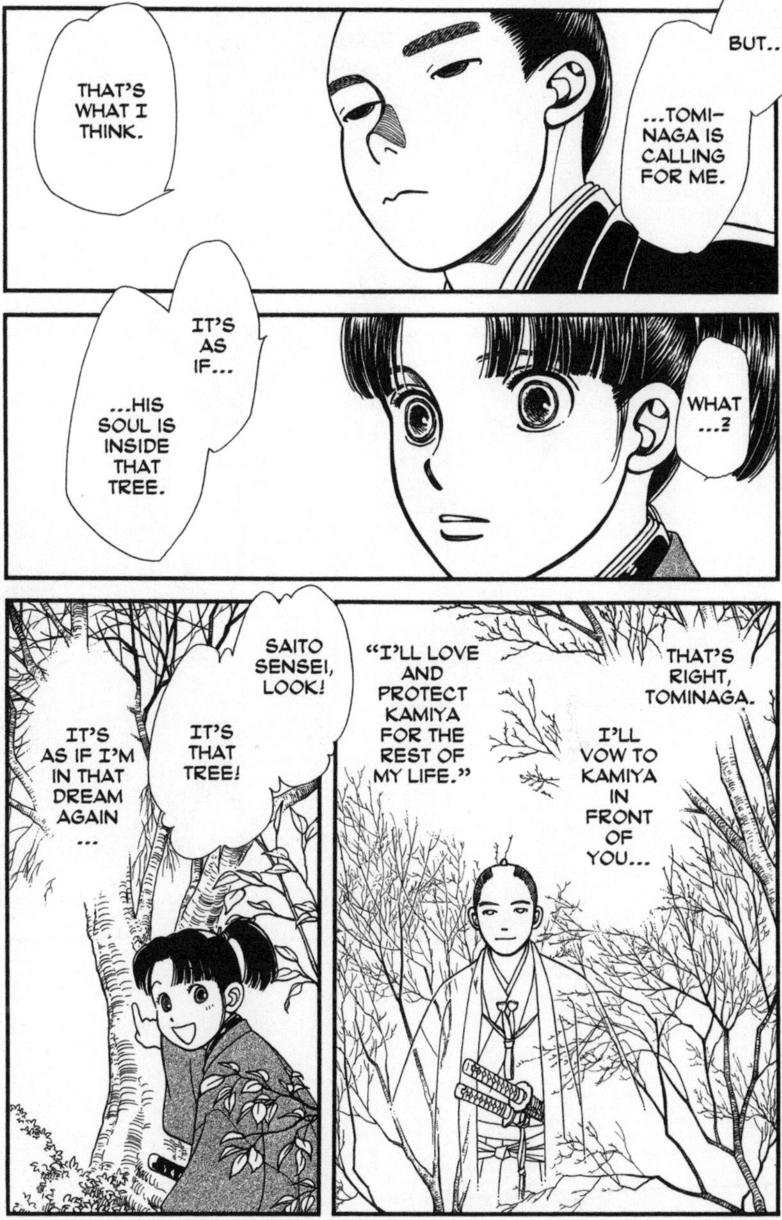
BUT...
...TOMI-NAGA IS CALLING FOR ME.
THAT'S WHAT I THINK.
WHAT ...?
IT'S AS IF...
...HIS SOUL IS INSIDE THAT TREE.
THAT'S RIGHT, TOMINAGA.
I'LL VOW TO KAMIYA IN FRONT OF YOU...
"I'LL LOVE AND PROTECT KAMIYA FOR THE REST OF MY LIFE."
SAITO SENSEI, LOOK!
IT'S THAT TREE!
IT'S AS IF I'M IN THAT DREAM AGAIN...

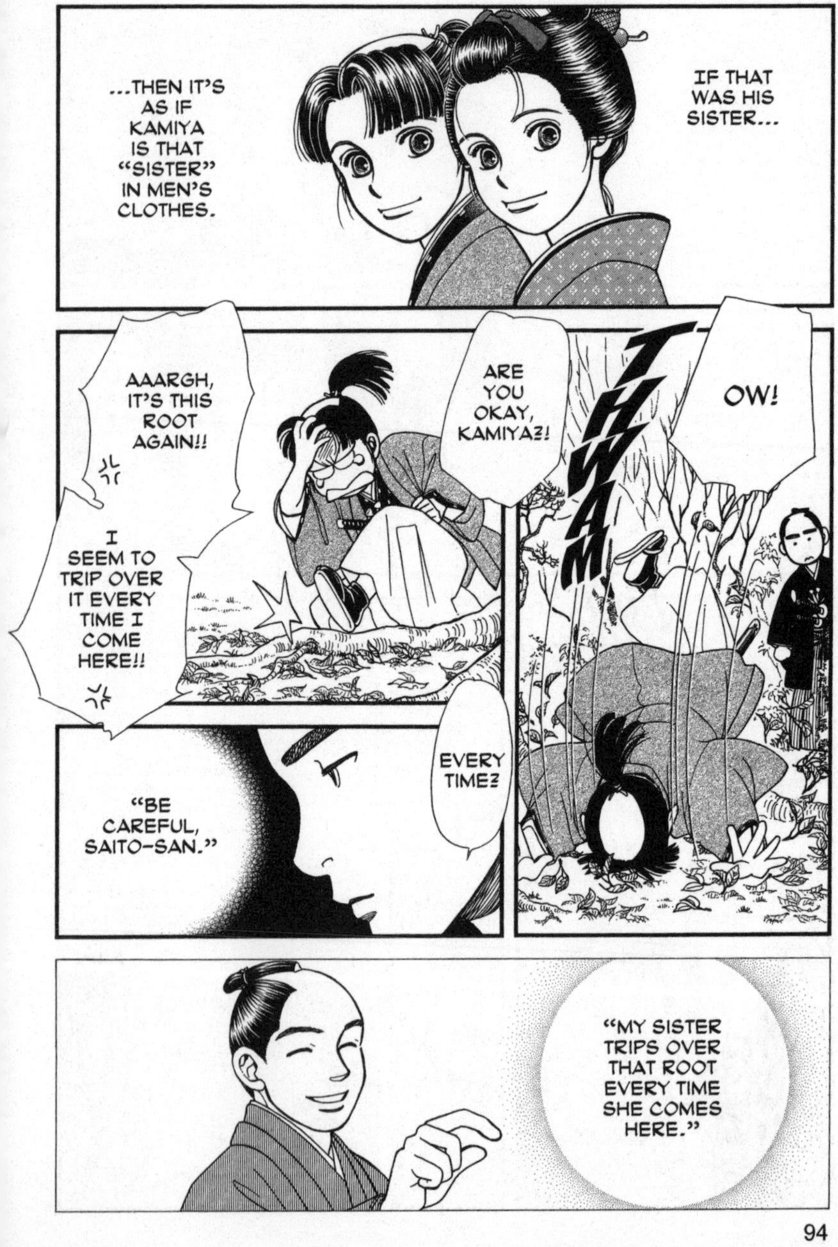
IF THAT WAS HIS SISTER...
...THEN IT'S AS IF KAMIYA IS THAT "SISTER" IN MEN'S CLOTHES.
OW!
ARE YOU OKAY, KAMIYA?!
AAARGH, IT'S THIS ROOT AGAIN!!
I SEEM TO TRIP OVER IT EVERY TIME I COME HERE!!
EVERY TIME?
"BE CAREFUL, SAITO-SAN."
"MY SISTER TRIPS OVER THAT ROOT EVERY TIME SHE COMES HERE."

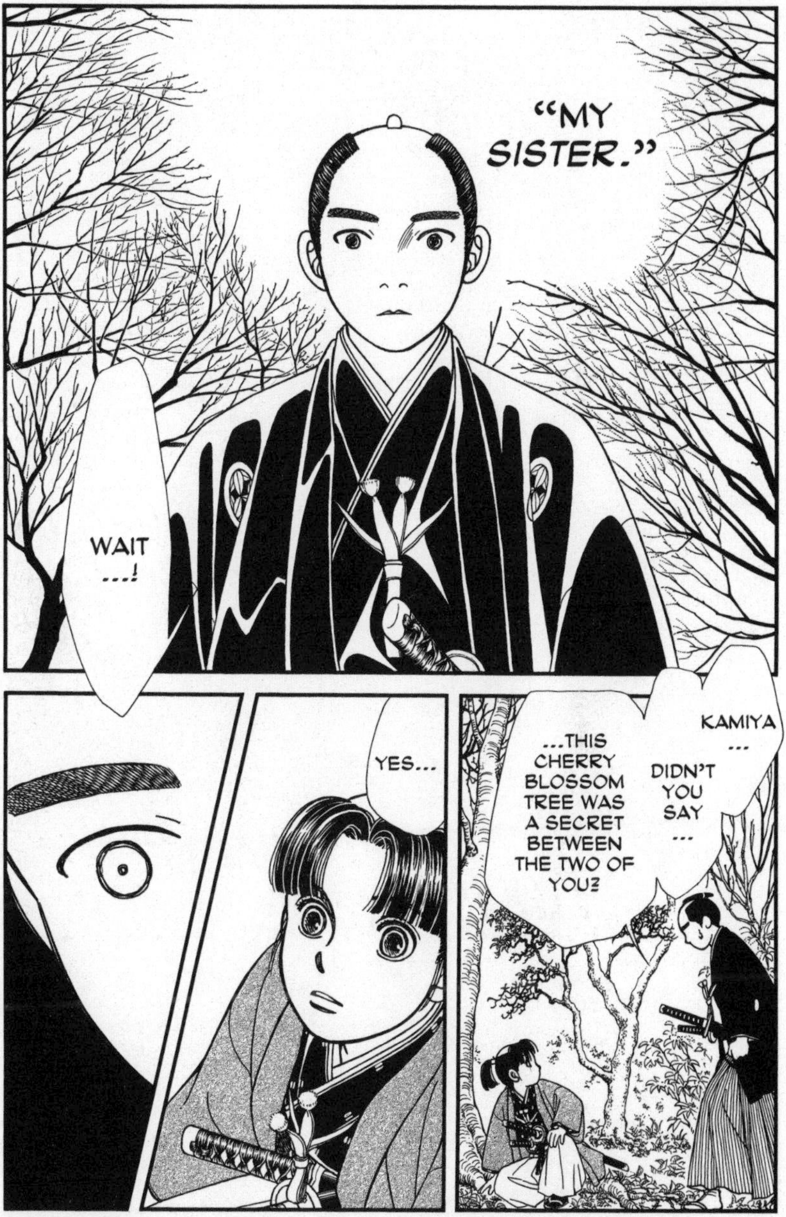
"MY SISTER."
WAIT ...!
KAMIYA ... DIDN'T YOU SAY ...
...THIS CHERRY BLOSSOM TREE WAS A SECRET BETWEEN THE TWO OF YOU?
YES...

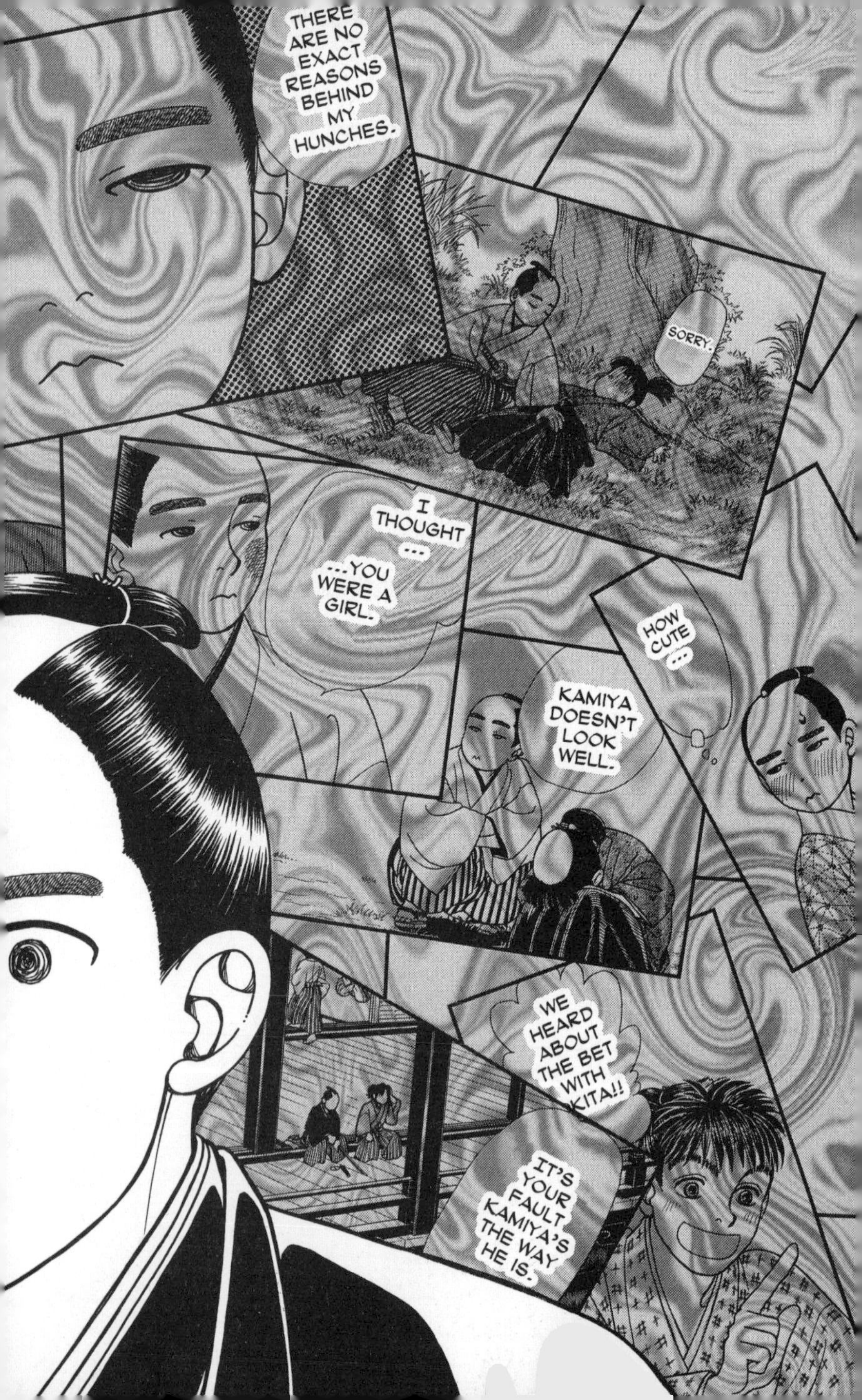
THERE ARE NO EXACT REASONS BEHIND MY HUNCHES.
SORRY.
I THOUGHT ...
...YOU WERE A GIRL.
HOW CUTE ...
KAMIYA DOESN'T LOOK WELL.
WE HEARD ABOUT THE BET WITH KITA!!
IT'S YOUR FAULT KAMIYA'S THE WAY HE IS.

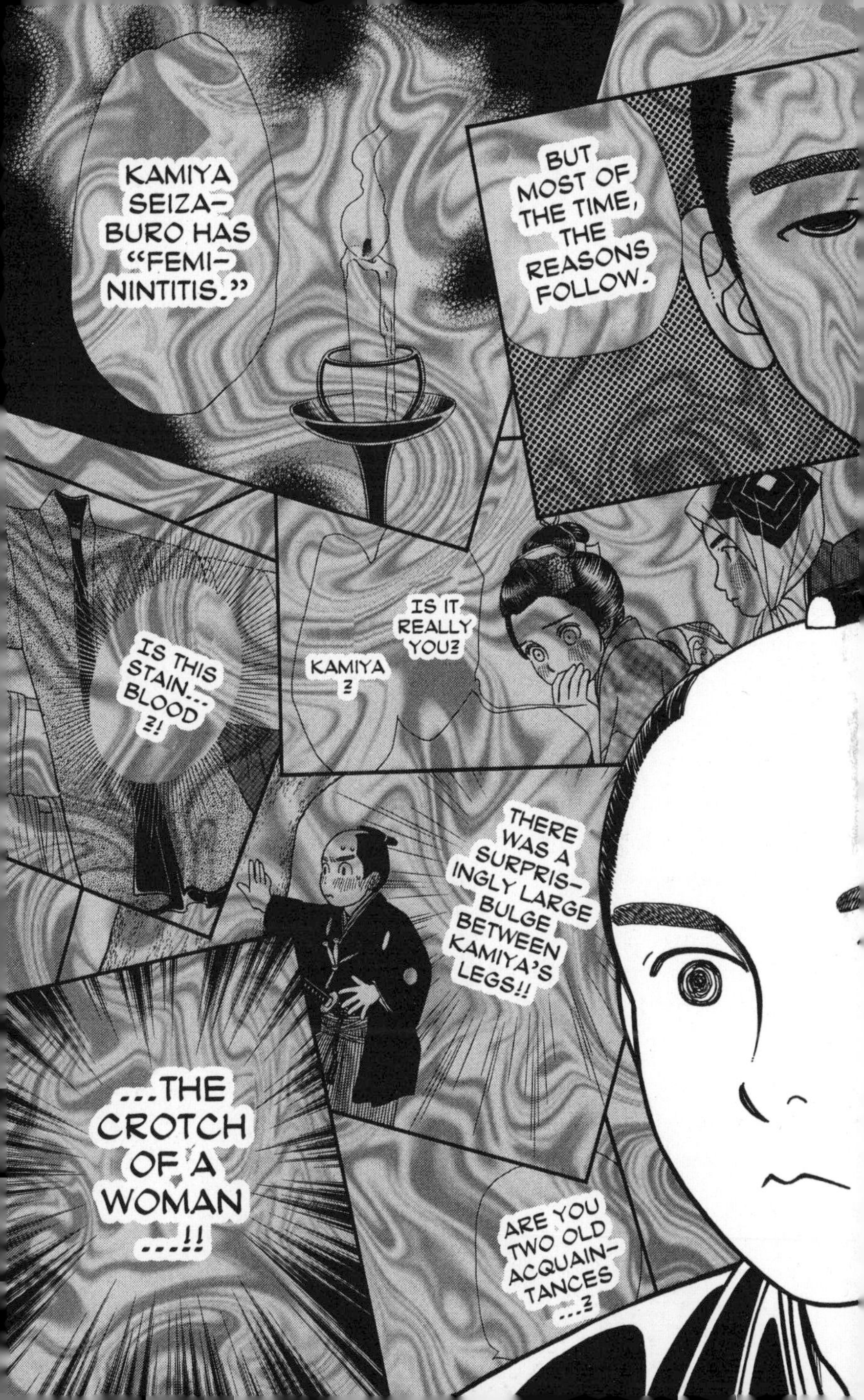
KAMIYA SEIZABURO HAS "FEMININTITIS."
BUT MOST OF THE TIME, THE REASONS FOLLOW.
IS IT REALLY YOU?
KAMIYA?
ARE YOU TWO OLD ACQUAINTANCES...?
IS THIS STAIN... BLOOD?!
THERE WAS A SURPRISINGLY LARGE BULGE BETWEEN KAMIYA'S LEGS!!
...THE CROTCH OF A WOMAN...!!

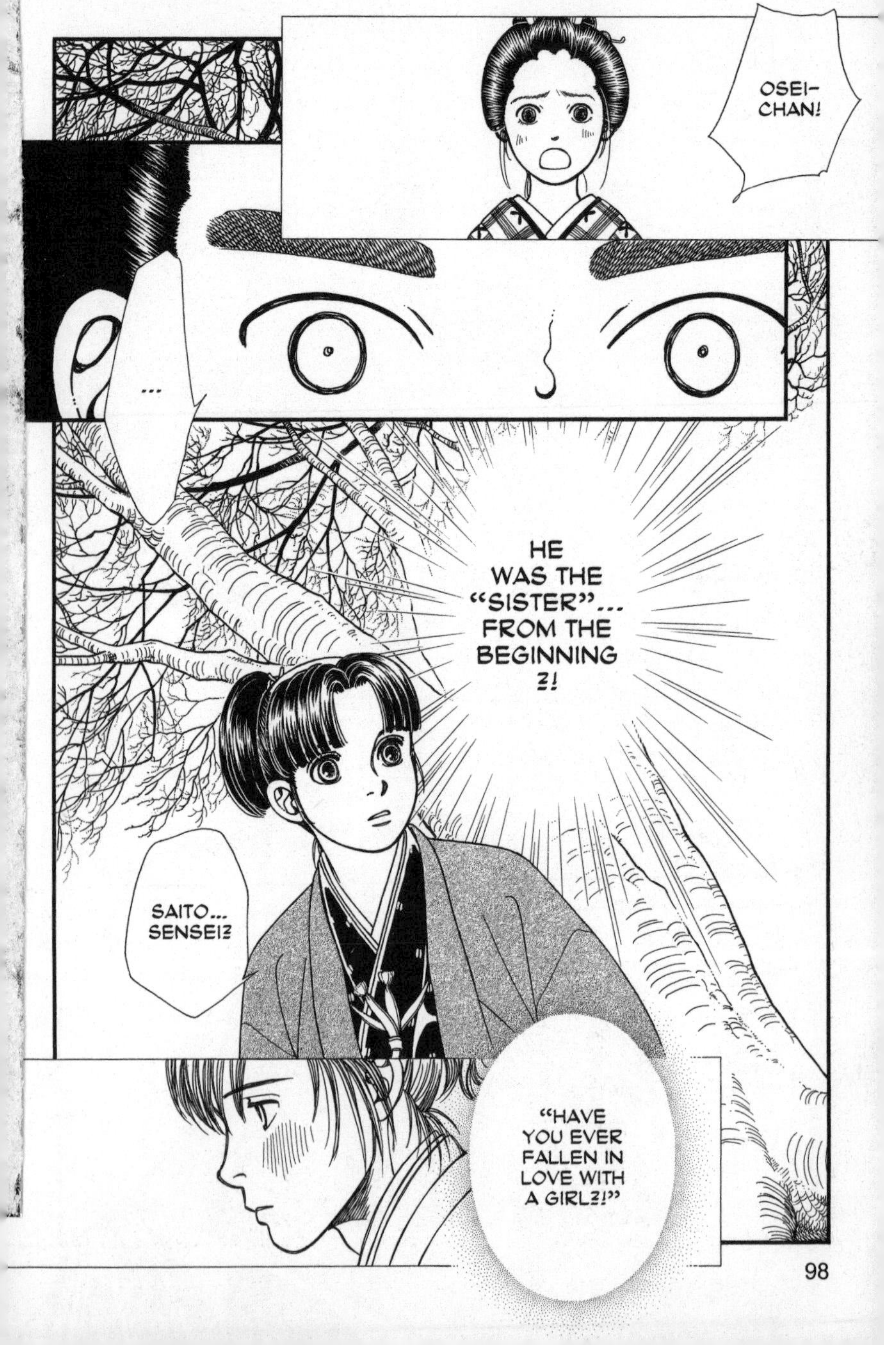
OSEI-CHAN!
...
HE WAS THE "SISTER"... FROM THE BEGINNING?!
SAITO... SENSEI?
"HAVE YOU EVER FALLEN IN LOVE WITH A GIRL?!"

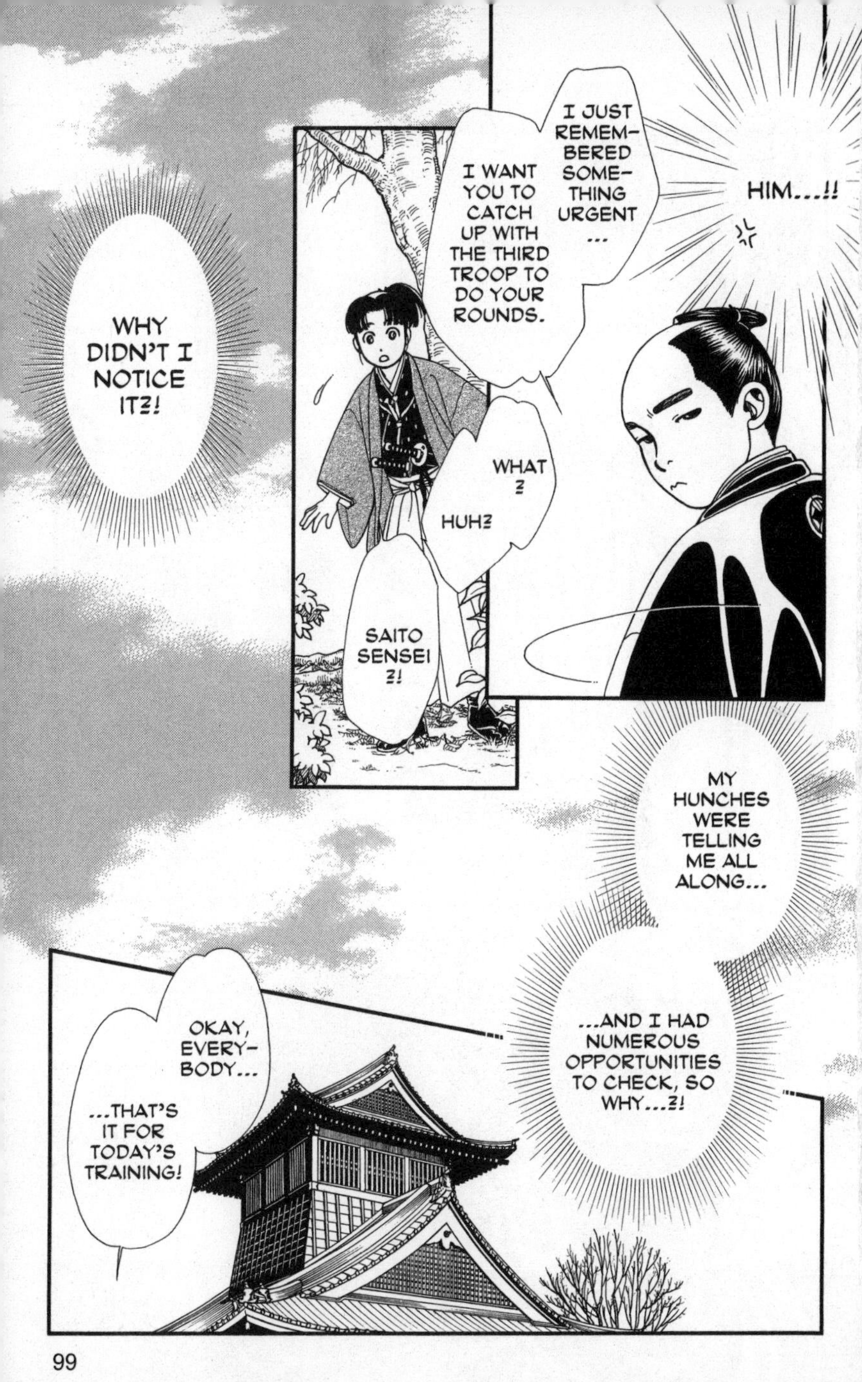
HIM...!!
I JUST REMEMBERED SOMETHING URGENT...
I WANT YOU TO CATCH UP WITH THE THIRD TROOP TO DO YOUR ROUNDS.
WHAT?
HUH?
SAITO SENSEI?!
WHY DIDN'T I NOTICE IT?!
MY HUNCHES WERE TELLING ME ALL ALONG...
...AND I HAD NUMEROUS OPPORTUNITIES TO CHECK, SO WHY...?!
OKAY, EVERYBODY...
...THAT'S IT FOR TODAY'S TRAINING!

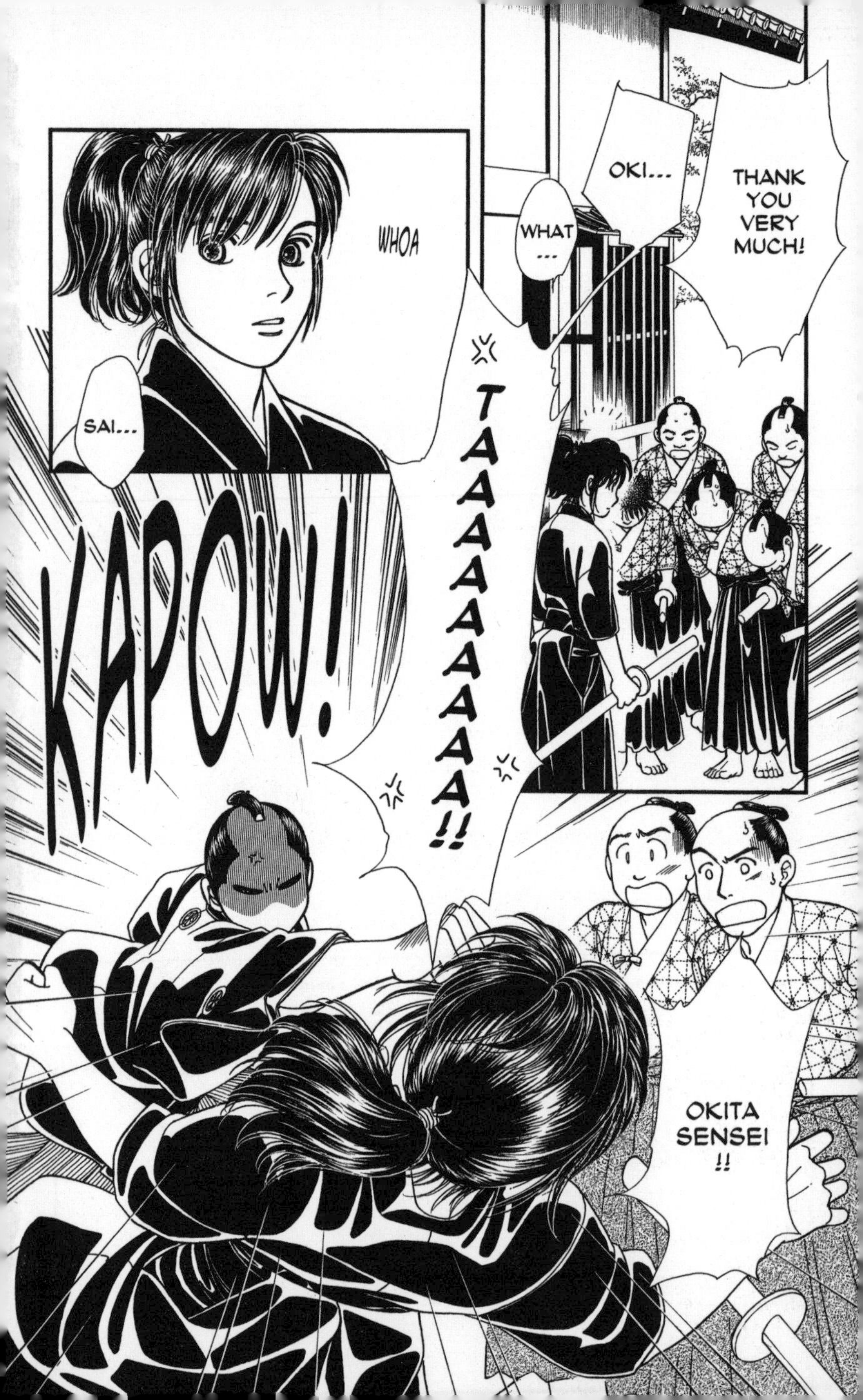
THANK YOU VERY MUCH!
OKI...
WHAT...
WHOA
SAI...
OKITA SENSEI!!
TAAAAAAAAAA!!
KAPOW!

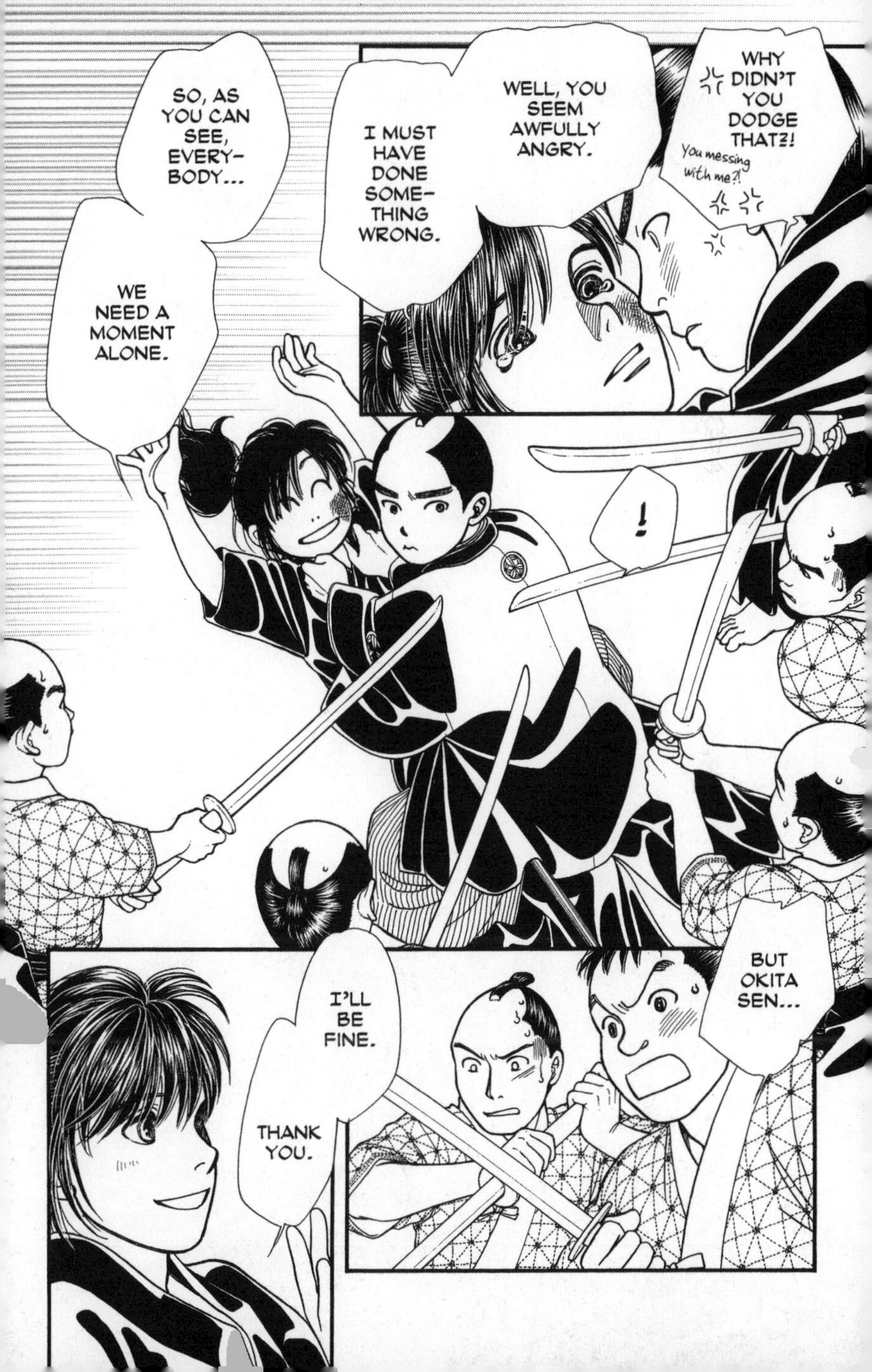
WHY DIDN'T YOU DODGE THAT?!
You messing with me?!
WELL, YOU SEEM AWFULLY ANGRY.
I MUST HAVE DONE SOMETHING WRONG.
SO, AS YOU CAN SEE, EVERYBODY...
WE NEED A MOMENT ALONE.
!
BUT OKITA SEN...
I'LL BE FINE.
THANK YOU.

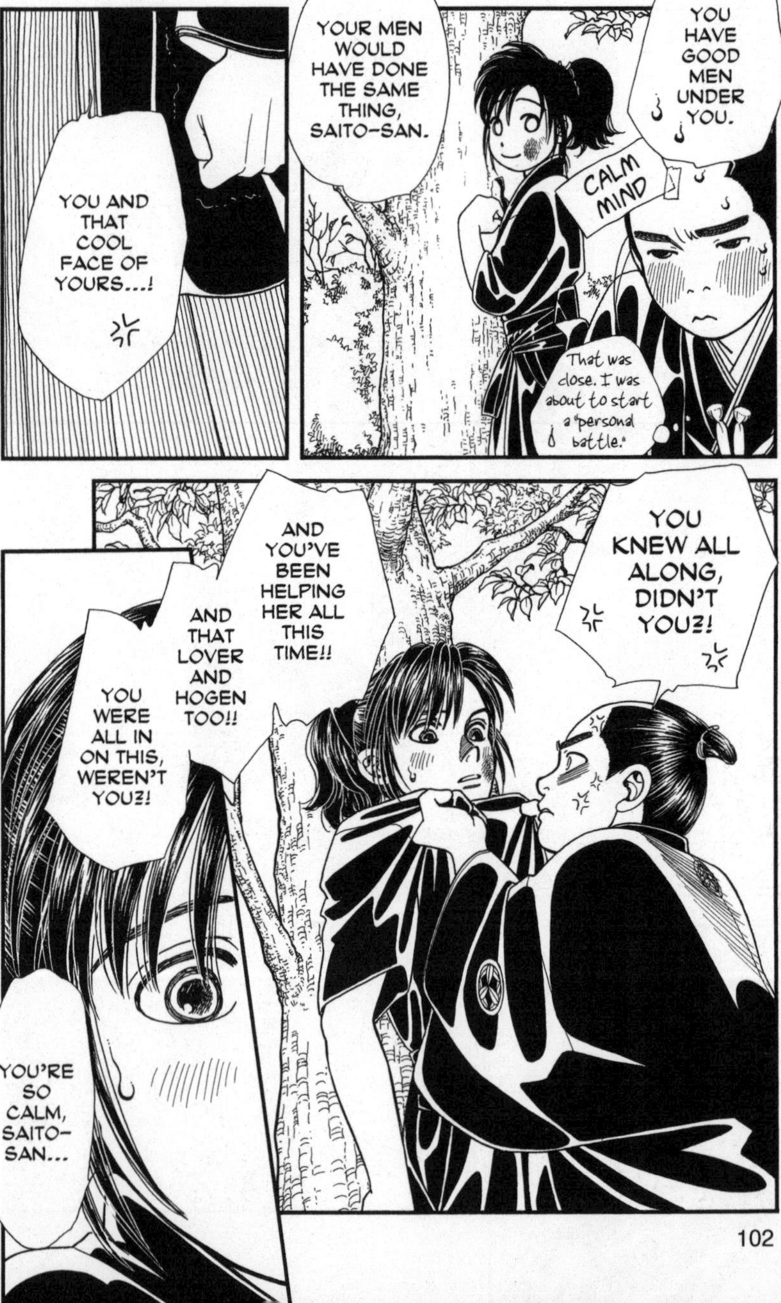
YOU HAVE GOOD MEN UNDER YOU.
CALM MIND
YOUR MEN WOULD HAVE DONE THE SAME THING, SAITO-SAN.
That was close. I was about to start a "personal battle."
YOU AND THAT COOL FACE OF YOURS...!
YOU KNEW ALL ALONG, DIDN'T YOU?!
AND YOU'VE BEEN HELPING HER ALL THIS TIME!!
AND THAT LOVER AND HOGEN TOO!!
YOU WERE ALL IN ON THIS, WEREN'T YOU?!
YOU'RE SO CALM, SAITO-SAN...

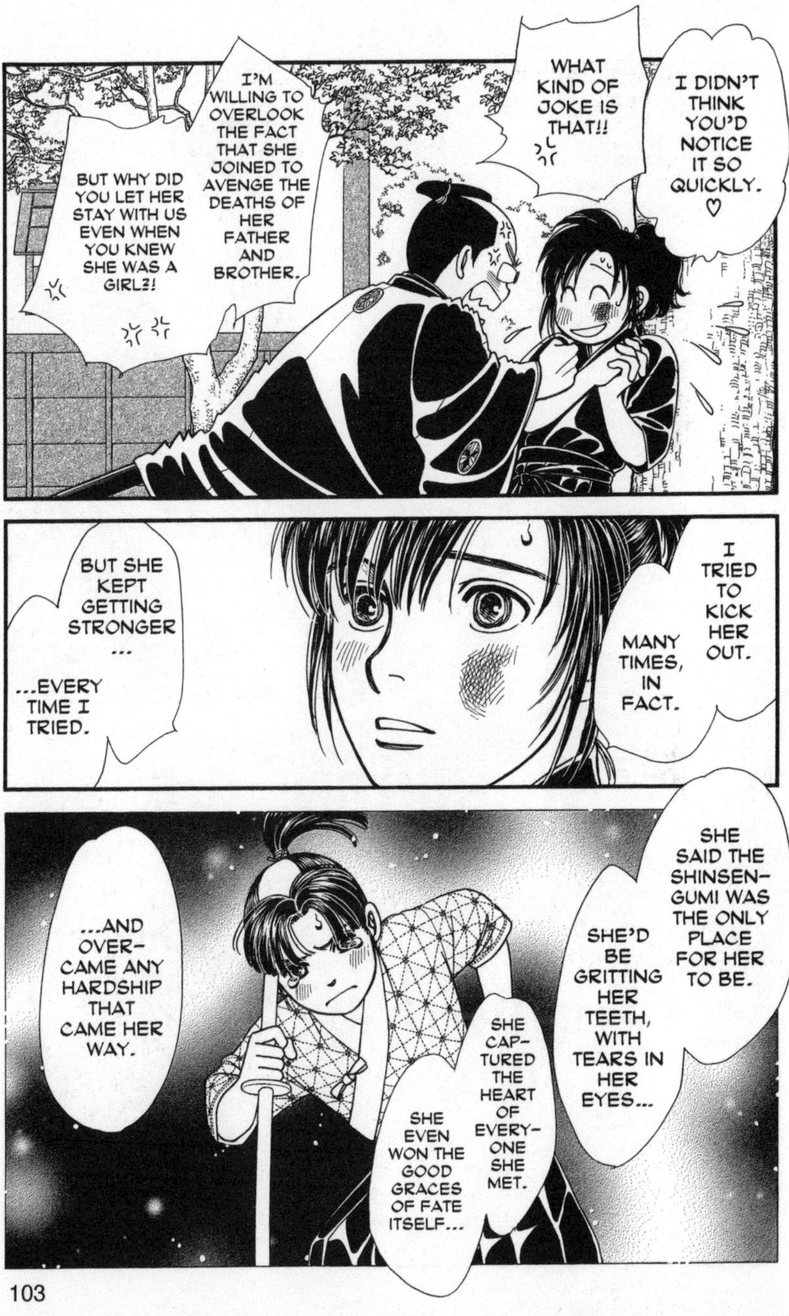

I DIDN'T THINK YOU'D NOTICE IT SO QUICKLY. ♡
WHAT KIND OF JOKE IS THAT!!
I'M WILLING TO OVERLOOK THE FACT THAT SHE JOINED TO AVENGE THE DEATHS OF HER FATHER AND BROTHER.
BUT WHY DID YOU LET HER STAY WITH US EVEN WHEN YOU KNEW SHE WAS A GIRL?!
I TRIED TO KICK HER OUT.
MANY TIMES, IN FACT.
BUT SHE KEPT GETTING STRONGER...
...EVERY TIME I TRIED.
SHE SAID THE SHINSEN-GUMI WAS THE ONLY PLACE FOR HER TO BE.
SHE'D BE GRITTING HER TEETH, WITH TEARS IN HER EYES...
...AND OVER-CAME ANY HARDSHIP THAT CAME HER WAY.
SHE CAP-TURED THE HEART OF EVERY-ONE SHE MET.
SHE EVEN WON THE GOOD GRACES OF FATE ITSELF...

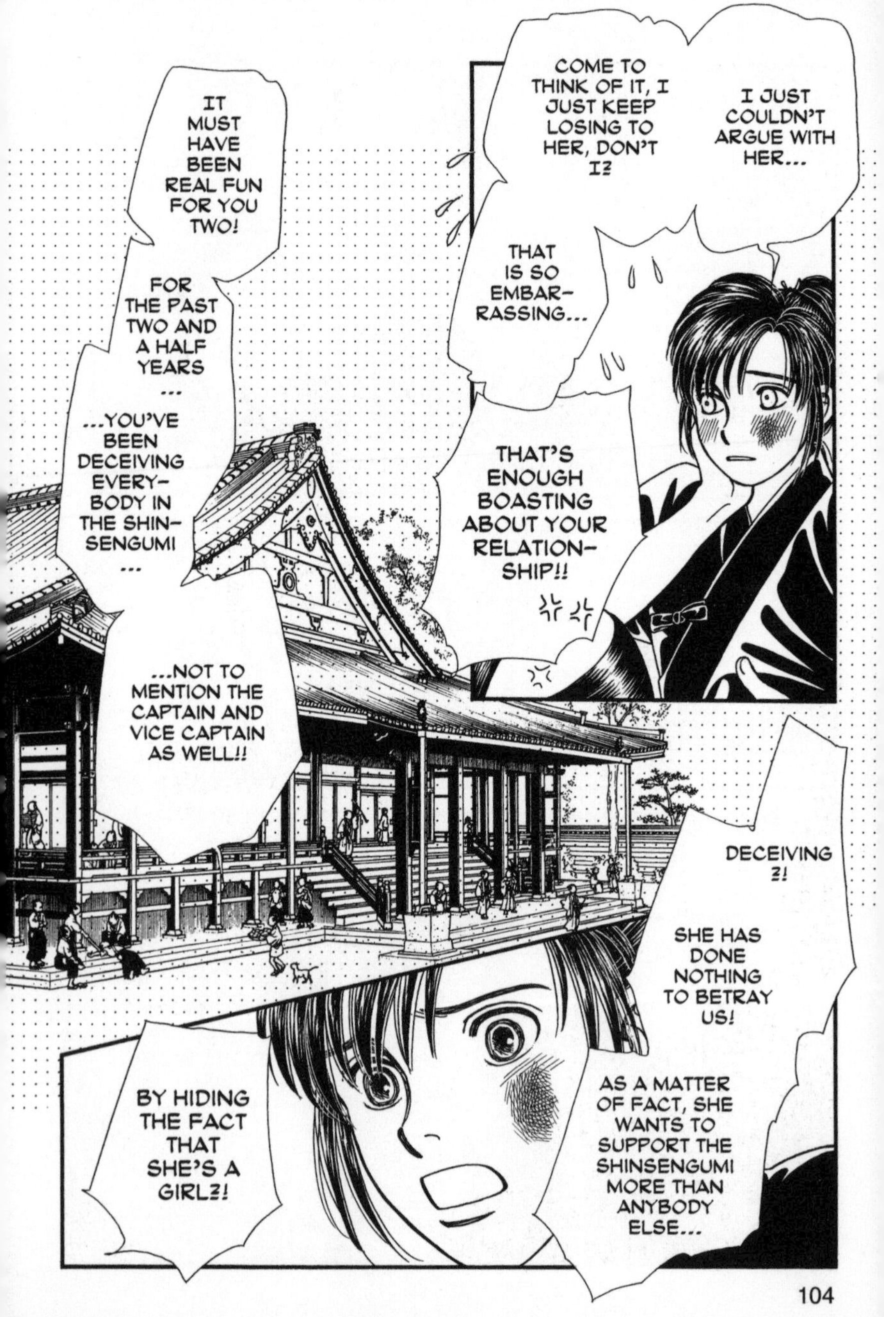
I JUST COULDN'T ARGUE WITH HER...
COME TO THINK OF IT, I JUST KEEP LOSING TO HER, DON'T I?
THAT IS SO EMBARRASSING...
THAT'S ENOUGH BOASTING ABOUT YOUR RELATIONSHIP!!
IT MUST HAVE BEEN REAL FUN FOR YOU TWO!
FOR THE PAST TWO AND A HALF YEARS...
...YOU'VE BEEN DECEIVING EVERYBODY IN THE SHINSENGUMI...
...NOT TO MENTION THE CAPTAIN AND VICE CAPTAIN AS WELL!!
DECEIVING?!
SHE HAS DONE NOTHING TO BETRAY US!
AS A MATTER OF FACT, SHE WANTS TO SUPPORT THE SHINSENGUMI MORE THAN ANYBODY ELSE...
BY HIDING THE FACT THAT SHE'S A GIRL?!

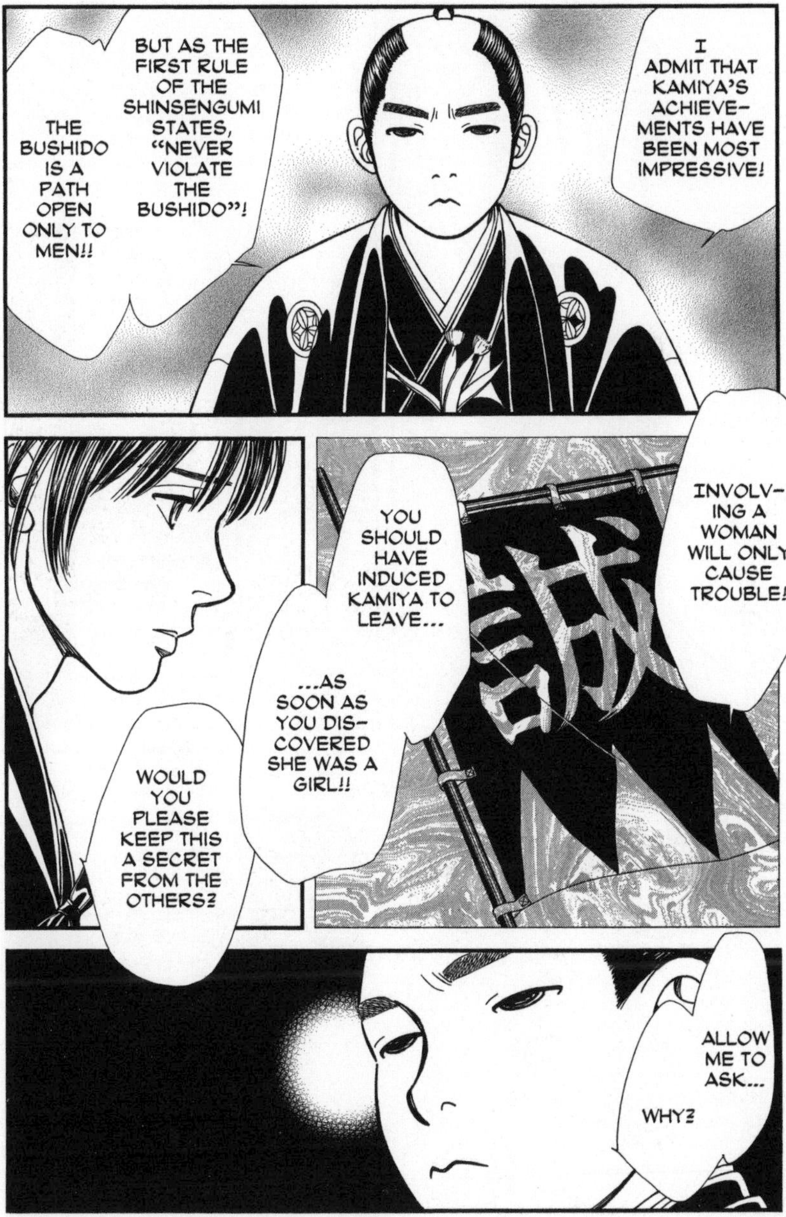
I ADMIT THAT KAMIYA'S ACHIEVEMENTS HAVE BEEN MOST IMPRESSIVE!
BUT AS THE FIRST RULE OF THE SHINSENGUMI STATES, "NEVER VIOLATE THE BUSHIDO"!
THE BUSHIDO IS A PATH OPEN ONLY TO MEN!!
INVOLVING A WOMAN WILL ONLY CAUSE TROUBLE!
YOU SHOULD HAVE INDUCED KAMIYA TO LEAVE...
...AS SOON AS YOU DISCOVERED SHE WAS A GIRL!!
WOULD YOU PLEASE KEEP THIS A SECRET FROM THE OTHERS?
ALLOW ME TO ASK...
WHY?

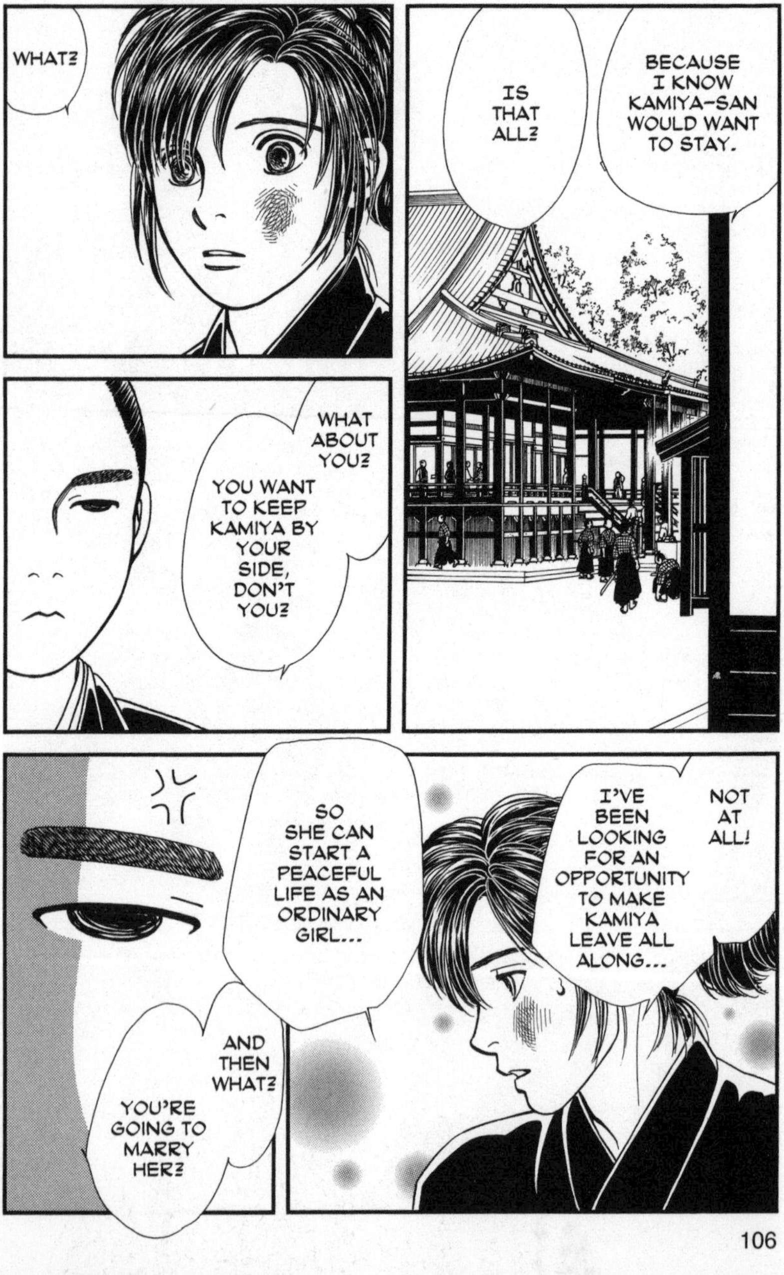
BECAUSE I KNOW KAMIYA-SAN WOULD WANT TO STAY.
IS THAT ALL?
WHAT?
WHAT ABOUT YOU?
YOU WANT TO KEEP KAMIYA BY YOUR SIDE, DON'T YOU?
NOT AT ALL!
I'VE BEEN LOOKING FOR AN OPPORTUNITY TO MAKE KAMIYA LEAVE ALL ALONG...
SO SHE CAN START A PEACEFUL LIFE AS AN ORDINARY GIRL...
AND THEN WHAT?
YOU'RE GOING TO MARRY HER?

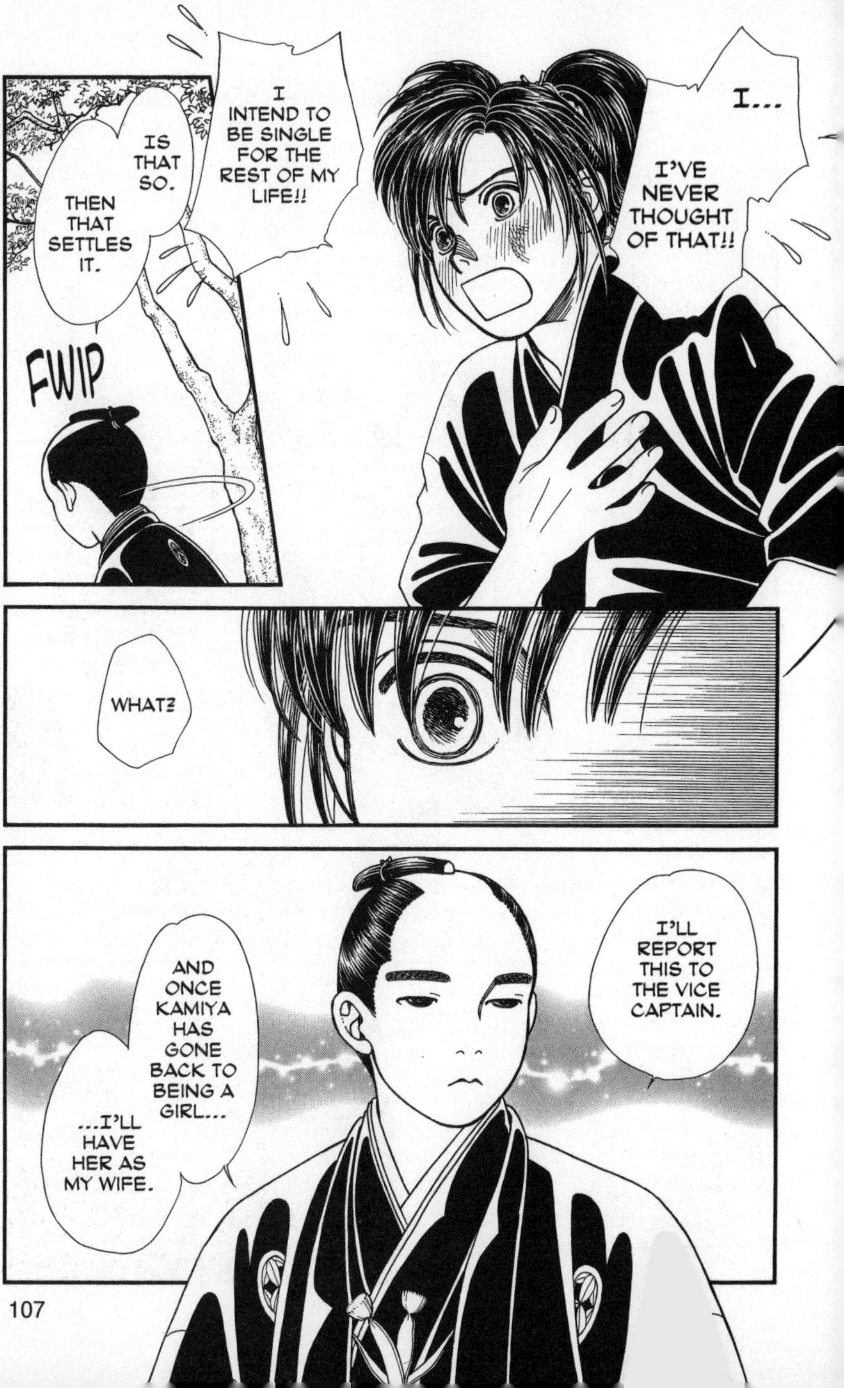
I...
I'VE NEVER THOUGHT OF THAT!!
I INTEND TO BE SINGLE FOR THE REST OF MY LIFE!!
IS THAT SO.
THEN THAT SETTLES IT.
FWIP
WHAT?
I'LL REPORT THIS TO THE VICE CAPTAIN.
AND ONCE KAMIYA HAS GONE BACK TO BEING A GIRL...
...I'LL HAVE HER AS MY WIFE.

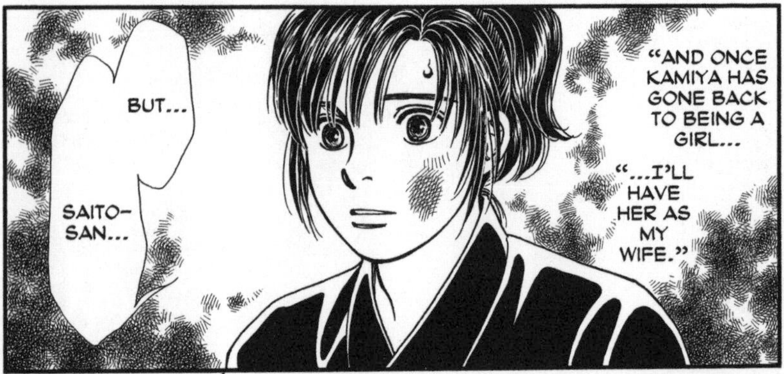
"AND ONCE KAMIYA HAS GONE BACK TO BEING A GIRL...
"...I'LL HAVE HER AS MY WIFE."
BUT...
SAITO-SAN...

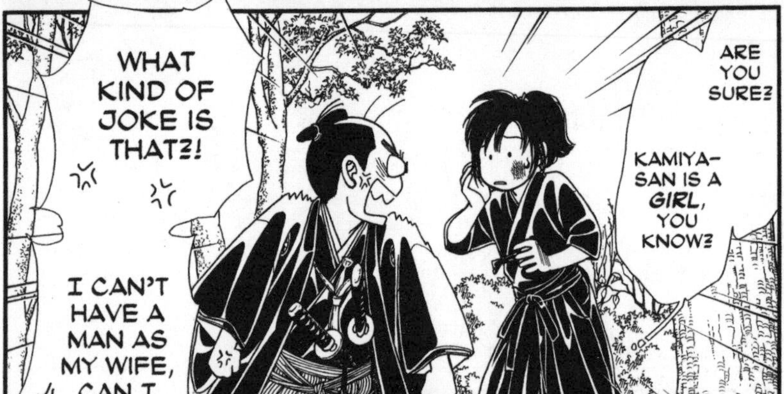
ARE YOU SURE?
KAMIYA-SAN IS A GIRL, YOU KNOW?
WHAT KIND OF JOKE IS THAT?!
I CAN'T HAVE A MAN AS MY WIFE, CAN I ?!

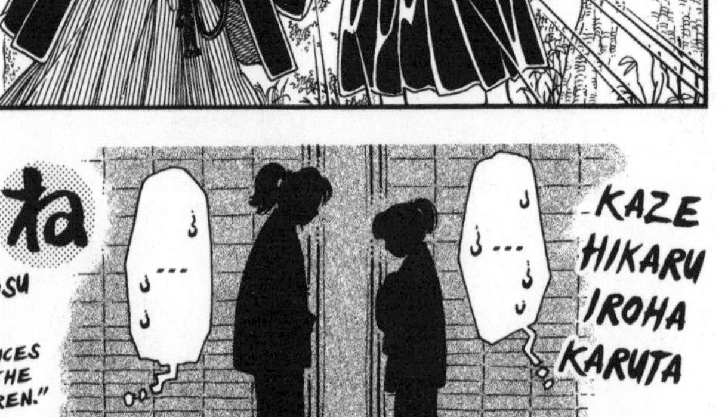
KAZE HIKARU IROHA KARUTA

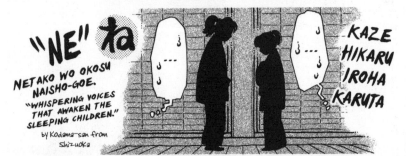

"NE" ね

NETAKO WO OKOSU NAISHO-GOE.

"WHISPERING VOICES THAT AWAKEN THE SLEEPING CHILDREN."

by Kodama-san from Shizuoka

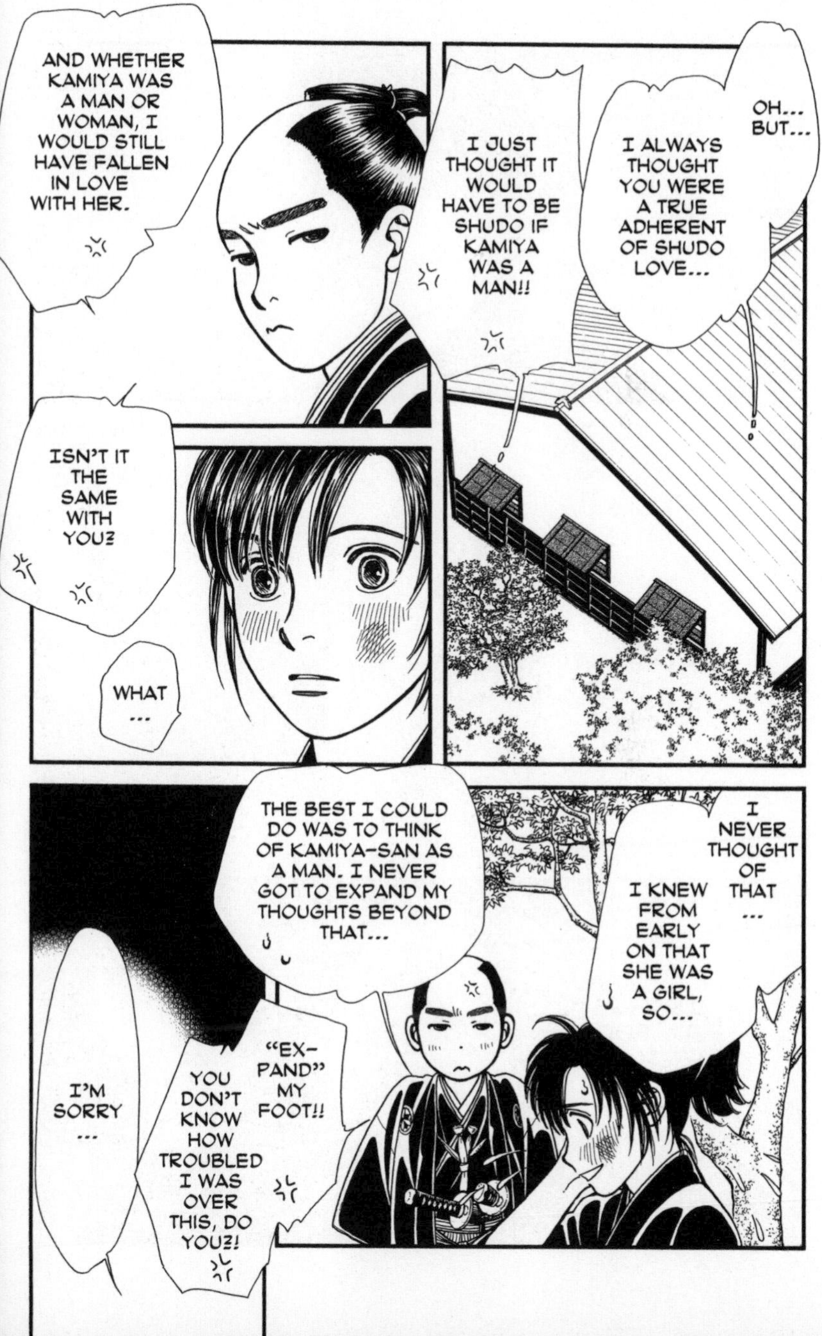
OH... BUT...
I ALWAYS THOUGHT YOU WERE A TRUE ADHERENT OF SHUDO LOVE...
I JUST THOUGHT IT WOULD HAVE TO BE SHUDO IF KAMIYA WAS A MAN!!
AND WHETHER KAMIYA WAS A MAN OR WOMAN, I WOULD STILL HAVE FALLEN IN LOVE WITH HER.
ISN'T IT THE SAME WITH YOU?
WHAT ...
I NEVER THOUGHT OF THAT ...
I KNEW FROM EARLY ON THAT SHE WAS A GIRL, SO...
THE BEST I COULD DO WAS TO THINK OF KAMIYA-SAN AS A MAN. I NEVER GOT TO EXPAND MY THOUGHTS BEYOND THAT...
"EX-PAND" MY FOOT!!
YOU DON'T KNOW HOW TROUBLED I WAS OVER THIS, DO YOU?!
I'M SORRY ...

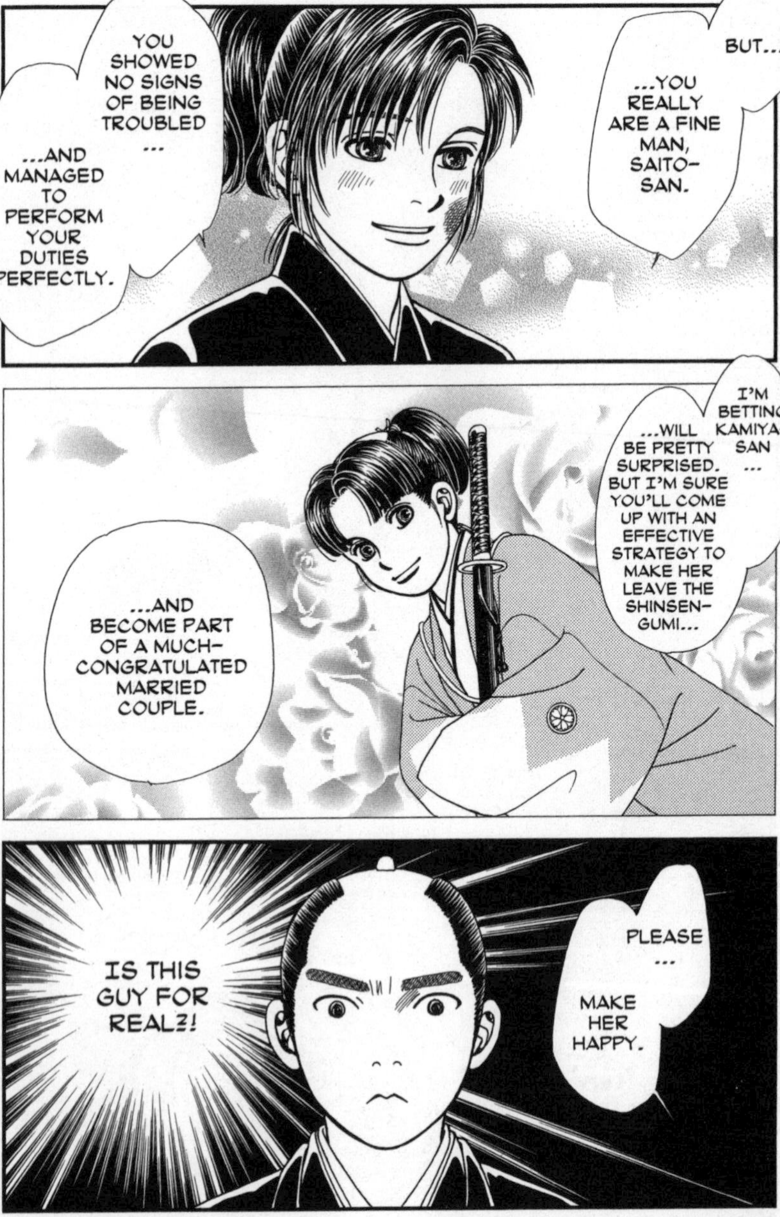
BUT...
...YOU REALLY ARE A FINE MAN, SAITO-SAN.
YOU SHOWED NO SIGNS OF BEING TROUBLED...
...AND MANAGED TO PERFORM YOUR DUTIES PERFECTLY.
I'M BETTING KAMIYA-SAN...
...WILL BE PRETTY SURPRISED. BUT I'M SURE YOU'LL COME UP WITH AN EFFECTIVE STRATEGY TO MAKE HER LEAVE THE SHINSEN-GUMI...
...AND BECOME PART OF A MUCH-CONGRATULATED MARRIED COUPLE.
PLEASE...
MAKE HER HAPPY.
IS THIS GUY FOR REAL?!

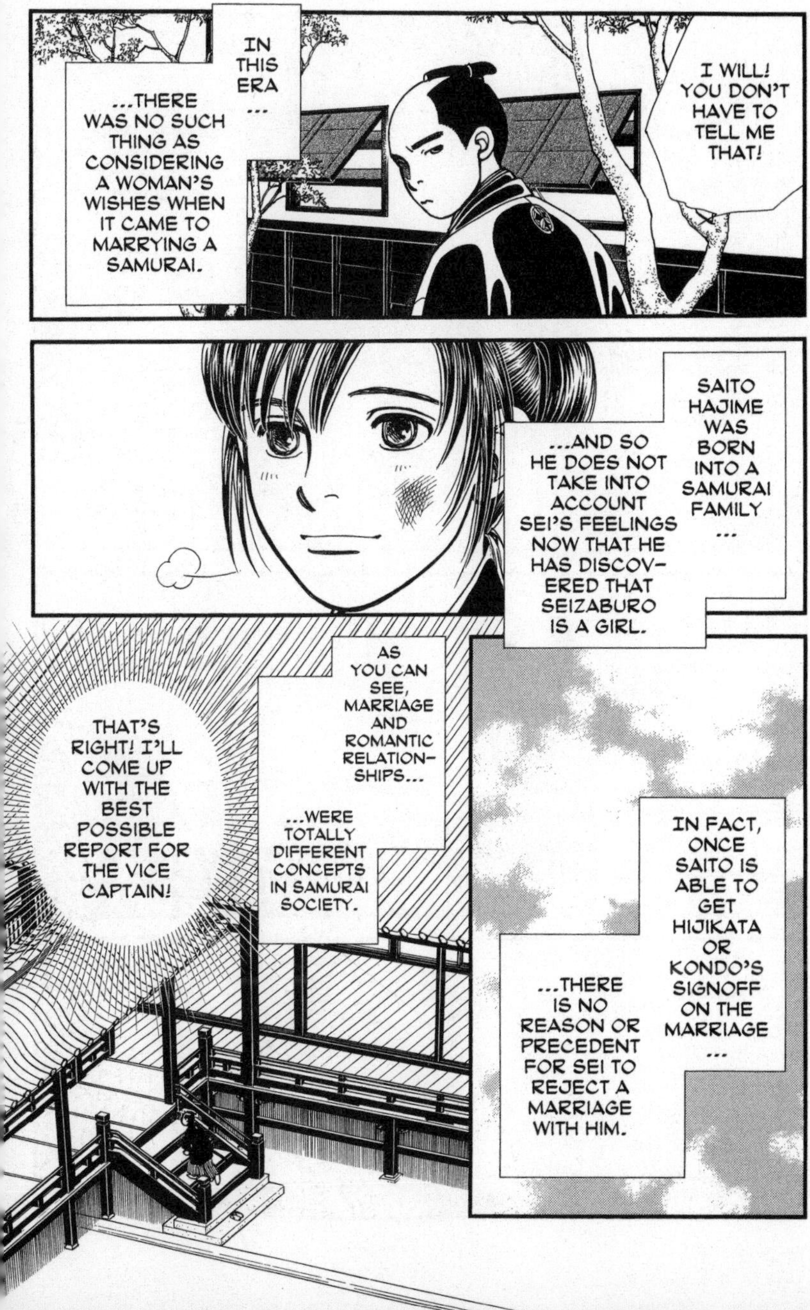
I WILL! YOU DON'T HAVE TO TELL ME THAT!
IN THIS ERA...
...THERE WAS NO SUCH THING AS CONSIDERING A WOMAN'S WISHES WHEN IT CAME TO MARRYING A SAMURAI.
SAITO HAJIME WAS BORN INTO A SAMURAI FAMILY...
...AND SO HE DOES NOT TAKE INTO ACCOUNT SEI'S FEELINGS NOW THAT HE HAS DISCOVERED THAT SEIZABURO IS A GIRL.
IN FACT, ONCE SAITO IS ABLE TO GET HIJIKATA OR KONDO'S SIGNOFF ON THE MARRIAGE...
...THERE IS NO REASON OR PRECEDENT FOR SEI TO REJECT A MARRIAGE WITH HIM.
AS YOU CAN SEE, MARRIAGE AND ROMANTIC RELATIONSHIPS...
...WERE TOTALLY DIFFERENT CONCEPTS IN SAMURAI SOCIETY.
THAT'S RIGHT! I'LL COME UP WITH THE BEST POSSIBLE REPORT FOR THE VICE CAPTAIN!

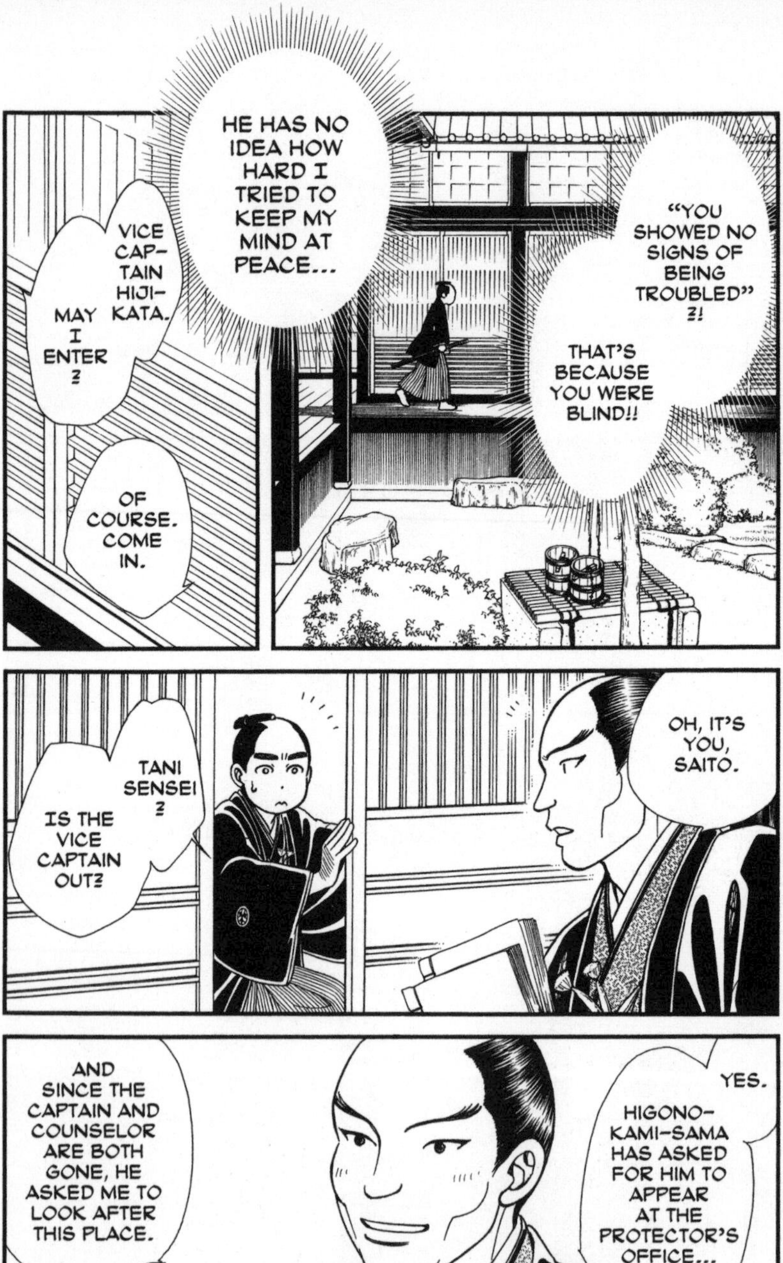

"YOU SHOWED NO SIGNS OF BEING TROUBLED"?!
THAT'S BECAUSE YOU WERE BLIND!!
HE HAS NO IDEA HOW HARD I TRIED TO KEEP MY MIND AT PEACE...
VICE CAPTAIN HIJIKATA.
MAY I ENTER?
OF COURSE. COME IN.
OH, IT'S YOU, SAITO.
TANI SENSEI?
IS THE VICE CAPTAIN OUT?
YES.
HIGONO-KAMI-SAMA HAS ASKED FOR HIM TO APPEAR AT THE PROTECTOR'S OFFICE...
AND SINCE THE CAPTAIN AND COUNSELOR ARE BOTH GONE, HE ASKED ME TO LOOK AFTER THIS PLACE.

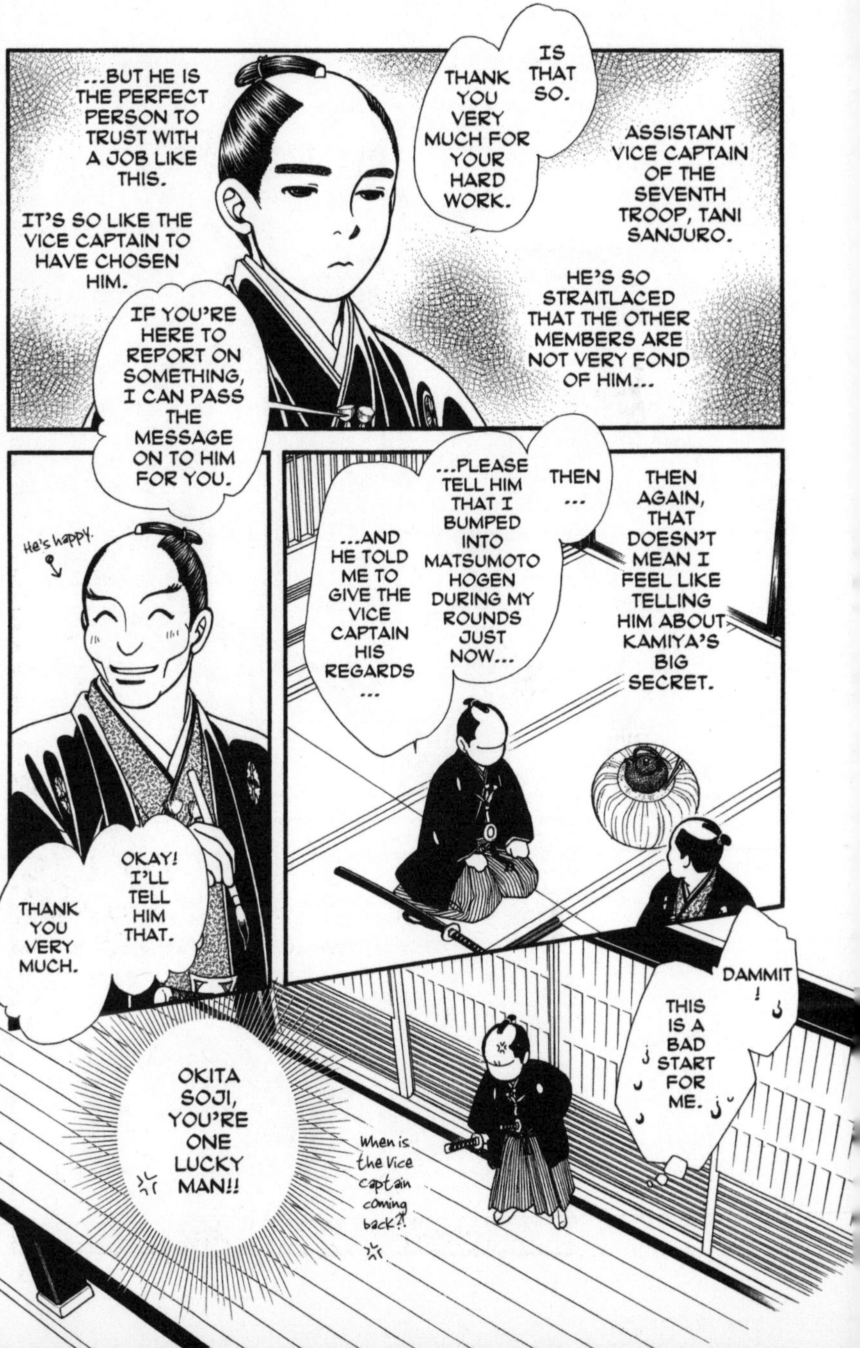
IS THAT SO.
THANK YOU VERY MUCH FOR YOUR HARD WORK.
ASSISTANT VICE CAPTAIN OF THE SEVENTH TROOP, TANI SANJURO.
HE'S SO STRAITLACED THAT THE OTHER MEMBERS ARE NOT VERY FOND OF HIM...
...BUT HE IS THE PERFECT PERSON TO TRUST WITH A JOB LIKE THIS.
IT'S SO LIKE THE VICE CAPTAIN TO HAVE CHOSEN HIM.
IF YOU'RE HERE TO REPORT ON SOMETHING, I CAN PASS THE MESSAGE ON TO HIM FOR YOU.
THEN AGAIN, THAT DOESN'T MEAN I FEEL LIKE TELLING HIM ABOUT KAMIYA'S BIG SECRET.
THEN ...
...PLEASE TELL HIM THAT I BUMPED INTO MATSUMOTO HOGEN DURING MY ROUNDS JUST NOW...
...AND HE TOLD ME TO GIVE THE VICE CAPTAIN HIS REGARDS ...
He's happy.
OKAY! I'LL TELL HIM THAT.
THANK YOU VERY MUCH.
DAMMIT!
THIS IS A BAD START FOR ME.
When is the Vice captain coming back?!
OKITA SOJI, YOU'RE ONE LUCKY MAN!!

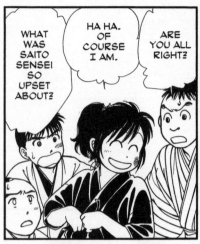

I'M SORRY I'M LATE.
OKITA SENSEI!
ARE YOU ALL RIGHT?
HA HA. OF COURSE I AM.
WHAT WAS SAITO SENSEI SO UPSET ABOUT?
EEEEH ...
LET ME SEE.
WHAT DID HE SAY?
In the end, we spoke of something deserving congratulations.
I THINK I CAN UNDERSTAND WHY SAITO SENSEI WOULD WANT TO PUNCH HIM...
YEAH.
STRANGE...

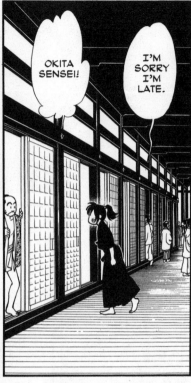

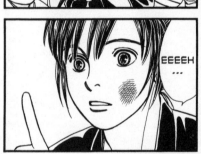

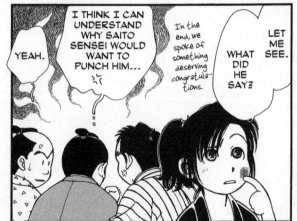

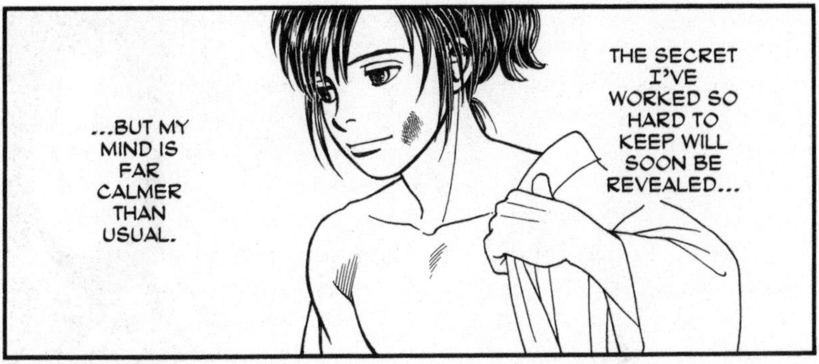
THE SECRET I'VE WORKED SO HARD TO KEEP WILL SOON BE REVEALED...
...BUT MY MIND IS FAR CALMER THAN USUAL.
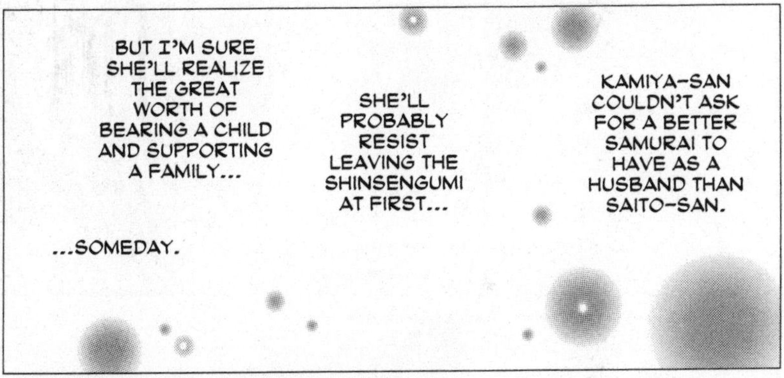
KAMIYA-SAN COULDN'T ASK FOR A BETTER SAMURAI TO HAVE AS A HUSBAND THAN SAITO-SAN.
SHE'LL PROBABLY RESIST LEAVING THE SHINSENGUMI AT FIRST...
BUT I'M SURE SHE'LL REALIZE THE GREAT WORTH OF BEARING A CHILD AND SUPPORTING A FAMILY...
...SOMEDAY.
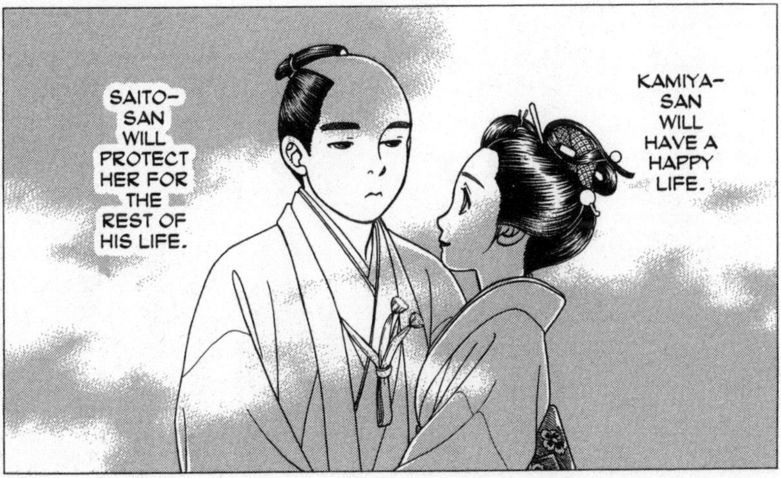
KAMIYA-SAN WILL HAVE A HAPPY LIFE.
SAITO-SAN WILL PROTECT HER FOR THE REST OF HIS LIFE.

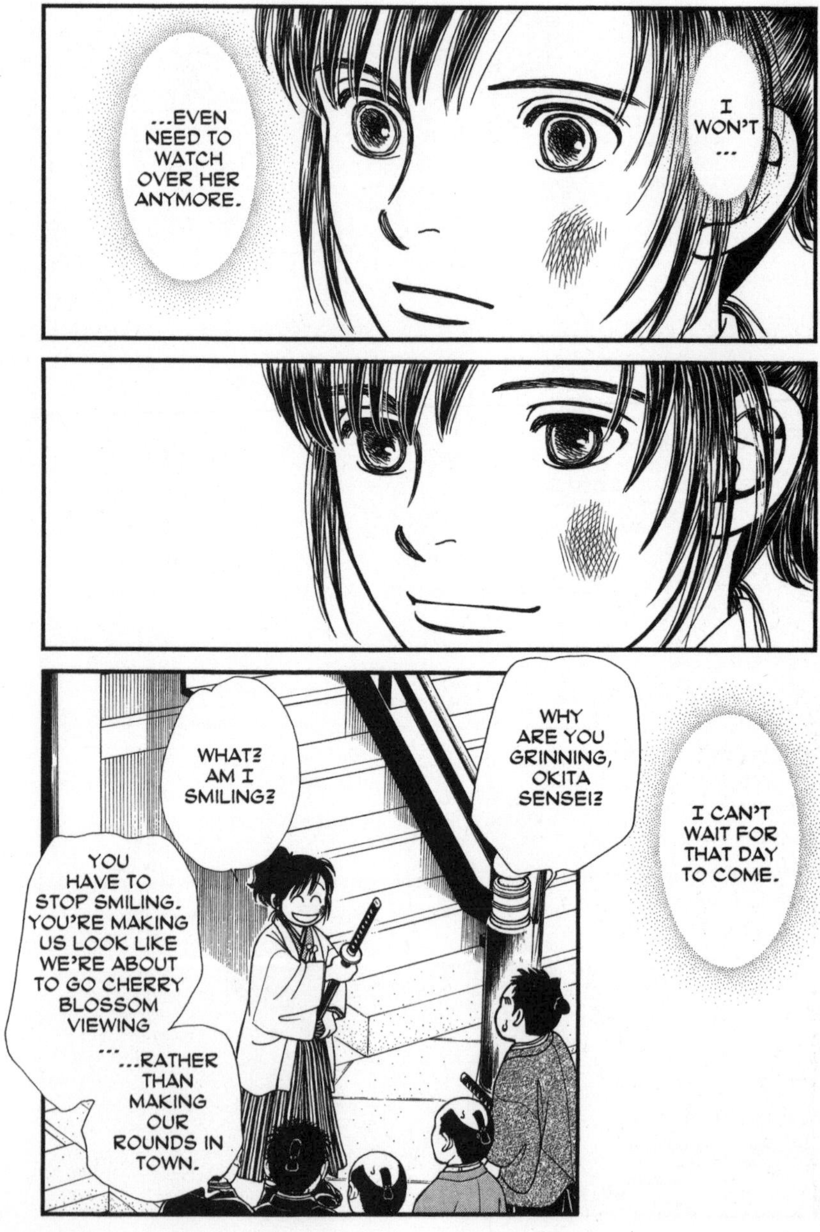
I WON'T...
...EVEN NEED TO WATCH OVER HER ANYMORE.
I CAN'T WAIT FOR THAT DAY TO COME.
WHY ARE YOU GRINNING, OKITA SENSEI!?
WHAT? AM I SMILING?
YOU HAVE TO STOP SMILING. YOU'RE MAKING US LOOK LIKE WE'RE ABOUT TO GO CHERRY BLOSSOM VIEWING... ...RATHER THAN MAKING OUR ROUNDS IN TOWN.

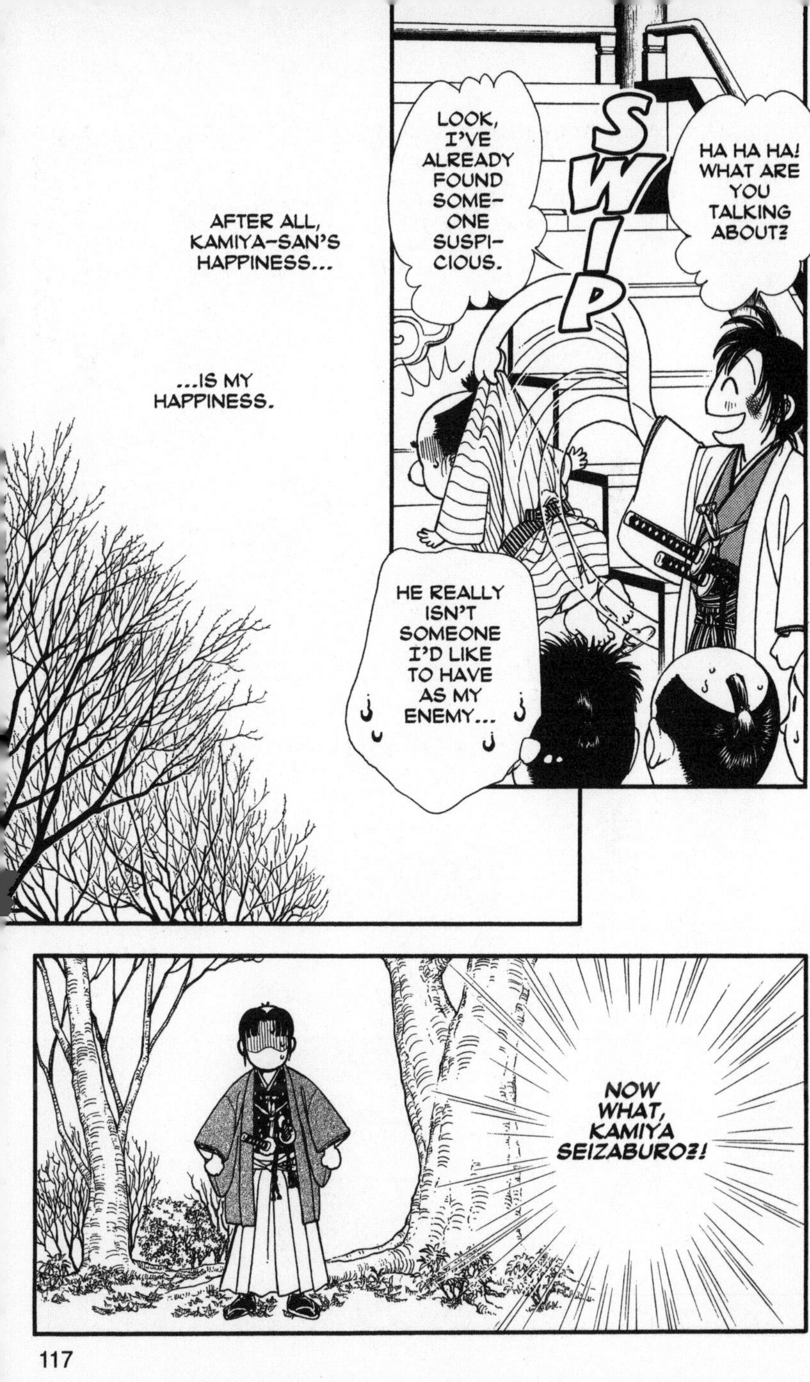
HA HA HA! WHAT ARE YOU TALKING ABOUT?
LOOK, I'VE ALREADY FOUND SOME-ONE SUSPICIOUS.
SWIP
HE REALLY ISN'T SOMEONE I'D LIKE TO HAVE AS MY ENEMY...
AFTER ALL, KAMIYA-SAN'S HAPPINESS...
...IS MY HAPPINESS.
NOW WHAT, KAMIYA SEIZABURO?!

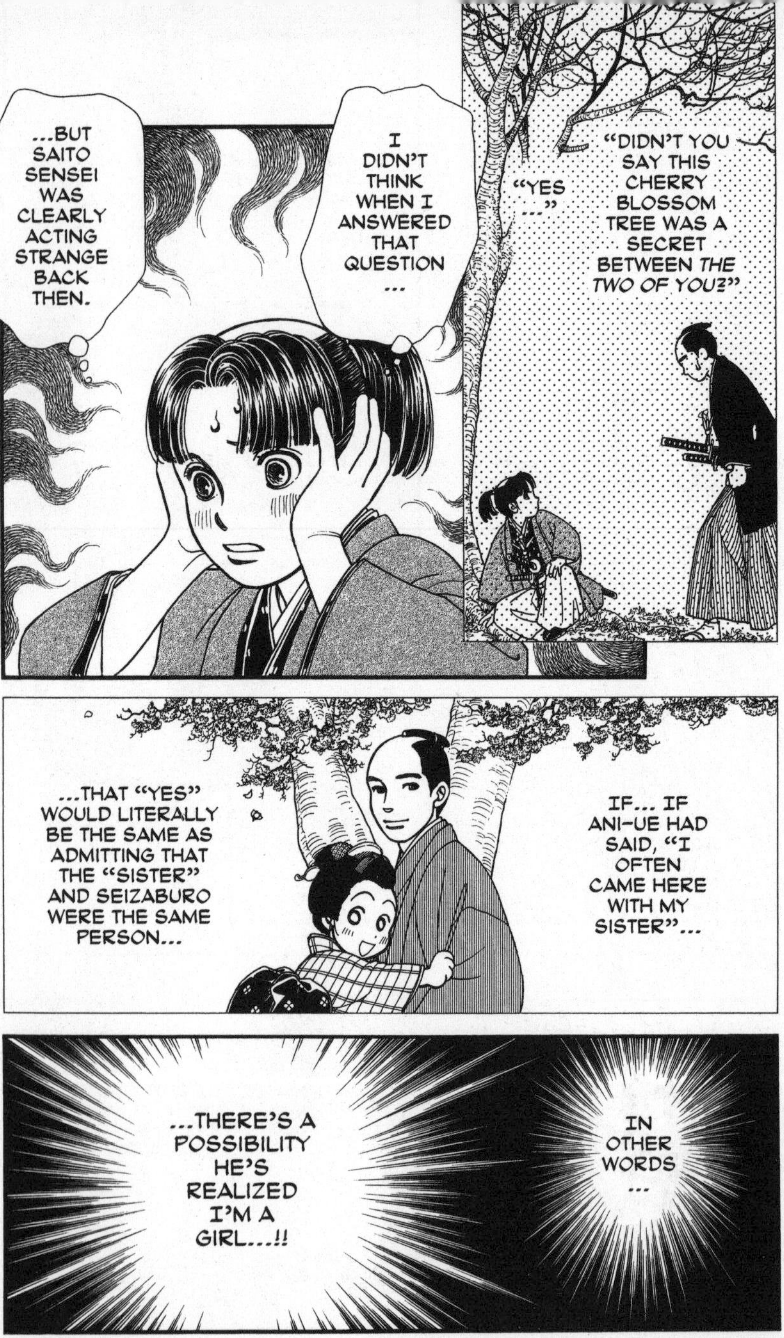
"DIDN'T YOU SAY THIS CHERRY BLOSSOM TREE WAS A SECRET BETWEEN *THE TWO OF YOU*?"
"YES..."
I DIDN'T THINK WHEN I ANSWERED THAT QUESTION...
...BUT SAITO SENSEI WAS CLEARLY ACTING STRANGE BACK THEN.
IF... IF ANI-UE HAD SAID, "I OFTEN CAME HERE WITH MY SISTER"...
...THAT "YES" WOULD LITERALLY BE THE SAME AS ADMITTING THAT THE "SISTER" AND SEIZABURO WERE THE SAME PERSON...
IN OTHER WORDS...
...THERE'S A POSSIBILITY HE'S REALIZED I'M A GIRL...!!

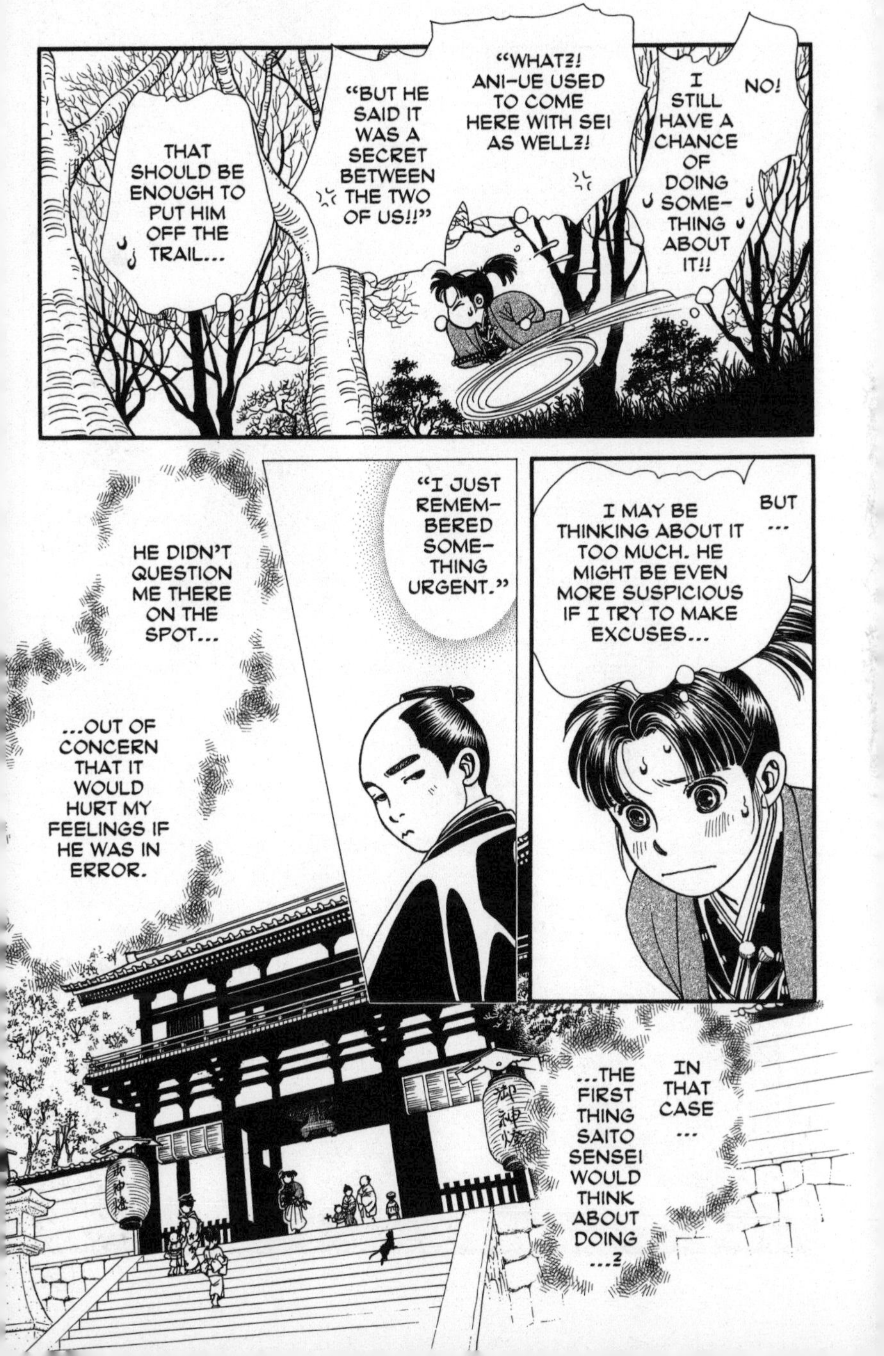
NO!
I STILL HAVE A CHANCE OF DOING SOMETHING ABOUT IT!!
"WHAT?! ANI-UE USED TO COME HERE WITH SEI AS WELL?!
"BUT HE SAID IT WAS A SECRET BETWEEN THE TWO OF US!!"
THAT SHOULD BE ENOUGH TO PUT HIM OFF THE TRAIL...
BUT...
I MAY BE THINKING ABOUT IT TOO MUCH. HE MIGHT BE EVEN MORE SUSPICIOUS IF I TRY TO MAKE EXCUSES...
"I JUST REMEMBERED SOMETHING URGENT."
HE DIDN'T QUESTION ME THERE ON THE SPOT...
...OUT OF CONCERN THAT IT WOULD HURT MY FEELINGS IF HE WAS IN ERROR.
IN THAT CASE...
...THE FIRST THING SAITO SENSEI WOULD THINK ABOUT DOING...?

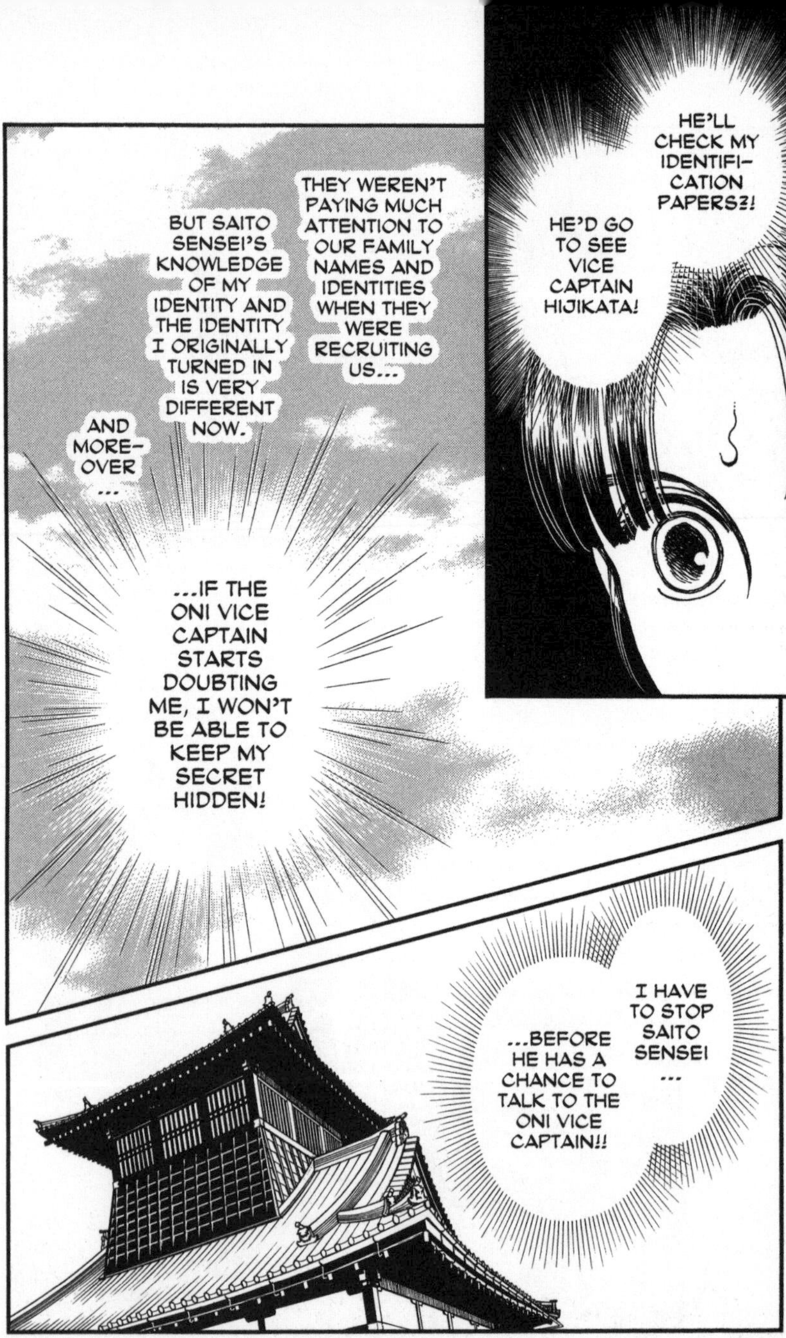
HE'LL CHECK MY IDENTIFI-CATION PAPERS?!
HE'D GO TO SEE VICE CAPTAIN HIJIKATA!
THEY WEREN'T PAYING MUCH ATTENTION TO OUR FAMILY NAMES AND IDENTITIES WHEN THEY WERE RECRUITING US...
BUT SAITO SENSEI'S KNOWLEDGE OF MY IDENTITY AND THE IDENTITY I ORIGINALLY TURNED IN IS VERY DIFFERENT NOW.
AND MORE-OVER ...
...IF THE ONI VICE CAPTAIN STARTS DOUBTING ME, I WON'T BE ABLE TO KEEP MY SECRET HIDDEN!
I HAVE TO STOP SAITO SENSEI ...
...BEFORE HE HAS A CHANCE TO TALK TO THE ONI VICE CAPTAIN!!

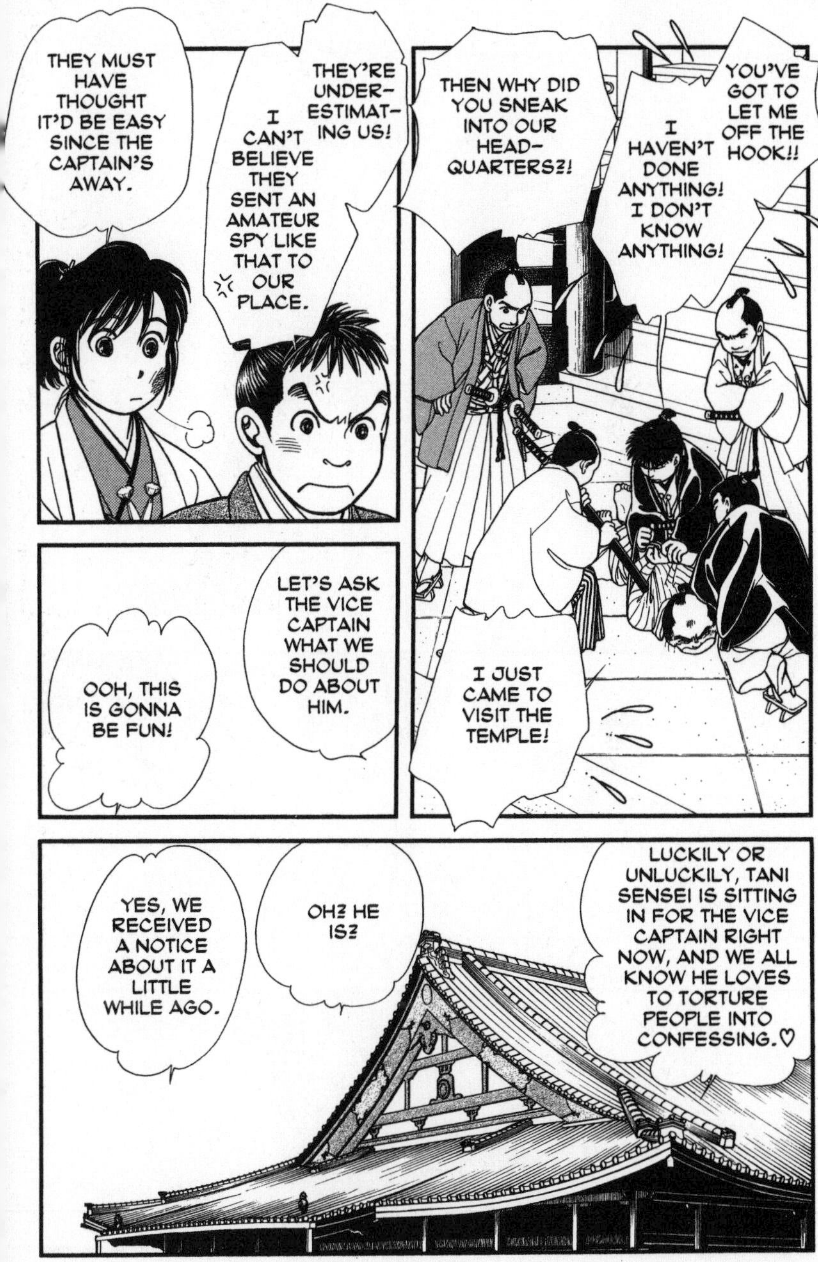
YOU'VE GOT TO LET ME OFF THE HOOK!!
I HAVEN'T DONE ANYTHING! I DON'T KNOW ANYTHING!
THEN WHY DID YOU SNEAK INTO OUR HEAD-QUARTERS?!
I JUST CAME TO VISIT THE TEMPLE!
THEY'RE UNDER-ESTIMATING US!
I CAN'T BELIEVE THEY SENT AN AMATEUR SPY LIKE THAT TO OUR PLACE.
THEY MUST HAVE THOUGHT IT'D BE EASY SINCE THE CAPTAIN'S AWAY.
LET'S ASK THE VICE CAPTAIN WHAT WE SHOULD DO ABOUT HIM.
OOH, THIS IS GONNA BE FUN!
LUCKILY OR UNLUCKILY, TANI SENSEI IS SITTING IN FOR THE VICE CAPTAIN RIGHT NOW, AND WE ALL KNOW HE LOVES TO TORTURE PEOPLE INTO CONFESSING.♡
OH? HE IS?
YES, WE RECEIVED A NOTICE ABOUT IT A LITTLE WHILE AGO.

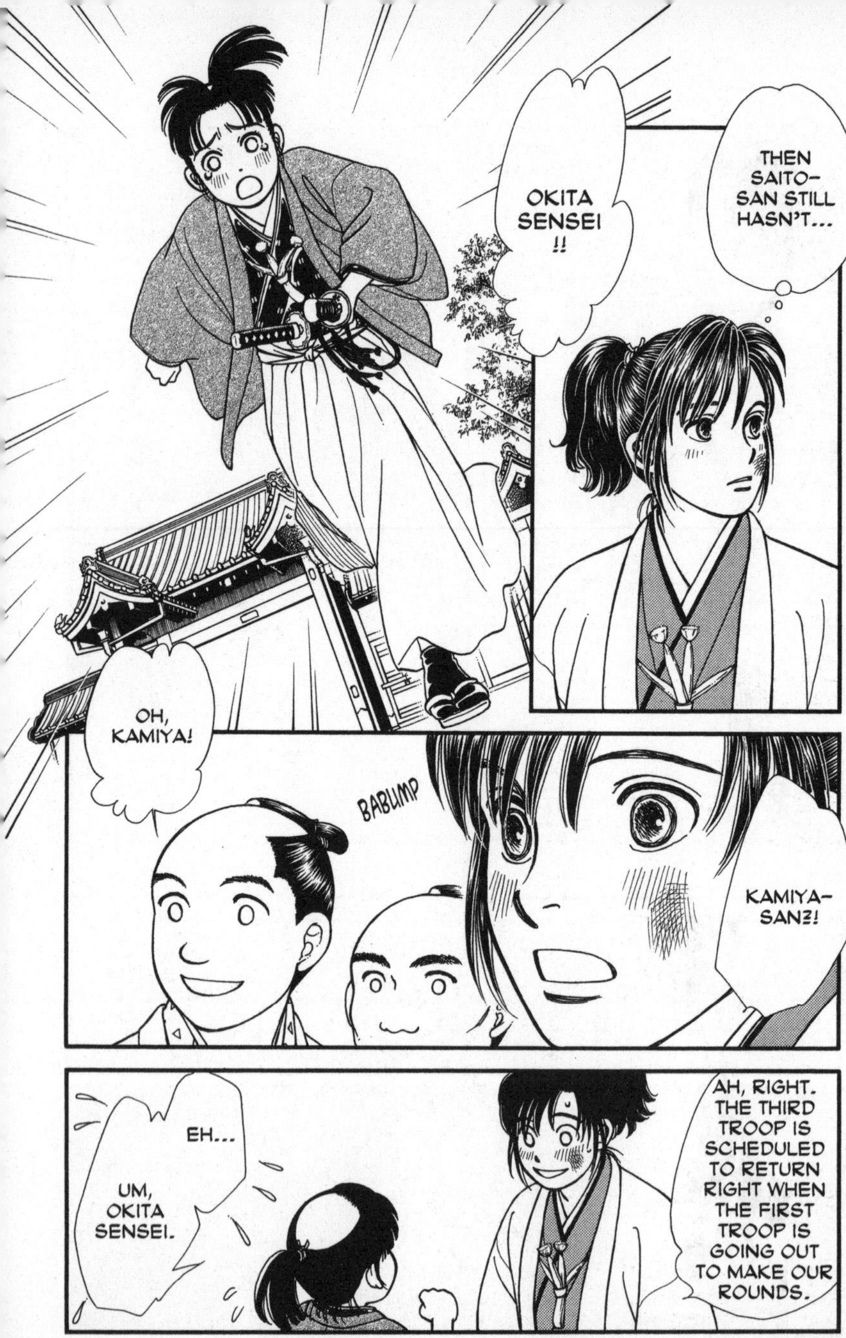
THEN SAITO-SAN STILL HASN'T...
OKITA SENSEI !!
OH, KAMIYA!
KAMIYA-SAN?!
BABUMP
AH, RIGHT. THE THIRD TROOP IS SCHEDULED TO RETURN RIGHT WHEN THE FIRST TROOP IS GOING OUT TO MAKE OUR ROUNDS.
EH...
UM, OKITA SENSEI.

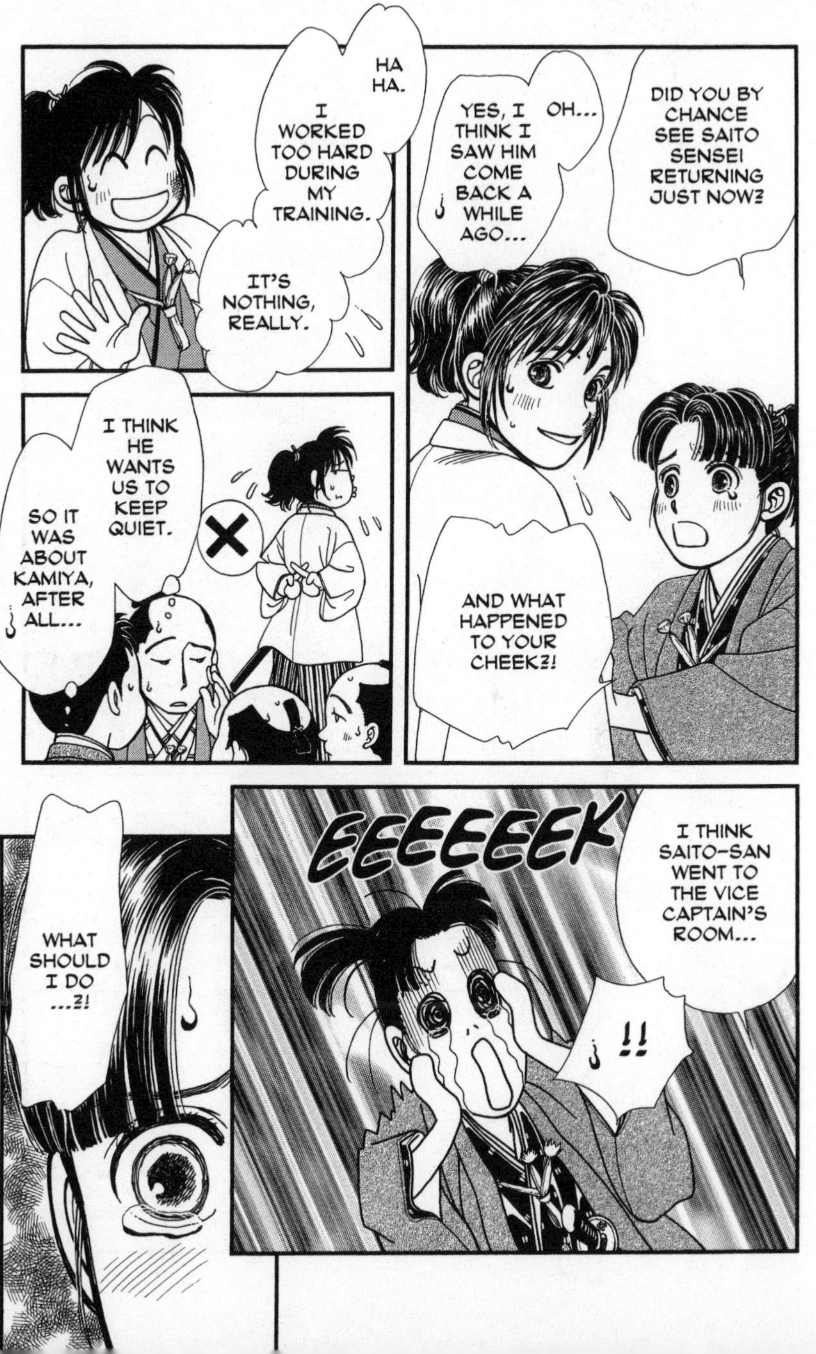
DID YOU BY CHANCE SEE SAITO SENSEI RETURNING JUST NOW?
OH...
YES, I THINK I SAW HIM COME BACK A WHILE AGO...
AND WHAT HAPPENED TO YOUR CHEEK?!
HA HA.
I WORKED TOO HARD DURING MY TRAINING.
IT'S NOTHING, REALLY.
I THINK HE WANTS US TO KEEP QUIET.
SO IT WAS ABOUT KAMIYA, AFTER ALL...
I THINK SAITO-SAN WENT TO THE VICE CAPTAIN'S ROOM...
EEEEEEK
!!
WHAT SHOULD I DO ...?!

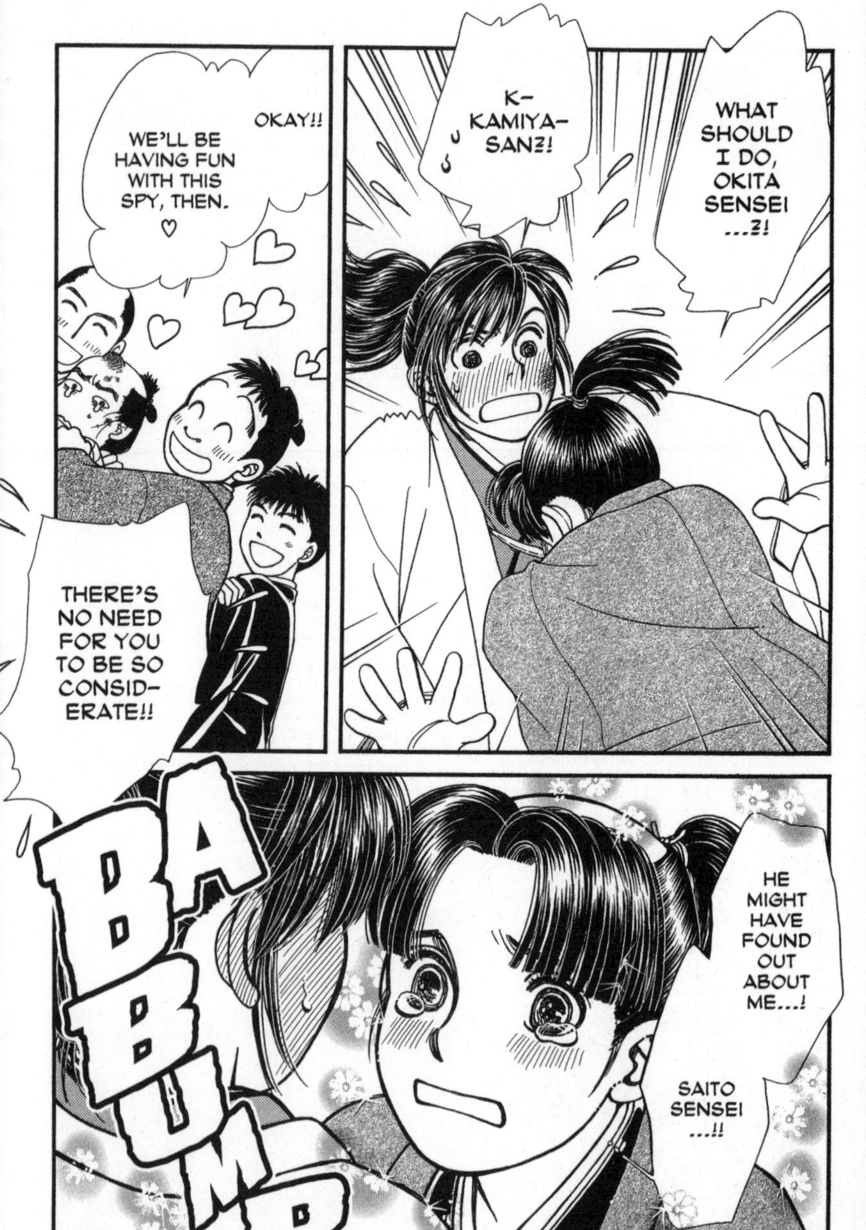
WHAT SHOULD I DO, OKITA SENSEI ...?!
K-KAMIYA-SAN?!
OKAY!!
WE'LL BE HAVING FUN WITH THIS SPY, THEN. ♡
THERE'S NO NEED FOR YOU TO BE SO CONSID-ERATE!!
HE MIGHT HAVE FOUND OUT ABOUT ME...!
SAITO SENSEI ...!!
BA BUMP

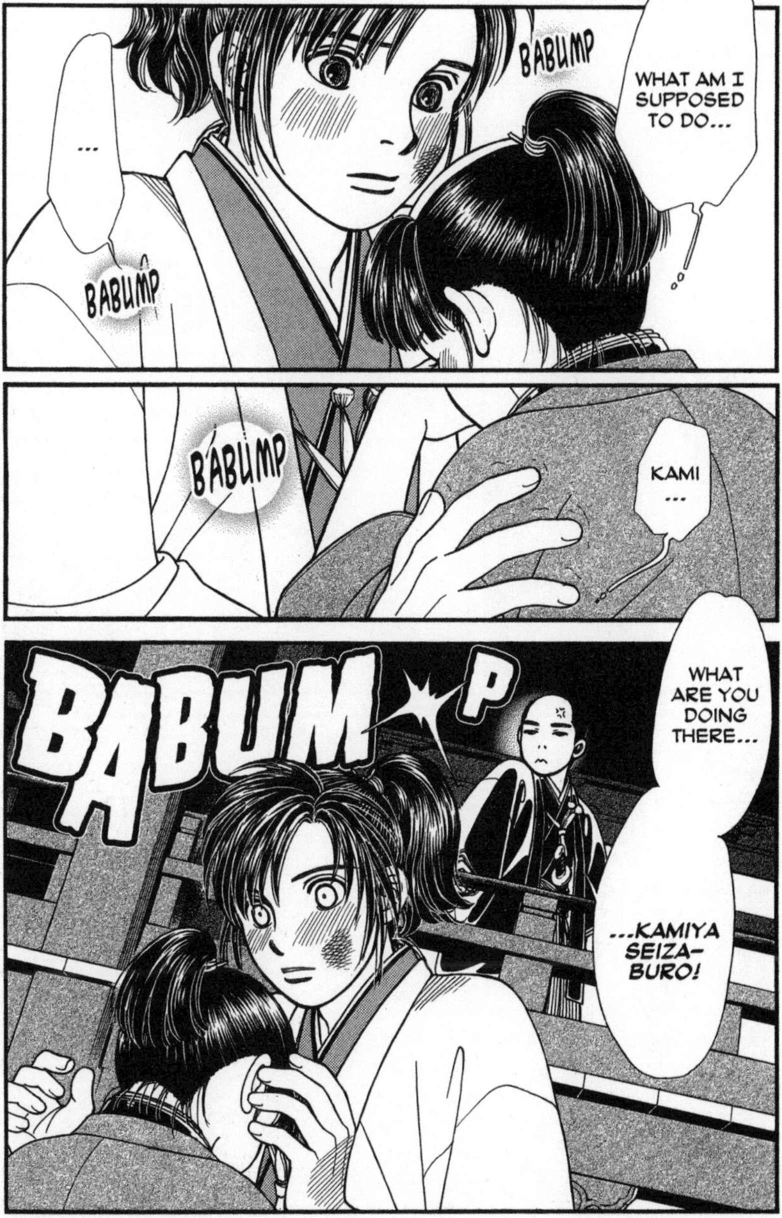
WHAT AM I SUPPOSED TO DO...
BABUMP
...
BABUMP
KAMI ...
BABUMP
WHAT ARE YOU DOING THERE...
...KAMIYA SEIZA-BURO!
BABUMP

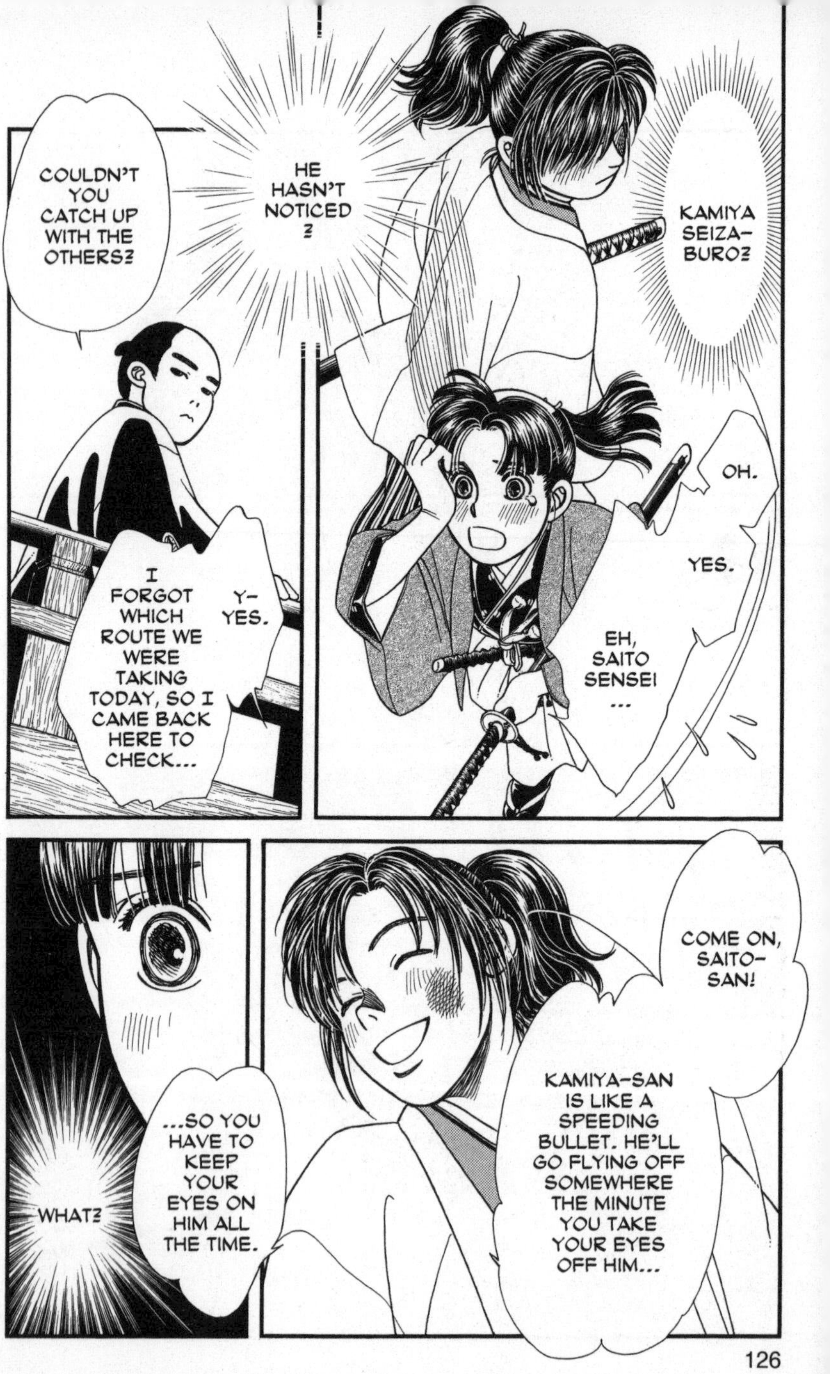
KAMIYA SEIZA-BURO?
HE HASN'T NOTICED?
OH.
YES.
EH, SAITO SENSEI...
COULDN'T YOU CATCH UP WITH THE OTHERS?
Y-YES.
I FORGOT WHICH ROUTE WE WERE TAKING TODAY, SO I CAME BACK HERE TO CHECK...
COME ON, SAITO-SAN!
KAMIYA-SAN IS LIKE A SPEEDING BULLET. HE'LL GO FLYING OFF SOMEWHERE THE MINUTE YOU TAKE YOUR EYES OFF HIM...
...SO YOU HAVE TO KEEP YOUR EYES ON HIM ALL THE TIME.
WHAT?

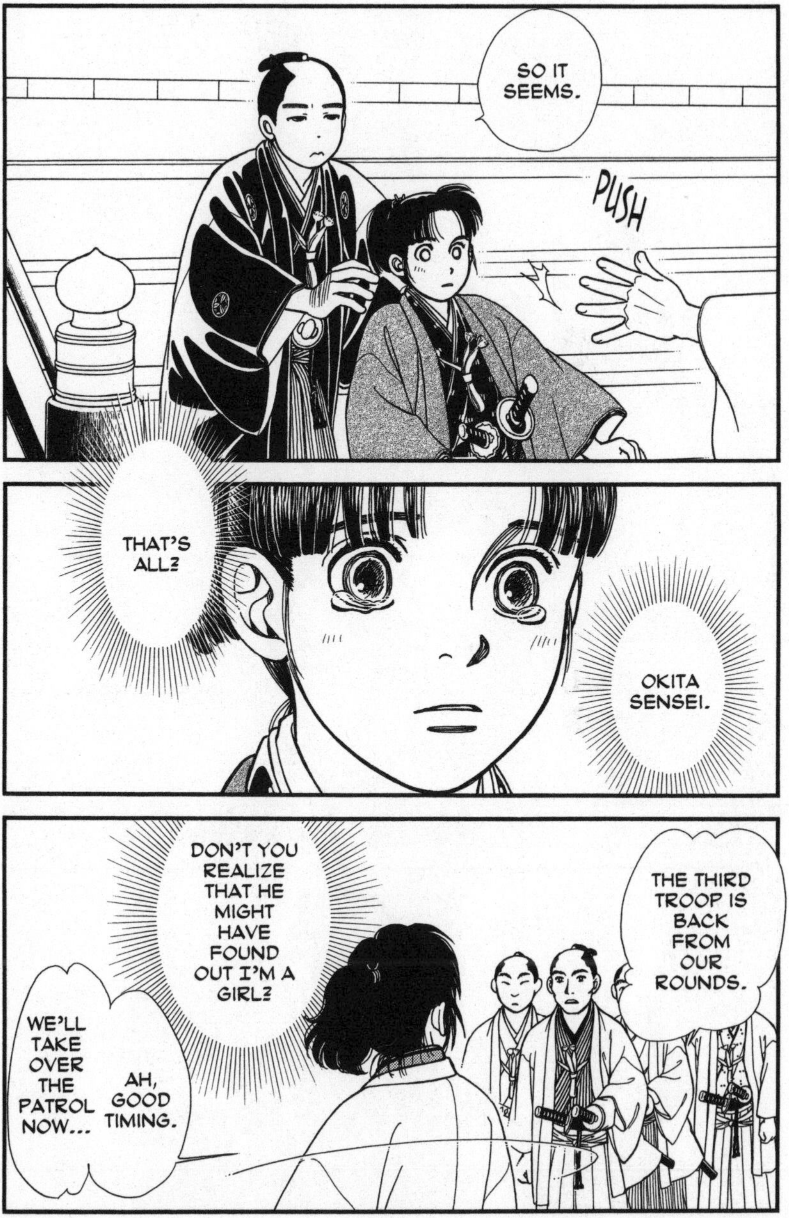
SO IT SEEMS.
PUSH
OKITA SENSEI.
THAT'S ALL?
THE THIRD TROOP IS BACK FROM OUR ROUNDS.
DON'T YOU REALIZE THAT HE MIGHT HAVE FOUND OUT I'M A GIRL?
AH, GOOD TIMING.
WE'LL TAKE OVER THE PATROL NOW...

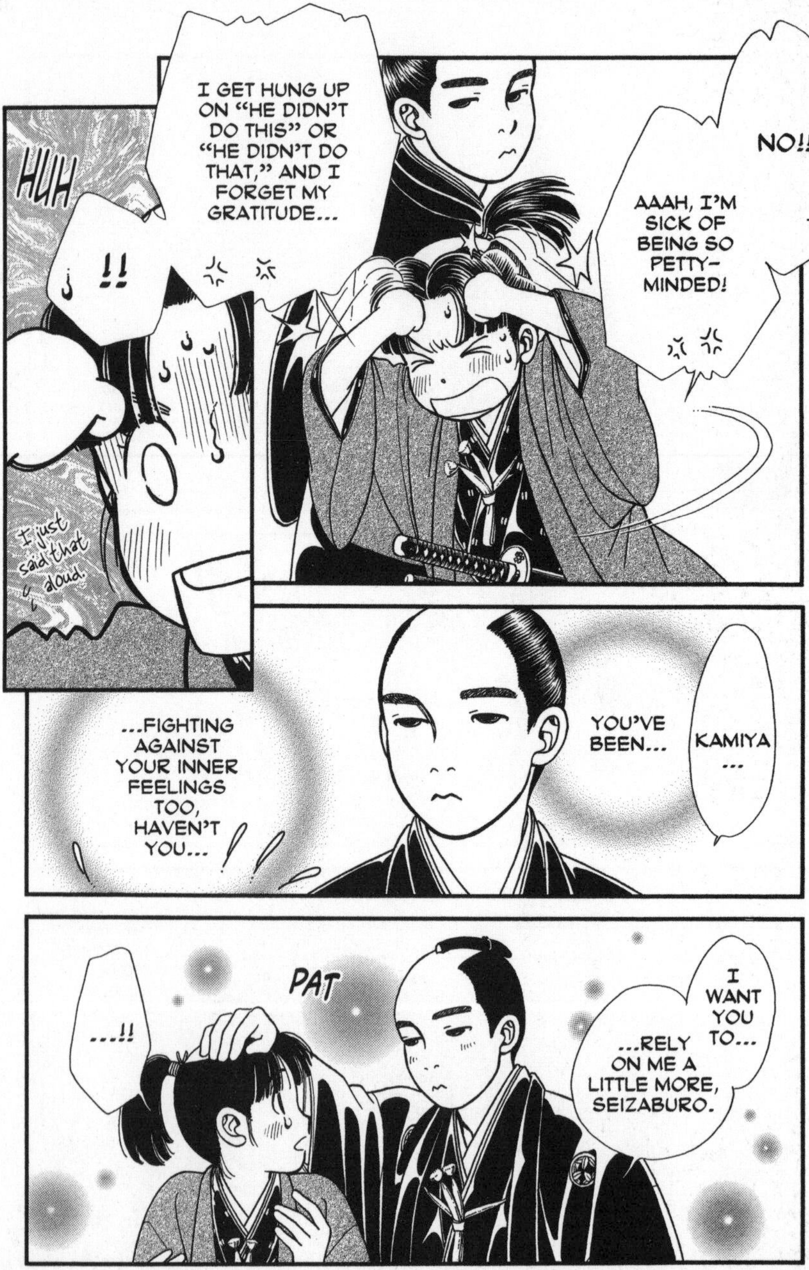
I GET HUNG UP ON "HE DIDN'T DO THIS" OR "HE DIDN'T DO THAT," AND I FORGET MY GRATITUDE...
NO!!
AAAH, I'M SICK OF BEING SO PETTY-MINDED!
HUH
!!
I just said that aloud.
KAMIYA...
YOU'VE BEEN...
...FIGHTING AGAINST YOUR INNER FEELINGS TOO, HAVEN'T YOU...
I WANT YOU TO...
...RELY ON ME A LITTLE MORE, SEIZABURO.
PAT
...!!

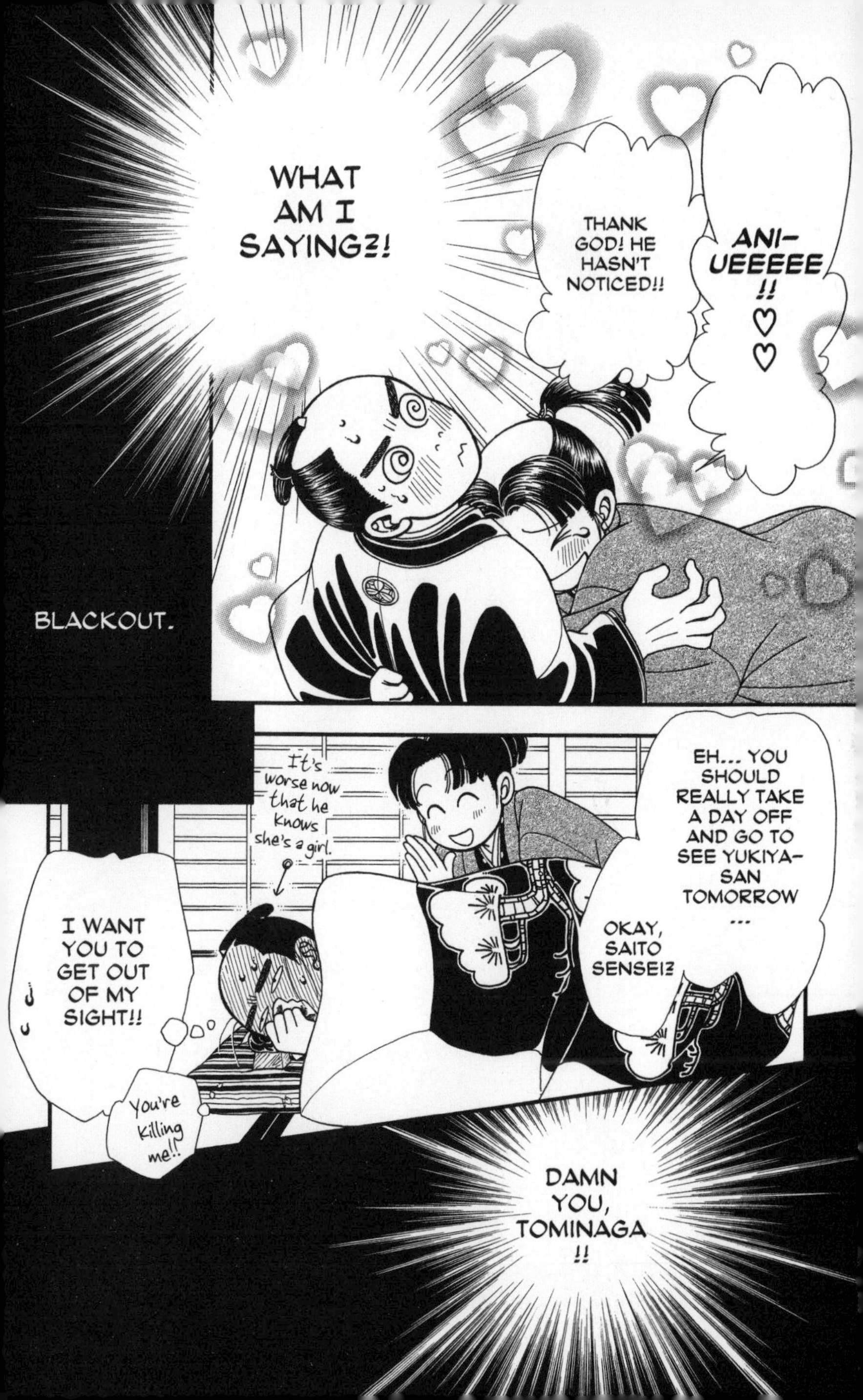
ANI-UEEEEE!! ♡ ♡
THANK GOD! HE HASN'T NOTICED!!
WHAT AM I SAYING?!
BLACKOUT.
EH... YOU SHOULD REALLY TAKE A DAY OFF AND GO TO SEE YUKIYA-SAN TOMORROW...
OKAY, SAITO SENSEI?
It's worse now that he knows she's a girl.
I WANT YOU TO GET OUT OF MY SIGHT!!
You're Killing me!!
DAMN YOU, TOMINAGA!!

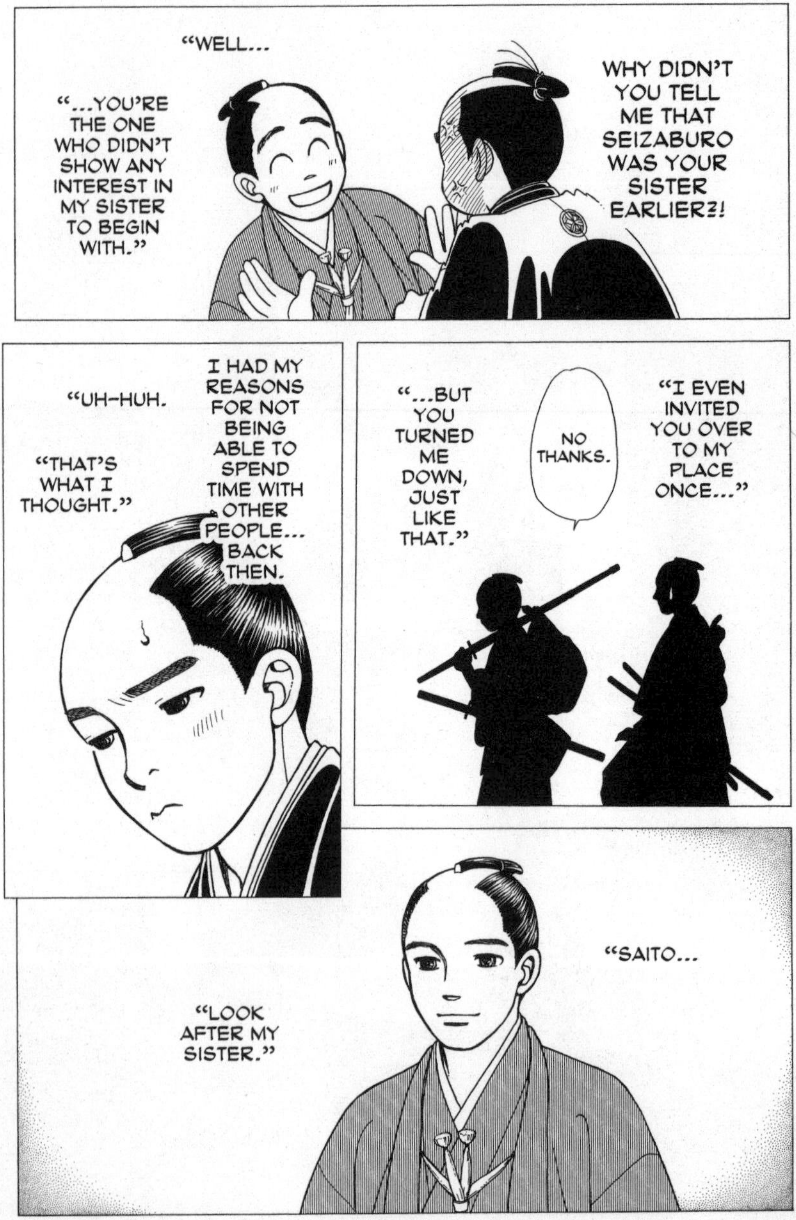
WHY DIDN'T YOU TELL ME THAT SEIZABURO WAS YOUR SISTER EARLIER?!
"WELL...
"...YOU'RE THE ONE WHO DIDN'T SHOW ANY INTEREST IN MY SISTER TO BEGIN WITH."
"I EVEN INVITED YOU OVER TO MY PLACE ONCE..."
NO THANKS.
"...BUT YOU TURNED ME DOWN, JUST LIKE THAT."
I HAD MY REASONS FOR NOT BEING ABLE TO SPEND TIME WITH OTHER PEOPLE... BACK THEN.
"UH-HUH.
"THAT'S WHAT I THOUGHT."
"SAITO...
"LOOK AFTER MY SISTER."

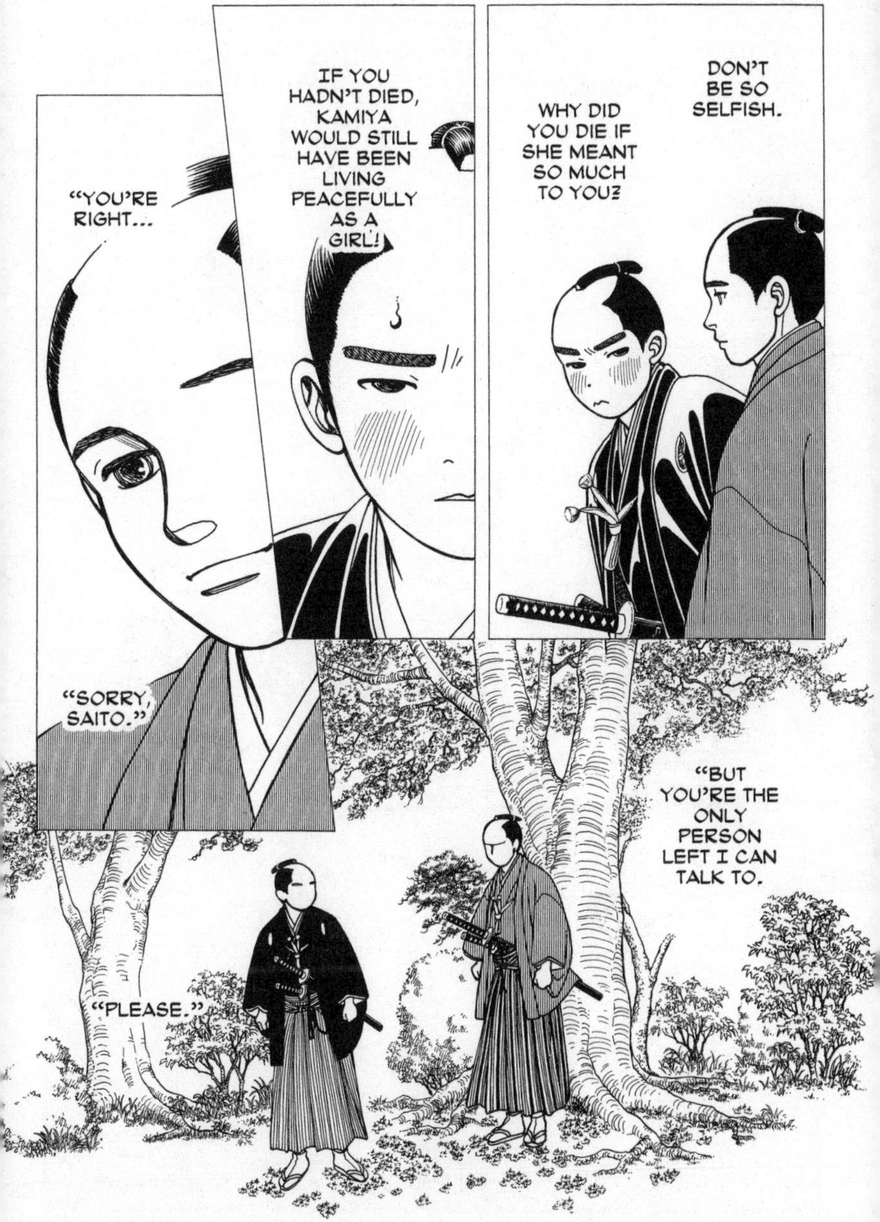
DON'T BE SO SELFISH.
WHY DID YOU DIE IF SHE MEANT SO MUCH TO YOU?
IF YOU HADN'T DIED, KAMIYA WOULD STILL HAVE BEEN LIVING PEACEFULLY AS A GIRL!
"YOU'RE RIGHT...
"SORRY, SAITO."
"BUT YOU'RE THE ONLY PERSON LEFT I CAN TALK TO.
"PLEASE."

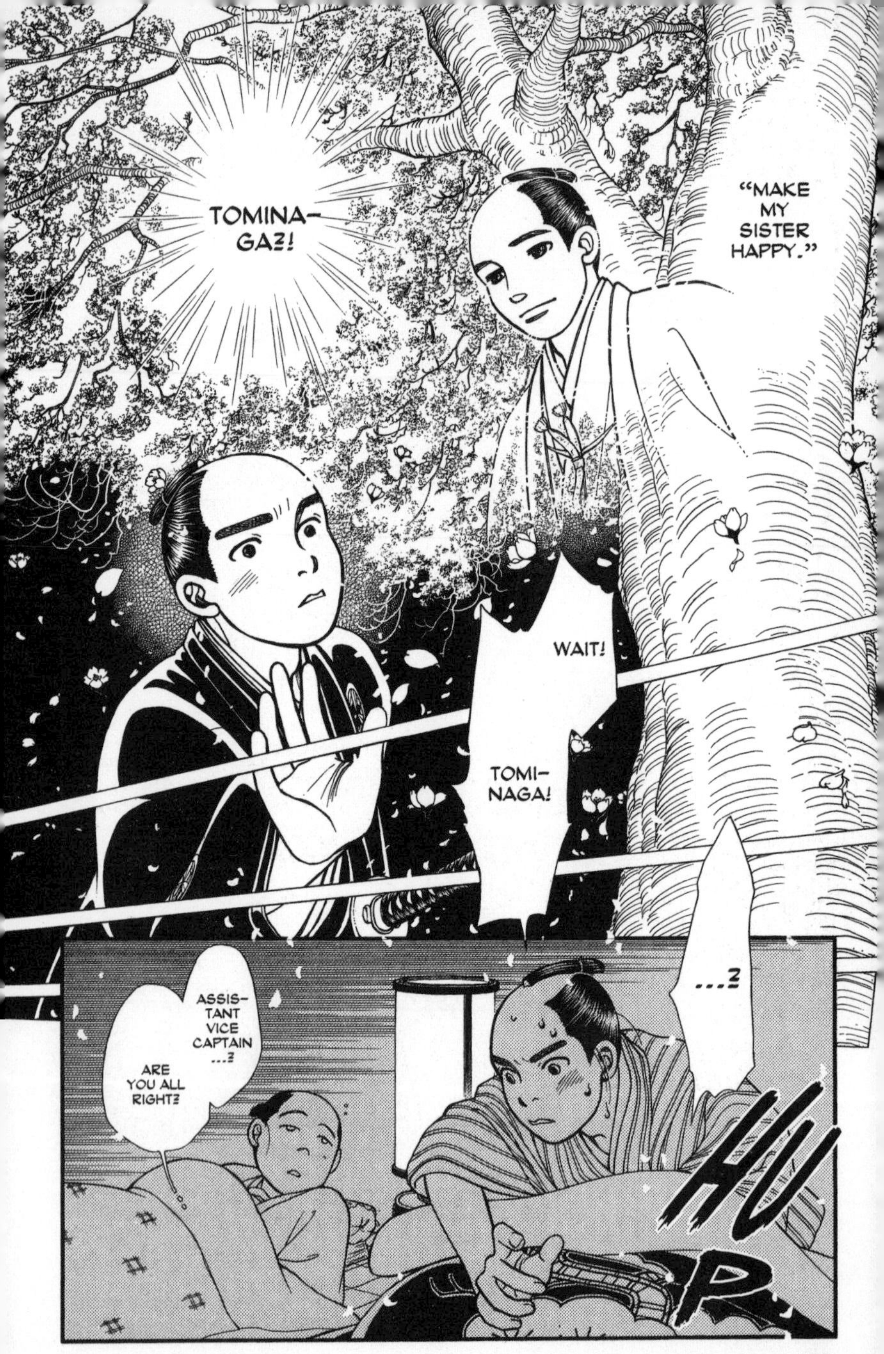
"MAKE MY SISTER HAPPY."
TOMINA-GA?!
WAIT!
TOMI-NAGA!
...?
ASSIS-TANT VICE CAPTAIN ...?
ARE YOU ALL RIGHT?
HUP

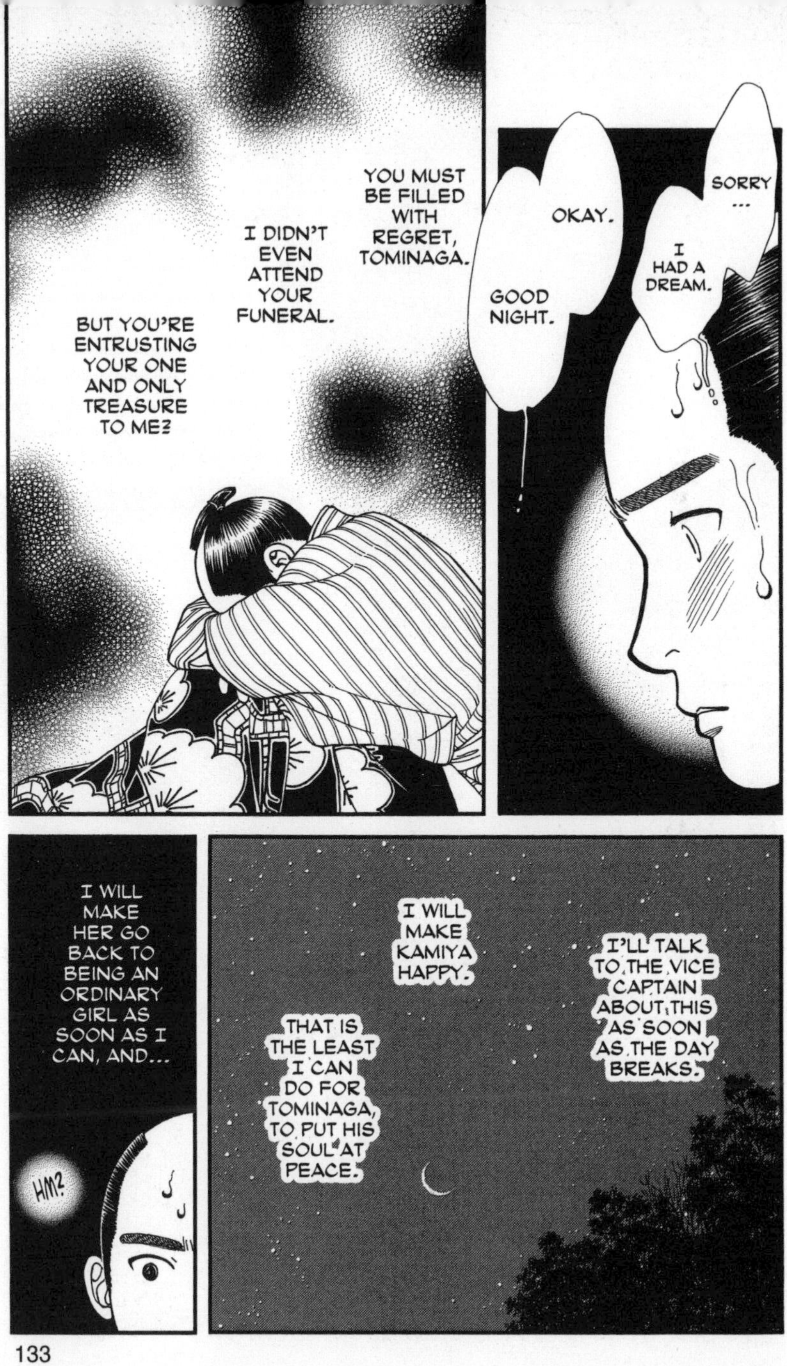
SORRY...
I HAD A DREAM.
OKAY.
GOOD NIGHT.
YOU MUST BE FILLED WITH REGRET, TOMINAGA.
I DIDN'T EVEN ATTEND YOUR FUNERAL.
BUT YOU'RE ENTRUSTING YOUR ONE AND ONLY TREASURE TO ME?
I'LL TALK TO THE VICE CAPTAIN ABOUT THIS AS SOON AS THE DAY BREAKS.
I WILL MAKE KAMIYA HAPPY.
THAT IS THE LEAST I CAN DO FOR TOMINAGA, TO PUT HIS SOUL AT PEACE.
I WILL MAKE HER GO BACK TO BEING AN ORDINARY GIRL AS SOON AS I CAN, AND...
HM?

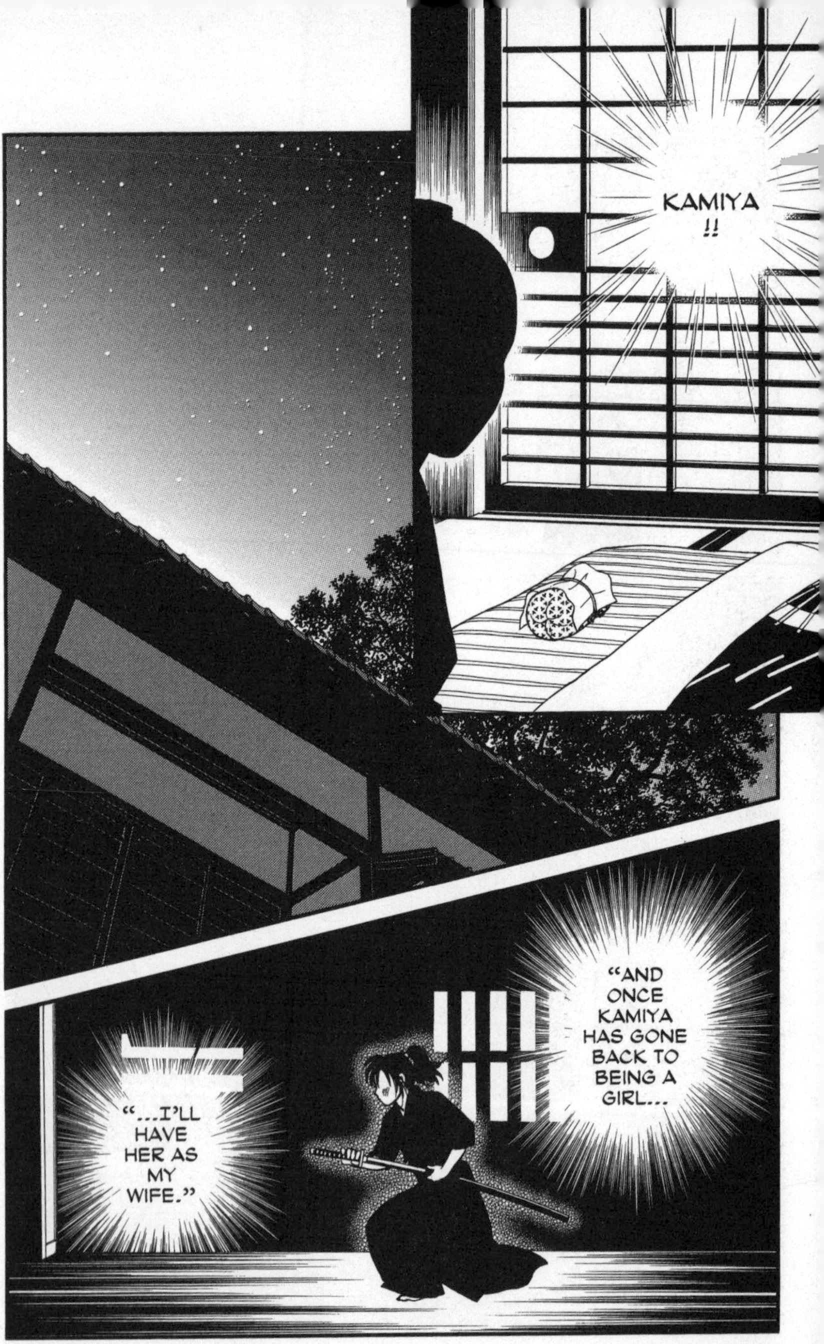
KAMIYA !!
"AND ONCE KAMIYA HAS GONE BACK TO BEING A GIRL...
"...I'LL HAVE HER AS MY WIFE."

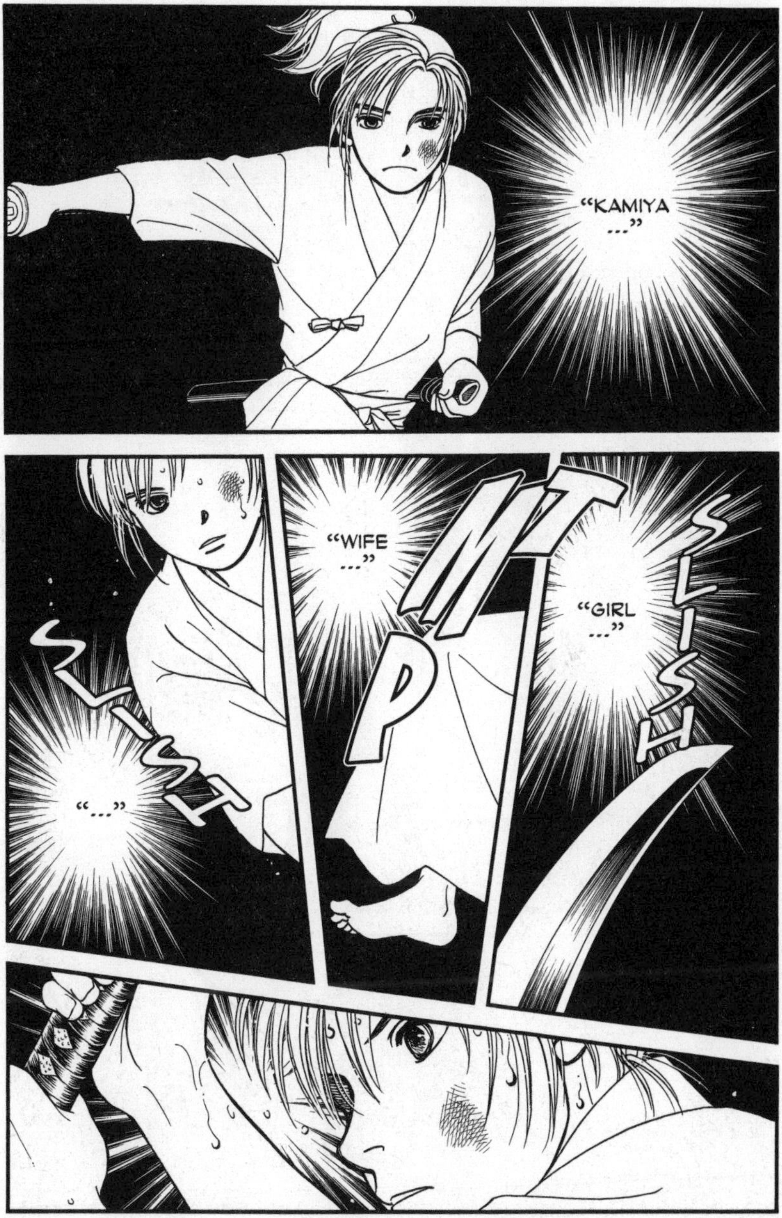
"KAMIYA ..."
SLISH
"GIRL ..."
"WIFE ..."
SLISH
"..."

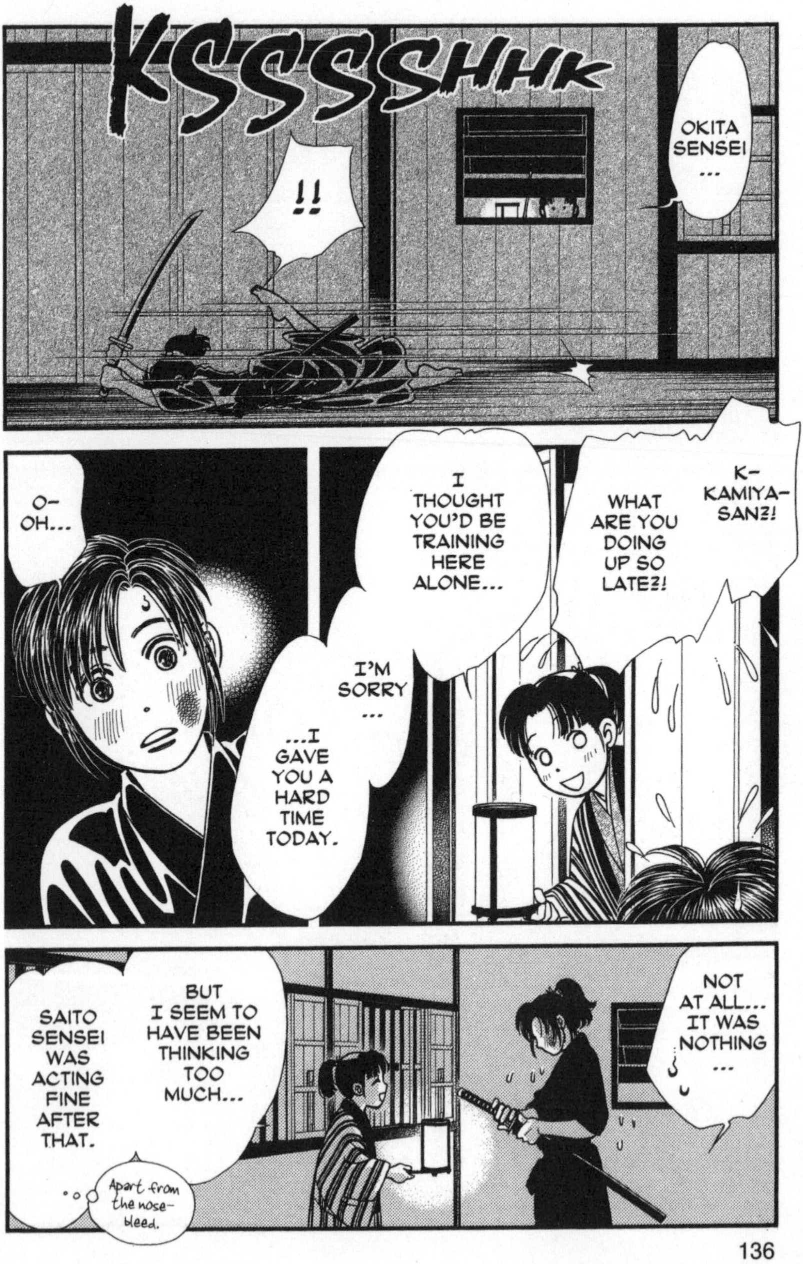
OKITA SENSEI ...
KSSSSHHK
!!
K-KAMIYA-SAN?!
WHAT ARE YOU DOING UP SO LATE?!
I THOUGHT YOU'D BE TRAINING HERE ALONE...
I'M SORRY ...
...I GAVE YOU A HARD TIME TODAY.
O-OH...
NOT AT ALL... IT WAS NOTHING ...
BUT I SEEM TO HAVE BEEN THINKING TOO MUCH...
SAITO SENSEI WAS ACTING FINE AFTER THAT.
Apart from the nose-bleed.

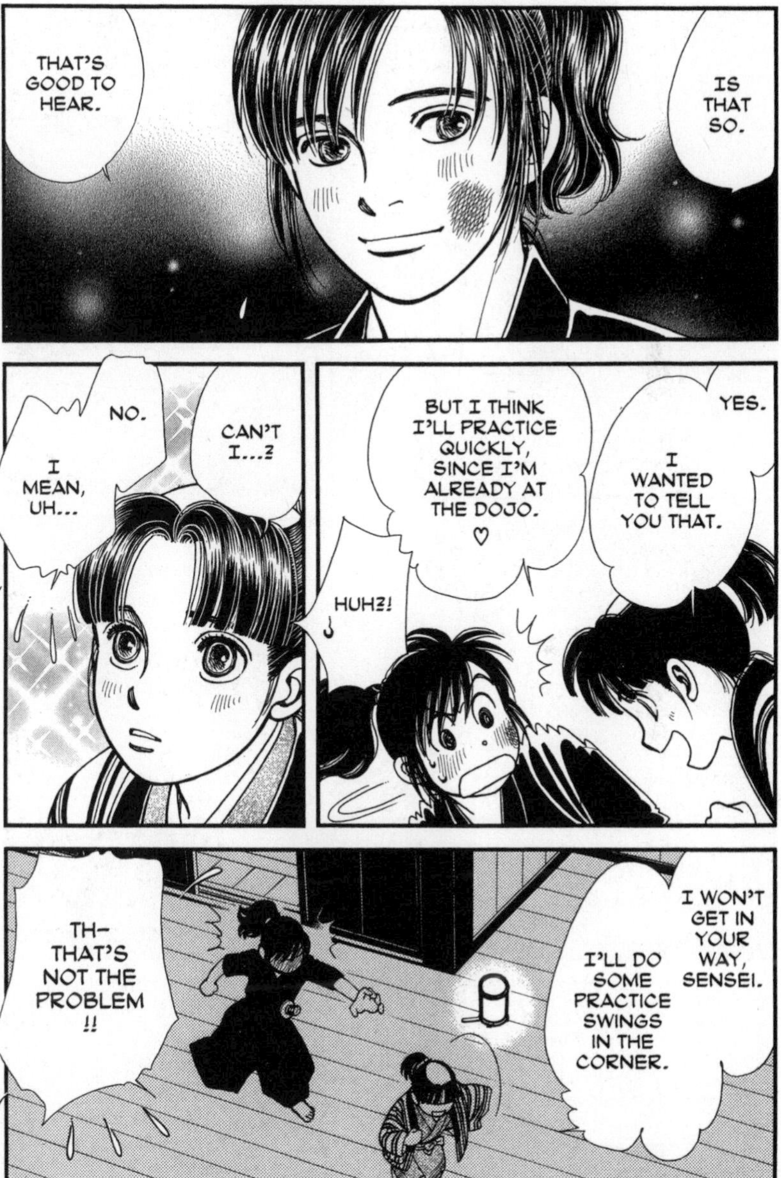
IS THAT SO.
THAT'S GOOD TO HEAR.
YES.
I WANTED TO TELL YOU THAT.
BUT I THINK I'LL PRACTICE QUICKLY, SINCE I'M ALREADY AT THE DOJO. ♡
HUH?!
CAN'T I...?
NO.
I MEAN, UH...
I WON'T GET IN YOUR WAY, SENSEI.
I'LL DO SOME PRACTICE SWINGS IN THE CORNER.
TH-THAT'S NOT THE PROBLEM!!

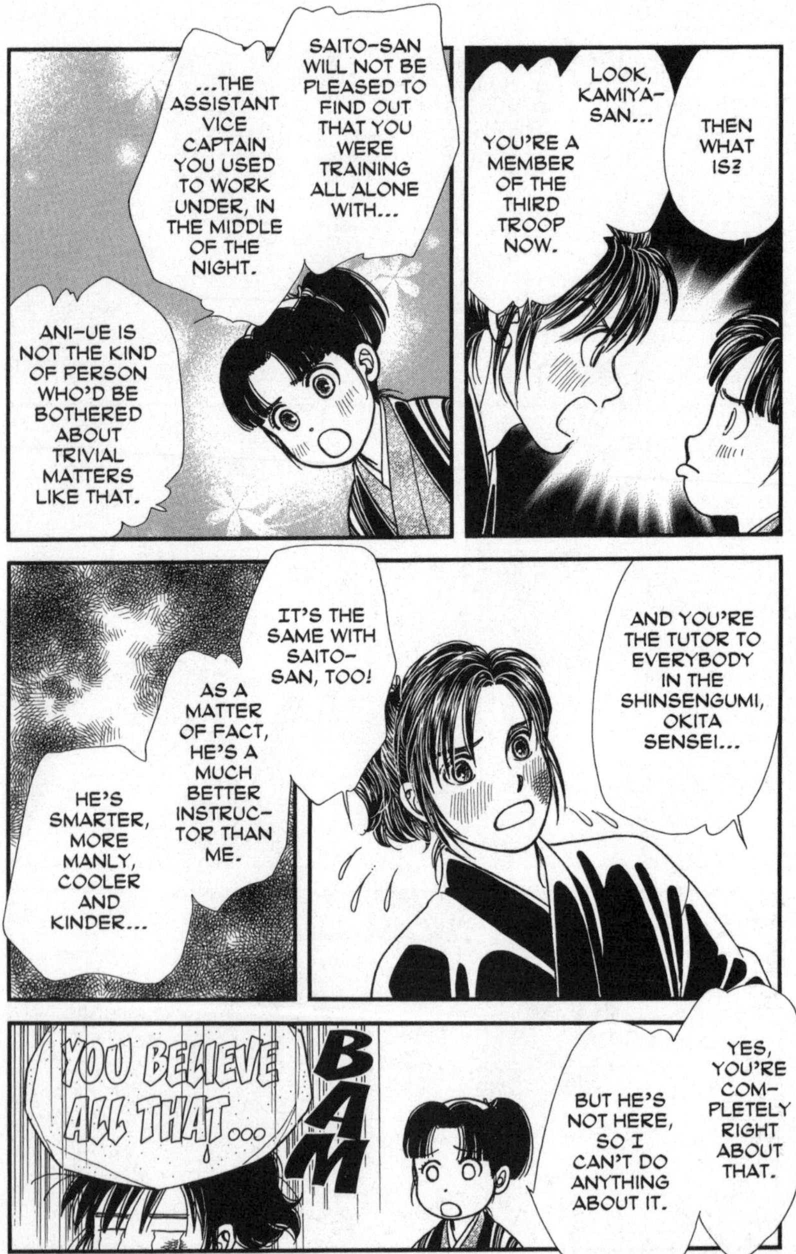
THEN WHAT IS?
LOOK, KAMIYA-SAN...
YOU'RE A MEMBER OF THE THIRD TROOP NOW.
SAITO-SAN WILL NOT BE PLEASED TO FIND OUT THAT YOU WERE TRAINING ALL ALONE WITH...
...THE ASSISTANT VICE CAPTAIN YOU USED TO WORK UNDER, IN THE MIDDLE OF THE NIGHT.
ANI-UE IS NOT THE KIND OF PERSON WHO'D BE BOTHERED ABOUT TRIVIAL MATTERS LIKE THAT.
AND YOU'RE THE TUTOR TO EVERYBODY IN THE SHINSENGUMI, OKITA SENSEI...
IT'S THE SAME WITH SAITO-SAN, TOO!
AS A MATTER OF FACT, HE'S A MUCH BETTER INSTRUC-TOR THAN ME.
HE'S SMARTER, MORE MANLY, COOLER AND KINDER...
YES, YOU'RE COM-PLETELY RIGHT ABOUT THAT.
BUT HE'S NOT HERE, SO I CAN'T DO ANYTHING ABOUT IT.
BAM
YOU BELIEVE ALL THAT...

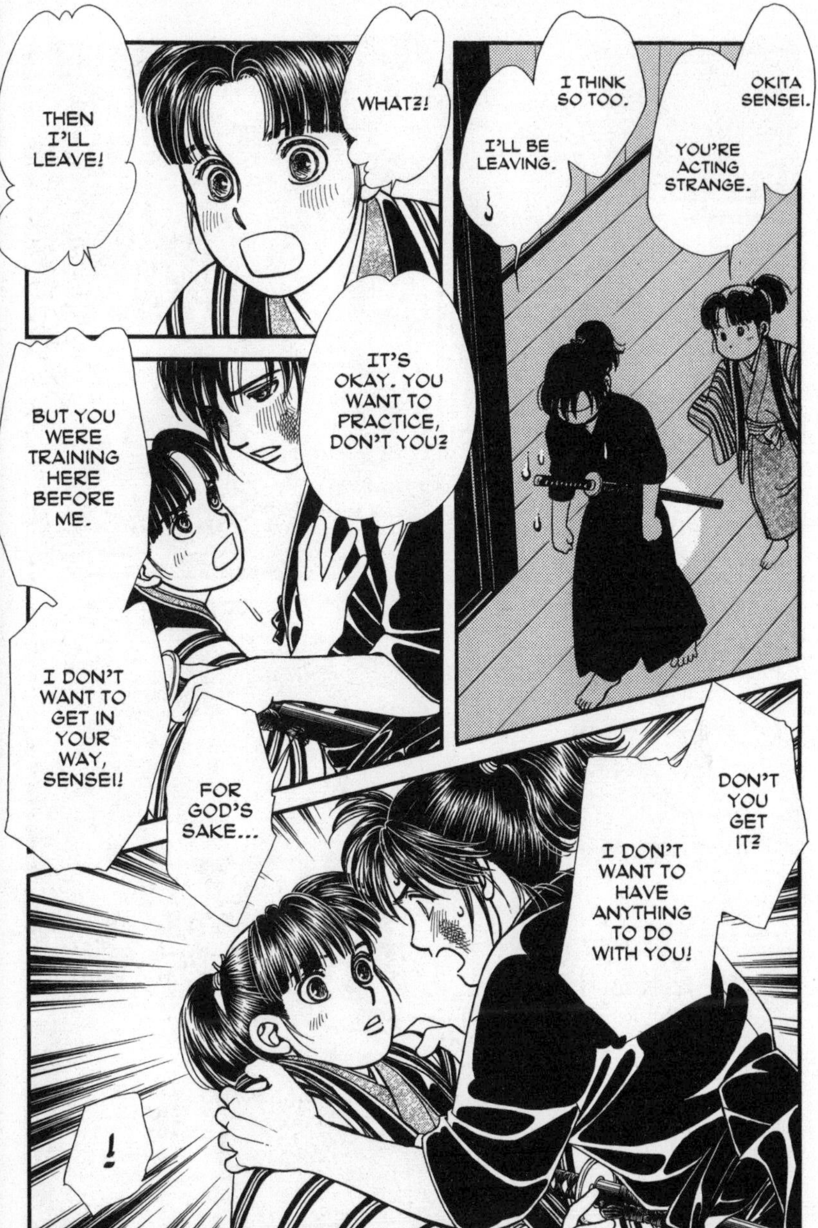
OKITA SENSEI.
YOU'RE ACTING STRANGE.
I THINK SO TOO.
I'LL BE LEAVING.
WHAT?!
THEN I'LL LEAVE!
IT'S OKAY. YOU WANT TO PRACTICE, DON'T YOU?
BUT YOU WERE TRAINING HERE BEFORE ME.
I DON'T WANT TO GET IN YOUR WAY, SENSEI!
DON'T YOU GET IT?
I DON'T WANT TO HAVE ANYTHING TO DO WITH YOU!
FOR GOD'S SAKE...
!

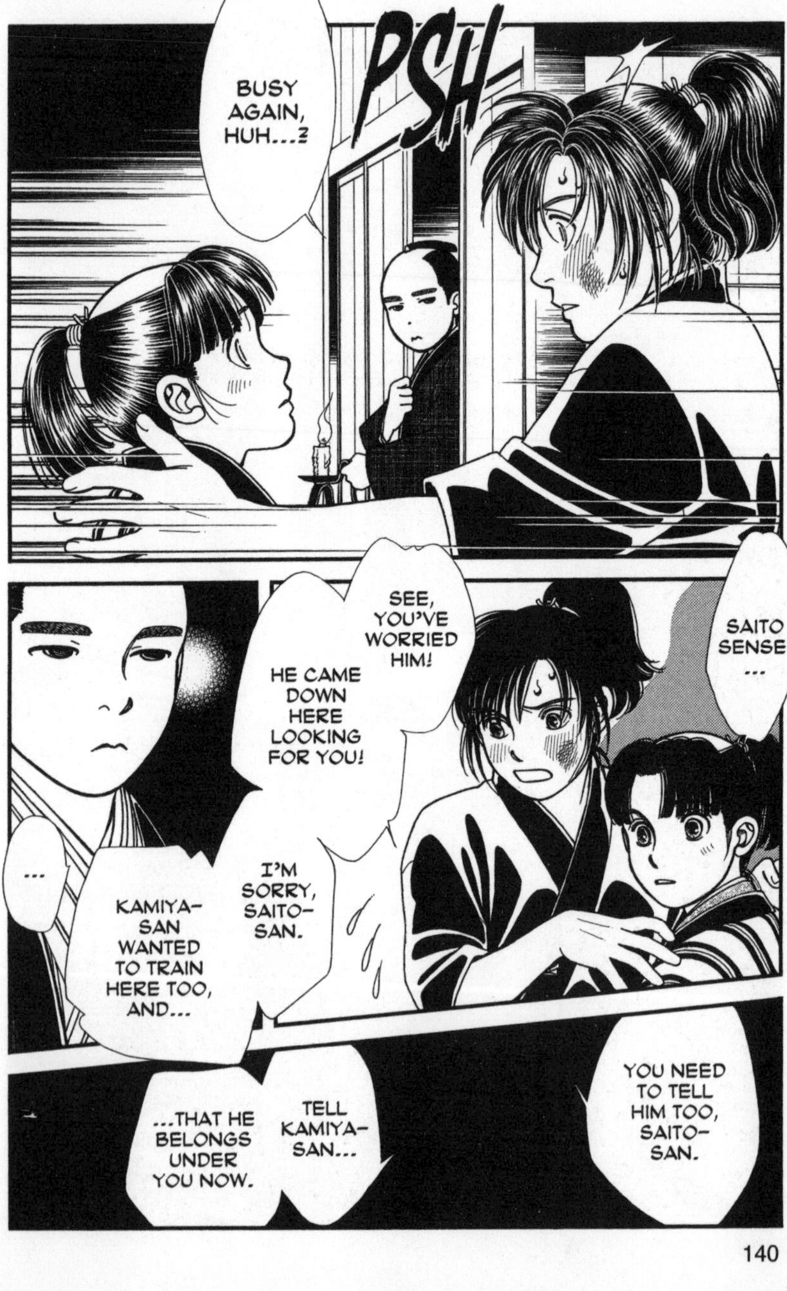
PSH
BUSY AGAIN, HUH...?
SAITO SENSEI ...
SEE, YOU'VE WORRIED HIM!
HE CAME DOWN HERE LOOKING FOR YOU!
I'M SORRY, SAITO-SAN.
KAMIYA-SAN WANTED TO TRAIN HERE TOO, AND...
...
YOU NEED TO TELL HIM TOO, SAITO-SAN.
TELL KAMIYA-SAN...
...THAT HE BELONGS UNDER YOU NOW.

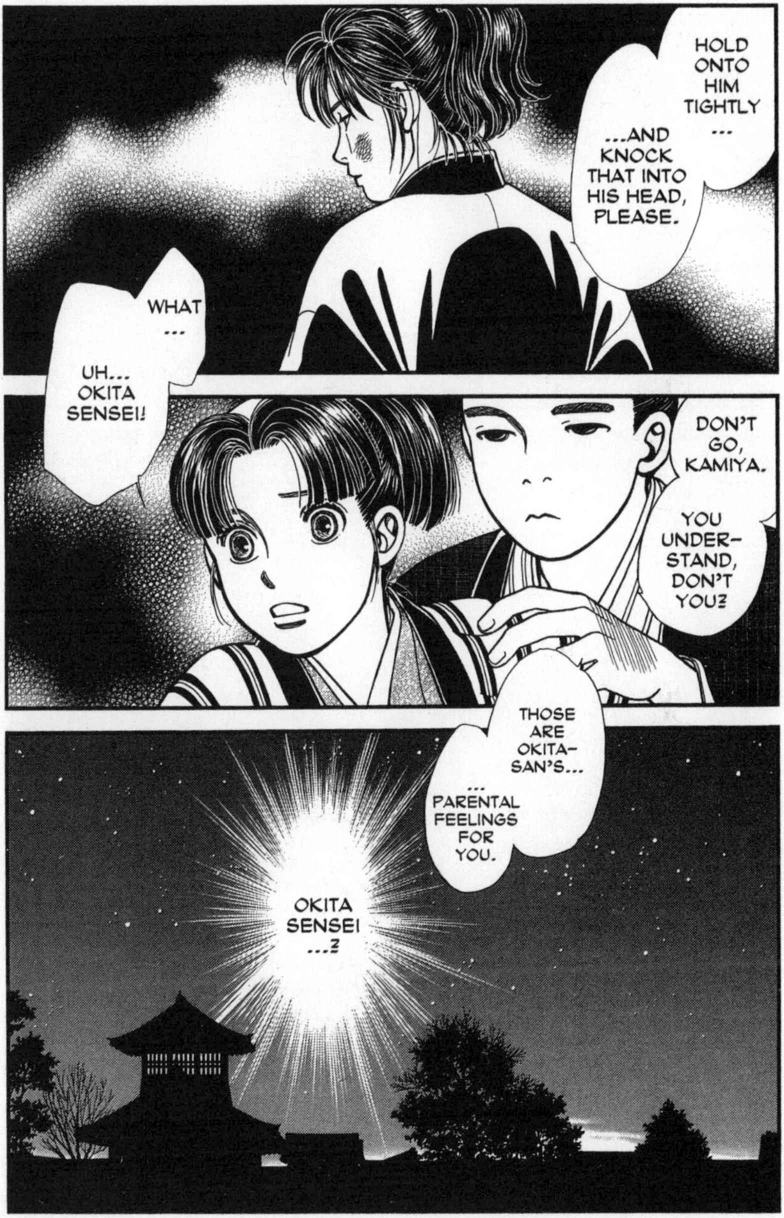
HOLD ONTO HIM TIGHTLY...
...AND KNOCK THAT INTO HIS HEAD, PLEASE.
WHAT... UH... OKITA SENSEI!
DON'T GO, KAMIYA.
YOU UNDERSTAND, DON'T YOU?
THOSE ARE OKITA-SAN'S...
...PARENTAL FEELINGS FOR YOU.
OKITA SENSEI...?

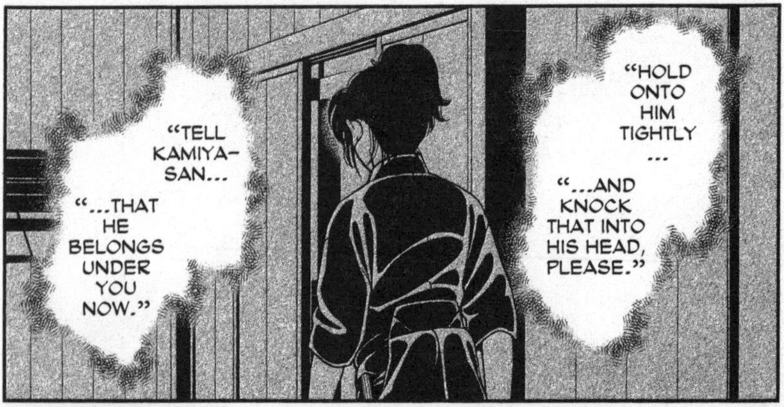
"HOLD ONTO HIM TIGHTLY...
"...AND KNOCK THAT INTO HIS HEAD, PLEASE."
"TELL KAMIYA-SAN...
"...THAT HE BELONGS UNDER YOU NOW."

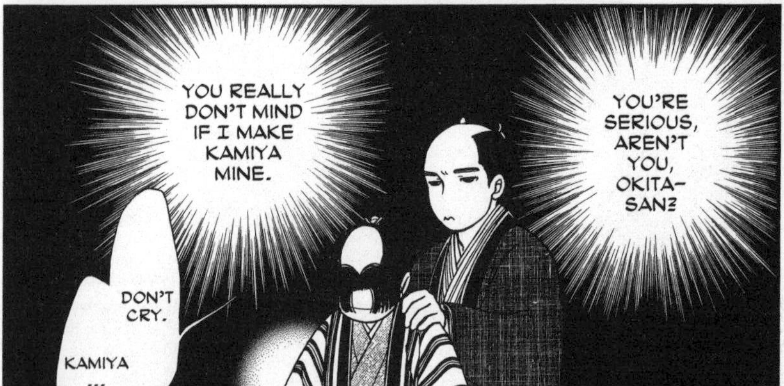
YOU'RE SERIOUS, AREN'T YOU, OKITA-SAN?
YOU REALLY DON'T MIND IF I MAKE KAMIYA MINE.
DON'T CRY.
KAMIYA...

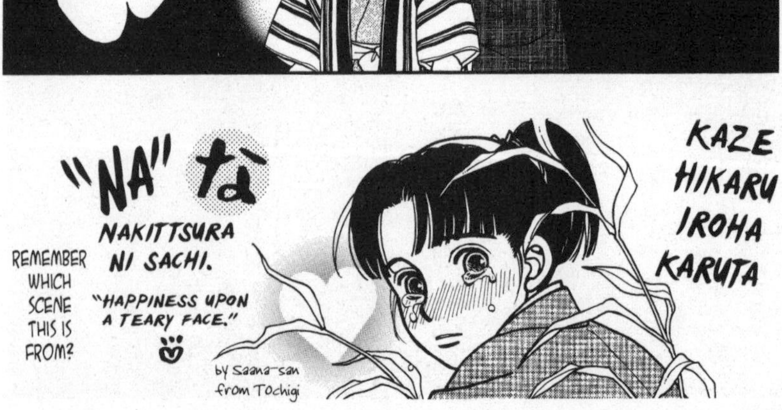
KAZE HIKARU IROHA KARUTA
"NA" な
NAKITTSURA NI SACHI.
"HAPPINESS UPON A TEARY FACE."
REMEMBER WHICH SCENE THIS IS FROM?
by Saana-san from Tochigi

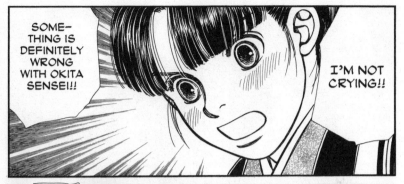

I'M NOT CRYING!!
SOMETHING IS DEFINITELY WRONG WITH OKITA SENSEI!!
HUH?
HE SEEMS TO BE OVERLY CONSCIOUS OF YOU, SAITO SENSEI!!
ACK
UH, I HAVEN'T DONE ANYTHING...
TING!
OKITA SENSEI'S CHEEK!!
WERE YOU THE ONE WHO DID THAT, SAITO SENSEI?!
EH... WELL, UM... I GOT A BIT CARRIED AWAY WHEN WE WERE TRAINING...
She's so quick...
THAT'S NOT A MARK LEFT BEHIND FROM A SHINAI OR WOODEN SWORD!
I KNEW IT!
YOU GOT INTO A FIGHT WITH OKITA SENSEI, DIDN'T YOU?!

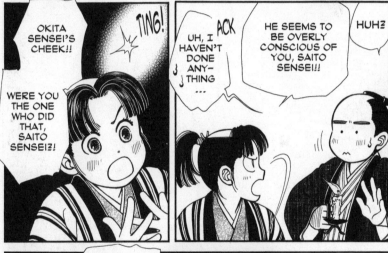

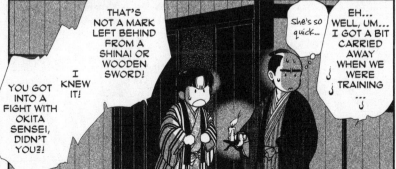

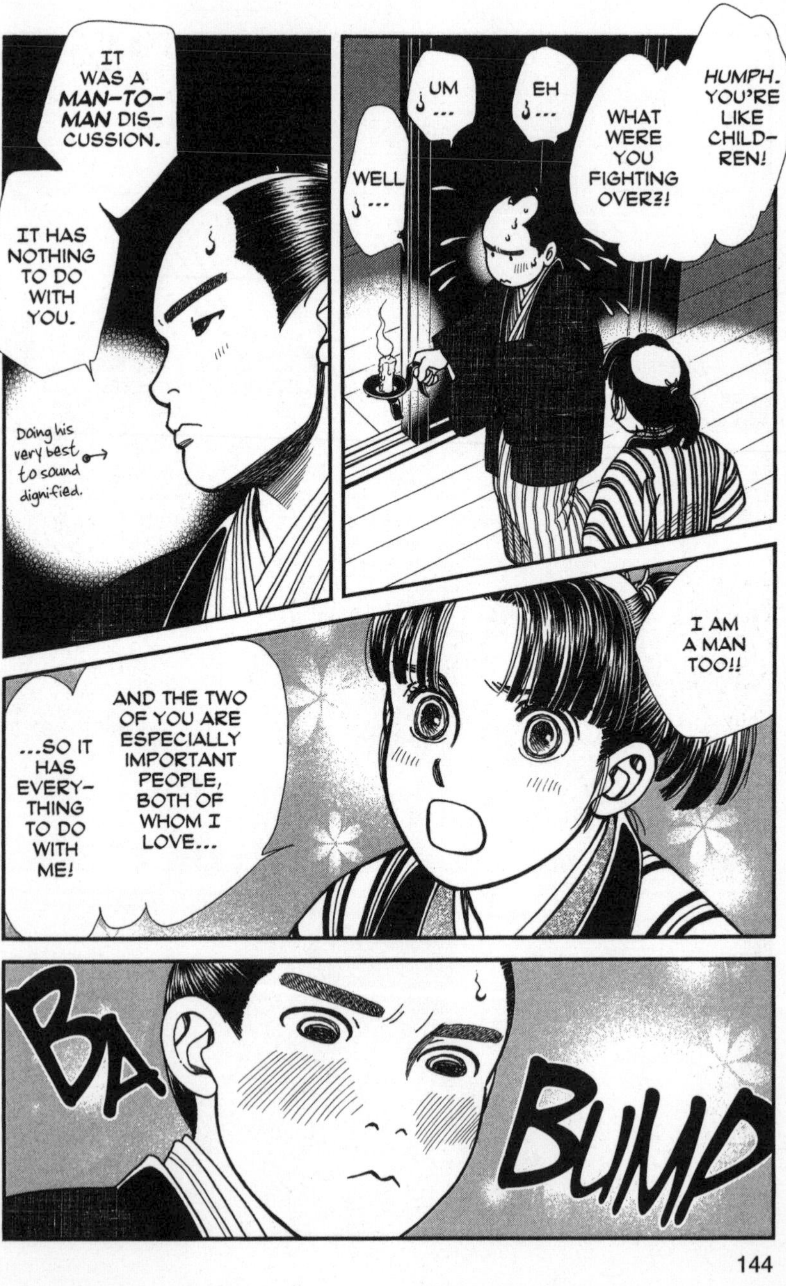
HUMPH. YOU'RE LIKE CHILDREN!
WHAT WERE YOU FIGHTING OVER?!
EH...
UM...
WELL...
IT WAS A MAN-TO-MAN DISCUSSION.
IT HAS NOTHING TO DO WITH YOU.
Doing his very best to sound dignified.
I AM A MAN TOO!!
AND THE TWO OF YOU ARE ESPECIALLY IMPORTANT PEOPLE, BOTH OF WHOM I LOVE...
...SO IT HAS EVERYTHING TO DO WITH ME!
BA
BUMP

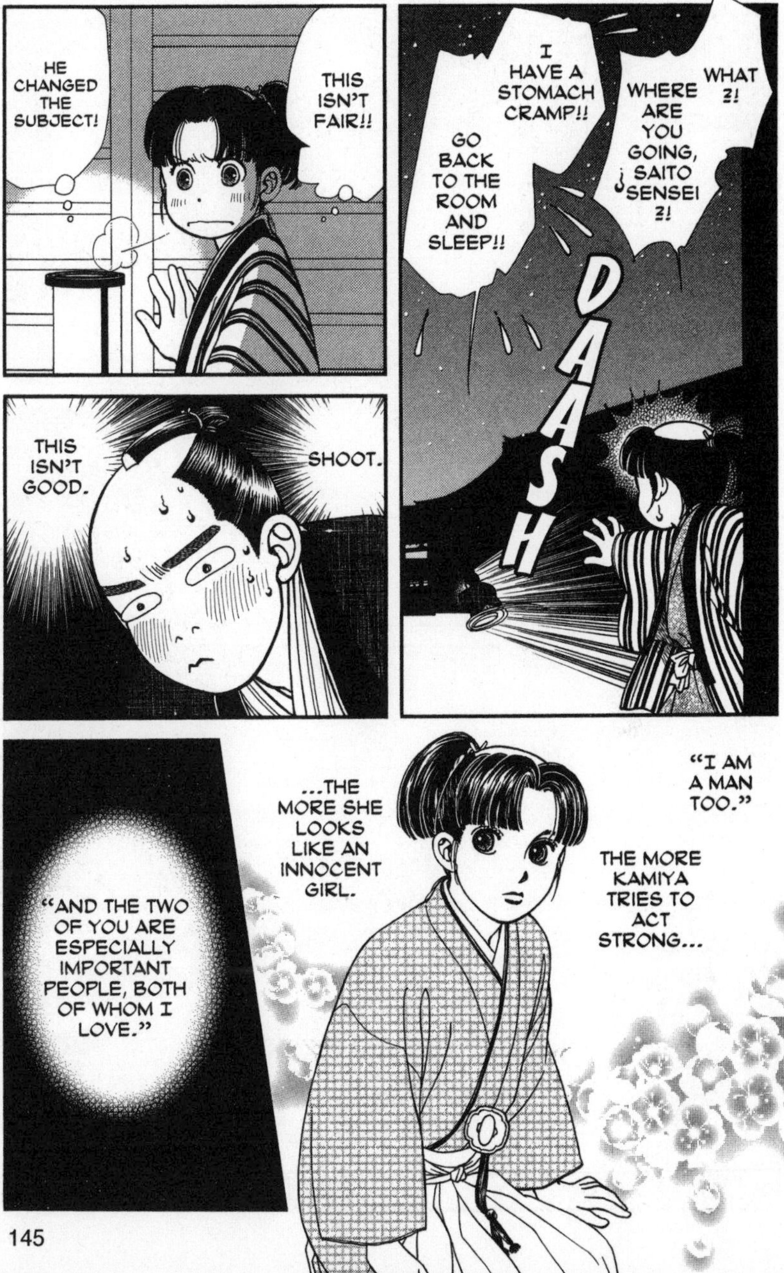
WHAT ?!
WHERE ARE YOU GOING, SAITO SENSEI ?!
I HAVE A STOMACH CRAMP!!
GO BACK TO THE ROOM AND SLEEP!!
DAAASH
THIS ISN'T FAIR!!
HE CHANGED THE SUBJECT!
SHOOT.
THIS ISN'T GOOD.
"I AM A MAN TOO."
THE MORE KAMIYA TRIES TO ACT STRONG...
...THE MORE SHE LOOKS LIKE AN INNOCENT GIRL.
"AND THE TWO OF YOU ARE ESPECIALLY IMPORTANT PEOPLE, BOTH OF WHOM I LOVE."

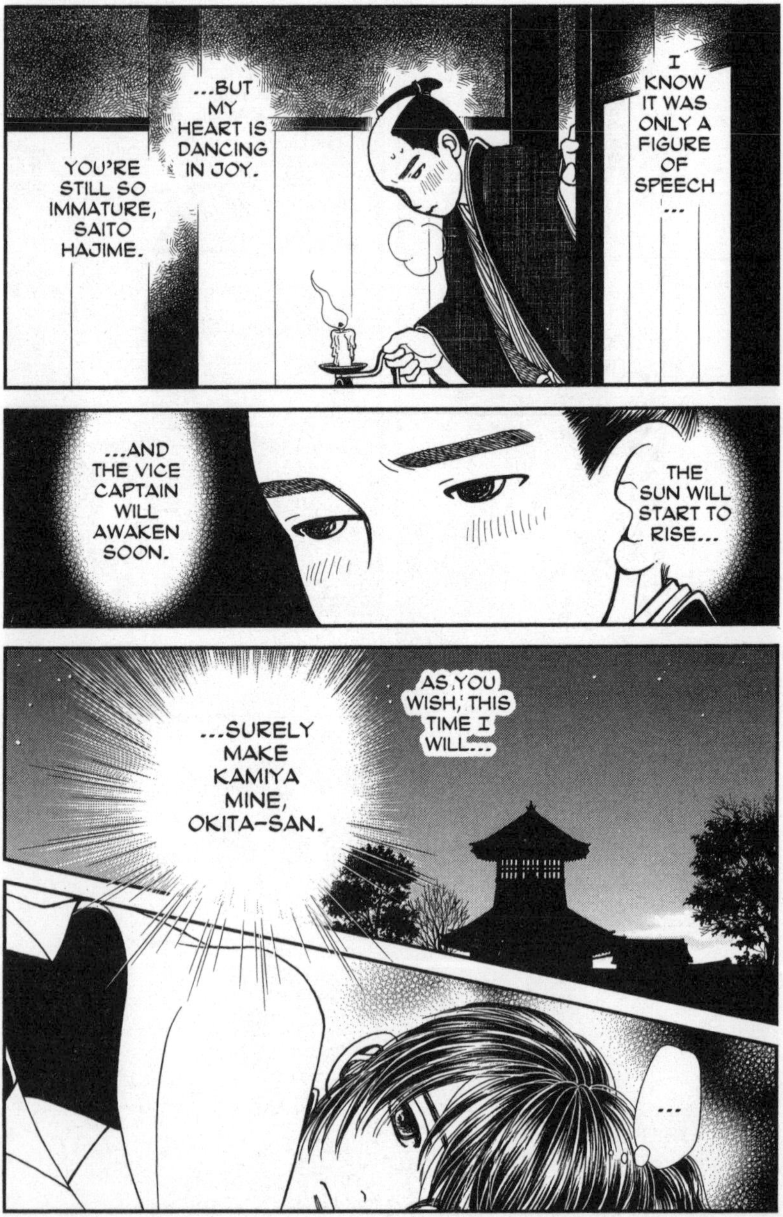
I KNOW IT WAS ONLY A FIGURE OF SPEECH...
...BUT MY HEART IS DANCING IN JOY.
YOU'RE STILL SO IMMATURE, SAITO HAJIME.
THE SUN WILL START TO RISE...
...AND THE VICE CAPTAIN WILL AWAKEN SOON.
AS YOU WISH, THIS TIME I WILL...
...SURELY MAKE KAMIYA MINE, OKITA-SAN.
...

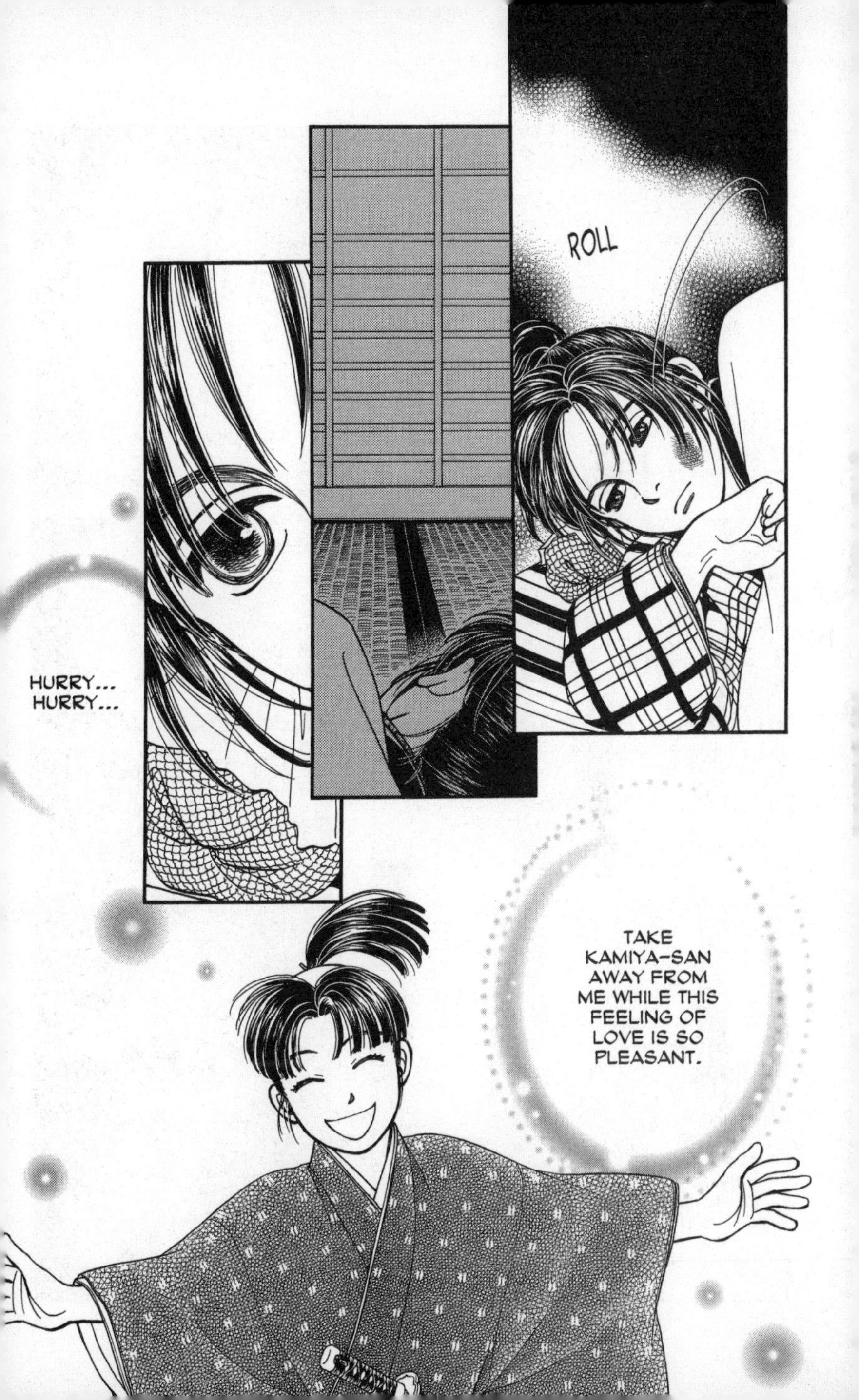
ROLL
HURRY... HURRY...
TAKE KAMIYA-SAN AWAY FROM ME WHILE THIS FEELING OF LOVE IS SO PLEASANT.

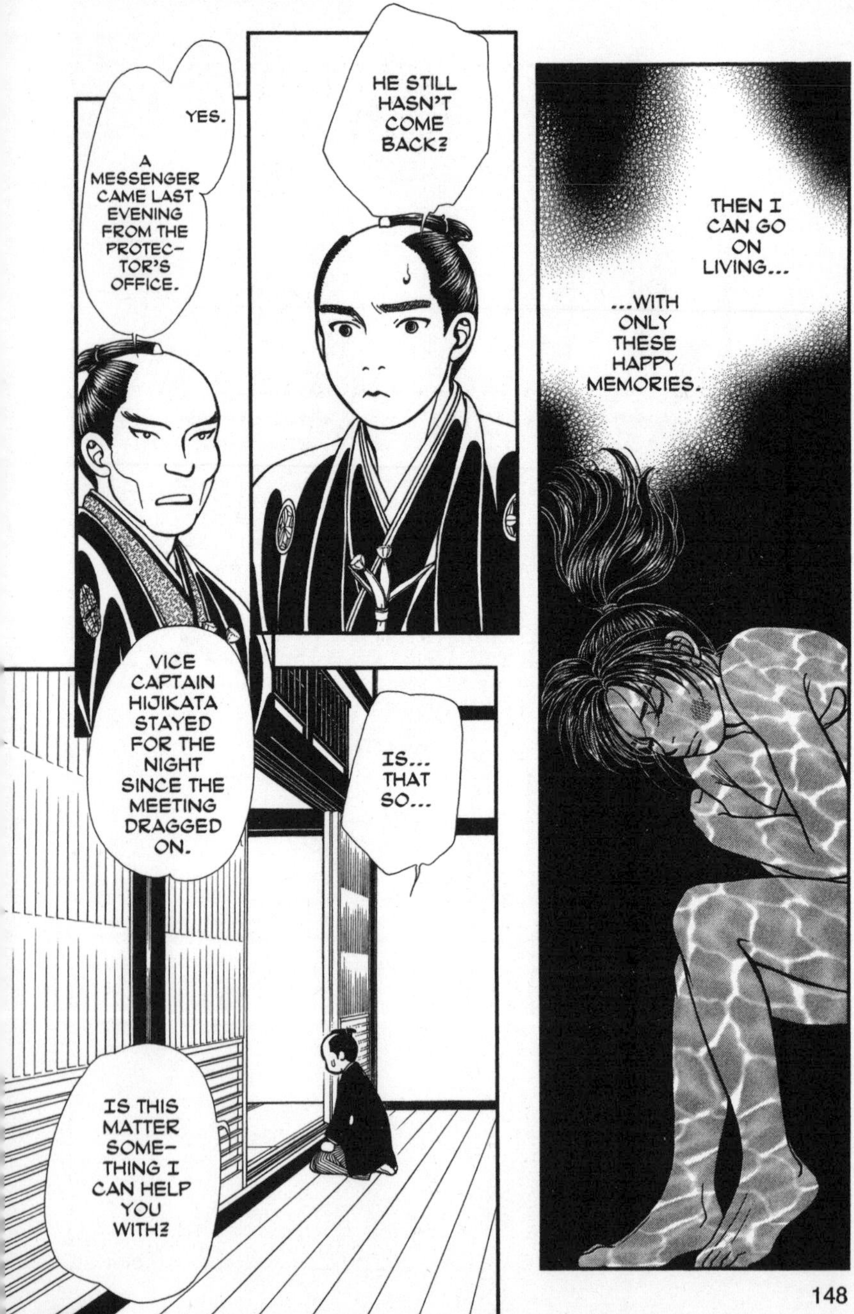
THEN I CAN GO ON LIVING...
...WITH ONLY THESE HAPPY MEMORIES.
HE STILL HASN'T COME BACK?
YES.
A MESSENGER CAME LAST EVENING FROM THE PROTECTOR'S OFFICE.
VICE CAPTAIN HIJIKATA STAYED FOR THE NIGHT SINCE THE MEETING DRAGGED ON.
IS... THAT SO...
IS THIS MATTER SOMETHING I CAN HELP YOU WITH?

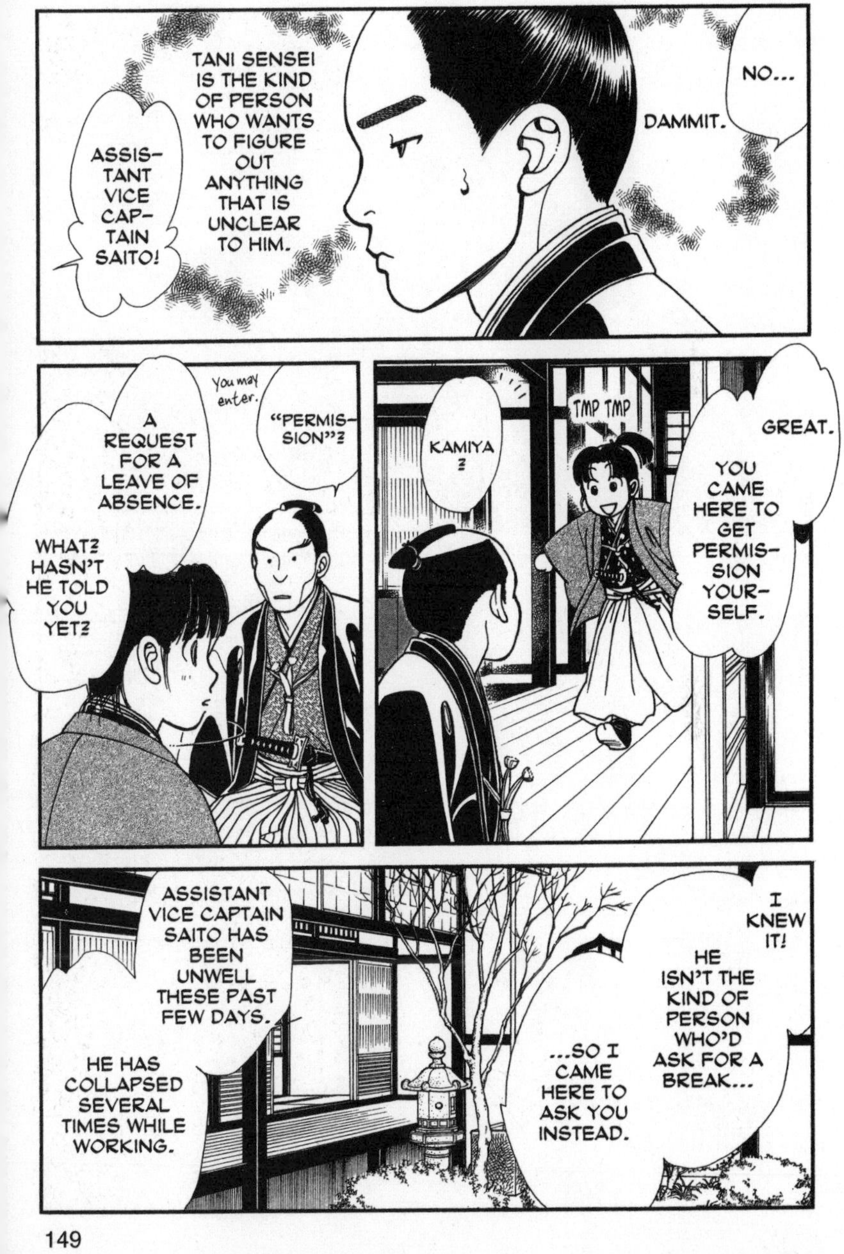
NO... DAMMIT.
TANI SENSEI IS THE KIND OF PERSON WHO WANTS TO FIGURE OUT ANYTHING THAT IS UNCLEAR TO HIM.
ASSISTANT VICE CAPTAIN SAITO!
GREAT. YOU CAME HERE TO GET PERMISSION YOURSELF.
TMP TMP
KAMIYA?
"PERMISSION"?
You may enter.
A REQUEST FOR A LEAVE OF ABSENCE.
WHAT? HASN'T HE TOLD YOU YET?
I KNEW IT! HE ISN'T THE KIND OF PERSON WHO'D ASK FOR A BREAK...
...SO I CAME HERE TO ASK YOU INSTEAD.
ASSISTANT VICE CAPTAIN SAITO HAS BEEN UNWELL THESE PAST FEW DAYS.
HE HAS COLLAPSED SEVERAL TIMES WHILE WORKING.

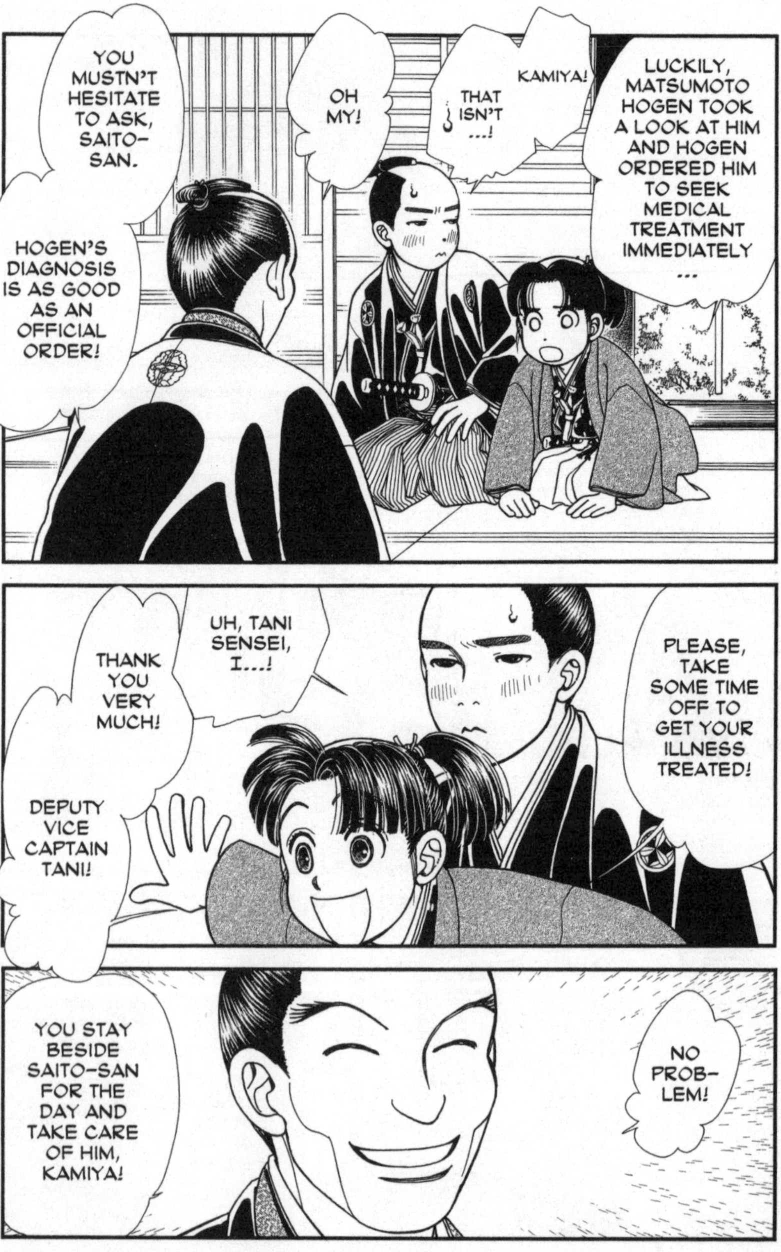
LUCKILY, MATSUMOTO HOGEN TOOK A LOOK AT HIM AND HOGEN ORDERED HIM TO SEEK MEDICAL TREATMENT IMMEDIATELY ...
KAMIYA!
THAT ISN'T ...!
OH MY!
YOU MUSTN'T HESITATE TO ASK, SAITO-SAN.
HOGEN'S DIAGNOSIS IS AS GOOD AS AN OFFICIAL ORDER!
PLEASE, TAKE SOME TIME OFF TO GET YOUR ILLNESS TREATED!
UH, TANI SENSEI, I...!
THANK YOU VERY MUCH!
DEPUTY VICE CAPTAIN TANI!
NO PROB-LEM!
YOU STAY BESIDE SAITO-SAN FOR THE DAY AND TAKE CARE OF HIM, KAMIYA!

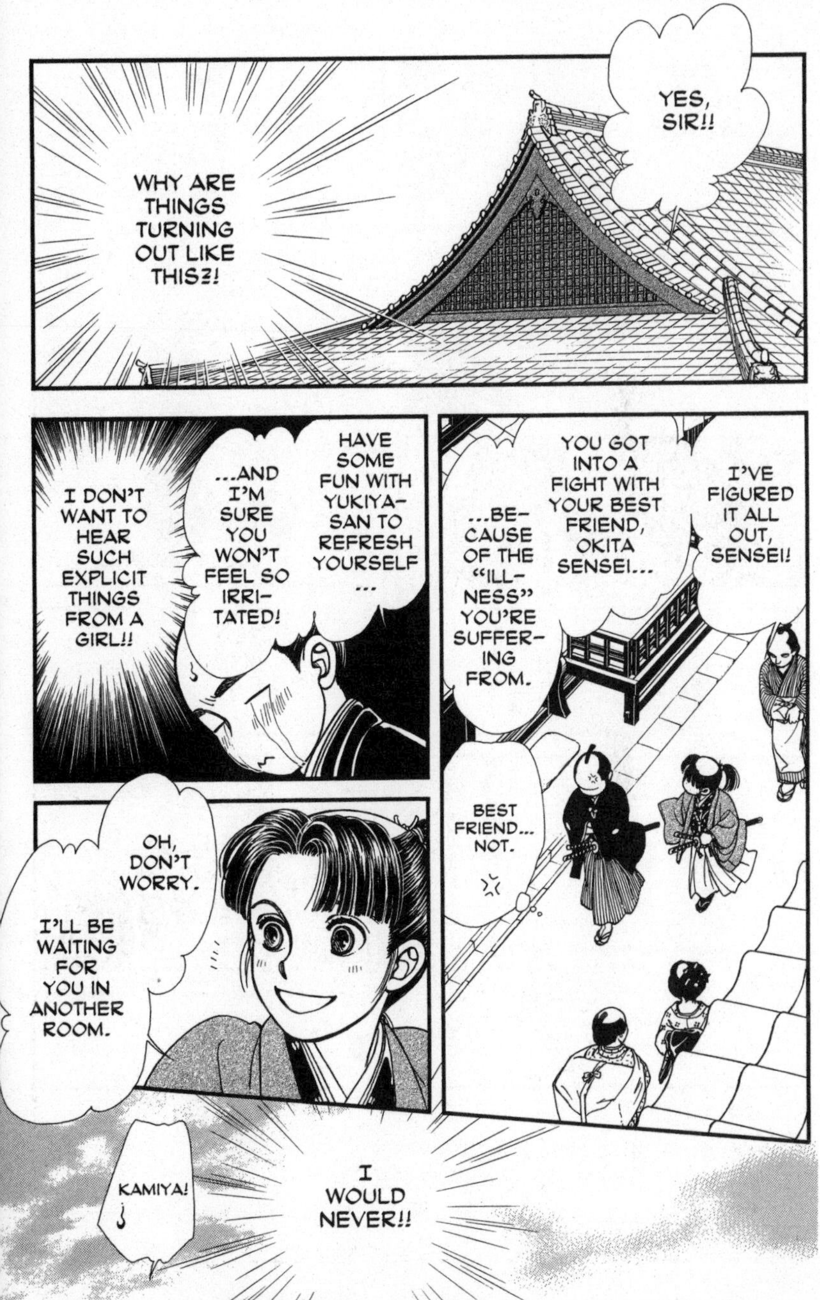
YES, SIR!!
WHY ARE THINGS TURNING OUT LIKE THIS?!
I'VE FIGURED IT ALL OUT, SENSEI!
YOU GOT INTO A FIGHT WITH YOUR BEST FRIEND, OKITA SENSEI...
...BECAUSE OF THE "ILLNESS" YOU'RE SUFFERING FROM.
BEST FRIEND... NOT.
HAVE SOME FUN WITH YUKIYA-SAN TO REFRESH YOURSELF...
...AND I'M SURE YOU WON'T FEEL SO IRRITATED!
I DON'T WANT TO HEAR SUCH EXPLICIT THINGS FROM A GIRL!!
OH, DON'T WORRY.
I'LL BE WAITING FOR YOU IN ANOTHER ROOM.
I WOULD NEVER!!
KAMIYA!

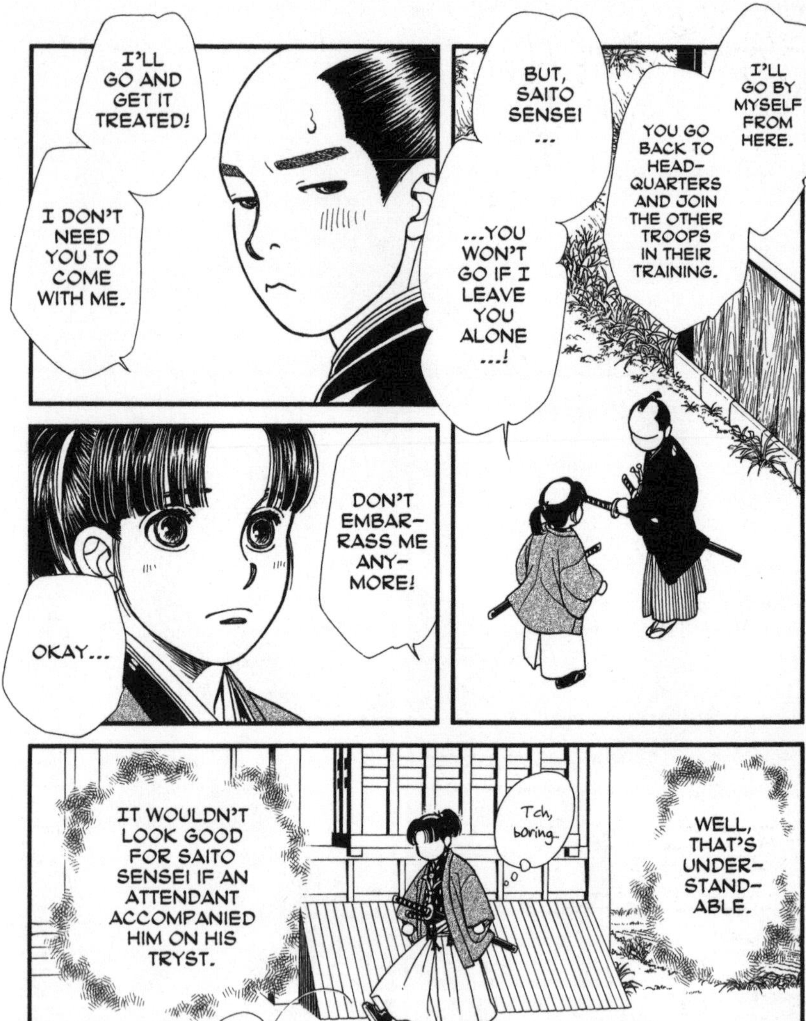
I'LL GO BY MYSELF FROM HERE.
YOU GO BACK TO HEAD-QUARTERS AND JOIN THE OTHER TROOPS IN THEIR TRAINING.
BUT, SAITO SENSEI...
...YOU WON'T GO IF I LEAVE YOU ALONE...!
I'LL GO AND GET IT TREATED!
I DON'T NEED YOU TO COME WITH ME.
DON'T EMBAR-RASS ME ANY-MORE!
OKAY...
WELL, THAT'S UNDER-STAND-ABLE.
Tch, boring..
IT WOULDN'T LOOK GOOD FOR SAITO SENSEI IF AN ATTENDANT ACCOMPANIED HIM ON HIS TRYST.

BUT...

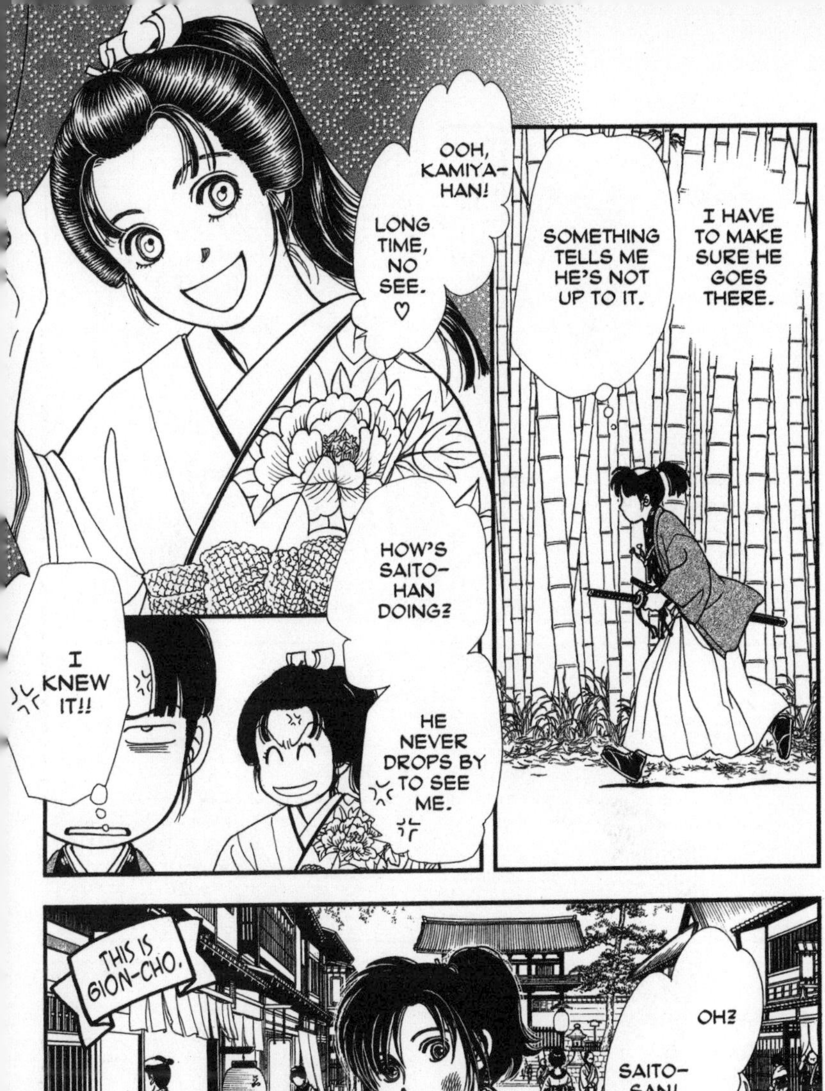
I HAVE TO MAKE SURE HE GOES THERE.
SOMETHING TELLS ME HE'S NOT UP TO IT.
OOH, KAMIYA-HAN!
LONG TIME, NO SEE. ♡
HOW'S SAITO-HAN DOING?
HE NEVER DROPS BY TO SEE ME.
I KNEW IT!!
OH?
SAITO-SAN!
THIS IS GION-CHO.

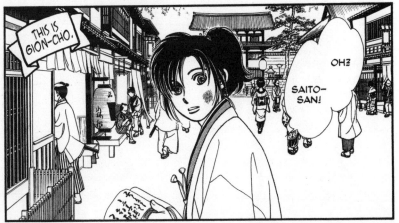

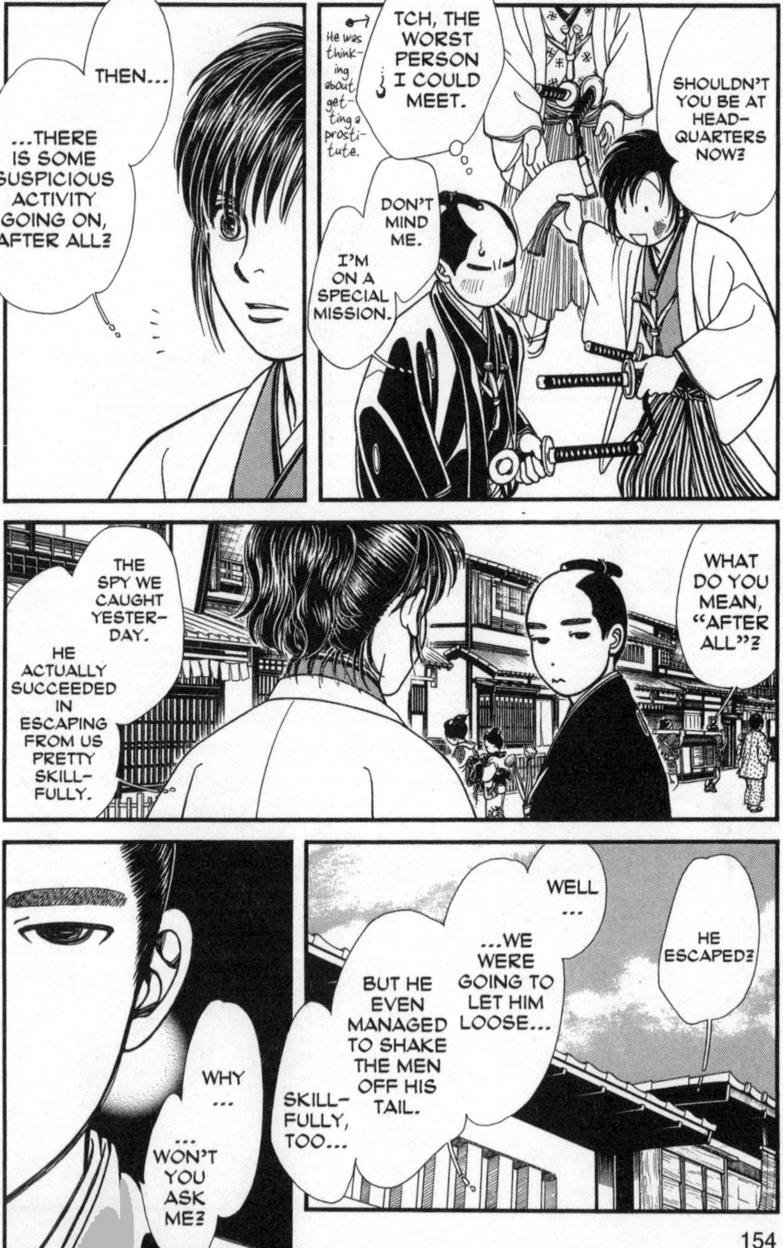
SHOULDN'T YOU BE AT HEADQUARTERS NOW?
TCH, THE WORST PERSON I COULD MEET.
He was thinking about getting a prostitute.
DON'T MIND ME.
I'M ON A SPECIAL MISSION.
THEN...
...THERE IS SOME SUSPICIOUS ACTIVITY GOING ON, AFTER ALL?
WHAT DO YOU MEAN, "AFTER ALL"?
THE SPY WE CAUGHT YESTERDAY.
HE ACTUALLY SUCCEEDED IN ESCAPING FROM US PRETTY SKILLFULLY.
HE ESCAPED?
WELL...
...WE WERE GOING TO LET HIM LOOSE...
BUT HE EVEN MANAGED TO SHAKE THE MEN OFF HIS TAIL.
SKILLFULLY, TOO...
WHY...
...WON'T YOU ASK ME?

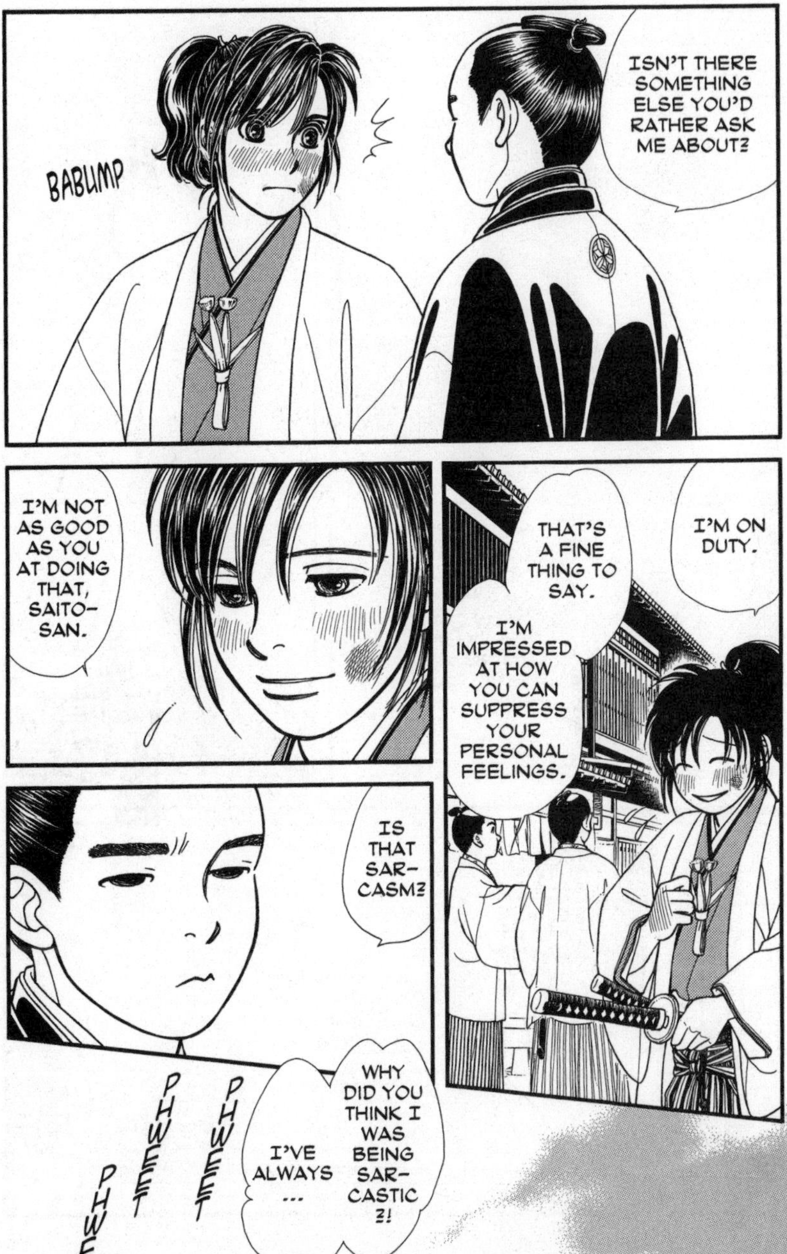
ISN'T THERE SOMETHING ELSE YOU'D RATHER ASK ME ABOUT?
BABUMP
I'M ON DUTY.
THAT'S A FINE THING TO SAY.
I'M IMPRESSED AT HOW YOU CAN SUPPRESS YOUR PERSONAL FEELINGS.
I'M NOT AS GOOD AS YOU AT DOING THAT, SAITO-SAN.
IS THAT SAR-CASM?
WHY DID YOU THINK I WAS BEING SAR-CASTIC?!
I'VE ALWAYS ...
PHWEET
PHWEET
PHWEET

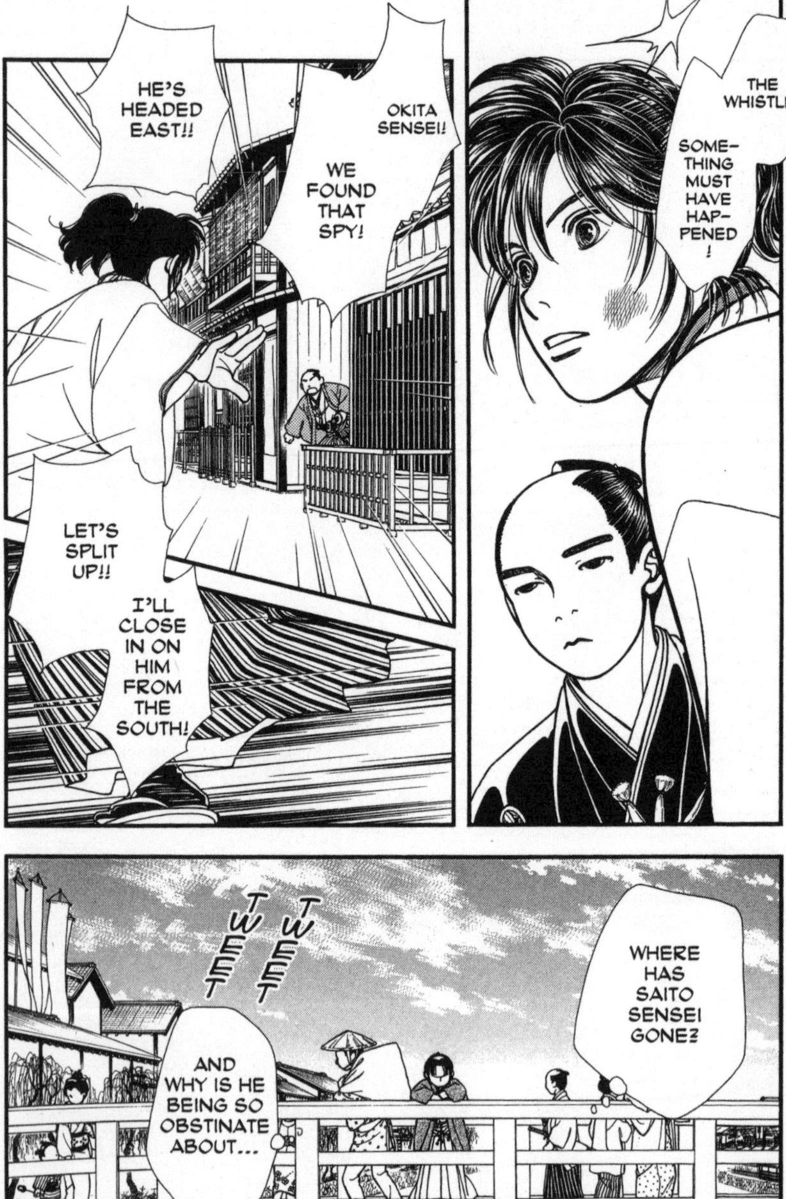
THE WHISTLE!
SOMETHING MUST HAVE HAPPENED!
OKITA SENSEI!
WE FOUND THAT SPY!
HE'S HEADED EAST!!
LET'S SPLIT UP!!
I'LL CLOSE IN ON HIM FROM THE SOUTH!
TWEET
TWEET
WHERE HAS SAITO SENSEI GONE?
AND WHY IS HE BEING SO OBSTINATE ABOUT...

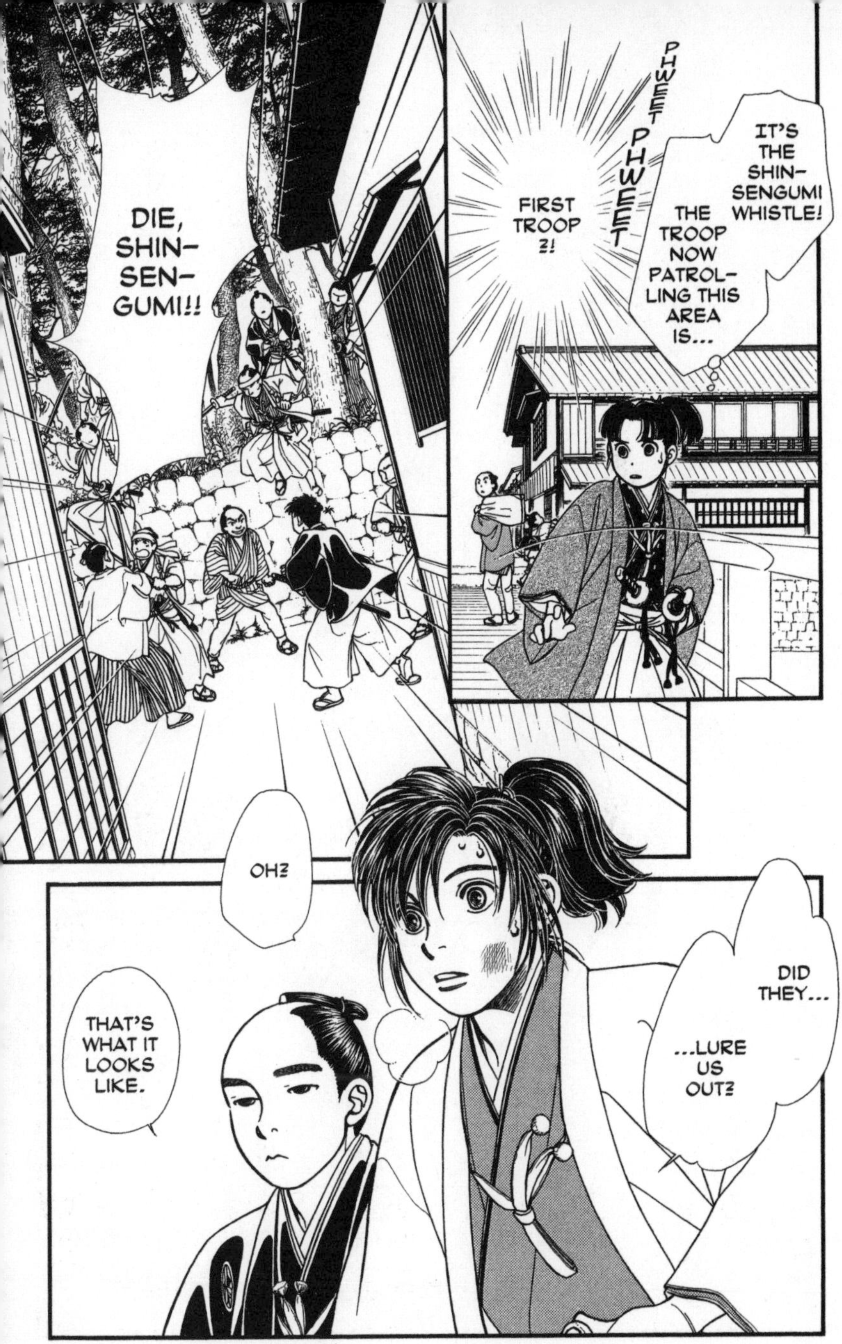
PHWEET PHWEET PHWEET
IT'S THE SHINSENGUMI WHISTLE!
THE TROOP NOW PATROLLING THIS AREA IS...
FIRST TROOP?!
DIE, SHINSENGUMI!!
DID THEY...
...LURE US OUT?
OH?
THAT'S WHAT IT LOOKS LIKE.

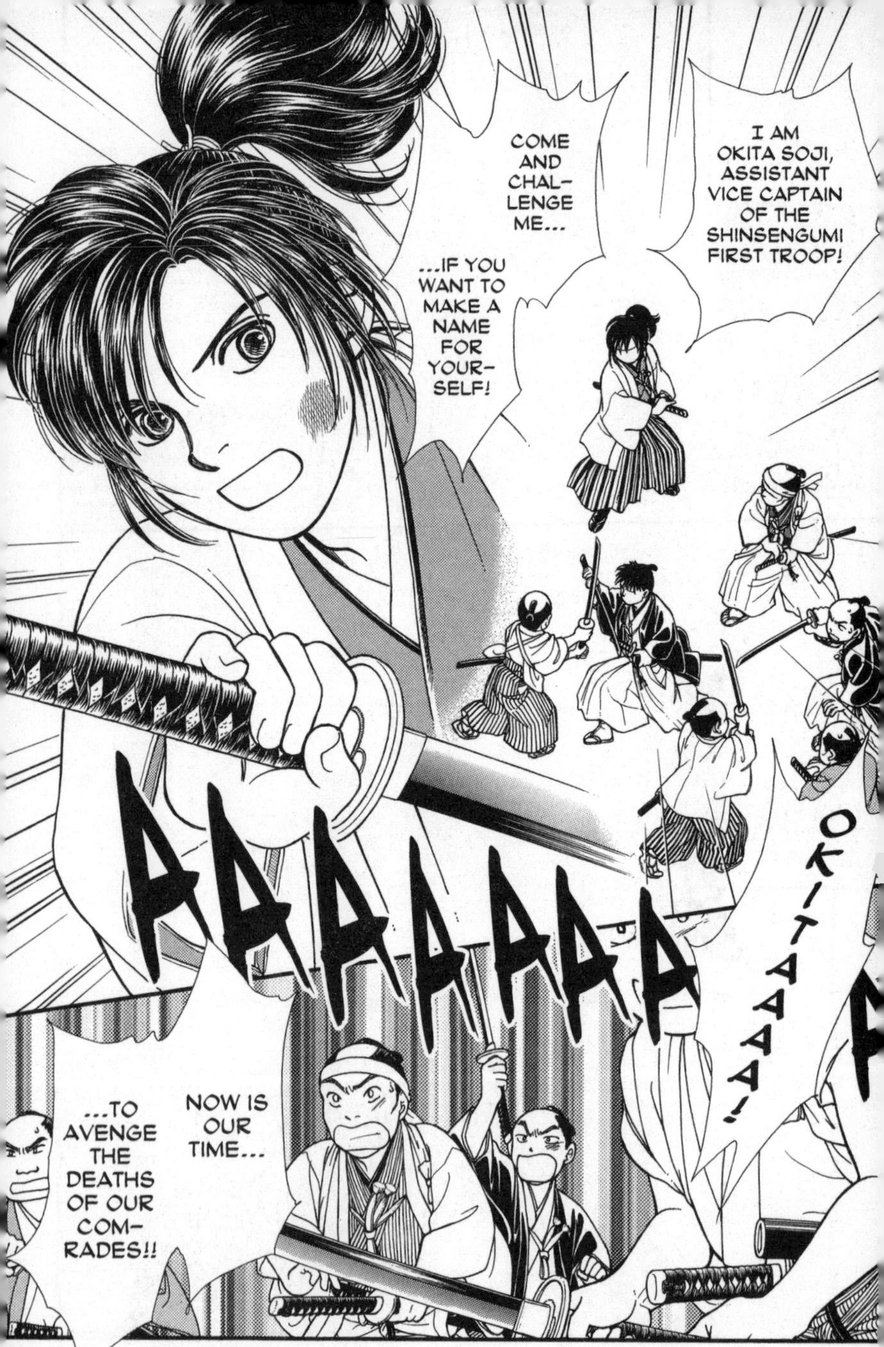
I AM OKITA SOJI, ASSISTANT VICE CAPTAIN OF THE SHINSENGUMI FIRST TROOP!
COME AND CHAL-LENGE ME...
...IF YOU WANT TO MAKE A NAME FOR YOUR-SELF!
OKITAAAAA!
AAAAAAA
NOW IS OUR TIME...
...TO AVENGE THE DEATHS OF OUR COM-RADES!!

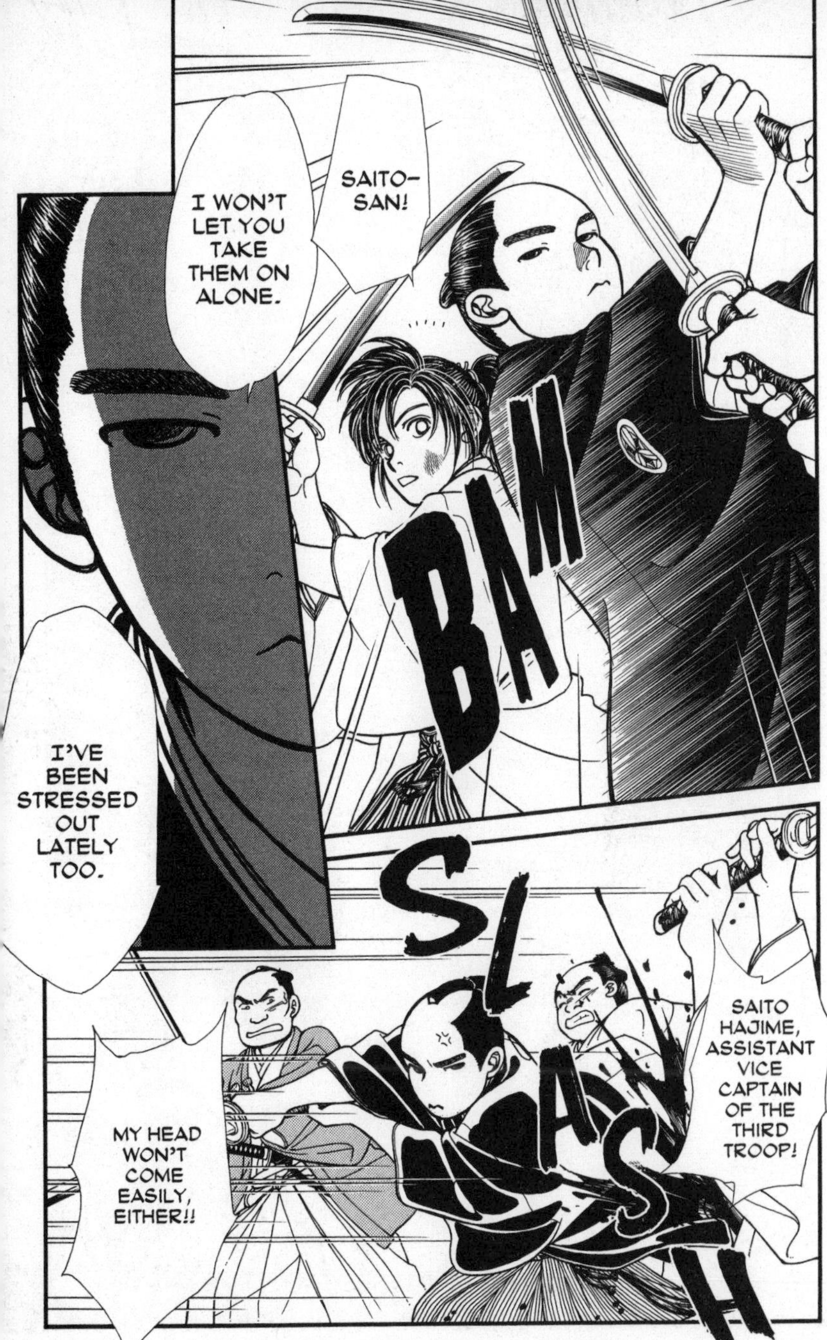
SAITO-SAN!
I WON'T LET YOU TAKE THEM ON ALONE.
BAM
I'VE BEEN STRESSED OUT LATELY TOO.
SLASH
SAITO HAJIME, ASSISTANT VICE CAPTAIN OF THE THIRD TROOP!
MY HEAD WON'T COME EASILY, EITHER!!

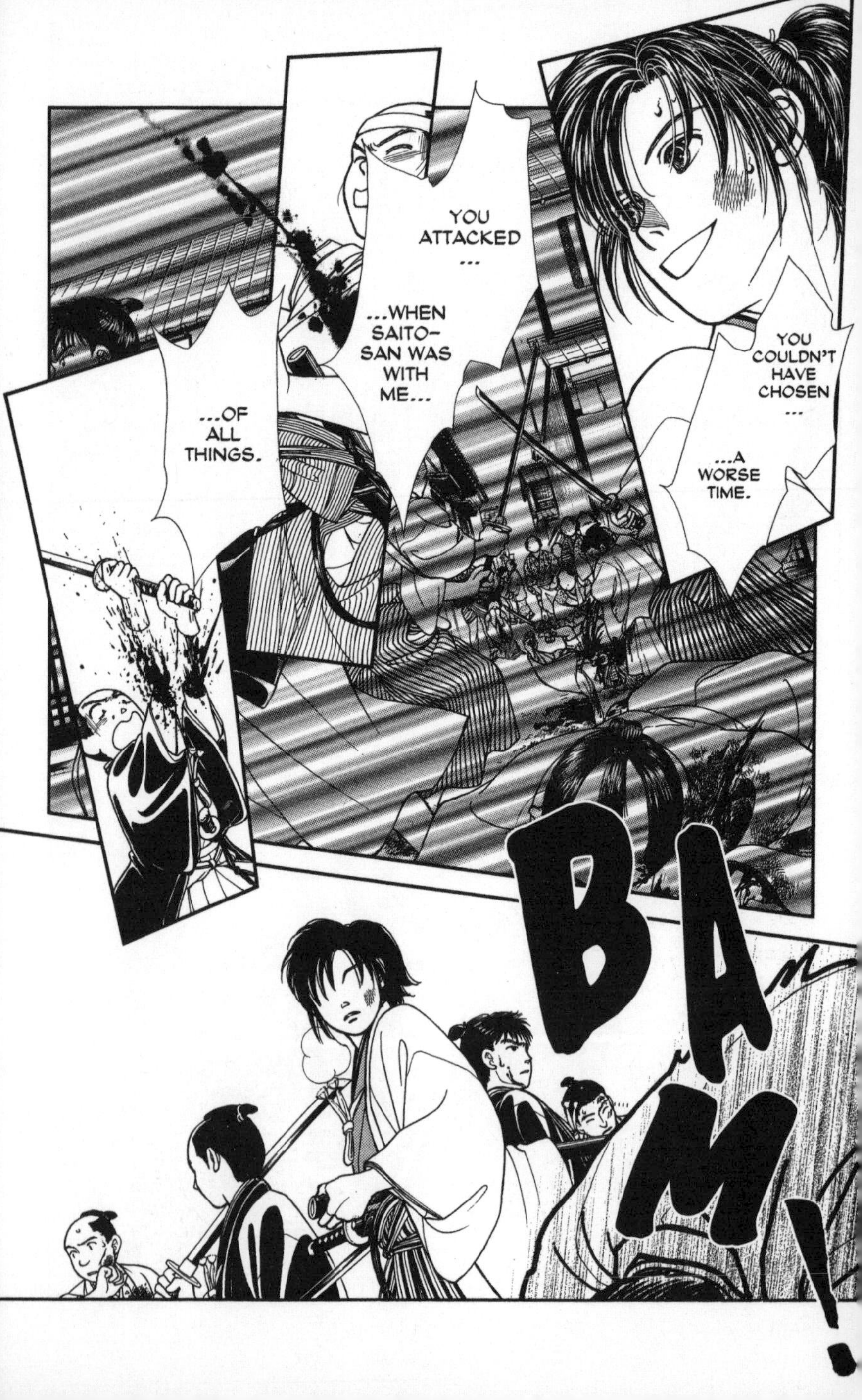
YOU COULDN'T HAVE CHOSEN ...
...A WORSE TIME.
YOU ATTACKED ...
...WHEN SAITO-SAN WAS WITH ME...
...OF ALL THINGS.
BAM!

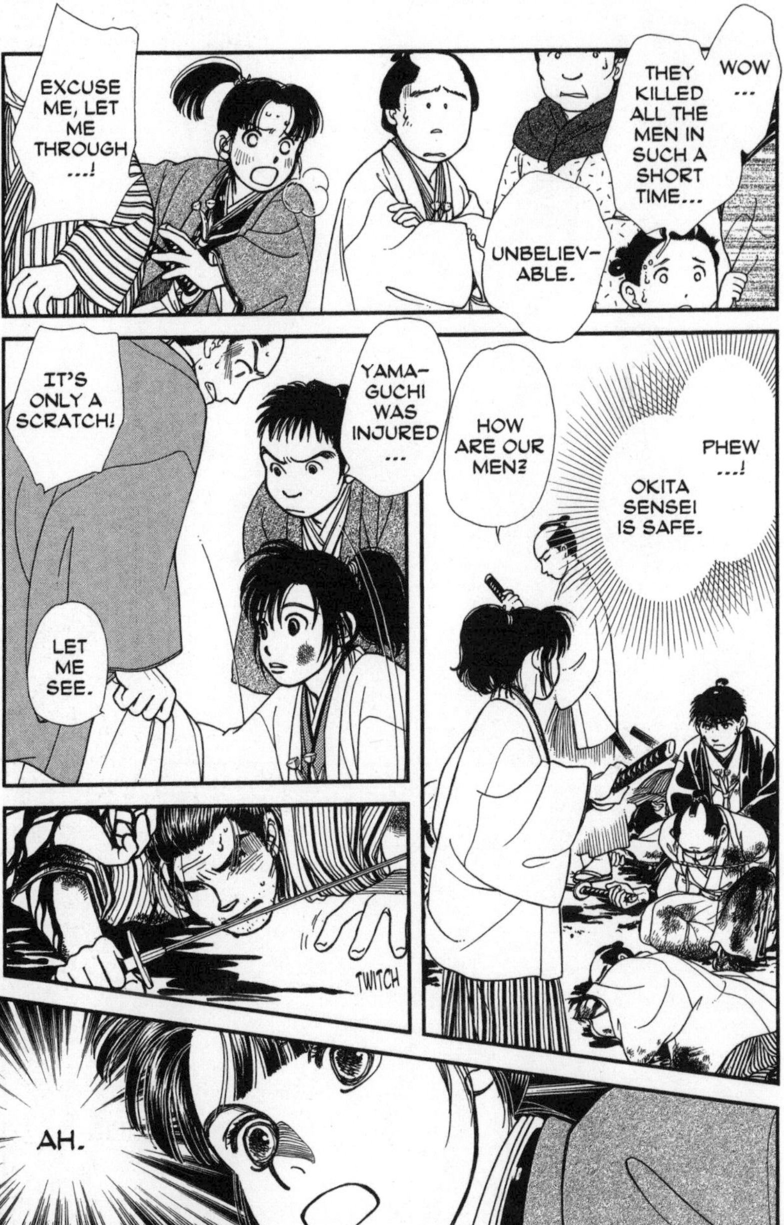
WOW ...
THEY KILLED ALL THE MEN IN SUCH A SHORT TIME...
UNBELIEVABLE.
EXCUSE ME, LET ME THROUGH ...!
PHEW ...!
OKITA SENSEI IS SAFE.
HOW ARE OUR MEN?
YAMAGUCHI WAS INJURED ...
IT'S ONLY A SCRATCH!
LET ME SEE.
TWITCH
AH.

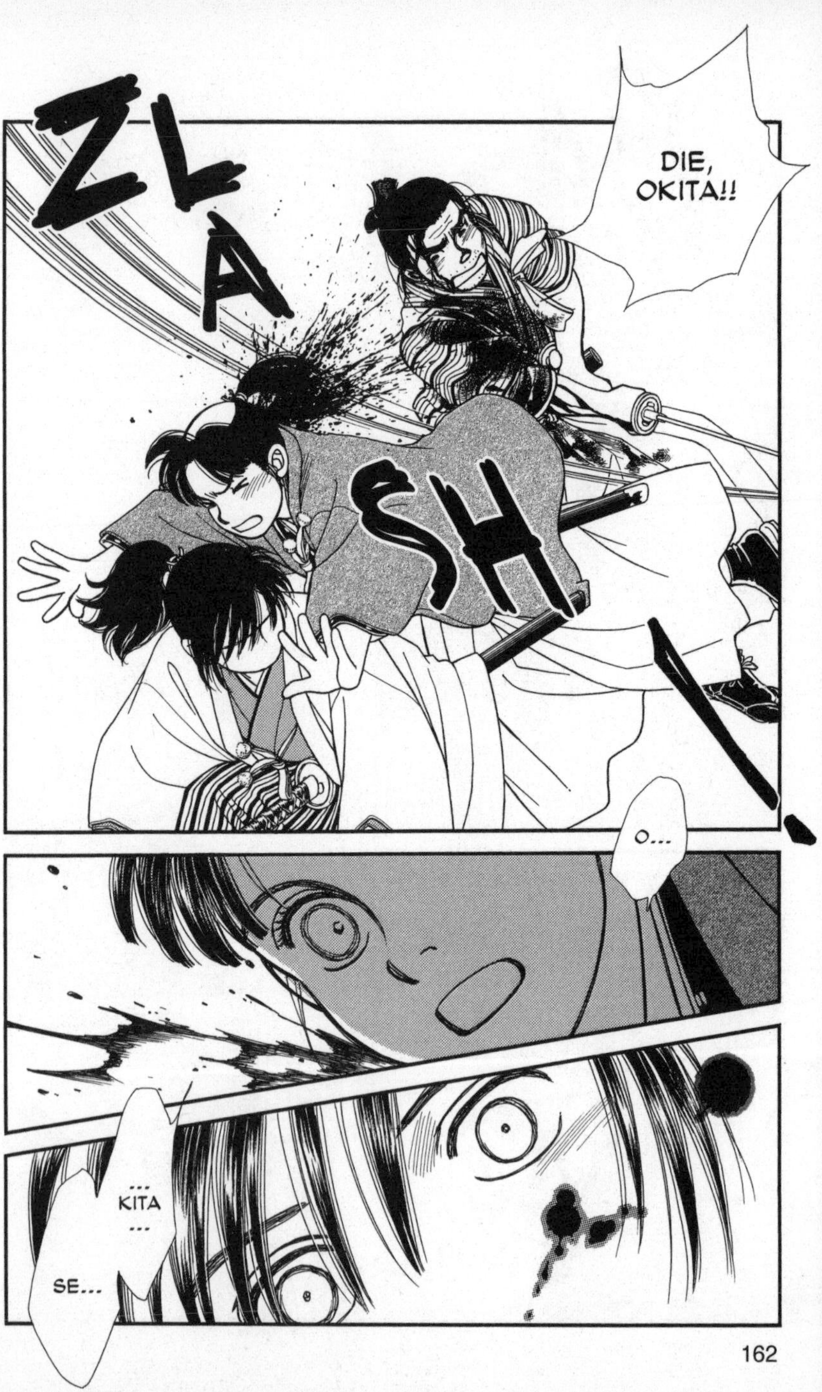
DIE, OKITA!!
ZLASH
O...
...KITA...
SE...

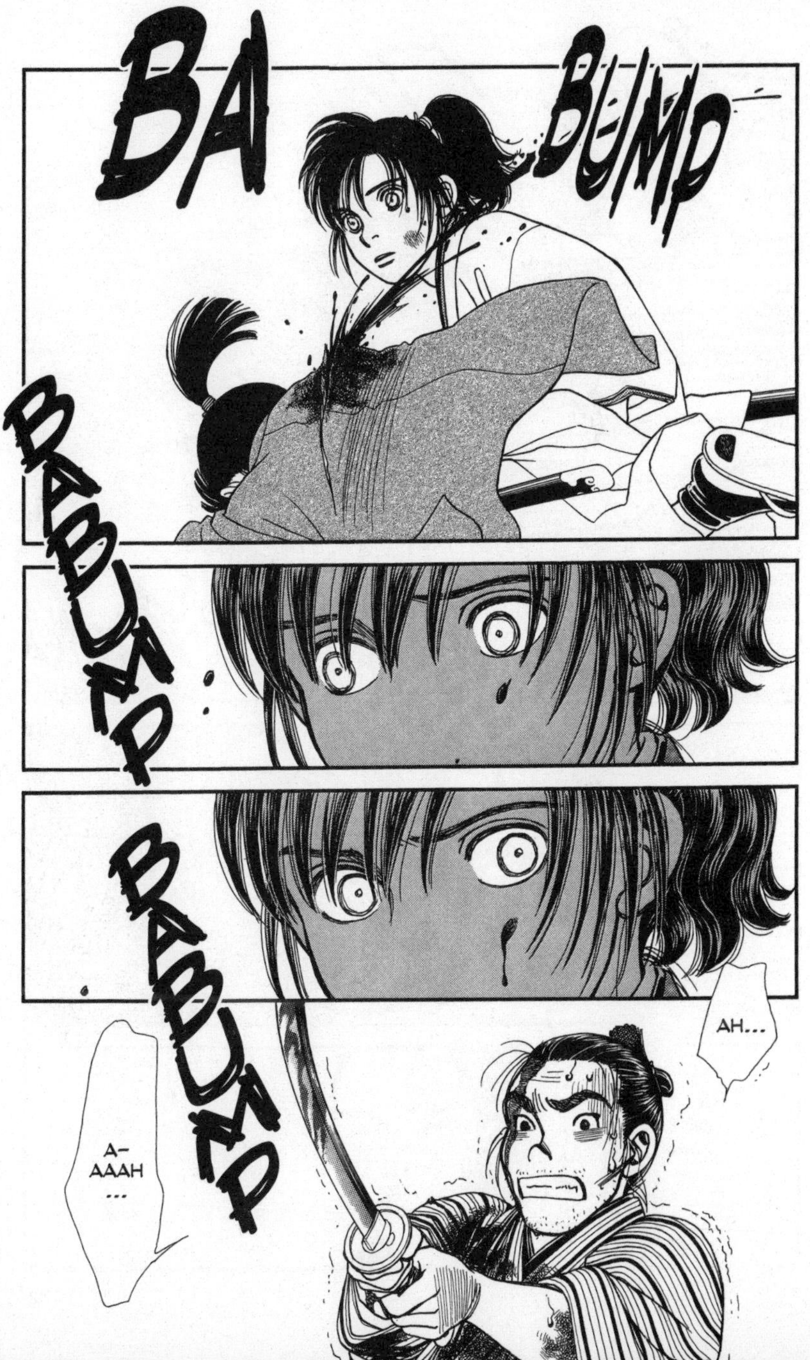
BA BUMP
BABUMP
BABUMP
AH...
A-AAAH...

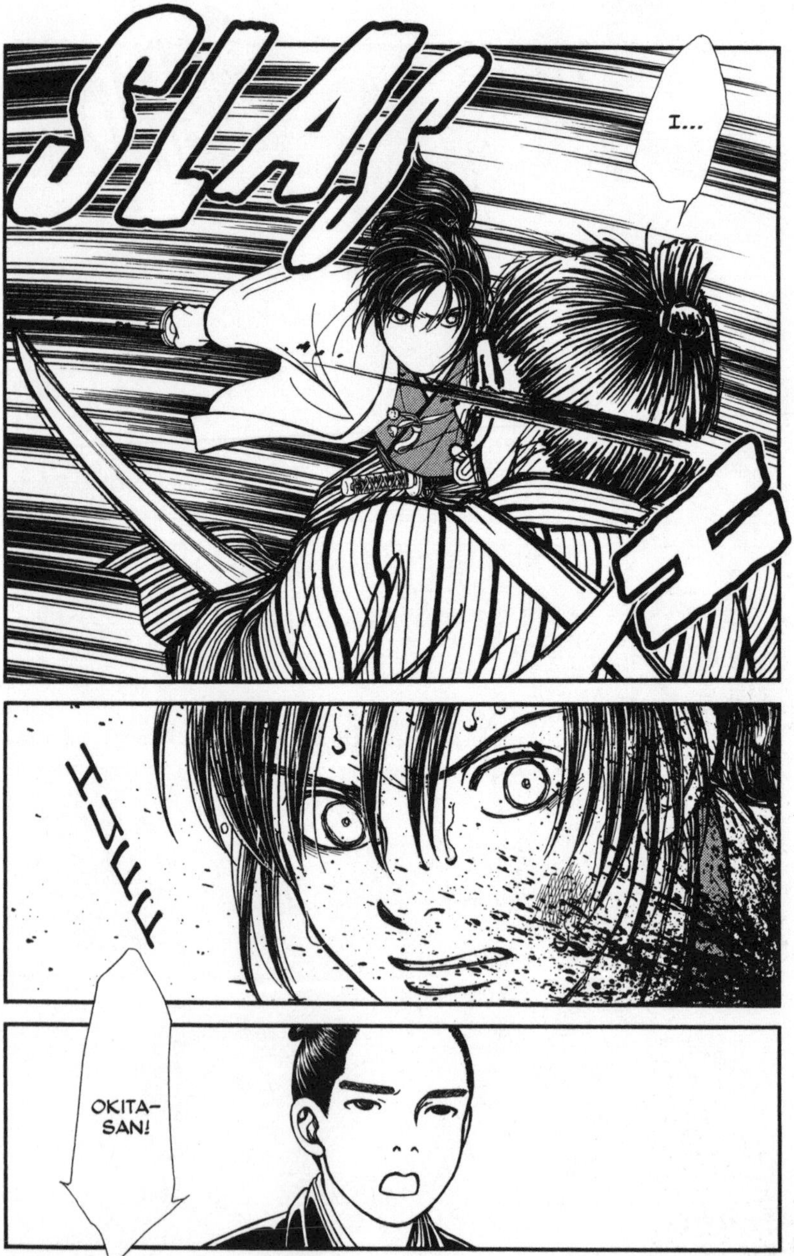
SLAP
I...
HUFF
OKITA-SAN!

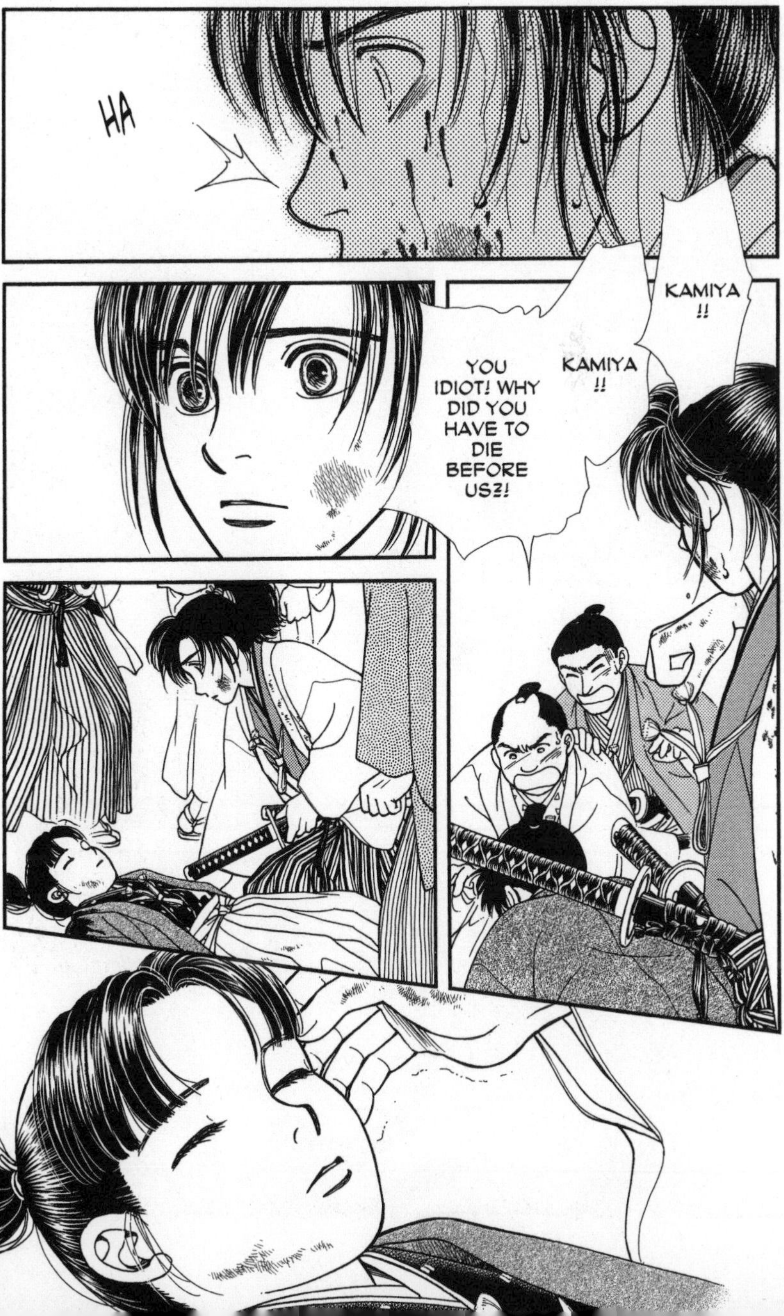
HA
KAMIYA !!
KAMIYA !!
YOU IDIOT! WHY DID YOU HAVE TO DIE BEFORE US?!

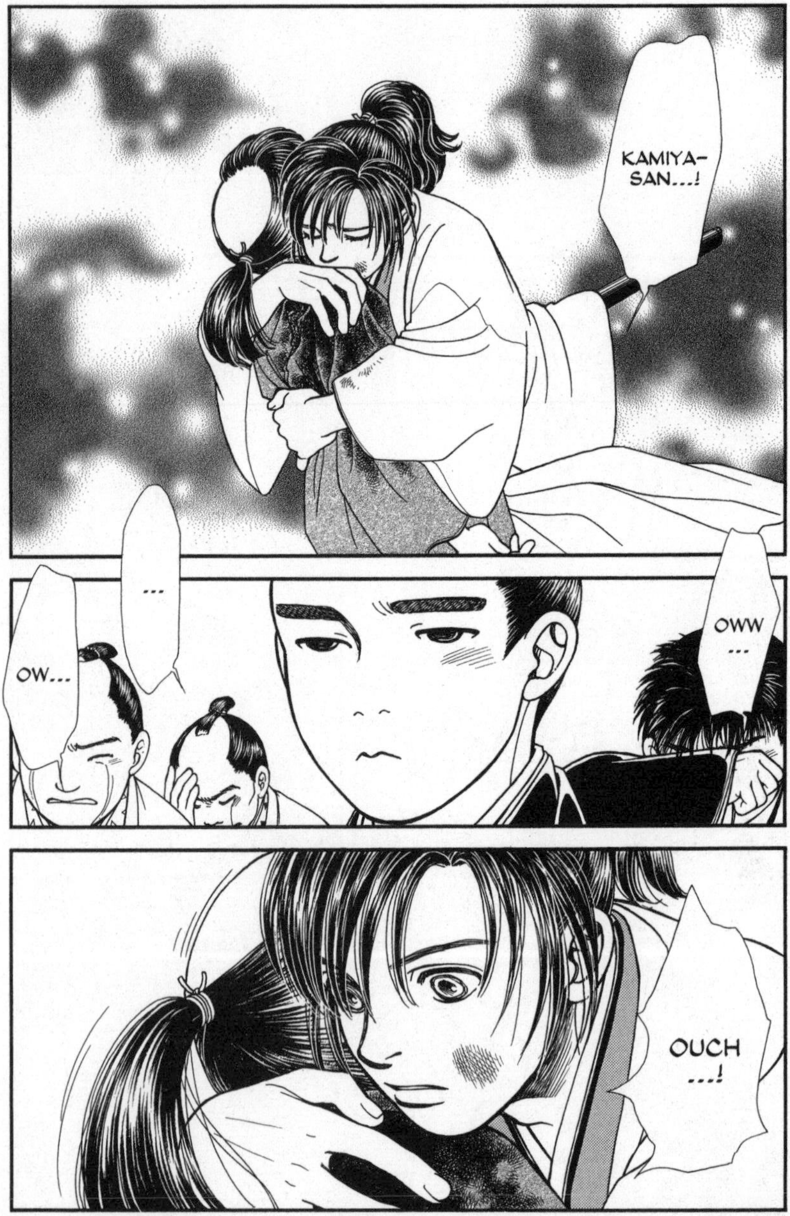
KAMIYA-SAN...!
OWW ...
...
OW...
OUCH ...!

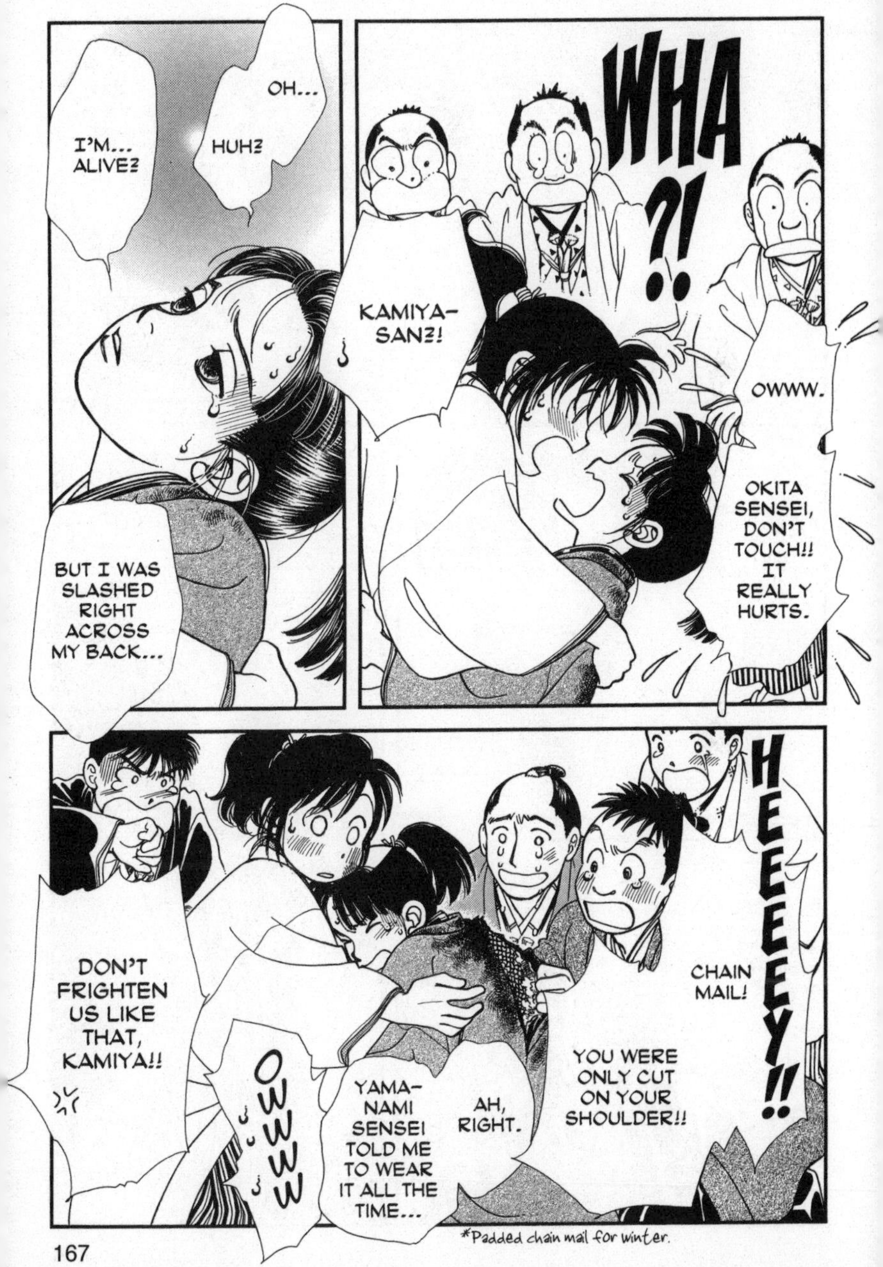
WHA?!
KAMIYA-SAN?!
OWWW.
OKITA SENSEI, DON'T TOUCH!! IT REALLY HURTS.
OH...
HUH?
I'M... ALIVE?
BUT I WAS SLASHED RIGHT ACROSS MY BACK...
HEEEEEY!!
CHAIN MAIL!
YOU WERE ONLY CUT ON YOUR SHOULDER!!
AH, RIGHT.
YAMA-NAMI SENSEI TOLD ME TO WEAR IT ALL THE TIME...
OWWWW
DON'T FRIGHTEN US LIKE THAT, KAMIYA!!

*Padded chain mail for winter.

BUT AT ANY RATE, I'M GLAD...

...THAT YOU'RE ALL RIGHT, OKITA SENSEI.

...!

OKITA SENSEI...

YOU SHOULD GET IT TREATED...

SOMEONE TAKE HER TO MATSUMOTO HOGEN'S PLACE!

IT WOULDN'T HURT TO SAY A WORD OF THANKS TO HIM.

BUT I'M NOT GRATEFUL ABOUT WHAT HE DID!!

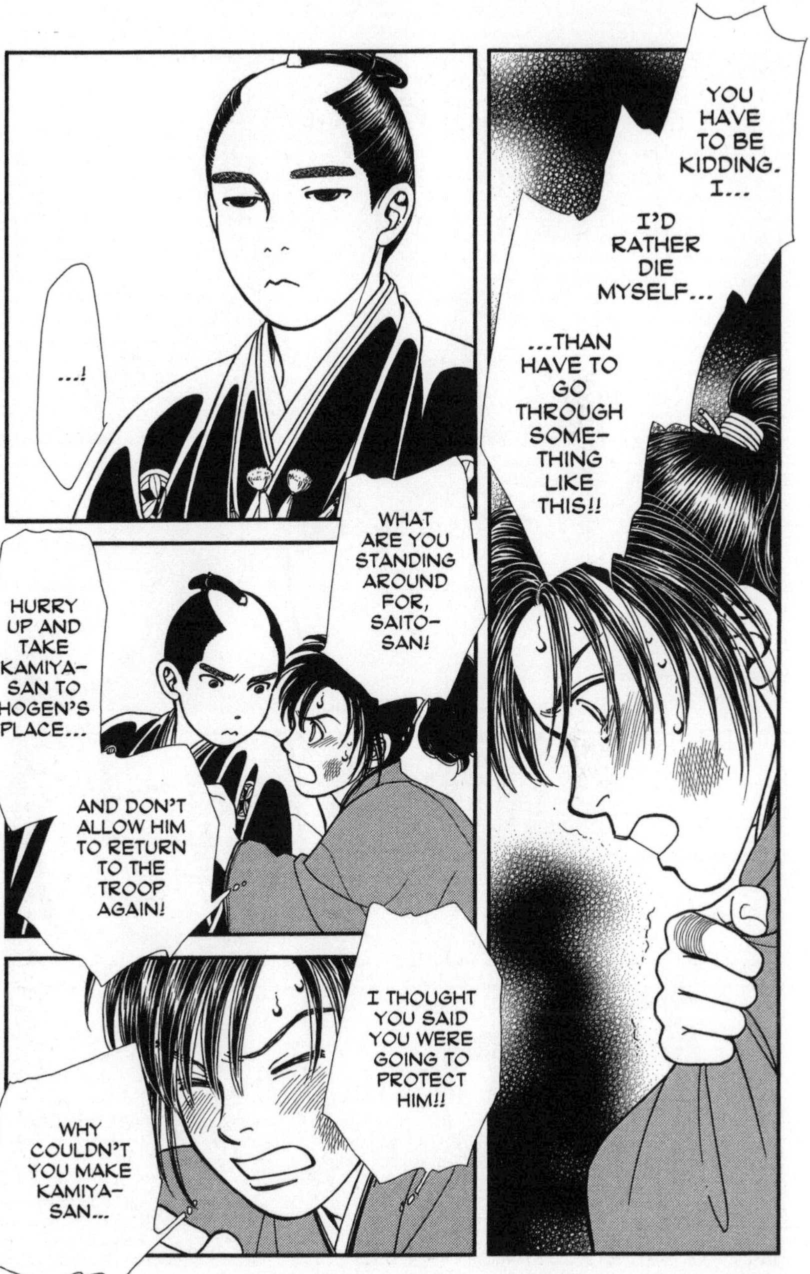
YOU HAVE TO BE KIDDING. I...
I'D RATHER DIE MYSELF...
...THAN HAVE TO GO THROUGH SOME-THING LIKE THIS!!
...!
WHAT ARE YOU STANDING AROUND FOR, SAITO-SAN!
HURRY UP AND TAKE KAMIYA-SAN TO HOGEN'S PLACE...
AND DON'T ALLOW HIM TO RETURN TO THE TROOP AGAIN!
I THOUGHT YOU SAID YOU WERE GOING TO PROTECT HIM!!
WHY COULDN'T YOU MAKE KAMIYA-SAN...

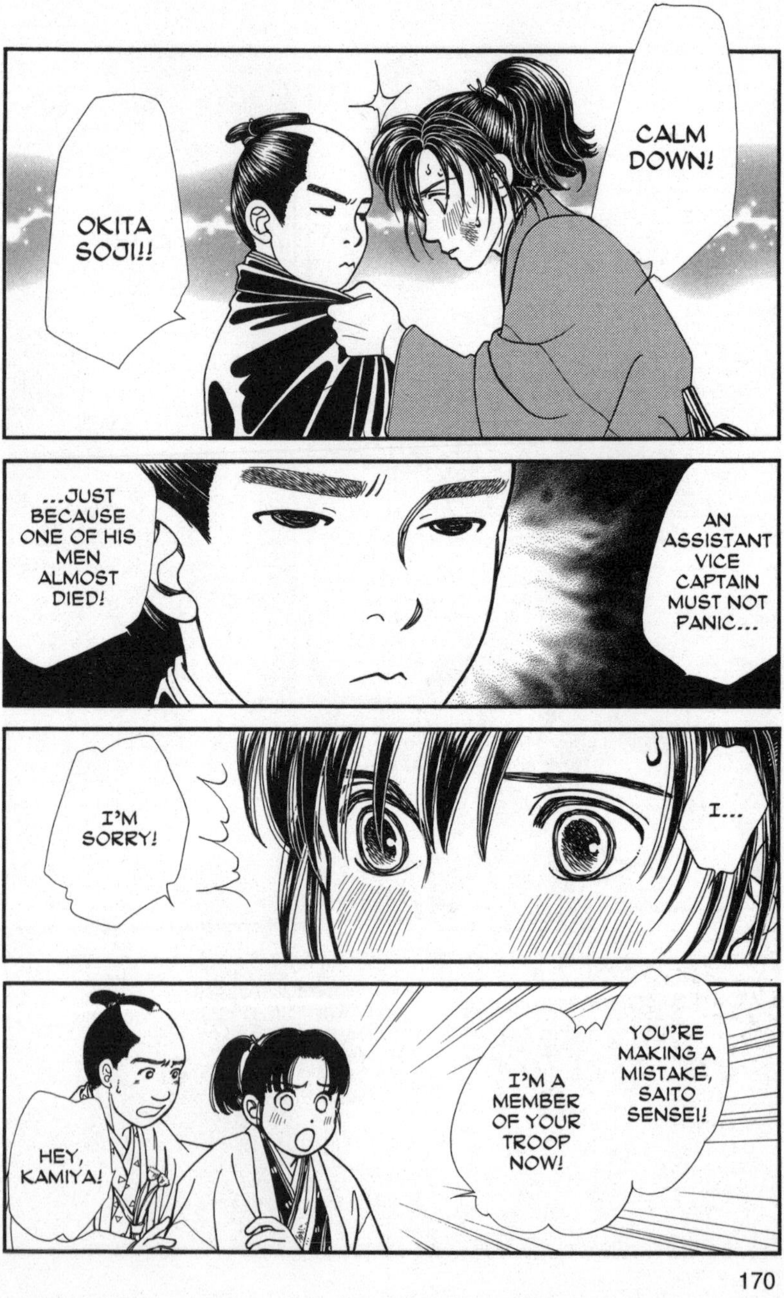
CALM DOWN!
OKITA SOJI!!
AN ASSISTANT VICE CAPTAIN MUST NOT PANIC...
...JUST BECAUSE ONE OF HIS MEN ALMOST DIED!
I...
I'M SORRY!
YOU'RE MAKING A MISTAKE, SAITO SENSEI!
I'M A MEMBER OF YOUR TROOP NOW!
HEY, KAMIYA!

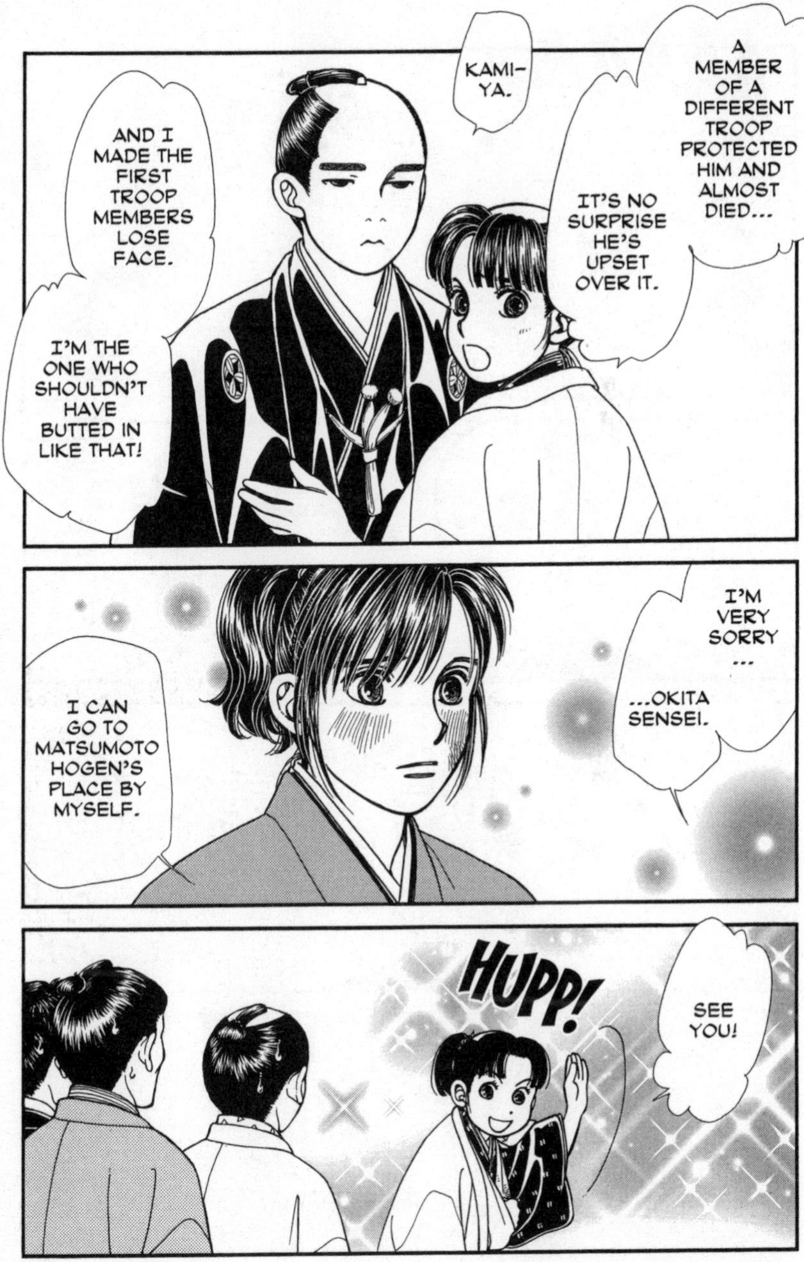
A MEMBER OF A DIFFERENT TROOP PROTECTED HIM AND ALMOST DIED...
IT'S NO SURPRISE HE'S UPSET OVER IT.
KAMI-YA.
AND I MADE THE FIRST TROOP MEMBERS LOSE FACE.
I'M THE ONE WHO SHOULDN'T HAVE BUTTED IN LIKE THAT!
I'M VERY SORRY ...
...OKITA SENSEI.
I CAN GO TO MATSUMOTO HOGEN'S PLACE BY MYSELF.
SEE YOU!
HUPP!

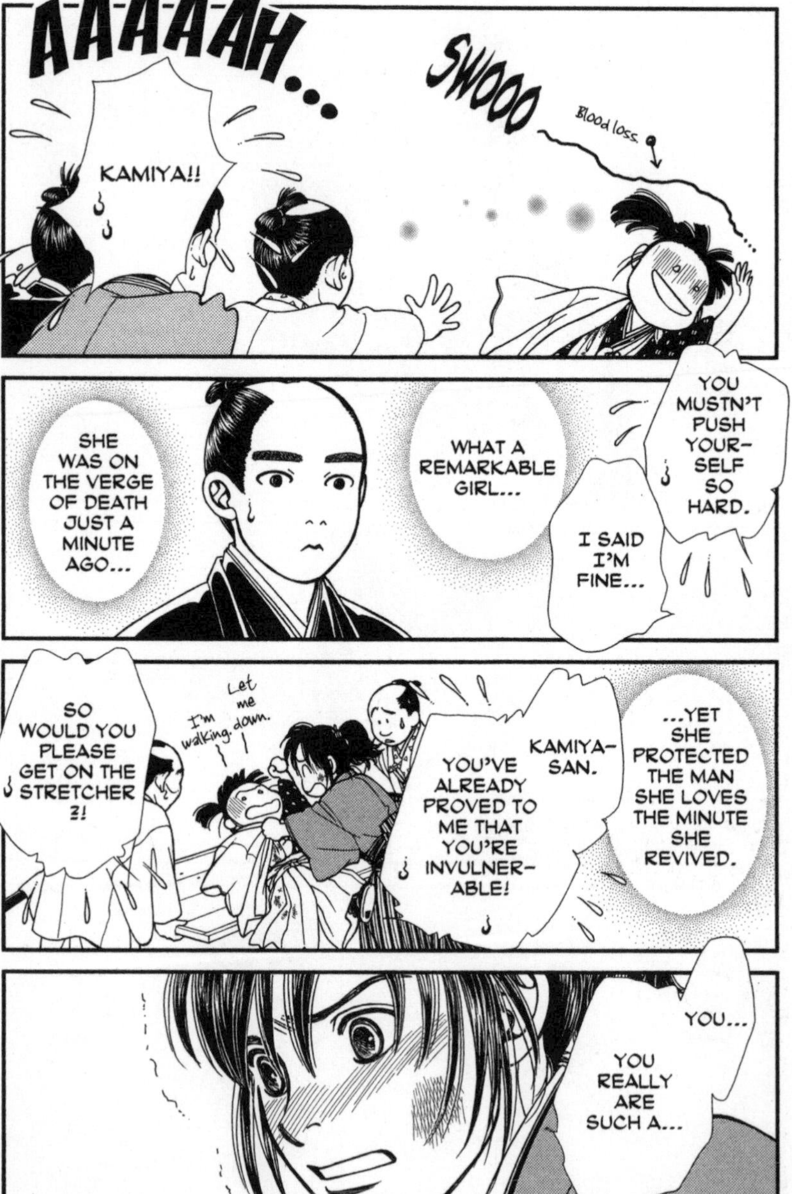

SWOOO
Blood loss.
AAAAAH...
KAMIYA!!
YOU MUSTN'T PUSH YOURSELF SO HARD.
I SAID I'M FINE...
WHAT A REMARKABLE GIRL...
SHE WAS ON THE VERGE OF DEATH JUST A MINUTE AGO...
...YET SHE PROTECTED THE MAN SHE LOVES THE MINUTE SHE REVIVED.
KAMIYA-SAN.
YOU'VE ALREADY PROVED TO ME THAT YOU'RE INVULNERABLE!
Let me down.
I'm walking.
SO WOULD YOU PLEASE GET ON THE STRETCHER?!
YOU...
YOU REALLY ARE SUCH A...

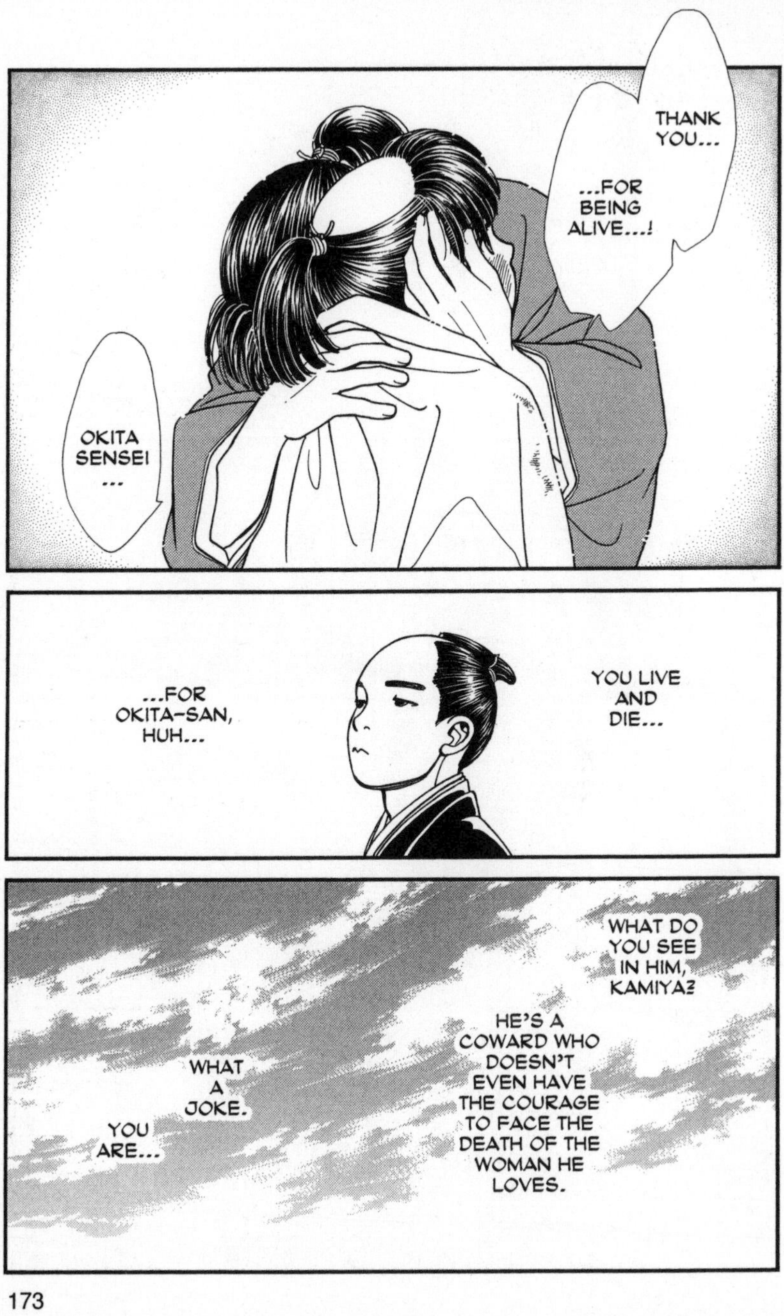
THANK YOU...
...FOR BEING ALIVE...!
OKITA SENSEI ...
YOU LIVE AND DIE...
...FOR OKITA-SAN, HUH...
WHAT DO YOU SEE IN HIM, KAMIYA?
HE'S A COWARD WHO DOESN'T EVEN HAVE THE COURAGE TO FACE THE DEATH OF THE WOMAN HE LOVES.
WHAT A JOKE.
YOU ARE...

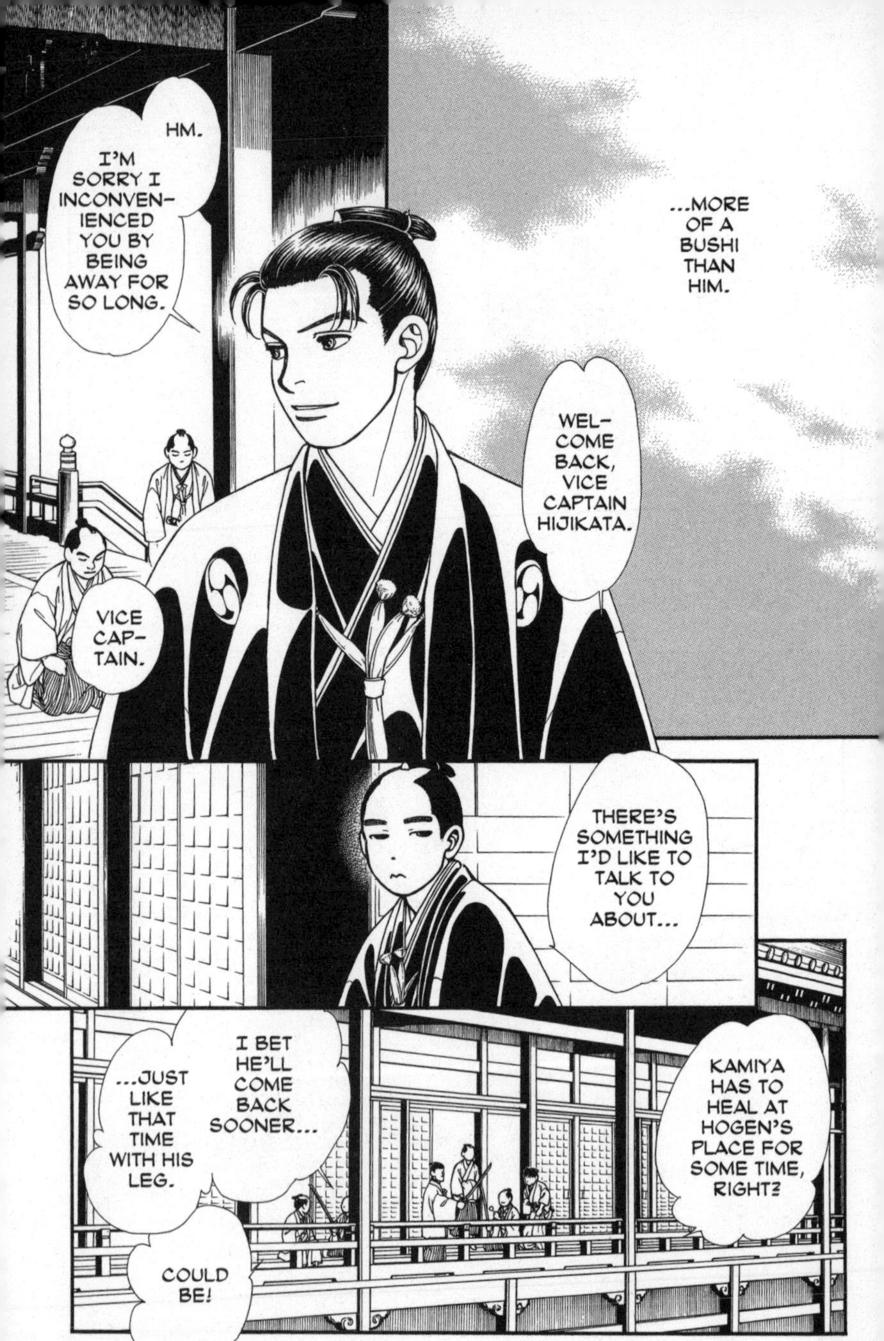
...MORE OF A BUSHI THAN HIM.
WEL-COME BACK, VICE CAPTAIN HIJIKATA.
HM. I'M SORRY I INCONVEN-IENCED YOU BY BEING AWAY FOR SO LONG.
VICE CAP-TAIN.
THERE'S SOMETHING I'D LIKE TO TALK TO YOU ABOUT...
KAMIYA HAS TO HEAL AT HOGEN'S PLACE FOR SOME TIME, RIGHT?
I BET HE'LL COME BACK SOONER...
...JUST LIKE THAT TIME WITH HIS LEG.
COULD BE!

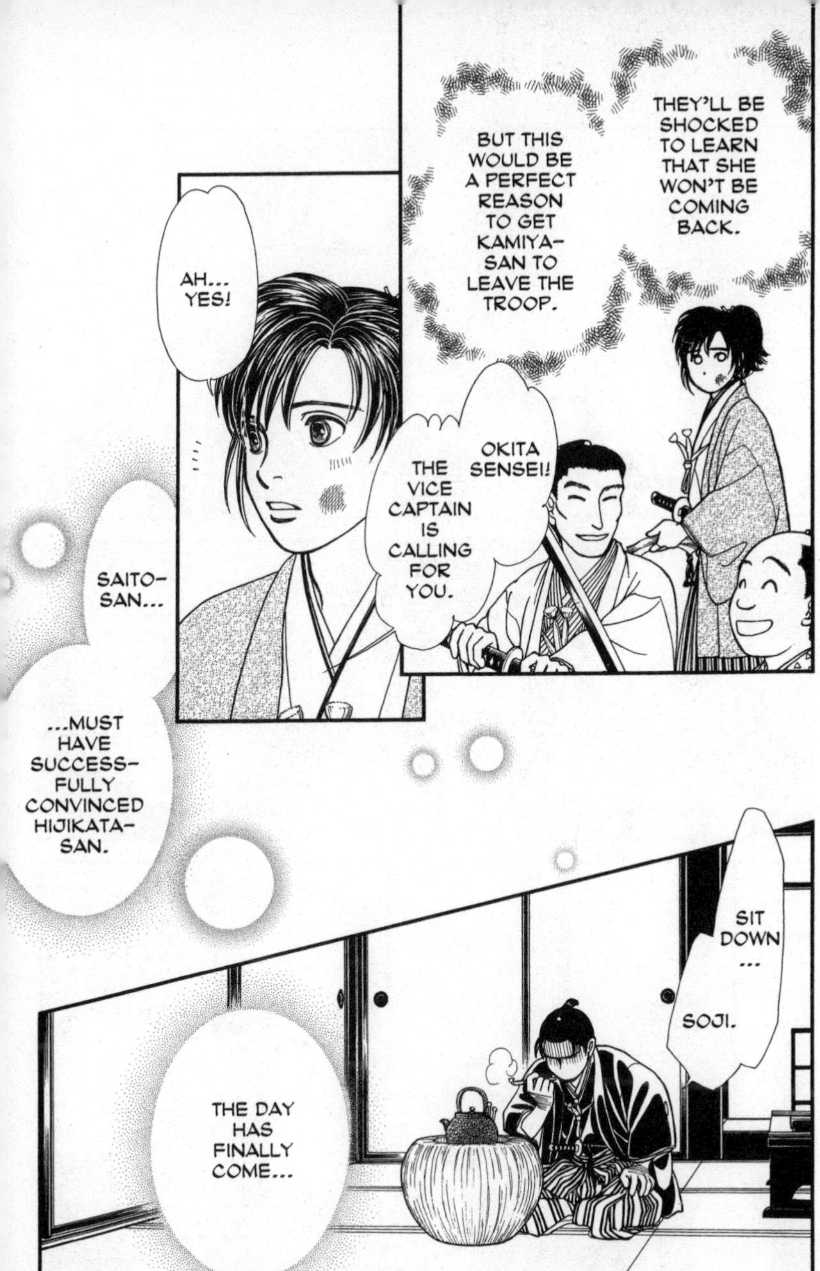
THEY'LL BE SHOCKED TO LEARN THAT SHE WON'T BE COMING BACK.
BUT THIS WOULD BE A PERFECT REASON TO GET KAMIYA-SAN TO LEAVE THE TROOP.
OKITA SENSEI! THE VICE CAPTAIN IS CALLING FOR YOU.
AH... YES!
SAITO-SAN...
...MUST HAVE SUCCESSFULLY CONVINCED HIJIKATA-SAN.
SIT DOWN... SOJI.
THE DAY HAS FINALLY COME...

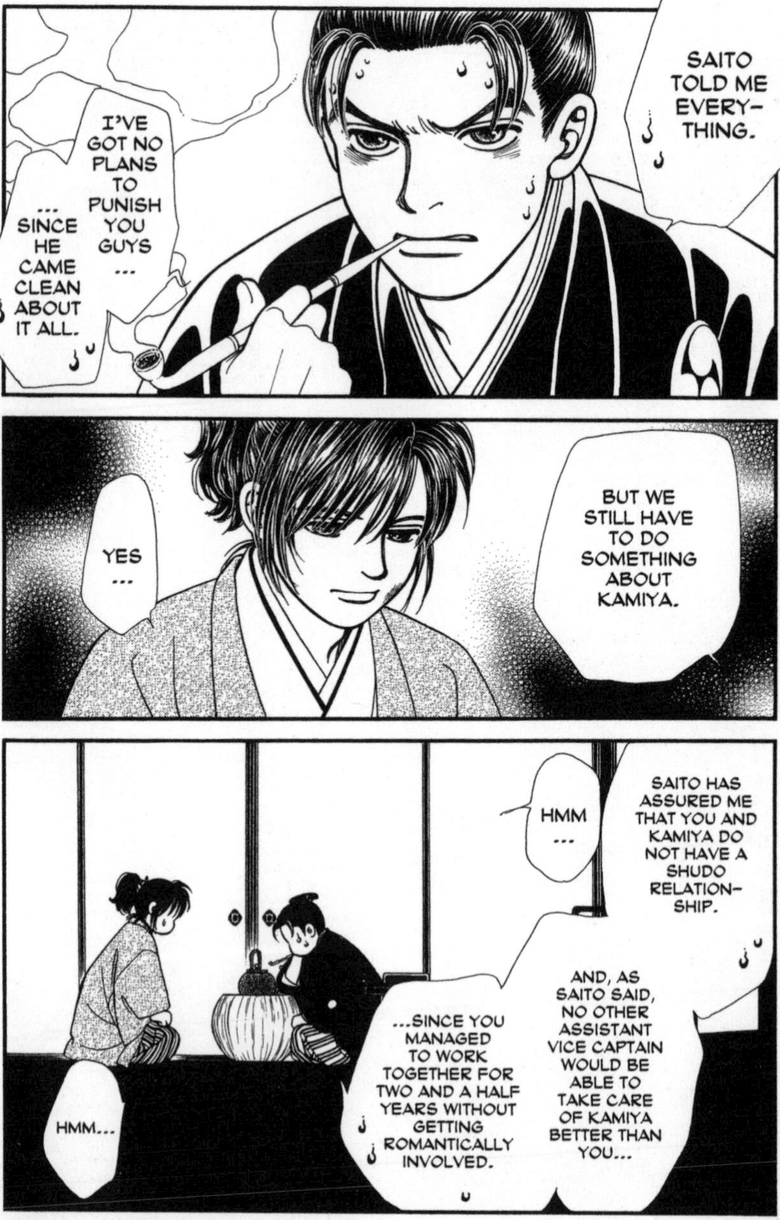
SAITO TOLD ME EVERYTHING.
I'VE GOT NO PLANS TO PUNISH YOU GUYS...
...SINCE HE CAME CLEAN ABOUT IT ALL.
BUT WE STILL HAVE TO DO SOMETHING ABOUT KAMIYA.
YES...
SAITO HAS ASSURED ME THAT YOU AND KAMIYA DO NOT HAVE A SHUDO RELATIONSHIP.
HMM...
AND, AS SAITO SAID, NO OTHER ASSISTANT VICE CAPTAIN WOULD BE ABLE TO TAKE CARE OF KAMIYA BETTER THAN YOU...
...SINCE YOU MANAGED TO WORK TOGETHER FOR TWO AND A HALF YEARS WITHOUT GETTING ROMANTICALLY INVOLVED.
HMM...

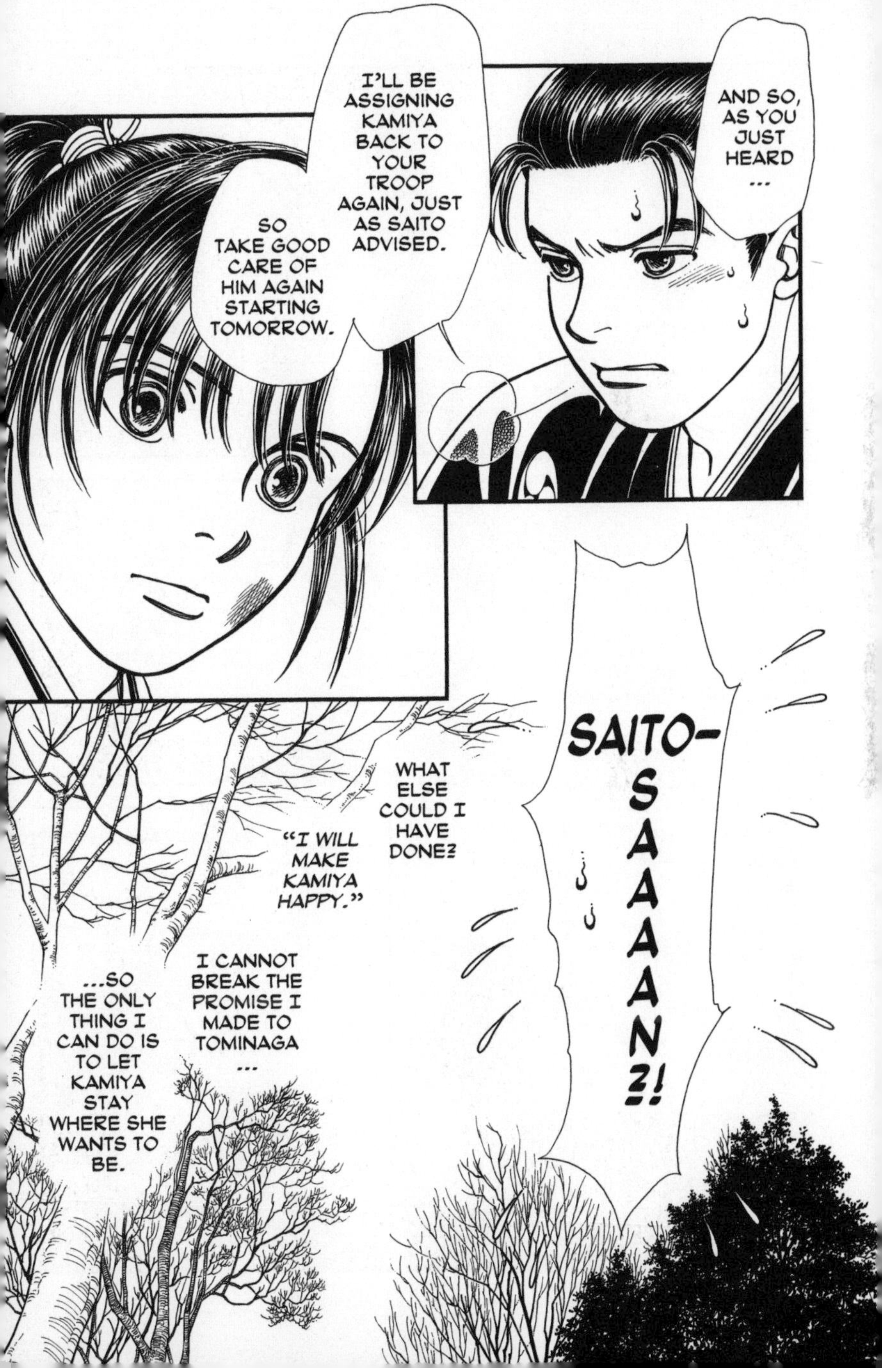
AND SO, AS YOU JUST HEARD...
I'LL BE ASSIGNING KAMIYA BACK TO YOUR TROOP AGAIN, JUST AS SAITO ADVISED.
SO TAKE GOOD CARE OF HIM AGAIN STARTING TOMORROW.
SAITO-SAAAAAN?!
WHAT ELSE COULD I HAVE DONE?
"I WILL MAKE KAMIYA HAPPY."
I CANNOT BREAK THE PROMISE I MADE TO TOMINAGA...
...SO THE ONLY THING I CAN DO IS TO LET KAMIYA STAY WHERE SHE WANTS TO BE.

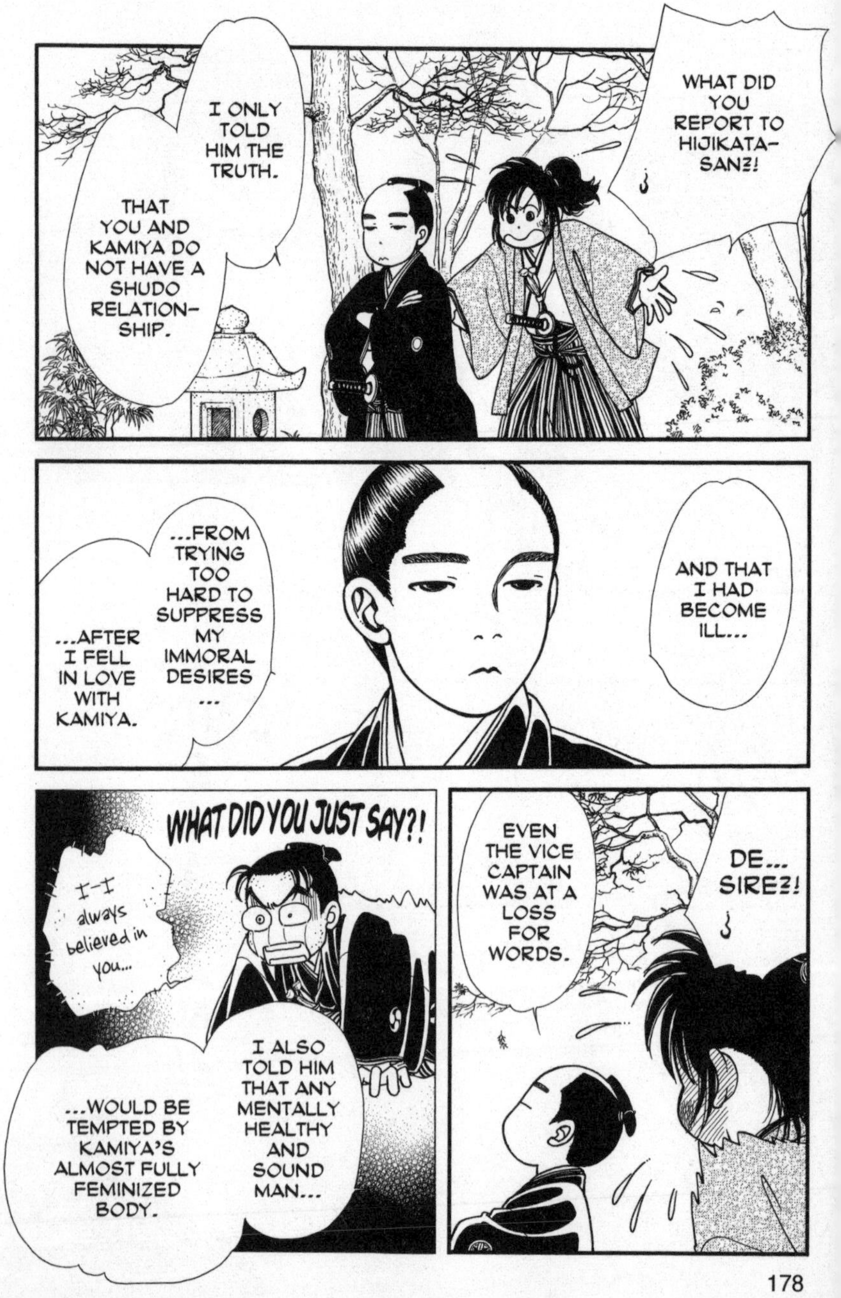
WHAT DID YOU REPORT TO HIJIKATA-SAN?!
I ONLY TOLD HIM THE TRUTH.
THAT YOU AND KAMIYA DO NOT HAVE A SHUDO RELATIONSHIP.
AND THAT I HAD BECOME ILL...
...FROM TRYING TOO HARD TO SUPPRESS MY IMMORAL DESIRES...
...AFTER I FELL IN LOVE WITH KAMIYA.
DE... SIRE?!
EVEN THE VICE CAPTAIN WAS AT A LOSS FOR WORDS.
WHAT DID YOU JUST SAY?!
I-I always believed in you...
I ALSO TOLD HIM THAT ANY MENTALLY HEALTHY AND SOUND MAN...
...WOULD BE TEMPTED BY KAMIYA'S ALMOST FULLY FEMINIZED BODY.

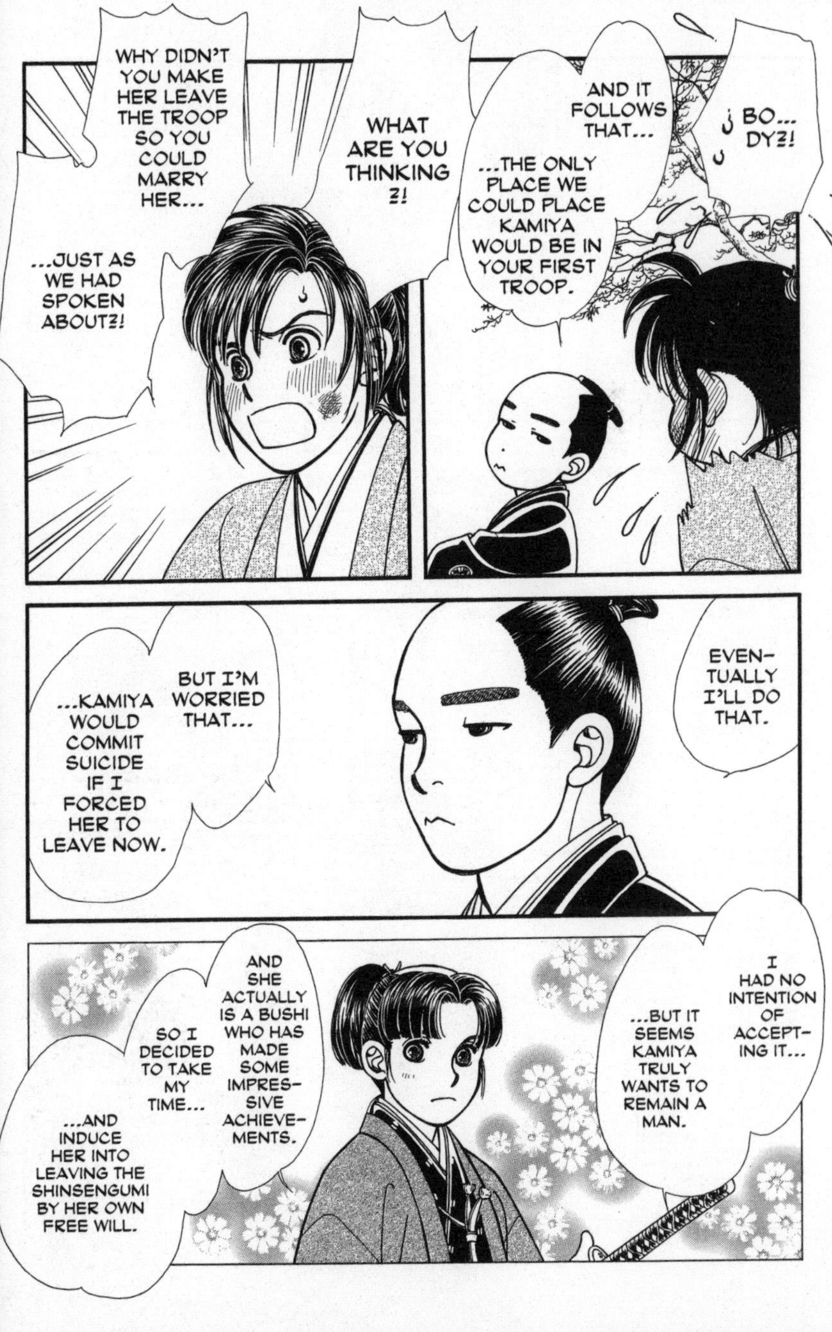
BO... DY?!
AND IT FOLLOWS THAT...
...THE ONLY PLACE WE COULD PLACE KAMIYA WOULD BE IN YOUR FIRST TROOP.
WHAT ARE YOU THINKING?!
WHY DIDN'T YOU MAKE HER LEAVE THE TROOP SO YOU COULD MARRY HER...
...JUST AS WE HAD SPOKEN ABOUT?!
EVEN-TUALLY I'LL DO THAT.
BUT I'M WORRIED THAT...
...KAMIYA WOULD COMMIT SUICIDE IF I FORCED HER TO LEAVE NOW.
I HAD NO INTENTION OF ACCEPT-ING IT...
...BUT IT SEEMS KAMIYA TRULY WANTS TO REMAIN A MAN.
AND SHE ACTUALLY IS A BUSHI WHO HAS MADE SOME IMPRES-SIVE ACHIEVE-MENTS.
SO I DECIDED TO TAKE MY TIME...
...AND INDUCE HER INTO LEAVING THE SHINSENGUMI BY HER OWN FREE WILL.

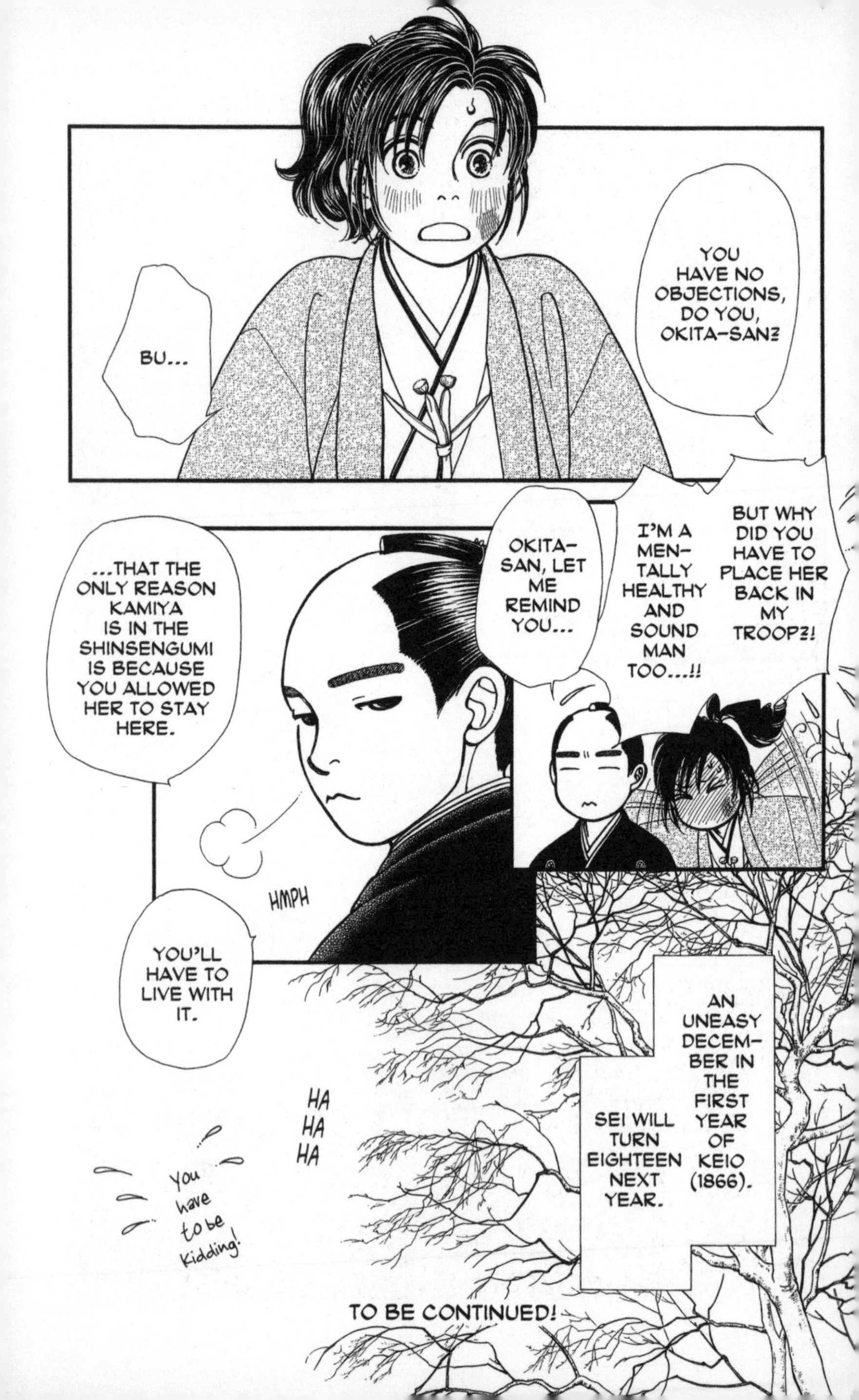
YOU HAVE NO OBJECTIONS, DO YOU, OKITA-SAN?
BU...
BUT WHY DID YOU HAVE TO PLACE HER BACK IN MY TROOP?!
I'M A MENTALLY HEALTHY AND SOUND MAN TOO...!!
OKITA-SAN, LET ME REMIND YOU...
...THAT THE ONLY REASON KAMIYA IS IN THE SHINSENGUMI IS BECAUSE YOU ALLOWED HER TO STAY HERE.
HMPH
YOU'LL HAVE TO LIVE WITH IT.
AN UNEASY DECEMBER IN THE FIRST YEAR OF KEIO (1866).
SEI WILL TURN EIGHTEEN NEXT YEAR.
HA HA HA
You have to be kidding!
TO BE CONTINUED!

TAEKO WATANABE PRESENTS

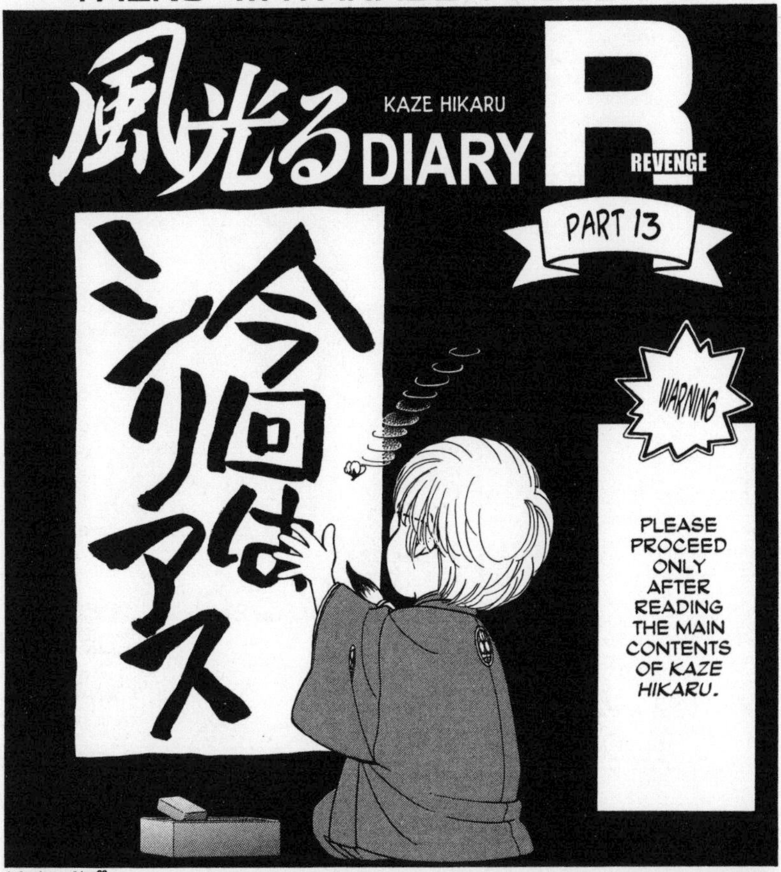
風光る
KAZE HIKARU
DIARY
R
REVENGE
PART 13
今回はシリアス
WARNING
PLEASE PROCEED ONLY AFTER READING THE MAIN CONTENTS OF KAZE HIKARU.

* Serious Stuff.

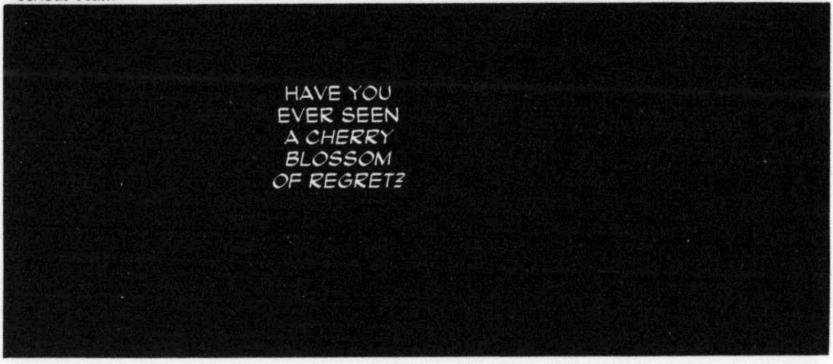
HAVE YOU EVER SEEN A CHERRY BLOSSOM OF REGRET?

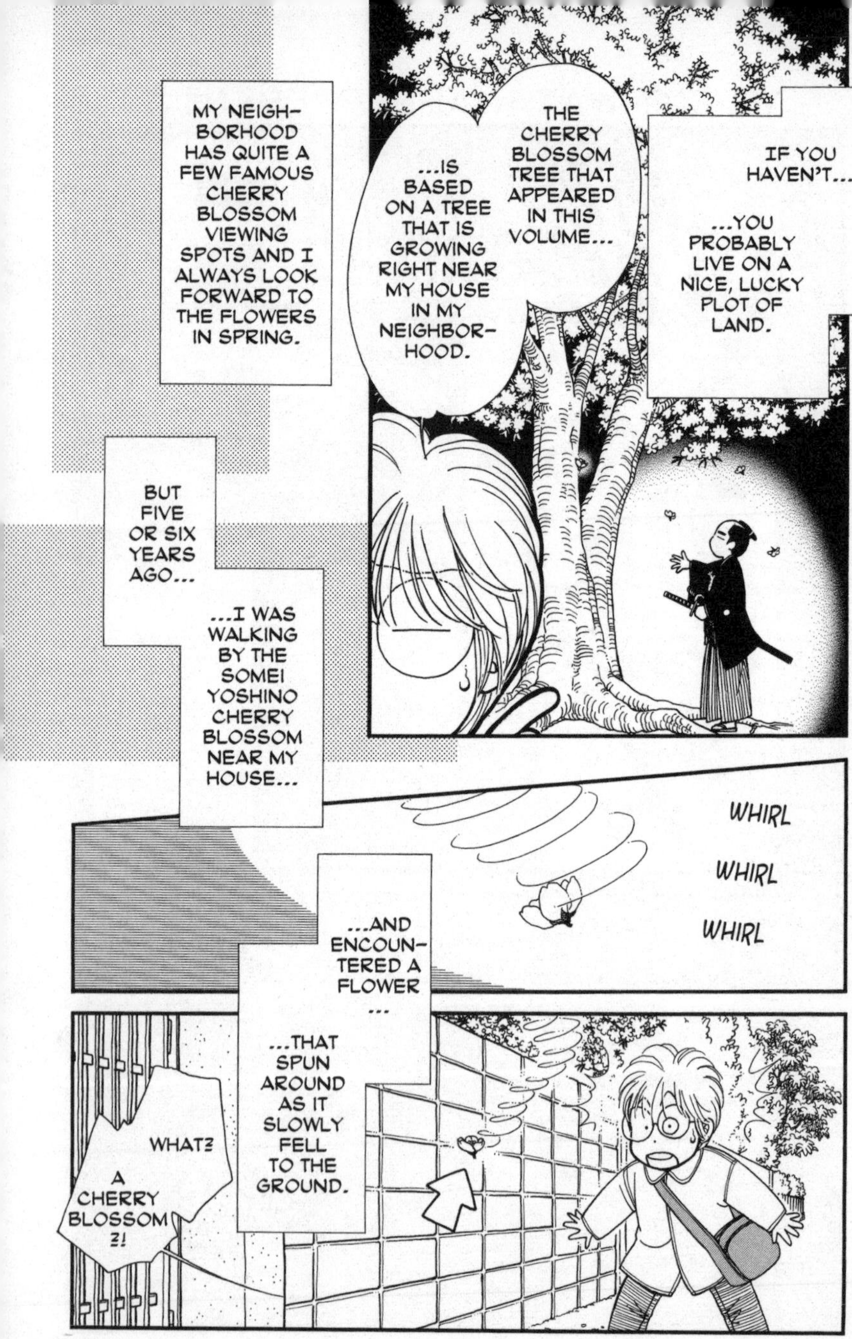
IF YOU HAVEN'T...
...YOU PROBABLY LIVE ON A NICE, LUCKY PLOT OF LAND.
THE CHERRY BLOSSOM TREE THAT APPEARED IN THIS VOLUME...
...IS BASED ON A TREE THAT IS GROWING RIGHT NEAR MY HOUSE IN MY NEIGHBOR-HOOD.
MY NEIGH-BORHOOD HAS QUITE A FEW FAMOUS CHERRY BLOSSOM VIEWING SPOTS AND I ALWAYS LOOK FORWARD TO THE FLOWERS IN SPRING.
BUT FIVE OR SIX YEARS AGO...
...I WAS WALKING BY THE SOMEI YOSHINO CHERRY BLOSSOM NEAR MY HOUSE...
WHIRL
WHIRL
WHIRL
...AND ENCOUN-TERED A FLOWER...
...THAT SPUN AROUND AS IT SLOWLY FELL TO THE GROUND.
WHAT?
A CHERRY BLOSSOM?!

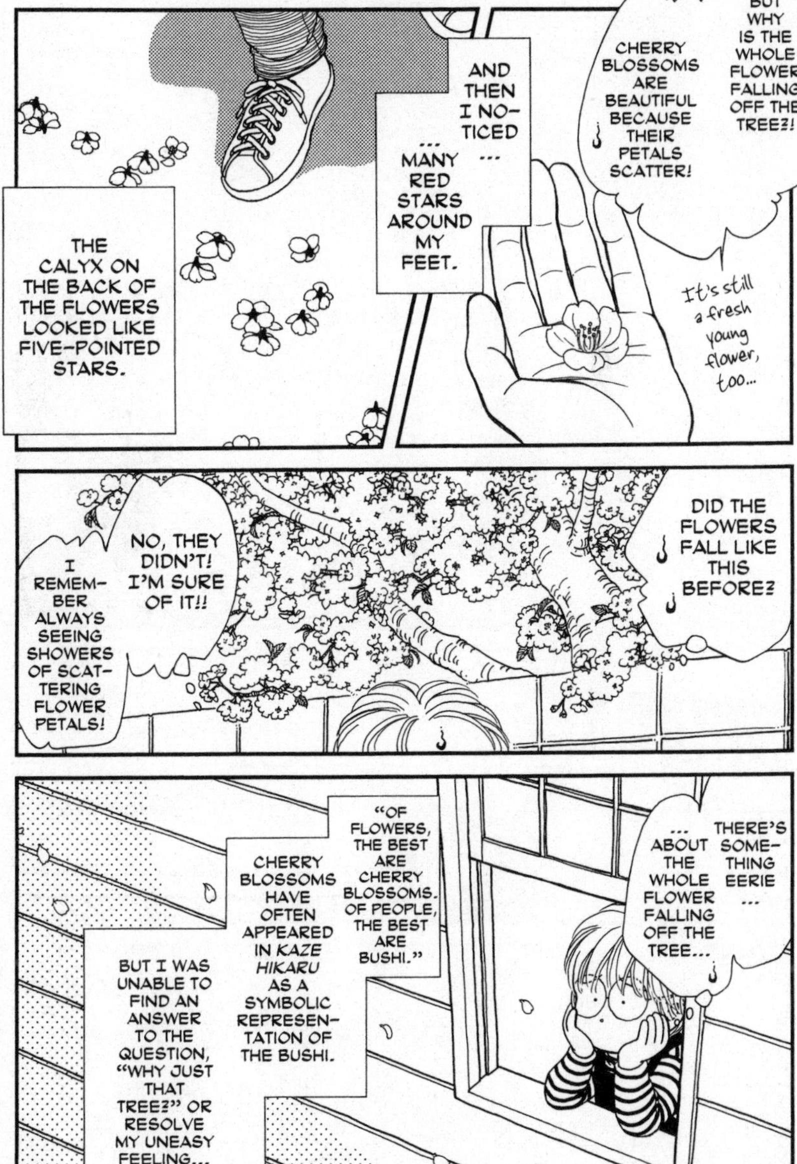
BUT WHY IS THE WHOLE FLOWER FALLING OFF THE TREE?!
CHERRY BLOSSOMS ARE BEAUTIFUL BECAUSE THEIR PETALS SCATTER!
It's still a fresh young flower, too...
AND THEN I NOTICED ... MANY RED STARS AROUND MY FEET.
THE CALYX ON THE BACK OF THE FLOWERS LOOKED LIKE FIVE-POINTED STARS.
DID THE FLOWERS FALL LIKE THIS BEFORE?
NO, THEY DIDN'T! I'M SURE OF IT!!
I REMEMBER ALWAYS SEEING SHOWERS OF SCATTERING FLOWER PETALS!
THERE'S SOMETHING EERIE ...
... ABOUT THE WHOLE FLOWER FALLING OFF THE TREE...
"OF FLOWERS, THE BEST ARE CHERRY BLOSSOMS. OF PEOPLE, THE BEST ARE BUSHI."
CHERRY BLOSSOMS HAVE OFTEN APPEARED IN *KAZE HIKARU* AS A SYMBOLIC REPRESENTATION OF THE BUSHI.
BUT I WAS UNABLE TO FIND AN ANSWER TO THE QUESTION, "WHY JUST THAT TREE?" OR RESOLVE MY UNEASY FEELING...

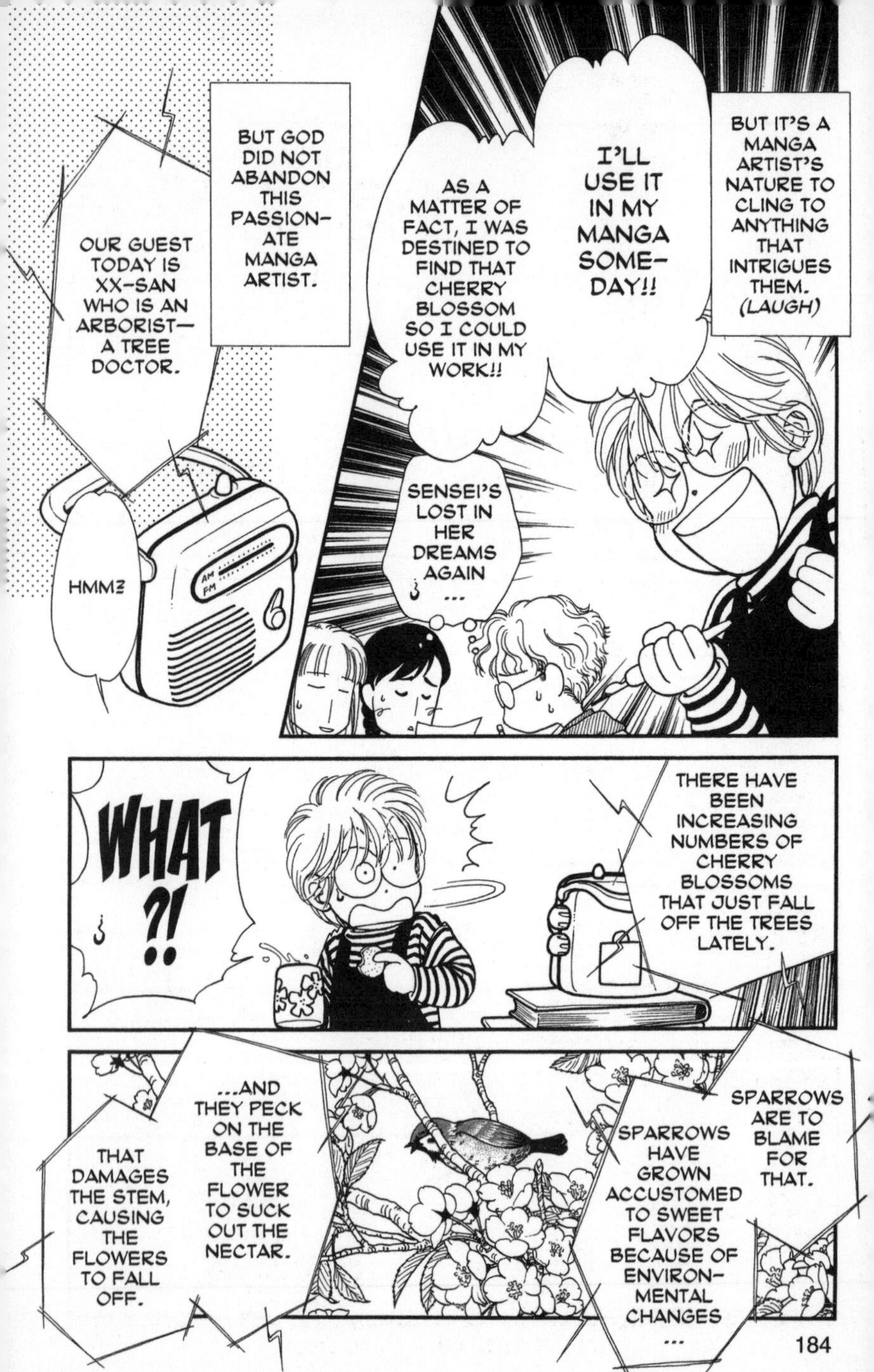

BUT IT'S A MANGA ARTIST'S NATURE TO CLING TO ANYTHING THAT INTRIGUES THEM. *(LAUGH)*
I'LL USE IT IN MY MANGA SOMEDAY!!
AS A MATTER OF FACT, I WAS DESTINED TO FIND THAT CHERRY BLOSSOM SO I COULD USE IT IN MY WORK!!
SENSEI'S LOST IN HER DREAMS AGAIN...
BUT GOD DID NOT ABANDON THIS PASSIONATE MANGA ARTIST.
OUR GUEST TODAY IS XX-SAN WHO IS AN ARBORIST—A TREE DOCTOR.
HMM?
AM
FM
THERE HAVE BEEN INCREASING NUMBERS OF CHERRY BLOSSOMS THAT JUST FALL OFF THE TREES LATELY.
WHAT?!
SPARROWS ARE TO BLAME FOR THAT.
SPARROWS HAVE GROWN ACCUSTOMED TO SWEET FLAVORS BECAUSE OF ENVIRONMENTAL CHANGES...
...AND THEY PECK ON THE BASE OF THE FLOWER TO SUCK OUT THE NECTAR.
THAT DAMAGES THE STEM, CAUSING THE FLOWERS TO FALL OFF.

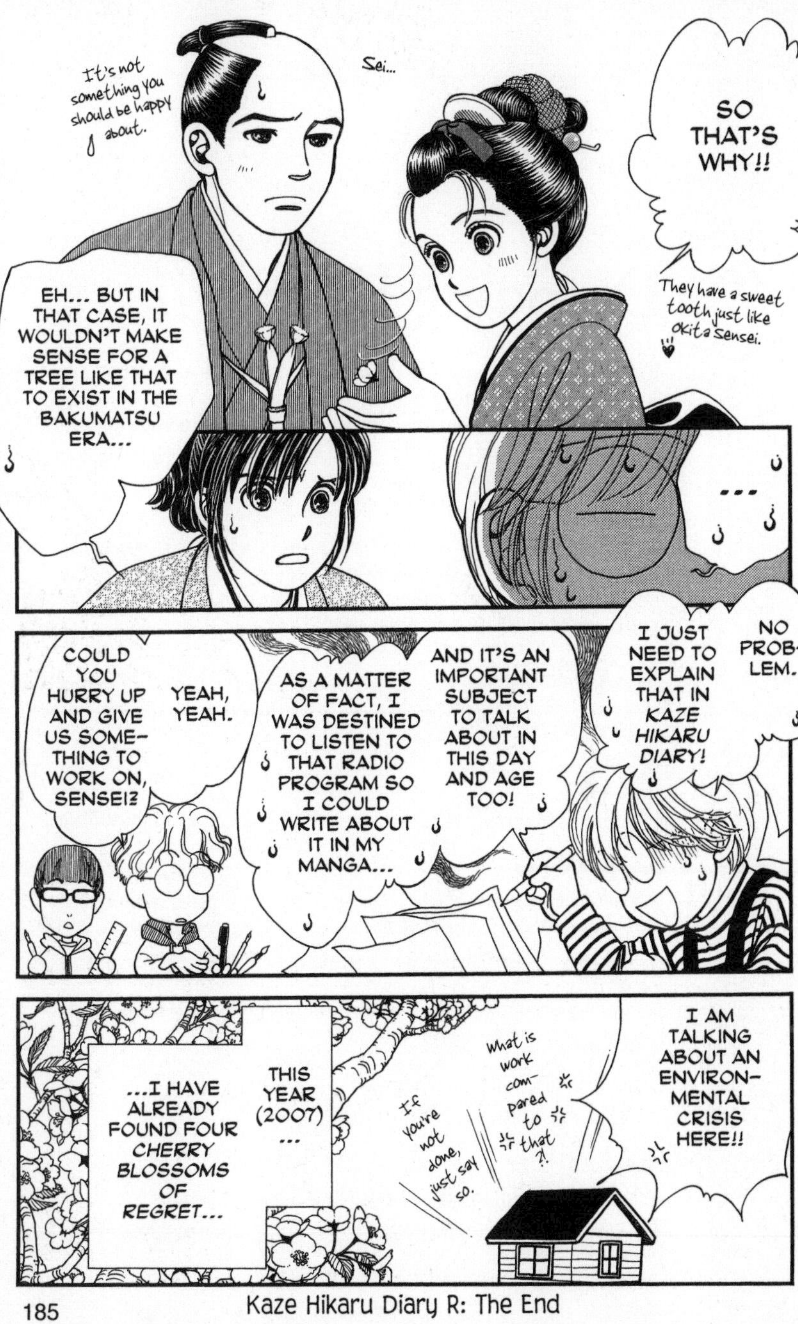
SO THAT'S WHY!!
They have a sweet tooth just like Okita sensei.
Sei...
It's not something you should be happy about.
EH... BUT IN THAT CASE, IT WOULDN'T MAKE SENSE FOR A TREE LIKE THAT TO EXIST IN THE BAKUMATSU ERA...
...
NO PROBLEM.
I JUST NEED TO EXPLAIN THAT IN KAZE HIKARU DIARY!
AND IT'S AN IMPORTANT SUBJECT TO TALK ABOUT IN THIS DAY AND AGE TOO!
AS A MATTER OF FACT, I WAS DESTINED TO LISTEN TO THAT RADIO PROGRAM SO I COULD WRITE ABOUT IT IN MY MANGA...
YEAH, YEAH.
COULD YOU HURRY UP AND GIVE US SOMETHING TO WORK ON, SENSEI!?
I AM TALKING ABOUT AN ENVIRONMENTAL CRISIS HERE!!
What is work compared to that?!
If you're not done, just say so.
THIS YEAR (2007)...
...I HAVE ALREADY FOUND FOUR CHERRY BLOSSOMS OF REGRET...

Kaze Hikaru Diary R: The End

Decoding Kaze Hikaru

Kaze Hikaru is a historical drama based in 19th century Japan and thus contains some fairly mystifying terminology. In this glossary we'll break down archaic phrases, terms and other linguistic curiosities for you so that you can move through life with the smug assurance that you are indeed a know-it-all.

First and foremost, because *Kaze Hikaru* is a period story, we kept all character names in their traditional Japanese form—that is, family name followed by first name. For example, the character Okita Soji's family name is Okita and his personal name is Soji.

AKO-ROSHI:
The *ronin* (samurai) of Ako; featured in the immortal Kabuki play *Chushingura* (Loyalty), aka *47 Samurai*.

ANI-UE:
Literally, "brother above"; an honorific for an elder male sibling.

BAKUFU:
Literally, "tent government." Shogunate; the feudal, military government that dominated Japan for more than 200 years.

BUSHI:
A samurai or warrior (part of the compound word *bushido*, which means "way of the warrior").

CHICHI-UE:
An honorific suffix meaning "father above."

DO:
In kendo (a Japanese fencing sport that uses bamboo swords), a short way of describing the offensive single-hit strike *shikake waza ippon uchi*.

-HAN:

The same as the honorific *-san*, pronounced in the dialect of southern Japan.

-KUN:

An honorific suffix that indicates a difference in rank and title. The use of *-kun* is also a way of indicating familiarity and friendliness between students or compatriots.

MEN:

In the context of *Kaze Hikaru*, *men* refers to one of the "points" in kendo. It is a strike to the forehead and is considered a basic move.

MIBU-ROSHI:

A group of warriors that supports the Bakufu.

NE'E-SAN:

Can mean "older sister," "ma'am" or "miss."

NI'I-CHAN:

Short for *oni'i-san* or *oni'i-chan*, meaning older brother.

OKU-SAMA:

This is a polite way to refer to someone's wife. *Oku* means "deep" or "further back" and comes from the fact that wives (in affluent families) stayed hidden away in the back rooms of the house.

ONI:

Literally "ogre," this is Sei's nickname for Vice Captain Hijikata.

RANPO:

Medical science derived from the Dutch.

RONIN:
Masterless samurai.

RYO:
At the time, one *ryo* and two *bu* (four *bu* equaled roughly one *ryo*) were enough currency to support a family of five for an entire month.

-SAN:
An honorific suffix that carries the meaning of "Mr." or "Ms."

SENSEI:
A teacher, master or instructor.

SEPPUKU:
A ritualistic suicide that was considered a privilege of the nobility and samurai elite.

SONJO-HA:
Those loyal to the emperor and dedicated to the expulsion of foreigners from the country.

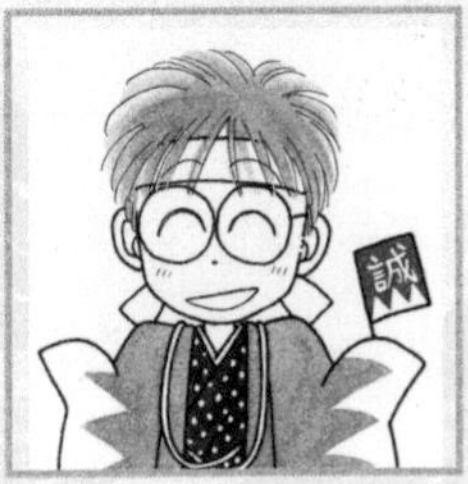
誠

Part two of the secret theme for the cover illustration. Maybe some of you have already figured it out, thinking "Hmm, maybe it's...?". That's right, it's you-know-what. It wasn't that difficult, was it? And for those of you who still haven't gotten it, wait for the next volume! (Heh)

And so, the seasonal word for this volume is Summer Willow. It's actually a lot greener, but I used a lighter green to give it a refreshing atmosphere for the summertime. Actually, my favorite time in Kyoto is the season of new green leaves. I can't enjoy the cherry blossoms or the crimson autumn foliage, but the layers of fresh green young leaves revives my tired body. Aaah, I feel like going to Kyoto again!!

Taeko Watanabe debuted as a manga artist in 1979 with her story *Waka-chan no Netsuai Jidai* (Love Struck Days of Waka). *Kaze Hikaru* is her longest-running series, but she has created a number of other popular series. Watanabe is a two-time winner of the prestigious Shogakukan Manga Award in the girls' category—her manga *Hajime-chan ga Ichiban!* (Hajime-chan Is Number One!) claimed the award in 1991, and *Kaze Hikaru* took it in 2003.

Watanabe read hundreds of historical sources to create *Kaze Hikaru.* She is from Tokyo.

KAZE HIKARU
VOL. 22
Shojo Beat Edition

STORY AND ART BY
TAEKO WATANABE

KAZE HIKARU Vol. 22
by Taeko WATANABE
© 1997 Taeko WATANABE
All rights reserved.
Original Japanese edition published by SHOGAKUKAN.
English translation rights in the United States of America and Canada arranged with
SHOGAKUKAN.

Translation & English Adaptation/Tetsuichiro Miyaki
Touch-up Art & Lettering/Rina Mapa
Design/Veronica Casson
Editor/Megan Bates

Printed in the U.S.A.

Published by VIZ Media, LLC
P.O. Box 77010
San Francisco, CA 94107

10 9 8 7 6 5 4 3 2 1
First printing, August 2014

www.viz.com

www.shojobeat.com